A MODERN APPROACH TO

OPERATIONS MANAGEMENT

A MODERN APPROACH TO OPERATIONS MANAGEMENT

Dr. RAM NARESH ROY
PhD.

NEW AGE MANAGEMENT
An Imprint of
NEW AGE INTERNATIONAL (P) LIMITED, PUBLISHERS
LONDON • NEW DELHI • NAIROBI
Bangalore • Chennai • Cochin • Guwahati • Hyderabad • Kolkata • Lucknow • Mumbai
Visit us at **www.newagepublishers.com**

Published by New Age International (P) Ltd., Publishers
First Edition: 2005
Reprint: 2020

GLOBAL OFFICES

- **New Delhi** — **NEW AGE INTERNATIONAL (P) LIMITED, PUBLISHERS**
  7/30 A, Daryaganj, New Delhi-110002, (INDIA)
  Tel.: (011) 23253771, 23253472, **Telefax:** 23267437, 43551305
  E-mail: contactus@newagepublishers.com • Visit us at www.newagepublishers.com
- **London** — **NEW AGE INTERNATIONAL (UK) LTD.**
  27 Old Gloucester Street, London, WC1N 3AX, UK
  E-mail: info@newacademicscience.co.uk • Visit us at www.newacademicscience.co.uk
- **Nairobi** — **NEW AGE GOLDEN (EAST AFRICA) LTD.**
  Ground Floor, Westlands Arcade, Chiromo Road (Next to Naivas Supermarket)
  Westlands, Nairobi, KENYA, **Tel.:** 00-254-713848772, 00-254-725700286
  E-mail: kenya@newagepublishers.com

BRANCHES

- **Bangalore** — 37/10, 8th Cross (Near Hanuman Temple), Azad Nagar, Chamarajpet, Bangalore- 560 018
  Tel.: (080) 26756823, **Telefax:** 26756820, **E-mail: bangalore@newagepublishers.com**
- **Chennai** — 26, Damodaran Street, T. Nagar, Chennai-600 017, **Tel.:** (044) 24353401, **Telefax:** 24351463
  E-mail: chennai@newagepublishers.com
- **Cochin** — CC-39/1016, Carrier Station Road, Ernakulam South, Cochin-682 016, **Tel.:** (0484) 2377303, **Telefax:** 4051304
  E-mail: cochin@newagepublishers.com
- **Guwahati** — Hemsen Complex, Mohd. Shah Road, Paltan Bazar, Near Starline Hotel, Guwahati-781 008,
  Tel.: (0361) 2513881, **Telefax:** 2543669, **E-mail: guwahati@newagepublishers.com**
- **Hyderabad** — 105, 1st Floor, Madhiray Kaveri Tower, 3-2-19, Azam Jahi Road, Near Kumar Theater, Nimboliadda
  Kachiguda, Hyderabad-500 027, **Tel.:** (040) 24652456, **Telefax:** 24652457
  E-mail: hyderabad@newagepublishers.com
- **Kolkata** — RDB Chambers (Formerly Lotus Cinema) 106A, 1st Floor, S N Banerjee Road, Kolkata-700 014
  Tel.: (033) 22273773, **Telefax:** 22275247, **E-mail: kolkata@newagepublishers.com**
- **Lucknow** — 16-A, Jopling Road, Lucknow-226 001, **Tel.:** (0522) 2209578, 4045297, **Telefax:** 2204098
  E-mail: lucknow@newagepublishers.com
- **Mumbai** — 142C, Victor House, Ground Floor, N.M. Joshi Marg, Lower Parel, Mumbai-400 013
  Tel.: (022) 24927869, **Telefax:** 24915415, **E-mail: mumbai@newagepublishers.com**
- **New Delhi** — 22, Golden House, Daryaganj, New Delhi-110 002, **Tel.:** (011) 23262368, 23262370, **Telefax:** 43551305
  E-mail: sales@newagepublishers.com

ISBN: 978-81-224-1627-5
C-19-04-12048

Printed in India at Ajit Printing Press, Delhi.
Typeset at Goswami Associates, Delhi.

NEW AGE INTERNATIONAL (P) LIMITED, PUBLISHERS
7/30 A, Daryaganj, New Delhi-110002
Visit us at **www.newagepublishers.com**
(CIN: U74899DL1966PTC004618)

Preface

While teaching the course on 'Production Operations Management (POM)' to my students in India and abroad, I have felt a huge shortage of books and relevant materials on this subject. The books available are mostly written with Western world perspective. The examples included in those books are not very relevant to the students of developing countries. This has motivated me to write this book which is based on my own teaching experiences and the feed back of my students.

The book includes the background, the core concepts, and the models of POM. It is readable, comprehensive, and contemporary in its approach. The concepts of Operations Management have been delivered to the readers in a simple, straightforward manner, and without mincing the words to avoid dilution of the materials itself.

The layout of the book has been organized to give the readers a sense of flow: (*i*) Beginning with fundamentals of Production systems, Productivity, Location of plant, layout issues; (*ii*) Core issues of POM like Forecasting, Operations planning, Purchasing systems and steps involved in it, Inventory models, and MRP, Quality control, TQM, Project Management; and finally (*iii*) the attention is focused to modern concepts on the subject like JIT, OPT, Automation, etc. This makes the book more comprehensive in nature.

Adequate number of solved problems have been included to give the readers a chance to enhance the learning process. Examples from local industries, agriculture sector, services (banking, airlines, hotels, transport, etc.) have been included to make the chapters interesting and palatable to the students' taste.

I thank my students and colleagues for their constructive comments in making the book more useful.

Lastly, I always believe in 'kaizen'—the continuous improvement process in everything I do and this goes with this book as well. I invite the readers, therefore, to send their comments and suggestions to improve this book in its next edition.

RAM NARESH ROY, PhD

ram_roy1959@yahoo.com

Contents

1

Production Systems and Operations Management

1.0 INTRODUCTION

In any manufacturing system, the job of an Operations Manager is to manage the process of converting inputs into the desired outputs. Therefore, **Operations Management** *can be defined as the management of the conversion process, which converts land, labor, capital, and management inputs into desired outputs of goods and services.* It is also concerned with the design and the operation of systems for manufacture, transport, supply or service.

1.1 RELATED ISSUES OF OPERATIONS MANAGEMENT

Some of the related issues of Operations management are production function, productivity, productivity measurements, types of production systems, production modeling, and so on. They all are discussed in this chapter.

1.1.1 PRODUCTION FUNCTION

Production is an organized activity of transforming raw materials into finished products. It is an intentional act of producing something useful. In production systems we have different resources as input. The inputs are processed in a series of operations. The sequence, number, and type of operations (mechanical, chemical, electrical, assembly, inspection, transportation, etc) are specified for each input. The output of the system will be complete parts products, chemicals etc. Production function shows the relationship between the input and the output of an organization. By the study of production function the maximum output which can be achieved with given inputs, or say resources with a given state of technology is determined. The production function can be represented by the simple mathematical equation which relates the outputs as the function of inputs , that is

$$Y = f(X_1, X_2, \ldots, X_n)$$

Where Y = units of output, which is the function of the quantity of two or more inputs

X_1 = unit of labor, and

X_2 = unit of machinery, and so on.

Some quantities of production are assumed as fixed, that is not varying with change of output, such quantities never enter in the equation.

1.1.2 PRODUCTIVITY

It is a very comprehensive concept, both in its aim and also in its operational content. It is a matter of common knowledge that *higher productivity leads to a reduction in cost of production, reduces the sales price of an item, expands markets, and enables the goods to compete effectively in the world market*. It yields more wages to the workers, shorter working hours and greater leisure time for the employees. In fact the strength of a country, prosperity of its economy, standard of living of the people and the wealth of the nation are very largely determined by the extent and measure of its production and productivity. By enabling an increase in the output of goods or services for existing resources, productivity decreases the cost of goods per unit, and makes it possible to sell them at lower prices, thus benefiting the consumers while at the same time leaving a margin for increase in the wages of the workers.

Productivity can be defined in many ways. Some of them are as follows:

- Productivity is nothing but the reduction in wastage of resources such as labor, machines, materials, power, space, time, capital, etc.
- Productivity can also be defined as human endeavor (effort) to produce more and more with less and less inputs of resources so that the products can be purchased by a large number of people at affordable price.
- Productivity implies development of an attitude of mind and a constant urge to find better, cheaper, easier, quicker, and safer means of doing a job, manufacturing a product and providing service.
- Productivity aims at the maximum utilization of resources for yielding as many goods and services as possible, of the kinds most wanted by consumers at lowest possible cost.
- Productivity processes more efficient works involving less fatigue to workers due to improvements in the layout of plant and work, better working conditions and simplification of work. In a wider sense productivity may be taken to constitute the ratio of all available goods and services to the potential resources of the group.

1.1.3 DIFFERENCE BETWEEN PRODUCTION AND PRODUCTIVITY

As discussed earlier, production is an organized activity of transforming raw materials into finished products which have higher value. Production of any commodity or service is the volume of output irrespective of the quantity of resources employed to achieve the level of output. Production in an industry can be increased by employing more labor, installing more machinery, and putting in more materials, regardless of the cost of production.

But increase of production does not necessarily mean increase in productivity. Higher productivity results when we put in production system an element of efficiency with which the resources are employed. The combined input of a number of factors such as land, materials, machines, capital, and labor gives an output in an industry. The ratio between output and one of these factors of input is usually known as productivity of the factor considered. Productivity may also be considered as a measure of performance of the economy as a whole. Mathematically,

Productivity = Output Value/Input Value

Factor Productivity = Output due to the factor/ Input factor employed

An example to illustrate the difference between production and productivity follows: For instance, 50 persons employed in an industry may be producing the same volume of goods over the same period as 75 persons working in another similar industry. Productions of these two industries are equal, but productivity of the former is higher than that of the latter.

In order to assure that productivity measurement captures what the company is trying to do with respect to such vague issues as customer satisfaction and quality, some firms redefined productivity as

Productivity = Effectiveness or value to customer/Efficiency or cost to producer

As it has been said so many times productivity measurement is the ratio of organizational outputs to organizational inputs. Thus productivity ratios can be

—Partial productivity measurement

—Multi-factor productivity measurement

—Total productivity measurement

Partial Productivity Measurement

Partial productivity measurement is used when the firm is interested in the productivity of a selected input factor. It is the ratio of output values to one class of input.

$$\text{PPM} = \frac{\text{Outputs}}{\text{Labor Input}} \text{ or } \frac{\text{Outputs}}{\text{Material Input}} \text{ or } \frac{\text{Outputs}}{\text{Capital}}$$

Multi-factor Productivity Measurement

This productivity measurement technique is used when the firm is interested to know the productivity of a group of input factors but not all input factors.

$$\text{MFPM} = \frac{\text{Outputs}}{\text{Labor + Capital}} \text{ or } \frac{\text{Outputs}}{\text{Labor + Material}}$$

Total (Composite) Productivity Measures

A firm deals about composite productivity when it is interested to know about the overall productivity of all input factors. This technique will give us the productivity of an entire organization or even a nation.

$$\text{TPM} = \frac{\text{Outputs}}{\text{Inputs}} \text{ or } \frac{\text{Goods and services provide}}{\text{All resources Used}}$$

The above measurement techniques can be grouped into two popular productivity measurement approaches the first uses a group-generated model and is called normative productivity measurement methodology. The second is less participative in that one model can be modified to fit any organization scheme. It is called multi-factor productivity measurement model.

1.1.4 EFFECTIVENESS

It is the degree of accomplishment of the objectives that is: How well a set of result is accomplished? How well are the resources utilized? Effectiveness is obtaining the desired results. It may reflect output quantities, perceived quality or both. *Effectiveness can also be defined as doing the right things.*

1.1.5 EFFICIENCY

This occurs when a certain output is obtained with a minimum of inputs. The desired output can be increased by minimizing the down times as much as possible (down times are coffee breaks, machine failures, waiting time, etc). But as we decrease down times the frequency of occurrence of defective products will increase due to fatigue. The production system might efficiently produce defective (ineffective) products. *Efficiency can be defined as doing things right. Operational efficiency refers to a ratio of outputs to inputs (like land, capital, labor, etc.)*

Example 1.1. Management of a hotel is concerned with labor efficiency, especially when labor is costly. To determine how efficient labor is in a given situation, management sets an *individual standard,* a goal reflecting an average worker's output per unit of time under normal working conditions. Say that the standard in a cafeteria is the preparation of 200 salads per hour. If a labor input produces 150 salads per hour, how efficient is the salad operation ?

$$\text{Labor efficiency} = \frac{\text{Labor Outputs}}{\text{Labor Input}} = \frac{150 \text{ salads}}{200 \text{ salads}} \times 100\% = 75\%$$

So, compared with the standard, this operation is 75% efficient in the preparation of salads.

1.2 OPERATIONS FUNCTION IN ORGANIZATIONS

The operations system of an organization is the part that produces the organization's products. In some organizations the product is a physical good (refrigerators, breakfast cereal), while in others it is a service (insurance, health care for the old people). However, these organizations have something in common as shown in Figure 1.1. They have a *conversion process*, some resource *inputs* into that process, the *outputs* resulting from the conversion of the inputs, and *information* feedback about the activities in the operations system. Once goods and services are produced, they are converted into cash (sold) to acquire more resources to keep the conversion process alive.

Example 1.2. On a farming situation, the *inputs* are: land, equipment, labor, etc and the *outputs* are: corn, wheat, milk, fruits, and so on.

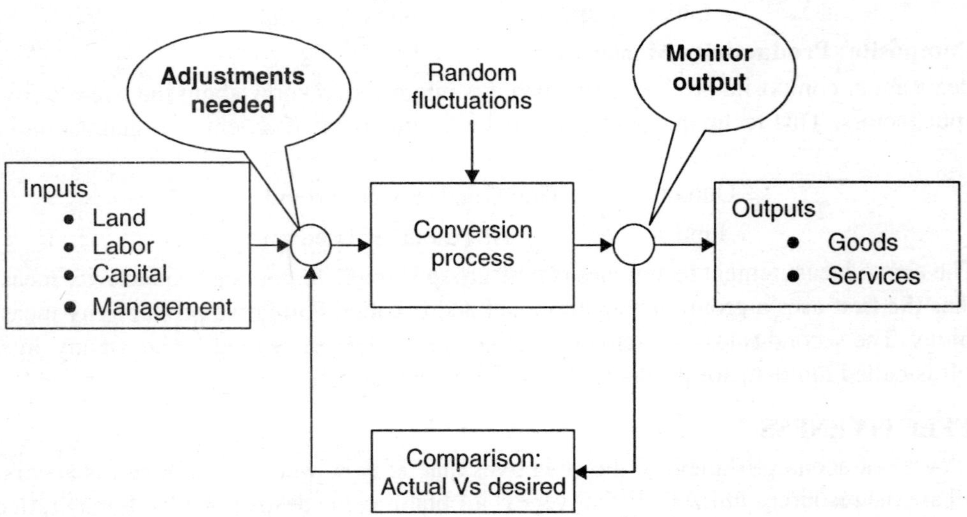

Figure 1.1

For all operations, the goal is to create some kind of *value-added*, so that the outputs are worth more to consumers than just the sum of the individual inputs. Some of the examples of input, conversion process, and output are shown in Table 1.1. Students are advised to collect some inputs and outputs of some of the industries visited by them. The *random fluctuations* in Figure 1.1 consist of unplanned or uncontrollable influences that cause the actual output to differ from the expected output. Random fluctuations can arise from external sources (fire, floods, earthquake, lightening, or even some diseases like SARS), or they can result from internal problems (defects in materials and equipment, human error). In fact, fluctuations are the rule rather than the exception in production system and reducing fluctuations (variations) is a major task of management. It may be noted that SARS (Severe Acute Respiratory Syndrome) has affected all aspects of life (airlines, tourism, schools, industries, etc.) in many countries especially in China.

Table 1.1

Input	*Conversion process*	*Output*
Elements	Transformation	Useful products
Materials	Machines	Products
Data	Interpretation	Knowledge
Energy	Skill	Services
Variable cost	Fixed cost	Revenue

An unit of output normally needs several types of inputs. The inputs account for most of the variable cost of production. Conversion process/facilities are associated with fixed cost, and the output produces the revenue.

Any system is a collection of interacting components. Each component could be a system unto itself in a descending order of simplicity. Systems are distinguished by their objectives; the objective of one system could be to produce a component which is to be assembled with other components to achieve the objective of a larger system.

1.2.1 MANUFACTURING OPERATIONS Vs SERVICE OPERATIONS

A conversion process that includes manufacturing (or production) yields a *tangible* output: a product. In contrast, a conversion process that includes service yields an *intangible* output: a deed, a performance, an effort. For example, Mesfin Industries produces a lot of tangible products, whereas Ethiopian Airlines provides air transport services to passengers which is an intangible output.

1.2.1.1 Distinguishing Between Manufacturing and Service Operations

Generally the following characteristics are used to distinguish between manufacturing and service operations:

- Tangible and intangible nature of output
- Consumption of output
- Nature of work (jobs)
- Degree of customer contact
- Customer participation in conversion
- Measurement of performance

Put simply, the manufacturing is characterized by tangible outputs (products), outputs that customers consume over time, jobs that use less labor and more equipment, little customer contact, no customer participation in the conversion process (in production), and sophisticated methods for measuring production activities and resource consumption as products are made.

Service, on the other hand, is characterized by intangible outputs, outputs that customers consume immediately, jobs that use more labor and less equipment, direct customer contact, frequent customer participation in the conversion process, and elementary methods for measuring conversion activities and resource consumption. However, some service is *equipment-based* like Computer software services, Internet services, telephone services, etc. Some service is people-based like tax accounting services, hair styling, and golf instruction.

Let's see the *customers' participation* aspects in conversion process. In service operations, managers sometimes find it useful to distinguish between *output* and *throughput* types of customer participation. Output is a generated service, throughput is an item going through the process. In a *pediatrics clinic* the output is the medical service to the child, who by going through the conversion process, is also a throughput. Same is the case with the students undergoing training in Addis Ababa University. *At a fast-food restaurant*, in contrast, the customer does not go through the conversion process. The outputs are burgers, pizzas, and French fries served in a hurry (both goods and services), while the throughputs are the food items as they are prepared and converted. The customer is neither a throughput nor an output. Both the clinic and the restaurant provide services, even though the outputs and throughputs differ considerably.

We will use the term **operations** to include both manufacturing and service in this book.

1.2.1.2 Historical Background of Production and Operations Management

For over two centuries, operations management has been recognized as an important factor in economic development of a country. POM has passed through a series of names like: *manufacturing management, production management*, and *operations management*. All of these describe the same general discipline.

The traditional view of *manufacturing management* began in the 8th century when Adam Smith recognized the economic benefits of specialization of labor. He recommended breaking jobs down into subtasks and reassigning workers to specialized tasks in which they become highly skilled and efficient. In the early 20th century, Fredrick W. Taylor implemented Smith's theories and crusaded for scientific management in the manufacturing sectors of his day. From then until about 1930, the traditional view prevailed, and many techniques we still use today were developed. A brief sketch of thee and other contributions to manufacturing management is given in Table 1.2.

Table 1.2. Historical summary of Operations Management

Date (approx)	*Contribution*	*Contributor*
1776	Specialization of labor in manufacturing	Adam Smith
1799	Interchangeable parts, cost accounting	Eli Whitney and others
1832	Division of labor by skill; assignment of jobs by skill; basics of time study	Charles Babbage
1900	Scientific management; time study and work study developed; dividing planning and doing of work	Frederick W. Taylor
1900	Motion study of jobs	Frank B. Gilbreth
1901	Scheduling techniques for employees, machines, jobs in manufacturing	Henry L. Gantt
1915	Economic lot sizes for inventory control	F. W. Harris
1927	Human relations; the Hawthorne studies	Elton Mayo
1931	Statistical inference applied to product quality; quality control charts	Walter A. Shewhart
1935	Statistical sampling applied to quality control; inspection sampling plans	H. F. Dodge and H. G. Romig

1940	Operations research applications in World War II	P. M. S. Blacket and others
1946	Digital computer	John Mauchly and J. P. Eckert
1947	Linear programming	George B. Dantzig, William Orchard Hays, and others
1950	Mathematical programming, nonlinear and stochastic processes	A. Charnes, W. W. Cooper, H. Raiffa, and others
1951	Commercial digital computer; large-scale computations available	Sperry Univac
1960	Organizational behavior; continued study of people at work	L. Cummings, L. Porter, and others
1970	Integrating operations into overall strategy and policy Computer applications to manufacturing, scheduling, and control, material requirements planning (MRP)	W. Skinner J. Orlicky and O. Wright
1980	Quality and productivity applications from Japan; robotics, computer-aided design and manufacturing (CAD/CAM)	W. E. Deming and J. Juran

Production management became the more widely accepted term from 1930s through the 1950s. As Frederick Taylor's work became more widely known, managers developed techniques that focused on economic efficiency in manufacturing. Workers were 'put under a microscope' and studied in great detail to eliminate wasteful efforts and achieve greater efficiency. At this same time, however, management also began discovering that workers have multiple needs, not just economic needs. Psychologists, sociologists, and other social scientists began to study people and human behavior in the work environment. In addition, economists, mathematicians, and computer scientists contributed newer, more sophisticated analytical approaches.

With the 1970's emerges two distinct changes in our views. The most obvious of these, reflected in the new name-operations management-was a shift in the service and manufacturing sectors of the economy. As the service sector became more prominent, the change from 'production' to 'operations' emphasized the broadening of our field to service organizations. The second, more subtle change was the beginning of an emphasis on synthesis, rather than just analysis, in management practices. These days, organizational goals are more focused to meet consumers' needs throughout the world. Quality concepts like TQM, ISO-9000, Quality function deployment, etc. are all examples of this attitude of management.

1.2.2 TYPES OF PRODUCTION SYSTEM

There are eight types of production which may be classified in three or four broad groups according to the quantities of production involved [Samuel Eilon]. They are shown in Figure 1.2 in terms of product variety and production volume—the figure is self explanatory.

1. **Job Shop Production system which has the following features :**

   (*a*) A small number of items produced only once,

   (*b*) A small number of items produced intermittently when the need is felt,

   (*c*) A small number of items produced periodically at known time interval.

2. **Batch Production which has the following characteristics :**
   (*a*) A batch of items produced only once,
   (*b*) A batch of items produced at irregular intervals when a need is felt,
   (*c*) A batch of items produced periodically at known intervals to satisfy the continuous demand.
3. **Continuous Production which consists of**
   (*a*) Mass production
   (*b*) Flow production

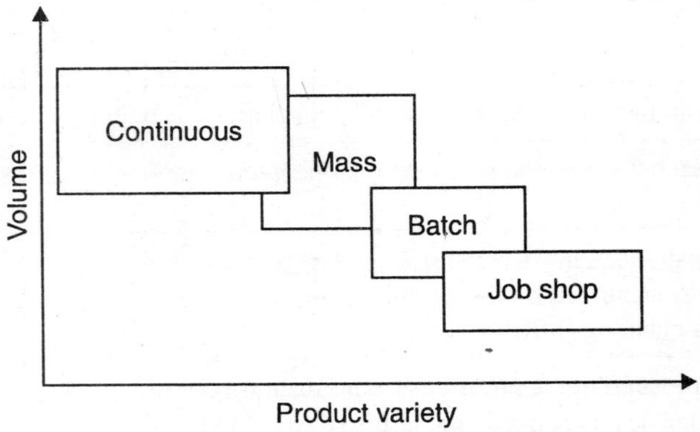

Figure 1.2. Different Types of Production Systems.

1.2.2.1 Job Production

This is the oldest method of production on a very small scale. It is also popularly known as 'job-shop or Unit' production. With this method individual requirements of consumers can be met. Each job order stands alone and may not be repeated. Some of the **examples** include manufacturing of aircrafts, ships, space vehicle, bridge and dam construction, ship building, boilers, turbines, machine tools, things of artistic nature, die work, etc. Some of the features of this system are as follows:

- This system has a lot of flexibility of operation, and hence general purpose machines are required.
- Generally no automation is used in this system, but computer-aided-design (CAD) is used.
- It deals with 'low volume and large variety' production. It can cater to specific customer order, or job of one kind at a time.
- It is known for rapid value addition.

Advantages

- Low risk of loss to the factory adopting this type of production. Due to flexibility, there is no chance of failure of factory due to reduction in demand. It can always get one or the other job orders to keep it going.
- Requires less money and is easy to start.
- Less or no management problem because of very small work force.

Disadvantages

- For handling different types of jobs, only workers with multiple skills are needed. This increases the labor cost.

- Low equipment utilization.
- As the raw materials are purchased in less quantity, the cost of material procurement is more.

1.2.2.2 Batch Production

The *batch production system* is generally adopted in medium size enterprises. Batch production is a stage in between **mass production** and **job-shop** production. As in this system, two or more than two types of products are manufactured in lots or batches at regular interval, which justifies its name the 'batch production system'. It has the following features:

- A batch production turns into flow production when the rest period vanishes. In flow production, the processing of materials is continuous and progressive.
- Batch production is bigger in scale than job production, but smaller than that of mass production.
- Material handling may be automated by robots as in case of CNC machining centers.
- A medium size lots (5 to 50) of same items is produced in this system. Lot may be produced once in a while or on regular interval generally to meet the continuous customer demands.
- Plant capacity generally is higher than demand.

Advantages

- It is flexible in the sense that it can go from one job to another with almost zero cost. It needs general purpose machine having high production rate.
- If demand for one product decreases then production rate for another product may be increased, thus the risk of loss is very less.
- Most suitable for computer-aided-manufacturing (CAM).

Disadvantages

- As the raw materials to be purchased are in smaller quantity than in case of mass production, the benefits of discount due to large lot purchasing is not possible.
- It needs specially designed jigs and fixtures.

1.2.2.3 Continuous Production

In this, the production activity continues for 24 hours or on three shifts a day basis. A steel plant, for **example**, belongs to this type. It is impossible to stop the production process on a short notice without causing a great damage to its blast furnace and related equipment. Other examples include bottling plant, soft drink industry, fertilizer plant, power plant, etc). *Mass production* and *Flow production* belong to continuous type only. They are explained below:

Mass production: In this type, a large number of identical items is produced, however, the equipment need not be designed to produce only this type of items. Both plant and equipment are flexible enough to deal with other products needing the same production processes. For **example,** a highly mechanized press shop that can be utilized to produce different types of components or products of steel metal without the need of major changes.

Flow production: In this type, the plant, its equipment, and layout have been chiefly designed to produce a particular type of product. Flexibility is limited to minor modifications in layout or design of models. Some famous **examples** are automobiles, engines, house-hold machinery, chemical plants, etc. If the management decides to switch over to a different type of product, it will result in extensive change in tooling, layout, and equipment.

Continuous production, in general, has the following *features*:

- It is very highly automated (process automation), and highly capital intensive. Items move from one stage to another automatically in a continuous manner.
- It has a fixed or hard automation which means there is very less or no flexibility at all. Layout of the plant is such that it can be used for only one type of product. Each machine in the system is assigned a definite nature of work.
- To avoid problem of material handling, use of cranes, conveyors etc. are made.
- Work-in-process (WIP) inventory in this system is zero.

Advantages

- It gives better quality, large volume but less variety of products.
- Wastage is minimum.
- As the raw materials are purchased on a large scale, higher margin of profit can be made on purchase.
- Only a few skilled, and many semi-skilled workers are required. This reduces the labor cost substantially.

Disadvantages

- During the period of less demand, heavy losses on invested capital may take place.
- Because all the machines are dedicated and special purpose type, the system is not changeable to other type of production.
- Most of the workers handle only a particular operation repetitively, which can make them feel monotonous.
- As this type of production is on the large scale, it cannot fulfill individual taste.

1.3 ROLE OF MODELS IN OPERATIONS MANAGEMENT

The context in which we use the term *mathematical modeling* refers to the creation of mathematical representations of management problems and organizations in order to determine outcomes of proposed courses of action. In spite of their utility, we must recognize that models cannot duplicate the real environment completely. However, this shortcoming should not be taken as a negative feature in a strict sense. In fact, it can be desirable, because it clears away extraneous elements and frills, and concentrates on the core problem. The modeling process can give us a simplified version of the situation with clear visibility of major factors.

1.3.1 TYPES OF MODELS IN PRODUCTION OPERATIONS MANAGEMENT (POM)

In operations management, we use several types of models of varying levels of sophistication.

1.3.1.1 Verbal Models

Verbal or written models express in words the relationships among variables. Verbal models are descriptive. Suppose a passing motorist asks you to give directions to the nearest gas station. If you tell him the way, you are giving a verbal model. If you write the directions in words (not pictures), you are giving a descriptive model.

1.3.1.2 Schematic Models

Schematic models show a pictorial relationship among variables. If you give the passing motorist a map showing the way to the nearest gas station, you would be giving a schematic model. Charts and diagrams are also schematic; they are very useful for showing relationships among variables, as long as all the legends, symbols, and scales are explained.

1.3.1.3 Iconic Models

Iconic models are scaled physical replicas of objects or processes. Architectural models of new buildings and highway engineering replicas of a proposed overpass system are iconic models.

1.3.1.4 Mathematical Models

Mathematical models show functional relationships among variables by using mathematical symbols and equations. In any equation, x, y, and similar symbols are used to express precise functional relationships among the variables.

1.3.2 MATHEMATICAL MODELS IN PRODUCTION AND OPERATIONS MANAGEMENT

Optimization: Operations managers often use models to help analyze problems and suggest solutions. To assist, they find it helpful to use an *algorithm*, a prescribed set of steps (a procedure) that attains a goal. In *optimization models*, for example, we want to find the best solution (the goal), and an *optimization algorithm* identifies the steps for doing so. In operations management we strive for optimization algorithms as aids in problem solving.

Heuristics: In other cases, a *heuristic* approach is used. A heuristic is a way (a strategy) of using *rules of thumb* or defined decision procedures to attack a problem. In general, when we use heuristics we do not expect to attain the best possible solution to a problem; instead, we hope for a *satisfactory* solution *quickly*. Formally developed heuristic procedures are called *heuristic algorithms*. They are useful for problems for which optimization algorithms have not yet been developed.

1.3.3 MODELING BENEFITS

The extensive use of models, especially schematic and mathematical models, is sometimes questioned by students and practitioners of POM. Using models often requires making questionable assumptions, applying hard-to-get cost and other data, and figuring in future events that are not easily predicted. Even so, the knowledge gained from working with models and attempting to apply them can yield valuable insights about a particular problem and what types of decisions are required. Simply recognizing the decision points can be a major step forward in many situations. Moreover, by using models, managers can recognize

- Variables that can be controlled to affect performance of the system
- Relevant costs and their magnitudes, and
- The relationship of costs to variables, including important tradeoffs among costs.

1.4 CLASSIFYING PROBLEMS

Since the operations analyst comes across different types of problems, it is a good idea to classify them into some groups. This will make it easier to select models and criteria to use in the analysis. There can be two ways of classifying problems: by the degree to which the outcome is uncertain, and by the degree to which the decisions are independent.

1.4.1 UNCERTAINTY OF OUTCOMES

When we know for sure what the outcome of each decision will be, we are dealing with a problem under control of *certainty*. When a decision has more than one possible outcome and we know the likelihood of each outcome, we are dealing with a problem under conditions of *risk*. Finally, when a decision has more than one possible outcome and we do not know the likelihood of each outcome, we are dealing with a problem under conditions of *uncertainty.* Some examples may clarify these conditions of certainty, risk, and uncertainty.

Example1.3. (Certainty) A chain of supermarkets is going to open a new store at one of four possible locations. Management wishes to select the location that will maximize profitability over the next ten years. An extensive analysis was performed to determine the costs, revenues, and profits for each alternative. The results are shown below.

Table 1.3

Location	*10 year annual profit ($ millions)*
1	0.70
2	0.95
3	0.60
4	0.84

Management has a high degree of confidence in these figures. The decision criterion (profit) has been explicitly identified and accurately calculated for each alternative. Management's strategy is to select the alternative with the highest criterion value, in this case location 2.

Solution. Under conditions of certainty, the best location is easily identified. Location 2 clearly yields the highest profit.

Example 1.4. (Risk) Further analysis of the supermarket chain's problem reveals that the profit associated with each location is not known for sure. Management is convinced that the ten-year profitability of each location will depend upon regional population growth. Therefore management cannot predict the outcome with certainty. Three possible rates of population growth were identified: *low, medium, and high.* The profitability ($ millions) associated with each location and each rate of population growth was calculated, as shown below.

Table 1.4

Location	*Rate of population growth*		
	Low (5% or less)	*Medium (above 5% but below 10%)*	*High (10% or more)*
1	0.3 million $	0.8 million $	0.9 million $
2	0.2	0.6	1.1
3	0.4	0.5	0.6
4	0.6	0.7	0.8
Probability (*p*)	0.2	0.3	0.5

The figures at the bottom of the table gives the probability (likelihood) of each rate of population growth. Decision strategy in this situation is more difficult than it is under conditions of certainty.

Solution. Under conditions of risk, the choice is not so easy. We do not know which location will be best because the rate of future population growth is not known for certain. In analyzing this situation, the data need to be arranged differently (see Table 1.4). The table arranged like this is called a *matrix.* Which alternative is the best?

If population growth turns out to be low, then location 4 is the best (0.6 million $). If growth is medium, then location 1 is the best (0.8 million $), and if the growth is high, then location 2 is the best (1.1 million $). In the analyst's language, the three rates of population growth are called *states of nature.*

Table 1.5. Calculation of Expected Value in $ million

Alternative	*Low*	*Medium*	*High*	*Expected Value (Profit)*
1	0.3	0.8	0.9	(.3*.2) + (.8*.3) + (.9*.5) = .75
2	0.2	0.6	1.1	(.2*.2) + (.6*.3) + (1.1*.5)= .77
3	0.4	0.5	0.6	(.4*.2) + (.5*.3 + (.6*.5) = .53
4	0.6	0.7	0.8	(.6*.2) + (.7*.3 + (.8*.5) = .73
p	0.2	0.3	0.5	

A concept of *expected value* has been applied to our problem (Table 1.5). The expected value is highest for alternative 2 ($ .77 million). If management faced this situation many times and always chose alternative 2, its average profit would be higher than for any other alternative.

Example 1.5. (Uncertainty) Even further analysis has cast doubt on the probability of the rates of population growth. New management doesn't know the probabilities of low, medium, or high growth, and is faced with a problem under conditions of uncertainty. Obviously, strategy is much harder to come by in this case.

Solution. We discuss three approaches from a set of several options that analysts use in the situation of uncertainty: *maximax, maximin,* and *principles of insufficient reason.*

(*i*) The *maximax* is an optimistic approach. Here the analyst considers only the best outcome for each alternative regardless of probability. Looking at Table 1.4 and ignoring the probability row, the outcomes that would be considered are: $.9 million for alternative1, $1.1 million for alternative 2, $.6 million for alternative 3, and $.8 million for alternative 4. Among these, *alternative 2* gives the best profit, and thus selected in this situation.

(*ii*) The second approach is *maximin* - a pessimistic approach. Here, the analyst considers only the worst outcome for each alternative and selects the '*best of the worst*'. In Table 1.4, the outcomes to be considered are: $.3 million for alternative1, $.2 million for alternative 2, $.4 million for alternative 3, and $.6 million for alternative 4. The best of these is *alternative 4*.

(*iii*) The third approach, the *principles of insufficient reason*, assumes that since we know absolutely nothing about the probabilities of any state of nature, we should treat each with equal probability, calculate the expected values accordingly, and choose the alternative whose expected value is highest. Using this approach, we would select *alternative 4*.

Table 1.6. Calculation of Expected Value in $ million

Alternative	*Low*	*Medium*	*High*	*Expected Value (Profit)*
1	0.3	0.8	0.9	(.3*.33) + (.8*.33) + (.9*.33) = .660
2	0.2	0.6	1.1	(.2*.33) + (.6*.33) + (1.1*.33)= .627
3	0.4	0.5	0.6	(.4*.33) + (.5*.33 + (.6*.33) = .495
4	0.6	0.7	0.8	(.6*.33) + (.7*.33 + (.8*.33) = .693
p	0.33	0.33	0.33	

1.4.2 MAXIMIN RULE *(WEATHER PROBLEM)*

A person needs to go to his office. The two possible *states of weather* are: (A) it may rain, (B) it might shine. The following threes possible *strategies* for the person are: X: go without protection, Y: go with an umbrella, Z: go with an umbrella and a rain coat. The *pay-off matrix* is given as follows:

Table 1.7. Pay-off matrix

Strategy	*A (Rain)*	*B (Shine)*
X (No Protection)	– 10	10
Y (Umbrella)	5	1
Z (Umbrella + Coat)	12	– 5

Decide on the basis of (*i*) Maximin , and (*ii*) Maximax what decision the person should take under the given situation?

Solution. (*i*) **Decision based on Maximin rule**

Strategy	*Minimum satisfaction for strategy*	*Maximum of these minima*
X	– 10	
Y	1	1 (the person will go with umbrella)
Z	– 5	

(*ii*) **Decision based on Maximax rule**

Strategy	*Max. satisfaction for the strategy*	*Maximum of these maxima*
X	10	
Y	5	
Z	12	12 (The person will go with umbrella and coat)

1.4.3 INTERDEPENDENCE AMONG DECISIONS

A second way to classify problems relates to the number of decision stages that must be considered. At one extreme are *single-stage* (or static) problems; at the other are *multistage* (or sequential) problems. Static problems entail essentially 'one-time-only' decisions. Decisions concerning inventory, 'make-vs-buy', product mix, and location of new facility are often treated as static problems. Our supermarket chain example was treated this way. To simplify the situation, the decision is treated as if it were independent of other decisions.

Multistage problems, on the other hand, entail several sequential decisions related to one another. The outcome of the first decision affects the attractiveness of choices at the next decision stage, and so on down the line at each decision point. With multistage problems, the concern is not how to get the best outcome at any single stage but how to make a series of choices that will finally result in the best overall set of outcomes from beginning to end. Some of the examples of multistage problems are encountered by operation managers in project management, capacity planning, and aggregate scheduling.

UNSOLVED PROBLEMS

1.1 The labor output standard for an *Insurance claims office* is 150 claims processes per day. So far this week, 160, 125, 140, and 100 claims have been processed daily. The claims backlog is building up. Prepare a graph of daily efficiency. What does the graph indicate?

1.2 The manager of a bottling plant came to work early on Friday, having been out of town throughout the week. Before others arrived, he checked the daily labor efficiency report for the bottling plant. He finds that daily efficiency was 102 % on Monday, 94 % on Tuesday, and 87 % on Wednesday. Going to the assistant manager's desk, he found that on Thursday employees worked 96 hours and bottled 1,025 cases. The standard for labor output is 12.5 cases per hour. What, if any, questions should the manager ask when employees arrive on Friday ?

1.3 A company is thinking to purchase a used truck. Its useful service life is estimated to be 3 years with a probability of 0.1; 4 years with a probability of 0.4; 5 years with a probability of 0.3; and 6 years with a probability of 0.2. what is the expected useful life of the used truck?

1.4 A cab company is considering three makes of autos-A,B, or C-to add to its taxi fleet The daily operating cost of each make depends on daily usage rate (demand) as shown here:

Make	*Daily Usage Rate*		
	Low	*Moderate*	*High*
A	$100	$200	$300
B	190	200	220
C	150	190	230

Which make is best according to the principles of insufficient reason? If the probabilities of low, moderate, and high usage are .5, .2, and.3, respectively, which make has the highest expected value?

1.5 Four alternative manufacturing methods are being considered for a new product. Profitability, which depends on method of manufacture and level of consumer acceptance, is anticipated as shown here.

Manufacturing Method	*Projected Consumer Acceptance*			
	Low	*Moderate*	*High*	*Very high*
1	$100	$200	$300	$600
2	175	300	400	500
3	250	300	350	425
4	100	300	400	450
Probability	.25	.35	.20	.20

(*a*) What is the best manufacturing method according to each of these approaches?

- Expected value
- Maximin
- Maximax
- Insufficient reason

(*b*) Which manufacturing method should be selected and why?

1.6 A glass factory is experiencing a substantial backlog, and the management is considering three courses of action: (A) arrange for subcontracting, (B) begin overtime production, or (C) construct new facilities. The correct choice depends largely upon future demand, which may be low, medium, or high. By consensus, the management ranks the respective probabilities as 0.1, 0.5, and 0.4. A cost analysis reveals the effect upon profits that is shown in Table 1.

	Profit ($000) If demand is		
	Low (p = 0.1)	*Medium (p = 0.5)*	*High (p = 0.4)*
A = Arrange for subcontracting	10	50	50
B = Begin overtime production	– 20	60	100
C = Construct new facilities	– 150	20	200

(*a*) State which course of action would be taken under a criterion of (*i*) maximax, (*ii*) maximin, (*iii*) maximum probability, and (*iv*) maximum expected value.

(*b*) Show this decision situation schematically in the form of a decision tree.

2

Location of Production and Service Facilities

2.0 INTRODUCTION

The problem of how many facilities to have and where they should be located is encountered by service and product organization in both the public and private sectors. Banks, restaurants, recreation agencies, and manufacturing companies are all concerned with selecting sites that will best enable them to meet their long-term goals. Since the operation managers fixes many costs with the location decision, both the efficiency and effectiveness of the conversion process are dependent upon location. This chapter will examine the facilities location issues in details by taking into account the reasons for location changes and the factors affecting the selection of location. We shall also discuss the procedure for facility location and related issues in the sections to follow.

2.1 REASONS FOR LOCATION CHANGES

Different situations for location change could be (*i*) a new plant is just being started, (*ii*) a new branch of an existing plant is to be located, or (*iii*) a new location for an existing plant is being sought. In addition to the need for greater capacity, there are other reasons for changing or adding locations:

- Changes in resources may occur. The cost or availability of labor, raw materials, and supporting resources (such as subcontractors) may change.
- The geography of demand may shift. As product markets change, it may be desirable to change facility location to provide better service to customers.
- Some companies may merge, making facilities location redundant.
- New products may be introduced, changing the availability of resources and markets.
- Political and economic conditions may change.

Location decision should be based on long range policy and forecasts, *e.g.* company's expansion policy, anticipated diversification of products, changing markets, changing sources of raw materials, etc.

Other decisions to be made before a plant selection/construction are: *(a) products or services to be made or offered in the plant, (b) type of equipment required, (c) type of structure needed, and (d) location of the plant.*

2.2 GENERAL FACTORS INFLUENCING LOCATION

The factors to be taken into account depend on the type of industry to be located. Thus the factors important for locating a steel plant may be different from the factors to be considered in locating a computer assembly plant. However, the general factors affecting the location of plant or facility are as mentioned below.

Proximity to Good Highways

This consists of the quality of highway system, its relationship to markets, raw materials, and labor supply. It is obvious that availability of inter state super highways makes the suburbs, small communities, and country easily accessible.

Abundant Labor Supply

It is always preferable to locate the plant in an area where skilled, semi-skilled, an unskilled labor are available. This explains why the glass and bangles industries are located in Firozabad (India) where skilled manpower in this field are available. The same reasons are true for carpets industry in Mirzapur, and silk sarees in Kanziwaram. It is also desirable to have no labor problem. Location of facility will also depend on the prevalent wage rate, facilities for labor, history of relationship between trade-union and management in the area under consideration. Rural labors can be hired at lower wages and Steel industry needs a lot of rural labor. Perhaps this is why most of the steel plants in India are located in rural areas.

Proximity to Markets

Plant should be located nearer to the consumers' market. Plants related to cement, bricks, roofing, and gypsum board are located nearer to the market. However, for those companies producing items like fountain pens, jewelry, and watches in which the costs of materials and labor are high, shipping costs are of secondary importance, and the location of plant is not on the basis of proximity of markets.

For many firms it is extremely important to locate the plant near customers. Specially, service organizations, like drugstores, restaurants, post offices, or barbers, find proximity to market as the primary location factor. Manufacturing firms find it useful to be close to customers when transporting finished goods is expensive or difficult (perhaps because they are bulky, heavy, or fragile). Further, with the trend toward JIT production, suppliers want to locate near users to speed up deliveries.

Availability of Suitable Land and Land Cost

Cost of land is usually a minor factor in the location of a plant. In the communities that are interested in attracting new plants, land may be offered at a reduced price or at no cost, which may influence some plants to locate there.

Adequate Water Supply

Water is necessary for almost all kinds of plants. However, some plants heavily depend on water supply. For example, thermal power plant, Hydroelectric power plant, steel plant need lots of water for its day to day operation. This needs the plant to be located nearer to the water sources like lake or river.

Nearness to Raw Materials and Suppliers

In general, bulky or perishable products manufacturing companies are located near to the source of the raw materials. For example, food processing industry should be located nearer to canning factories, meat packing plants and creameries. Firms locate near their suppliers because of the perishability of raw materials and products, and transportation costs. Bakeries, dairy plants, and frozen seafood processors deal with perishable raw materials, so they often locate themselves close to suppliers.

The Guiding principle in such cases is '*weight losing*'. If the raw material loses a lot of weight in processing, then the plant should be located nearer to the source of raw materials. Another principle is '*weight balancing*' i.e. relative cost of transporting raw materials must be weighed against the cost of shipping the finished products. Thus, steel industry should be located near the coal and iron ore supply. Most of the steel plants in India are located in the region where coal, iron ores, and other raw materials are available. Tata steel, and steel plants under SAIL are also examples to justify this guidelines.

Nearness to an Existing Plant

It is advisable to keep the new plant reasonably close to the parent plant. Thus the truck assembly plant can be kept close to a steel plant because the two plants can act as complementary to each other. Product of one becomes the raw materials for the other. Again one can see why Telco and Tata steel in Jamshedpur are located nearer to each other. This way, executive supervision and staff consultations can be made common and cost reduction will be possible. Engineers and executives can make frequent trips to do the consultation and supervision work.

Transportation

Some companies find it desirable to be located near the seaport or near one of the inland waterways to take advantage of the lower cost of transporting materials (e.g., coal, iron ore, petroleum products, etc.) by boat, barge, or ship. Access to railroad or trucking facilities is also desirable.

Power Supply

It is desirable to have power supply at low cost for the operation of the plant. Cost of power supply per unit is generally cheaper in rural location than its urban counterpart. Some companies prefer to maintain their own standby power station.

Water Disposal and Pollution

Anti-pollution law should be followed to avoid water pollution. Waste materials dumped into the rivers or stream may create problems for new company needing a supply of fresh and pure water.

For example, companies manufacturing antibiotics, steel, chemicals, and those using radioactive materials are confronted with waste disposal problems. Some of the examples related to environment issues include: three mile island (USA), Cello field (UK), Chernobyl (USSR), and Union carbide (India).

Most countries have laws to prevent the companies from dumping the industrial wastes into rivers. Some of the site related problems in India that have surfaced in media are: Mathura oil refinery vs The Taj Mahal, Barauni oil refinery vs The Ganges river, Paradip port *vs* Cyclone effect, Narmada dam vs environmental issues. Similarly, the environment issues in Mugher Cement Plant in Addis Ababa (Ethiopia) calls for relocation of this plant or convert the plant into an environment friendly one.

Taxes

Kinds and amounts of taxes (*e.g.*, excise duty, sales tax, income tax, etc.) levied by a state should also be considered in locating a plant. The kinds of taxes and the basis for fixing them should be investigated before hand. Some states and territories offer tax exemption for a stipulated period of time to attract the investors to set up their plants to produce certain priority products.

Climate

Companies requiring controlled temperature, humidity, and ventilation should consider the climatic factor while locating the plant. For example, textile factories in India needing high humidity are located in Maharashtra, Gujarat, etc which are near the sea coast and have adequate humidity for the textile mills. Even the choice of the executives may affect the plant location. Similarly, *companies interested in manufacturing computer components may be interested in a place with moderate climate and dust free environment.*

National Defense

Industry related to defense or military hardware should be located on the basis of national defense interest and may preferably be away from the country's borders.

Community Administration and Attitude

Local authorities and people should be willing to have the plant located in their area. Community should also provide the necessary municipal services, *e.g.* police and fire protection, maintenance of streets, waste disposal, etc. Worker attitude may also differ from country to country, region to region, and small town to city. Worker views about turnover, unions, and absenteeism are all relevant factors.

Schools, Churches, Parks, and Residential Area

It makes sense to pick up a town or locality that will provide the best services and living conditions for their employees and their families. Excellent schools, parks, hospitals, residential areas, etc. should be desirable.

Space for Future Expansions

Demand of products is dynamic in nature. It may be required to increase the production capacity of the plant in future if the demand increases or change the product altogether if the demand is very low. Thus, there should be an adequate space for future expansion or diversification of the plant.

2.2.1 RURAL AND URBAN SITES COMPARED

It has been seen above that some points are favorable in rural site, and some are good in an urban site. None of them is entirely good or bad from all points of view. A comparison between a rural and a urban sites with respect to various factors can be done as shown in Table 2.1.

Table 2.1. Comparison of Rural and Urban sites

Urban site (located in city)	Rural site (located in village)
Very well connected by rail, roads, and air.	Just the opposite. Rural sites are not easily accessible.
Provides good market for the final products.	Products need to be transported to some nearby markets.
Labor force with right kind of skill may be available.	Mostly labor force of low skill or no skill are available.
Power and water available in adequate quantity.	Water may be adequate but one may not be lucky with the power supply.
Good hospitals, marketing centers, schools, banks, recreation clubs, etc. are available.	Almost nothing of this sort exists on rural site.
Training centers available for all kinds of labor force.	No such facility exists here.
Services of experts, specialists available from other companies or consultants.	Can't think of such facility in rural sites.
Ancillary units available to support the main plant.	This may exist in rural sites too.
Land for the building is limited and costly.	Land is cheaper and available in plenty.

Local taxes are high.	Taxes are low.
Expansion of industry may be difficult.	Expansion and diversification will not be challenged by land availability.
Labor cost is high.	Labor cost is cheap.
Union labor problems related may be more, employer-employees relation not good.	This problem is not so acute in rural sites because the labor union may not be as right conscious as their urban counterparts.

A compromising solution will be to go for sub-urban site which has good points of both rural and urban locations.

2.3 GENERAL PROCEDURES FOR FACILITY LOCATION

Location of a plant or an organization can be seen as a two step decision. First, one has to select a **region**, and second a choice of a **site** has to be made within the region. The first step depends on the plant's long-term strategies like technological, marketing, resource mobilization, and financial strategies. However, the choice of a site within a region can be decided by comparing the relative availability and costs of required resources like: power, transport, labor, water, land, raw materials, in alternative sites. While comparing various sites, one has to take into account both tangible and intangible costs (climate, labor relations, community support, recreational facility, and presence of good schools, etc.) related to the sites. These are all discussed subsequently under the headings: *preliminary screening*, and *selection of exact site*.

2.3.1 PRELIMINARY SCREENING

It consists of decision about: *(a) zone to which the plant should belong, (b) region in which it should be placed,* and (c) *the exact site* where the plant be erected. A preliminary screening to identify feasible sites begins the planning process. For some kinds of facilities, particular environmental or labor considerations are crucial. Breweries, for example, need an adequate supply of clear water. Aircraft manufacturers must be located near a variety of subcontractors; and basic aluminum producers need electrical power and aluminum ores.

2.3.1.1 Sources of Information

After identifying several key location requirements (outlined in Section 2.2), management starts looking for alternative locations that are consistent with these requirements. The possible sources of information could be: *local chambers of commerce and industries, local communities, relevant ministries, Government agencies, and trade journals.* The data available with these wings could be geographic breakdowns of labor availability, population, transportation facilities, types of commerce, and similar information.

2.3.1.2 Detailed Analysis

Once the preliminary screening narrows down the alternative sites to just a few, more detailed analysis begins. At each potential site a labor survey may be conducted to assess the local skills. Community response can be obtained by survey. Community response is important, for example, in deciding where to locate a nuclear reactor, recreation area, commercial bank, state prison, or restaurant. Among the many considerations, each company must identify which ones are most pertinent for their location strategies.

2.3.2 SELECTION OF EXACT SITE

Different sites should be compared on the basis of various factors by asking relevant questions on each issues. Some of them are discussed below:

Transportation facilities

- Is the location easily accessible by vehicles from the main highways?
- Are the railroad facilities sufficient for quick receipt and shipment of goods?
- Can a railroad siding be made available?

Availability of water, power, gas and sewerage

- Is water available in sufficient quantity and of required quality?
- Is adequate power available or not?
- Is gas and sewer system adequate to the plant's needs?

Soil characteristics

- Is the bearing capacity of soil suitable to support the building and equipment?
- Will the soil provide adequate drainage?

Drainage

- Will the area drain away all surface water so that the buildings or work area will not be flooded?

Parking space

- Is adequate space available to provide for employees and visitors' vehicles parking?

Space for expansion

- Is enough space available for future expansion of the plant?

Accessibility by workers

- Can the sites be reached by public transport ?
- Is the road and street network suitable for speedy entrance and exit of employees during rush hours or emergency?

Cost of land

- Does the cost of land justify the selected site for the intended product?
- Can the location be shifted to some cheaper site with similar facilities?

Existing buildings

- Are the existing buildings suitable for company's operation on rent or final purchase basis?

2.3.2.1 Factors Ratings

Factor ratings are used to evaluate location alternatives because (*i*) their simplicity helps decide why one site is better than another; (*ii*) they enable managers to bring diverse locational considerations into the evaluation process; and (*iii*) they foster consistency of judgment about location alternatives. The following **steps** are involved in factor rating:

- Develop *a list of relevant factors.*
- Assign a *weight to each factor* to indicate its relative importance (weights may total 1.00).
- Assign a common scale to each factor (*e.g.*, 0 to 100 points), and designate any minimums.
- Score each potential location according to the designated scale, and multiply the scores by the weights.
- Total the points for each location, and choose the location with the maximum points.

Example 2.1. A glass company is evaluating four locations *A*, *B*, *C*, and *D* for a new plant and has weighted the relevant factors as shown in Table 2.2. Scores have been assigned with higher values indicative of preferred conditions. Using these scores, develop a qualitative factor comparison for the four locations.

Table 2.2

		A		*B*		*C*		*D*	
Relevant Factor	*Assigned weight*	*Score*	*Weighted score*	*Score*	*Weighted score*	*Score*	*Weighted score*	*Score score*	*Weighted*
Production cost	0.33	50	16.5	40	13.2	35	11.55	30	9.9
Raw material supply	0.25	70	17.5	80	20.0	75	18.75	80	20.0
Labor availability	0.20	55	11.0	70	14.0	60	12.00	45	9.0
Cost of living	0.05	80	4.0	70	3.5	40	2.00	50	2.5
Environment	0.02	60	1.2	60	1.2	60	1.20	90	1.8
Markets	0.15	80	12.0	90	13.5	85	12.75	50	7.5
Totals	1.00		62.2		65.4		58.25		50.7

Weighted scores are computed by multiplying the scores with the assigned weight (for example, 50 ×.33 = 16.50) and the totals are scored by summing those products. On the basis of this data, B is the best location, and thus selected.

2.3.2.2 Cost Analysis

Estimates should also be made for all the costs entering into the operation of the plant in each of the locations. This cost will include: initial cost, cost of raw materials, cost of manufacturing, cost of distribution. Revenues and costs are both affected by facility location. A technique called break-even analysis can be used to relate the costs and revenue to facility location. This is discussed later in section 2.4.5.

2.4 SOME OTHER FACILITY LOCATION MODELS

Various quantitative models are used to help determine the best location of facilities. Sometimes, models are tailor-made to meet the specific circumstances of a unique problem. In New York City, for example, a mathematical model was developed to find the best locations of fire companies.

There are some general models that can be adapted to the needs of a variety of systems. In the next section, we briefly introduce three types of models that have been applied to the location problem. They are *(a) simple median model, (b) center of gravity model, (c) linear programming, and (d) simulation.* All these models focus on transportation costs, although each considers a different version of the basic problem.

2.4.1 SIMPLE MEDIAN MODEL

Suppose we want to locate a new plant that will annually receive shipments of raw materials from two sources: F_1 and F_2. The plant will create finished goods that must be shipped to two distribution warehouses, F_3 and F_4. Given these four facilities (Figure 2.1), where should we locate the new plant to minimize annual transportation costs for this network of facilities?

The Model

The *simple median model* (SMM) can help answer this question. This model considers the volume of loads transported on *rectangular* paths. All movements are made in east-west or north-south directions; diagonal moves are not considered. The SMM provides an optimal solution. This is discussed with the help of Figure 2.1 and the Table 2.3.

Let L_i = Loads to be shipped annually between each existing facility F_i, and

C_i = Cost to move a load one distance unit to or from F_i.

D_i = Distance units between facility F_i and the new plant.

Then, the total transit cost is the sum of the products $C_iL_iD_i$ for all *i*.

$$\text{Total cost of transportation} = \sum_{i=1}^{n} C_iL_iD_i \tag{2.1}$$

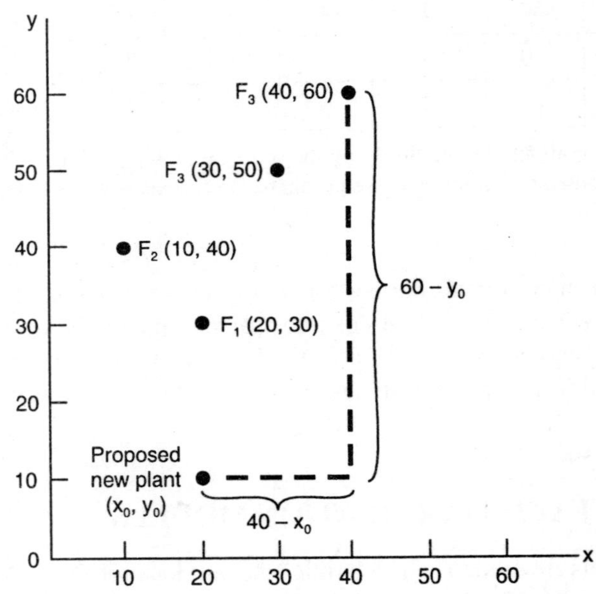

Figure 2.1. Sources of raw materials and distribution warehouses.

Table 2.3. Data related to C_i, L_i and D_i

F_i	L_i	C_i	(X_i, Y_i) of F_i
F_1	755	\$1	(20, 30)
F_2	900	1	(10, 40)
F_3	450	1	(30, 50)
F_4	500	1	(40, 60)
Total	2605		

Since all loads must be on rectangular paths, distance between each existing facility and the new plant will be measured by the difference in the x-coordinates and the difference in the y-coordinates (Figure 2.1). If we let (x_0, y_0) be the coordinates of a proposed new plant, then

$$D_i = | x_0 - x_i | + | y_0 - y_i | \quad (2.2)$$

Notice that we calculate the absolute value of the differences, because distance is always positive. We could have written Eqn.(2.2) as

$$D_i = | x_i - x_0 | + | y_i - y_0 | \quad (2.3)$$

Our goal is to find values for x_0 and y_0 for the *new plant* that result in minimum transportation costs. We follow three steps:

1. Identify the median value of the loads Li moved.
2. Find the x-coordinate of the existing facility that sends (or receives) the median load.
3. Find the y-coordinate value of the existing facility that sends or receives) the median load

The x and y coordinates found in steps 2 and 3 define the new plant's best location.

Example 2.2. (*Application of the SMM Model)*

Let us apply the three steps to the data in Table 2.3.

- *Identify the median load.* The total number of loads moved to and from the new plant will be 2,605. If we think of each load individually and number them from 1 to 2,605, then the median load number is the 'middle' number—that is, the number for which the same number of loads fall above and below. For 2,605 loads, the median load number is 1,303, since 1302 loads fall above and below load number 1,303. If the total number of loads were even we would consider both 'middle' numbers.
- *Find the x-coordinate of the median load.* First we consider movement of loads in the x-direction. Beginning at the origin of Figure 2.1 and moving to the right along the x-axis, observe the number of loads moved to or from existing facilities. Loads 1-900 are shipped by F_2 from location $x = 10$. Loads 901-1,655 are shipped by F_1 from $x = 20$. *Since the median load falls in the interval 901-1,655, $x = 20$ is the desired x-coordinate location for the new plant.*
- *Find y-coordinate of the median load.* Now consider the y-direction of load movements. Begin at the origin of Figure 2.1 and move upward along the y-axis. Movements in the y direction begin with loads 1-755 being shipped by F_1 from location $y = 30$. Loads 756-1,655 are shipped by F_2 from location $y = 40$. *Since the median load falls, in the interval 756-1,655, $y = 40$ is the desired y-coordinate for the new plant.*
- The optimal plant location, $x = 20$ and $y = 40$, results in minimizing annual transportation costs for this network of facilities. The calculation is shown in Table 2.4.

Remarks:

- First, we have considered the case in which only one new facility is to be added.
- Second, we have assumed that any point in x-y coordinate system is an eligible point for locating the new facility. *The model does not consider road availability, physical terrain, population densities, or any other considerations.*
- The task of blending model results with other major considerations to arrive at a location choice is managerial task.

Table 2.4. Calculation of total cost for optimal plant location (x = 20, y = 40)

F_i	x_i *of* F_i	y_i *of* F_i	$\mid 20 - x_i \mid$	$\mid 40 - y_i \mid$	$D_i = \mid x_0 - x_i \mid + \mid y_0 - y_i \mid$	L_i	C_i	$C_i L_i D_i$
F_1	20	30	0	10	10	755	$1	7,550
F_2	10	40	10	0	10	900	1	9,000
F_3	30	50	10	10	20	450	1	9,000
F_4	40	60	20	20	40	500	1	20,000
Total transportation cost = $\Sigma C_i L_i D_i$, where (i = 1 to 4) =								$45,550

2.4.2 CENTER OF GRAVITY (GRID) MODEL

This method assumes that the distribution cost is a function of the volumes shipped and the rectilinear distances (*i.e.*, X and Y coordinates). The distances in each of the X and Y coordinates are averaged, using the volumes as weights. The resultant coordinates then constitute the center of gravity for that grid.

If X_c = X coordinate of the center of gravity
Y_c = Y coordinate of the center of gravity
V_i = volume of goods transported to or from each of *i* destination
X_i = distances traveled by the goods in X direction
Y_i = distances traveled by the goods in Y direction

Then, $$X_c = \Sigma V_i X_i / \Sigma V_i \quad (2.4)$$

and $$Y_c = \Sigma V_i Y_i / \Sigma V_i \quad (2.5)$$

Once determined, the X_c, Y_c coordinates constitute a starting point for a new site. Locations in that vicinity may then be evaluated, changes suggested, and perhaps some recalculations done before the final choice is made.

Example 2.3. Table 2.5 shows eight market locations to which a manufacturer of wooden windows expects to ship its products. The shipment volumes, X and Y coordinates of the locations are shown in Table 2.5. Using the center of gravity method, (*a*) find the X_c and Y_c coordinates, and (*b*) suggest a possible warehouse location.

Table 2.5

Market Area	*Vi (tonne)*	*Xi (km)*	*Yi (km)*
A	8	2.5	10
B	20	3	5
C	12	6.5	8
D	10	11	10
E	30	11	8
F	20	10	4
G	40	13	3.5
H	30	12	2
	170		

Solution. The solution is shown in Table 2.6

Table 2.6

Market Area	V_i *(ton)*	X_i *(km)*	*Yi (km)*	$V_i X_i$ *(t-km)*	$V_i Y_i$ *(t-km)*	$X_c = \Sigma V_i X_i / \Sigma V_i$	$Y_c = \Sigma V_i Y_i / \Sigma V_i$
A	8	2.5	10	20	80	= 1678/170	= 896/170
B	20	3.0	5	60	100	= 9.87 km	= 5.3 km
C	12	6.5	8	78	96		
D	10	11	10	110	100		
E	30	11	8	330	240		
F	20	10	4	200	80		
G	40	13	3.5	520	140		
H	30	12	2	360	60		
	170			1678	896		

(*a*) Thus, $X_c = 9.87$ kms and $Y_c = 5.3$ kms

(*b*) Looking at the various coordinates in Table 2.6, we feel that ($X_c = 9.87$ and $Y_c = 5.3$) are very close to F, suggesting that it may be good to have the distribution center located here.

2.4.3 LINEAR PROGRAMMING (LP)

LP model may be helpful after the initial screening phase has narrowed the feasible alternative sites. The remaining candidates can then be evaluated, one at a time, to determine how well each would fit with existing facilities, and the alternative that leads to the best overall system (network) performance can be identified. Most often, overall transportation cost is the criterion used for performance evaluation. A special type of linear programming called the distribution or transportation method is particularly useful in location planning.

The linear programming model differs from the simple median model in two fundamental ways:

(*i*) **Number of alternative sites.** The simple median model assumes that all locations are eligible to be the new location. The linear programming model, in contrast, considers only a few locations pre-selected from preliminary feasibility studies.

(*ii*) **Direction of transportation movements.** The simple median model assumes that all shipments move in rectangular patterns. The linear programming model does not assume so.

Transportation adds no value to a good other than place utility. However, the transportation costs for raw materials and finished goods are often significant and merit special analysis. Before deciding on a plant location, management may want to know which plants will be used to produce what quantities and to which distribution warehouses all quantities should be shipped.

If the location problem can be formulated as one of minimizing a transportation cost, subject to satisfying overall supply and demand requirements, the transportation linear-programming (LP) method may be useful. The transportation model is a variation of the standard linear-programming approach and assumes the following:

1. The objective is to minimize total transportation costs.
2. Transportation costs are a linear function of the number of units shipped.

3. All supply and demand are expressed in homogeneous units.
4. Shipping costs per unit do not vary with the quantity shipped.
5. Total supply must equal total demand.
   - If demand is larger than supply, create a dummy supply and assign a zero transportation cost to it so that excess supply is absorbed.
   - If supply is larger than demand, create and assign a zero transportation cost to it so that excess supply is absorbed.

The Heuristic Model

To use the transportation (also called distribution) linear-programming format, (*i*) the demand requirements and supply availabilities are formulated in a rectangular matrix. (*ii*) The transportation costs between the supply and demand points are placed in the upper corner of each cell. (*iii*) Supply is then allocated to meet demand by placing entries, which express the number of units shipped from a supply source to a demand destination, into the cells. (*iv*) The solution procedure is an iterative one that begins with an initial solution that is feasible, but not necessarily optimal. (*v*) The solution is progressively tested and improved upon until an optimal solution is reached. The optimal solution satisfies demand at the lowest total cost.

Several methods of obtaining *initial* and *optimal* solutions have been developed:

Initial Solutions

1. Minimum cost (intuitive) method
2. Northwest corner method
3. Vogel's approximation method (VAM)

Optimal Solutions

1. Stepping-stone method
2. Modified distribution MODI)

The *minimum cost* method works well for simple problems, but VAM is likely to yield a better initial solution, which is often also the optimal solution. VAM works by sequential zeroing in on the most cost-advantageous row-and-column combinations. The *northwest-corner* method does not usually yield as good an initial solution as VAM, but it is extremely easy to apply. VAM is useful for hand calculation of relatively large-scale problems. However, most large problems are solved by computer, and numerous computer programs are available, so VAM is not covered in the examples that follow. The MODI method is well-suited to computer applications. It is a modified stepping-stone algorithm that uses index numbers to systematically reach an optimum solution. Example-2.4 uses the *northwest-corner* method for the initial solution and the *stepping-stone method* for the final solution.

Example 2.4. *(Distribution linear-programming methods or DLP)*

A company has production plants at A, B, and C, all of which manufacture similar products for the housing market. The products are currently distributed through plants at X and Y. The company is considering adding another distribution plant at Z, and has developed the transportation costs in dollars per unit, shown in Table 2.7.

Table 2.7

Production Plants	Cost to ship to distribution Plant at		
	X	*Y*	*Z*
A	$ 10	$ 14	$ 8
B	12	10	12
C	8	12	10

The production capacities at A, B, C are 20, 30, and 40 unit loads per week respectively. Management feels that a plant at Z could absorb 20 units per week, with X and Y claiming 40 and 30 units per week respectively. Determine the optimal distribution arrangement and cost if the Z site is selected.

Solution. We will use the north-west corner (NWC) method for the initial allocation and the stepping-stone method for the final solution. Table 2.9 shows supply on the horizontal rows, demand on the columns, and unit transportation cost ($) in the small boxes of the matrix. The initial allocation by the NWC method is made as follows:

- Assign as many units as possible to the NW-corner cell AX from the total available in row A. Given the 20 units available in row A and the 40 unit demand in column X, the maximum number of units that can be assigned to cell AX is 20. This is shown in the circle as initial allocation.

Table 2.8. Initial solution to DLP matrix

Production Plants	*X*	*Y*	*Z*	*Supply (units)*
A	[10] (20)	[14]	[08]	20
B	[12] (20)	[10] (10)	[12]	30
C	[08]	[12] (20)	[10] (20)	40
Demand (units)	40	30	20	90

- Assign additional units of supply from row B (or other rows) until the demand in column X is satisfied. This requires 20 additional units in cell BX and leaves 10 units of B's unassigned.
- Assign remaining units to BY. Since this does not satisfy demand in column Y, an additional 20 units are allocated from row C to CY.
- Continue down from the NW corner until the whole supply has been allocated to demand. The initial assignment is completed by assigning the 20 units remaining in row C to cell CZ.
- Check allocations to verify that all supply and demand conditions are satisfied. Since all row and column totals agree, the initial assignment is correct. Also, see that the number of entries should satisfy (R + C – 1), where R is number of rows, and C is number of columns. Here, R + C – 1 = 3 + 3 – 1 = 5 which is satisfied here.

The *transportation cost* for this arrangement is given as

$$TC_1 = (20 \times 10) + (20 \times 12) + (10 \times 10) + (20 \times 12) + (20 \times 10) = \$\ 980 \quad (2.6)$$

An optimal solution can be obtained by following a *stepping-stone approach*:

- It requires calculation of the net monetary gain or loss that can be obtained by shifting an allocation from one supply source to another. *The important rule to keep in mind is that every increase (or decrease) in supply at one location must be accompanied by a decrease (or increase) in supply at another.* The same holds true for demand. Thus *there must be two changes in every row or column that is changed* - one change increasing the quantity and one change decreasing it. This is easily done by evaluating reallocations in a closed-path sequence with only right-angle turns permitted and only on occupied cells.
- A cell must have an initial entry before it can be reduced in favor of another, but *empty (or filled) cells may be skipped over to get to a corner cell.* It is better to proceed systematically, evaluating each empty cell. When any changes are made, cells vacated earlier must be rechecked. This is because moves are restricted to occupied cells. Every time a vacant cell is filled, one previously occupied cell must become vacant. The initial and (continuing) number of entries is always maintained at (R + C – 1). When a move causes fewer entries (for example, when two cells become vacant at the same time but only one is filled), a 'zero' entry must be retained in one of the cells to avoid the situation of *degeneracy.*
- The zero entry (0) assigned to either cell should ensure that a closed path exists for all filled cells. The cell with the zero entry is then considered to be an occupied and potentially usable cell. If a cell evaluation reveals an improvement potential in a given cell, but no units are available because of a zero entry in the path to that cell, the zero (zero units) should be transported to the vacant cell, just as any other units would be shipped. Then the matrix should be reevaluated. Improvements may still be possible until the zero entries are relocated to where evaluations of all vacant cells are greater than or equal to 0.
- The criterion for making a reallocation is simply the desired effect upon costs. The net loss or gain is found by listing the unit costs associated with each cell (which is used as a corner in the evaluation path) and then summing over the path to find the net effect. Signs alternate from + to – depending upon whether shipments are being added or reduced at a given point. A negative sign on the net results indicates that cost can be reduced by making the change. The total savings are limited to the least number of units available for reallocation at any negative cell on the path.

Application of the model

From Table 2.8, *Filled cells are:* AX, BX, BY, CY and CZ, and *Empty cells are:* AY, AZ, BZ, and CX. We will evaluate the empty cells one by one.

Evaluate cell AY:

From Table 2.8*a*, Path: AY – BY – BX – AX – AY

Cost = +14 – 10 + 12 – 10 = + 6 (cost increase), thus, make no change.

Table 2.8a

Production Plants	*X*	*Y*	*Z*	*Supply (units)*
A	20 [10]	+ [14]	[08]	20
B	20 [12]	10 [10]	[12]	30
C	[08]	20 [12]	20 [10]	40
Demand (units)	40	30	20	90

Evaluate cell CX:

From Table 2.8*b*, Path: CX – BX – BY – CY – CX

Cost = + 8 – 12 + 10 – 12 = – 6 (cost savings). Therefore, this is a potential change. Evaluate remaining empty cells to see if other changes are more profitable.

Table 2.8b

Production Plants	*X*	*Y*	*Z*	*Supply (units)*
A	20 [10]	+ [14]	[08]	20
B	20 [12]	10 [10]	[12]	30
C	+ [08]	20 [12]	20 [10]	40
Demand (units)	40	30	20	90

Evaluate cell AZ:

From Table 2.8*c*, Path: AZ – CZ – CY – BY – BX – AX – AZ

Cost = + 8 – 10 + 12 – 10 + 12 – 10 = + 2 (cost increase). Thus, no change is needed.

Table 2.8c

Production Plants	*X*	*Y*	*Z*	*Supply (units)*
A	20 [10]	[14]	+ [08]	20
B	20 [12]	10 [10]	[12]	30
C	[08]	20 [12]	20 [10]	40
Demand (units)	40	30	20	90

Evaluate cell BZ:

From Table 2.8*d*, Path: BZ – CZ – CY – BY – BZ

Cost = + 12 – 10 + 12 – 10 = + 4 (cost increase). Thus, we will make no change.

Table 2.8d

Production Plants	*X*	*Y*	*Z*	*Supply (units)*
A	20 [10]	[14]	[08]	20
B	20 [12]	10 [10]	+ [12]	30
C	[08]	20 [12]	20 [10]	40
Demand (units)	40	30	20	90

Summary of evaluation:

AY = + 6, **CX = – 6**, AZ = + 2, and BZ = + 4

Therefore, cell CX presents the best opportunity for improvement. For each unit from C reallocated to X and from B reallocated to Y, a $6 savings results. Change the maximum number available in the loop (20) for a net savings of $6 × 20 = $120. *The maximum number will always be the smallest number in the cells where shipments are being reduced, that is, cells with negative coefficients.* The crossed circles with numbers above in Table 2.9 represents that changes have been made. Note that cells BX and CY have both become vacant (a degenerate situation), so a zero has been assigned to one of the vacant cells (BX) to maintain R + C – 1 requirement of 5.

Table 2.9. Revision of matrix

Production Plants	*X*	*Y*	*Z*	*Supply (units)*
A	(20) [10]	[14]	[08]	20
B	0 ~~(20)~~ [12]	30 ~~(10)~~ [10]	[12]	30
C	20 [08]	~~(20)~~ [12]	(20) [10]	40
Demand (units)	40	30	20	90

Because a reallocation was made, the empty cells are again evaluated for further improvement as shown below:

Cell AY: AY – BY – BX – AX = + 6 (no change)

Cell CY: CY – CX – BX – BY = + 6 (no change

Cell AZ: AZ – CZ – CX – AX = – 4 (possibility for savings)

Cell BZ: BZ – CZ – CX – BX = – 2 (possibility for savings)

Let's redraw Table 2.9 as Table 2.9*a*. Cell AZ has the greatest potential for improvement. *Note that the loop evaluating cell BZ has zero (Table 2.10a) units available for transfer from cell BX, so no reallocation could take place without first locating another route to BZ. This would be done by relocating the zero. However, in this example cell AZ offers the best improvement, so we capitalize upon the opportunity to load cell AZ.*

Table 2.9a. Revision of matrix

Production Plants	*X*	*Y*	*Z*	*Production capacity or Supply (units)*
A	(20) [10]	[14]	[08]	20
B	0 [12]	30 [10]	[12]	30
C	20 [08]	[12]	(20) [10]	40
Demand (units)	40	30	20	90

A reallocation of 20 units to cell AZ results in the matrix shown in Table 2.10. Note that a zero has again been retained in one of the vacated cells CZ to satisfy the R + C – 1 constraint. Further evaluation of the cells indicates that no additional savings are possible. The optimal solution is finally shown in Table 2.10. The transportation cost for this allocation is:

$$TC_2 = (40 \times 8) + (30 \times 10) + (20 \times 8) = \$\ 780 \tag{2.7}$$

$$\text{Net savings} = DTC = TC_2 - TC_1 = \$\ (980 - 780) = \$\ 200 \text{ per week}$$

Table 2.10. Optimal solution

Production Plants	*X*		*Y*		*Z*		*Supply (units)*
A		[10]		[14]	**20**	[08]	20
B	0	[12]	**30**	[10]		[12]	30
C	**40**	[08]		[12]	**0**	[10]	40
Demand (units)	40		30		20		90

2.4.4 SIMULATION

Although many quantitative models are available to deal with location problems, many real world problems are more complex than our examples. Some systems have multiple sources shipping to numerous plants; they in turn ship finished goods to warehouses from which further shipments are made to retailers. Multi-echelon (multilevel) production distribution systems such as these pose formidable problems. Even with the simplest revision of this system, adding or deleting one network component, the combinatorial aspects of the problem make it computationally difficult. More realistically, we may want to consider more drastic changes, such as total revision of the warehousing network. With problems of this complexity, no optimal solution is possible. Instead, approximation techniques like computer simulation are used.

2.4.5 BREAK EVEN ANALYSIS

In break even charts, the total cost (fixed costs + variable costs), and revenue are plotted against the output (either in units, dollar volume, or % of capacity). Such a graphical portrayal of revenue and costs, as a function of the output is called **'break even chart'**.

Example 2.5. A businessman is thinking of opening a factory in one of these places in Ethiopia: Nazereth, Debre Zeit, or on the outskirt of Addis Ababa to produce high quality electronic components for computer. He has gathered data on fixed cost and variable cost as given in Table 2.11.

Table 2.11

			Per unit costs	
Location	*Fixed cost/year*	*Material*	*Variable labor*	*Overhead*
Addis Ababa	$ 200,000	$ 0.20	$0.40	$0.40
Debre Zeit	180,000	0.25	0.75	0.75
Nazereth	170,000	1.00	1.00	1.00

(*a*) Represent the costs graphically.

(*b*) Over what range of annual volume is each location going to have a competitive advantage?

(*c*) What is the volume at the intersection?

Solution. (*a*) Let Q = quantity of components to be produced per year, then the total cost equations for all these sites can be written as shown in Table 2.12.

Table 2.12

Location	*Fixed cost/year*	*Material cost*	*Labor cost*	*Overhead*	*Variable cost/unit*	*Total Cost Equation*
Addis Ababa	$200,000	$0.20	$0.40	$0.40	$1.00	= 200,000 + 1.0Q
Debre Zeit	180,000	0.25	0.75	0.75	$1.75	= 180,000 + 1.75Q
Nazereth	170,000	1.00	1.00	1.00	$3.00	= 170,000 + 3.0Q

A graph of the total cost for all these locations have been shown in Figure 2.2.

(*b*) & (*c*). From Figure 2.2, we see that the cost line for Nazereth and Debre Zeit cross each other. At this point of intersection the total cost for both will be equal. Thus,

$$180{,}000 + 1.75Q = 170{,}000 + 3.0Q$$

or, $$1.25\,Q = 10{,}000$$

or, $$Q = 8{,}000$$

We see from the Figure 2.2 that *below 8000 units of production, Nazereth ensures a lower total cost than Debre Zeit*, and vice-versa for production more than 8000 units.

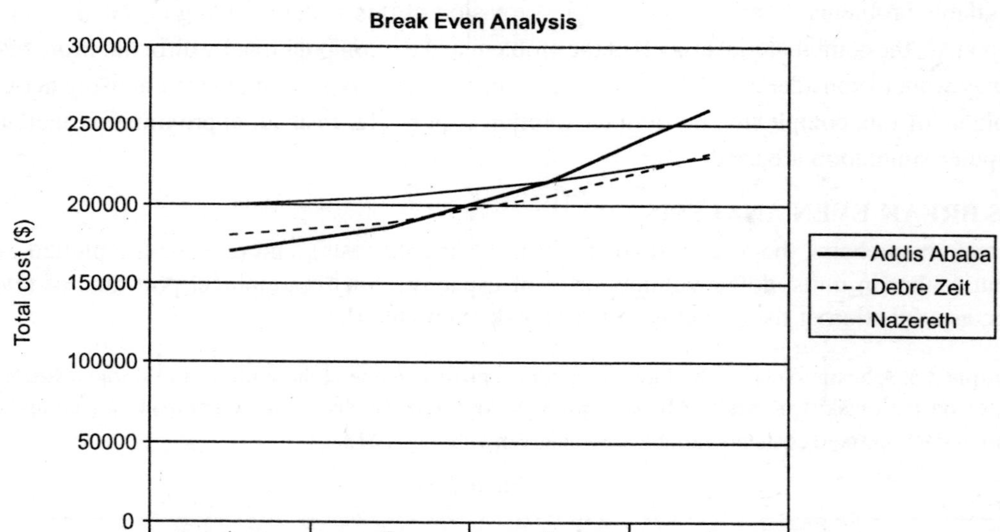

	1	2	3	4
—— Addis Ababa	200000	205000	215000	230000
---- Debre Zeit	180000	188750	206250	232500
—— Nazereth	170000	185000	215000	260000

Units of Components

Figure 2.2. Break Even Charts.

Similarly, the cost line for Debre Zeit and Addis Ababa cross each other. At this point of intersection the total cost for both will be equal. Thus

$$200{,}000 + 1.0Q = 180{,}000 + 1.75Q$$

or, $$0.75Q = 20{,}000$$

or, $$Q = 26{,}666$$

So, we see from the figure that *between 8000 units and 26,666 units of production, Debre Zeit has an advantage.*

Note. It has been assumed that delivery and intangible factors are constant regardless of the decision.

3

Layout Planning

3.0 INTRODUCTION

Decisions about layout are made only periodically, but since they have long-term consequences, they must be made with careful planning. The layout design affects the cost of producing goods and delivering services for many years into the future. The design of layouts begins with a statement of the goals of the facility. Layouts are designed to meet these goals. After initial designs are developed, improved designs are sought. This can be a tedious and cumbersome task because the number of possible designs is so large. For this reason, quantitative and computer-based models are often used.

Plant layout is defined as *the most effective physical arrangement of machines, processing equipment, and service departments to have the best co-ordination and efficiency of man, machine and material in a plant.* It is the spatial arrangement of physical resources used to create the product. It also means how the space needed for material movement, storage, indirect labor, etc is arranged in a factory.

For a factory which is already in operation, this may mean the arrangement that is already present. However, for a *new factory* this means the plan of how the machines, equipment, etc will be arranged in the different sections or shops. These should be arranged in such a way that material movement cost, cost of storage in between processes, the investment on machines and equipment etc should be optimal and the product is as cheap as possible.

Need to plan a layout can emerge due to various reasons. Some of them could be

- Need to make minor changes in present layout due to *method improvement, new type of inspection plan, and new type of product,*
- Need to rearrange the existing layout *due to marketing and technological change*,
- Re-allocating the existing facilities *due to new location*, or
- Building a new plant.

3.1 EFFECTS OF A PLANT LAYOUT

A good layout will result in the following:

- Material handling and transportation is *minimized* and efficiently controlled.
- The movements made by workers are *minimized.*

- Waiting time of the semi-finished products is minimized.
- Bottlenecks and point of congestion are eliminated (by line balancing) so that raw material and semi-finished goods move faster from one workstation to another.
- *Overall satisfaction & simplification* which will result in full utilization, minimum delay and congestion, ease in maintenance, and low manufacturing time.
- *Increased production,* safer working conditions, well ventilated rooms, clean environment,
- Increased flexibility for changes in product design, future expansion, and optimal use of space.
- A good layout provides maximum satisfaction to the employees, management, and share holders.
- Suitable spaces are allocated to production centers and service centers.
- Working conditions are safer, better (well ventilated rooms, etc.) and improved.
- There will be improved work methods and reduced production cycle time.
- There is an increased productivity, better product quality, and reduced capital cost.

In other words, the layout design must consider how to achieve the following:

- Higher utilization of space, equipment, and people.
- Improved flow of information, materials, and people.
- Improved employee morale and safer working conditions.
- Improved customer/client interaction.
- Flexibility to change the layout that exists anytime.

3.2 FACTORS AFFECTING LAYOUT

Layouts are affected by *types of industry, production systems, types of products, volume of production, and* types of manufacturing processes used to get the final products. They are elaborated below.

3.2.1 TYPES OF INDUSTRIES

Synthetic process based industry: In this, two or more materials are mixed to get a product, e.g. cement is obtained from the combination of limestone and clay.

Analytic process based industry: It is opposite of synthetic process. Here, the final products are obtained as a result of breaking of material into several parts. For example, the petroleum products are obtained from the fractional distillation (breaking process) of the crude oil.

Conditioning process based industry: Here, the form of raw material is changed into the desired products, e.g. jute products in the jute industry, or the milk products in the dairy farm.

Extractive process based industry: By applying heat, desired product is extracted from the raw material, e.g. Aluminum from bauxite, and steel from iron ores.

3.2.2 TYPES OF PRODUCTION SYSTEM

Continuous Production

They are characterized by standardized, high-volume, capital-intensive products made to store in inventory, by small product mix; by special purpose equipment; and by continuous product flow.

Job Shop Production

This is characterized by made-to-order, low volume, labor-intense products; by a large product mix; by general purpose equipment; by interrupted product flow; and by frequent schedule changes. The system should be flexible, which needs general purpose machines and highly skilled workers. Example; space vehicle, aircraft, special tools and equipment, prototype of future products.

Batch Production

They are characterized by medium size lots of the same type of item or product and has the following other features:

- lot may be produced once or on regular interval
- generally to meet continuous customer demand
- plant capacity generally higher than demand
- general purpose machine but having higher production rate
- specially designed jigs and fixtures
- most suitable for CAM

Example: industrial equipment, furniture, house-hold appliances, machine shop, casting, plastic molding, press work-shop, etc.

3.2.3 TYPE OF PRODUCT

Whether the product is heavy or light, large or small, liquid or solid, etc.

3.2.4 VOLUME OF PRODUCTION

Whether the production is in small quantity, or in lots or batches, or in huge quantity (mass production).

To deal with a plant layout for any kind of production situation, one has to step forward in a systematic and scientific manner. In the following section, one such method called **Systematic Layout Planning** is discussed in brief. A detailed treatment on this topic is a subject of another course called **Plant Design.**

3.3 SYSTEMATIC LAYOUT PLANNING (SLP)

SLP is a systematic approach to layout planning that was developed by Richard Muther and Associates. The steps of SLP are shown in Figure 3.1. As seen from the figure, one has to collect all data related to the current and forecasted production. Sometimes, it may be possible that 3 to 5 types of products account for 70 to 80 % of the total sales volume. The balance 20 to 30% can be grouped in such a way that only a few product groups need to be considered. Each product group and its respective volume for a projected horizon [Turner et al] should be listed. The projected horizon depends on how frequently the product or market changes, but a projection for each product for the next 5 years is sufficient. Any other information relevant to the layout should be included in the general comments.

The basic input data or information needed for making layout can be remembered by the following letters:

P — **Product** and type characteristic of the material needed for this

Q — **Quantity** of each type of product

R — **Route** i.e. sequence of operation & machines needed for completing these operations

S — **Supporting activities** like moving the material from one work place or machine to another and maintenance etc.

T — **Timing** as to how many times in the year and how quickly the products are to be made.

1. Having collected all the data, one can go for **Step 1** of the SLP procedure called the *preparation of the process charts*. This chart depicts the flow of material graphically through the plant. If the products are few, one can make separate operations process chart for each. But, if there are many products, a multi-product process chart may be used. An '*operation chart*' shows only the operations and inspection. But a '*flow process chart*' shows operations, inspections, transportations, delays and storages. These charts are thoroughly discussed under the topic 'Work Study' in any Industrial Engineering Book.

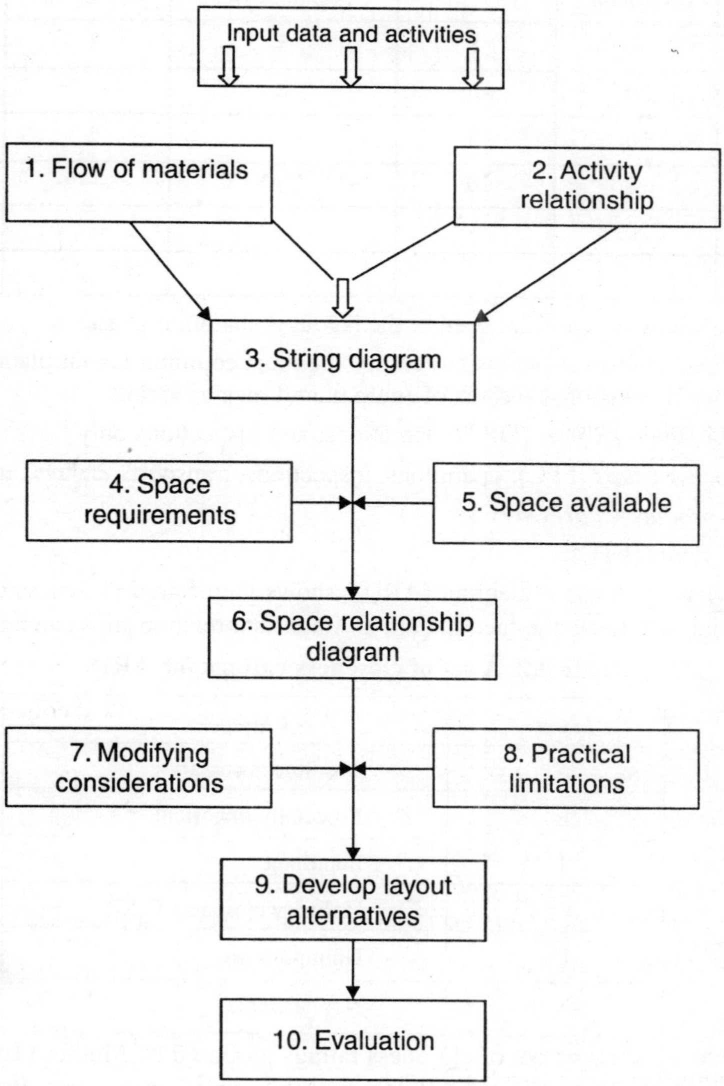

Figure 3.1. Systematic Layout Planning Procedure.

In some cases, for example a job shop, it will be difficult to represent all the flows with a few charts. So, one can go for a 'From-To Chart' in such situations. This chart shows the number of trips from one area to another area and is based on historical data or proposed production. The trips can be attached suitable weights depending on production volume or the degree of difficulty. Table 3.1 shows a 'From-To Chart' for an office situation. The number indicates the number of trips made by the person from one place to another. Based on these charts (flow chart, and From-To Chart), one can construct the layouts. But, sometimes, these charts are not enough. There may be some areas where the product flow is non-existent, and some in which the flow sequence differs for each of the many products. In such cases, one has to go for '*activity relationship diagram*'.

Table 3.1. From-To Chart of an Office

From\To	*Chairman*	*Secretary*	*Computer center*	*Staff room*	—	*Total*
Chairman	—	8	5	3		
Secretary	20	—	2	4		
Computer center	10	5	—	2		
Staff room	8	10	25	—		
—	—	—	—	—	—	—
Total						

In short, the following tools are used in the layout preparation phase:

- *Graphic and schematic analysis:* Perhaps the most common layout planning tools are *templates*—two dimensional cutouts of equipment drawn to scale.
- *Operation Process Chart* (OPC): operations, and inspections only
- *Flow Process Chart* (FPC): operations, inspections, transports, delays, and storage.
- *Multiple-product Chart* (MPC):
- *From-To Chart* (FTC):

2. An 'activity relationship diagram (ARD)' shows the desired closeness of departments and areas within the plant. It reflects the fact that not all important relationships can be shown by product flows. Table 3.2 shows a set of closeness ratings proposed by Muther [Turner et al]. For any paired combination, an **A** rating indicates that it is absolutely necessary to locate the two areas adjacent to each other. On the other hand, an **X** rating shows that keeping two areas adjacent to each other is not

Table 3.2. A set of closeness ratings for ARD

Letter	*Closeness*
A	Absolute necessary
E	Especially important
I	Important
O	Ordinary closeness O K
U	Unimportant
X	Not desirable

desirable. For example, a machining center and the conference room can be straightaway given an **X** rating to avoid their being placed together. To decide about the closeness ratings, it is a good idea to involve all the stake-holders in future layout. They can be asked to give ratings and finally an average closeness rating can be decided.

3. **Step 3** consists of using the information generated in Steps 1 and 2 to prepare a string diagram showing near optimal placement of the facilities without considering the space constraints. The placement is done by trial and error. Usually, the areas with an A closeness are shown first and are connected with 4 straight lines, then E with 3 straight lines, and so on. When an activity has to be close to several other areas, it can be stretched out or distorted. The areas may be moved around and interchanged until a final acceptable arrangement is obtained. It is helpful to imagine the straight lines as stretched rubber bands and the jagged lines as coiled springs representing varying attraction and repulsion forces. So, an A rating would imply 4 rubber bands pulling the areas together while an I rating would imply only 2 rubber bands [Turner et al].

Many diagrams and arrangements will have to be made before a good layout is obtained. Normally, two or more alternatives are developed. Space will have to be added and some modifications made, but the overall picture should not change much. Thus, **step 3** is supposed to be the most creative and important one.

4. **Step 4** may be called the 'adjustment step'. Here the adjustment must be made for space needs as related to space availability; so, the space requirements have to be determined. This can be done through calculations, adjustments of past areas, intuition or estimates.

5. Once these space requirements are known, it is necessary to consider the space available. In some cases, since the layout must fit into the existing buildings, the space available is highly restricted. In other cases, the capital budget is the main restriction, and, therefore, the space availability may be less restricted. In any case, one has to balance the space requirements and the space availability before going to step 6.

3.4 OTHER APPROACHES TO PLANT LAYOUT

Some authors [Heizer J. and Render B.] see the plant layout problem as a set of steps or phase as discussed below:

Phase-1

Location of area where the facilities are to be laid out. It is not necessary that the area be a completely new one. It may even be the existing layout of the plant.

Phase-II

Planning the general overall layout. This provides a block arrangement and the basic flow pattern for the area. It also gives an idea about the size, the relationship, and configuration of each major activity, department, and area.

Phase-III

Preparation of detailed layout plans. It includes planning where each piece of machinery, computer, and equipment will be placed.

Phase-IV

Installation. This involves both planning the installation and physically placing and hooking up the equipment.

The layout planner concentrates on Phase-II and III. Phase-I and IV are not part of the layout planning engineer's project. The layout plan depends on basic input data or factors of layout. For every layout the following **three considerations** are important:

(*a*) **Relationships:** It means the closeness desired between various activities or sections where different functions are performed.

For example, Figure 3.2*a* shows that maximum material moves from foundry section to milling, next is between pressing to milling, and so on. This means foundry should be closed to milling, milling should be closed to press, press closed to milling but also nearer to foundry and packing.

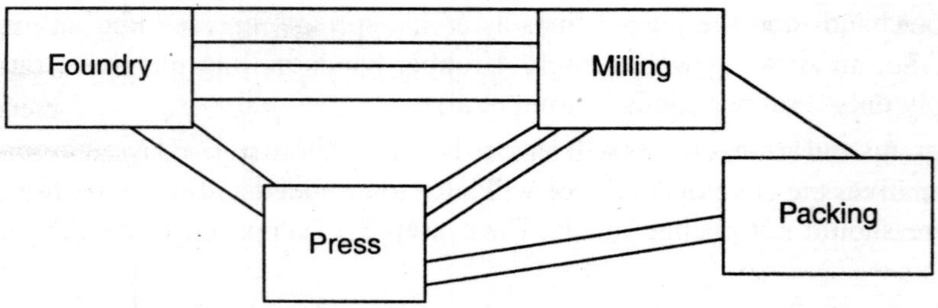

Figure 3.2. (*a*) Relationship diagram.

(*a*) **Space:** It is the area needed for the performance of every function satisfactorily as shown in Figure 3.2 (*b*). The total area needed by different sections = (A + B + C + D) m^2

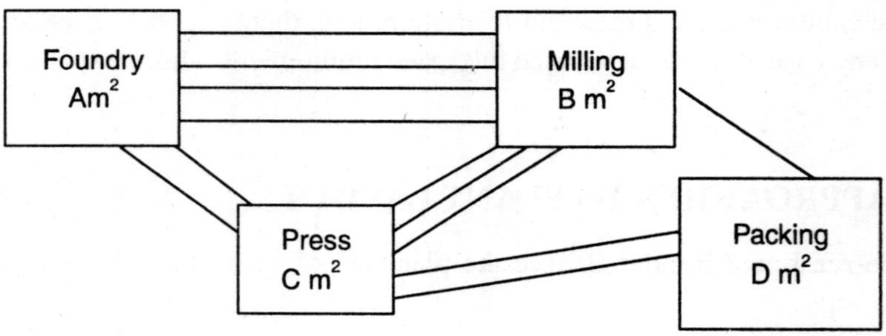

Figure 3.2. (*b*) Space required for various sections.

(*c*) **Adjustment:** It consists of arranging the activity areas in the actual plan of the building of the same area. For example, the total area needed is (A + B + C + D) square meter and based on the existing building space a possible layout plan is as shown in Figure 3.3.

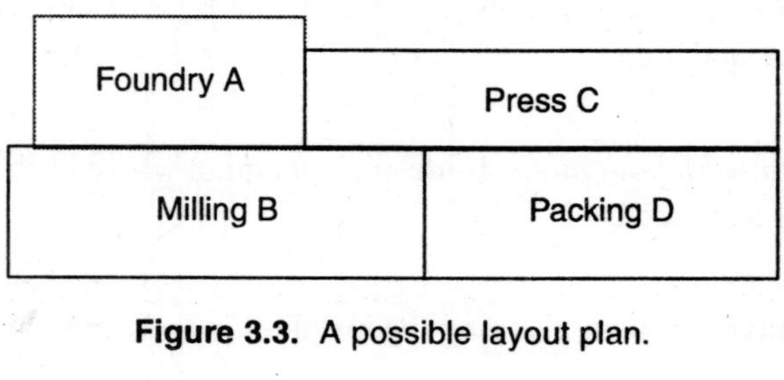

Figure 3.3. A possible layout plan.

3.4.1 PRINCIPLES OF PLANT LAYOUT

- Principle of overall integration (of man, materials, machine, supporting activities, etc)
- Principle of minimum distance between operations
- Principle of flow (arranging machines according to the sequence of operations)
- Principle of cubic space
- Principle of satisfaction and safety
- Principle of flexibility of rearrangement at a minimum cost.

3.4.2 TYPES OF FLOW PATTERNS

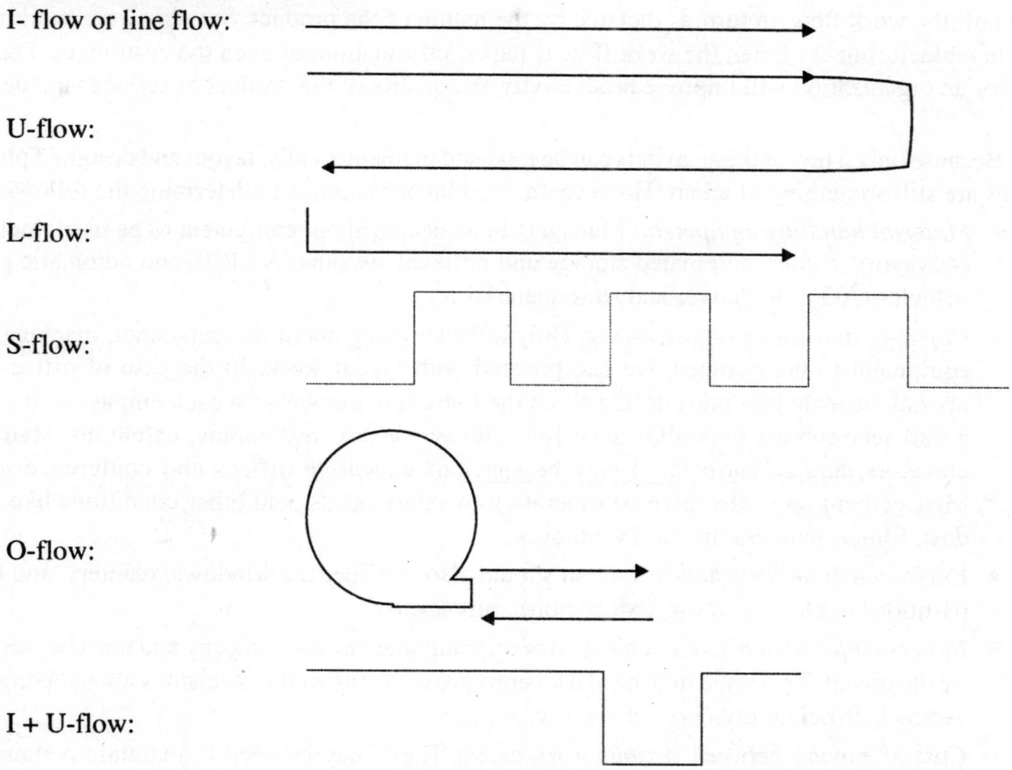

Figure 3.4. Types of Basic Flow.

Apart from this, one can combine this basic flows to get various combinations like (S + L) and (O + U), and so on.

3.5 TYPES OF LAYOUT

Layout decisions include the best placement of machines (in production settings), offices and furniture (in office settings), or service centers (in hospitals or department stores). We will discuss the following layouts in this chapter:

1. *Fixed position layout*: addresses the layout requirements of large, bulky projects such as ships and buildings.

2. *Process-oriented layout*: deals with low-volume, high-variety production (called as 'Job-shop' or intermittent production).
3. *Product-oriented*: seeks the best personnel and machine utilization in repetitive or continuous production.
4. *Office layout*: positions workers, their equipment, and spaces/offices to provide for movement and information.
5. *Retail layout*: allocates shelf space and responds to customer behavior.
6. *Warehouse layout*: addresses trade-offs between space and material handling.

The first three are called **the basic layouts**. They are differentiated by the types of work flows they entail; the work flow, in turn, is dictated by the nature of the product. Services have work flows, just as manufacturing do. Often the work flow is paper, information, or even the customers. The right layout for an organization will improve productivity, the quality of the product or service, and delivery rates.

Because only a few of these layouts can be modeled mathematically, layout and design of physical facilities are still something of an art. However, a good layout requires to determine the following:

- *Material handling equipment*: Managers must decide about equipment to be used, including conveyors, cranes, automated storage and retrieval systems (AS/RS), and automatic guided vehicles (AGV) to deliver and store material.
- *Capacity and space requirements*: Only after knowing about the personnel, machines, and equipment to be arranged, we can proceed with layout work. In the case of office work, operations managers must decide about the space requirements for each employee. It may be a 6x6 feet cubicle plus allowance for hallways, aisles, rest rooms, cafeterias, stairwells, elevators, and so forth, or it may be spacious executive offices and conference rooms. Management must also give consideration to safety needs, and other conditions like noise, dust, fumes, temperature, and ventilation.
- *Environment and aesthetics*: Layout should also consider the windows, planters, and height partitions to allow air flow, reduce noise, privacy, etc.
- *Flows of information*: Communication is very important to any company and must be facilitated by the layout. This issue may need decisions proximity as well as decisions about open spaces versus half-height dividers versus private offices.
- *Cost of moving between various work areas*: There may be need to maintain certain areas next to each other. For example, the movement of molten steel is more difficult than the movement of cold steel.

Table 3.3 summarizes the differences among basic layouts.

Table 3.3

Aspect of the conversion process	*Layout Type*		
	Product-oriented	*Process-oriented*	*Fixed position*
Product	standardized product, large volume, stable rate of output	diversified products using common operations, varying volumes, varying rate of output	made-to-order, low volume

Work flow	straight line of product; same sequence of operations for each unit	variable flow; each order (product) may require unique sequence of operations	little or no flow; equipment and resources brought to site as needed
Human skills	able to perform routine, repetitive tasks at fixed pace; highly specialized	primary skilled craftsmen; able to perform without close supervision and be moderately adaptable	great flexibility required; work assignments and locations vary
Support staff	large; schedule materials and people, monitor and maintain work	perform tasks of scheduling, materials handling, and production and inventory control	schedule and coordinate skillfully
Material handling	predictable, flow, systematized and often automated	flow variable; handling often duplicated	flow variable, often low; may require heavy duty, general purpose handling equipment
Inventory	high turnover of raw material and work-in-process inventories	low turnover of raw material and WIP inventories; high raw materials inventories	variable inventories and frequent tie-ups because production cycle is long
Space utilization	efficient utilization, large output per unit space	small output per unit space; large WIP requirements	small output per unit space if conversion is on site
Capital requirements	large investment in specialized equipment and processes	general purpose, flexible equipment and processes	general purpose, mobile equipment and processes
Product cost	relatively high fixed cost; low unit costs for direct labor and materials	relatively low fixed costs; high unit costs for direct labor, materials and materials handling	relatively low fixed costs; high unit labor and materials costs

3.5.1 FIXED POSITION LAYOUT

In this, the major part of the product remains in a fixed place. All the tools, machines, workers and smaller pieces of materials are brought to it and the product is completed with the major part staying in one place. Very heavy assemblies (e.g. ship, aircraft, cranes, rail coaches, highway, a bridge, a house, an oil well, etc) requiring small and portable tools are made by this method.

The techniques to deal with fixed-position layout are not well developed and are complicated by three factors:

- There is limited space at virtually all sites.
- At different stages in the construction process, different materials are needed; therefore, different items become critical as the project develops.
- The volume of materials needed is dynamic. For example, the rate of use of steel panels for the hull of a ship changes as the project progresses.

Because problems with fixed-position layouts are so difficult to solve on-site, an *alternative strategy is to complete as much of the project as possible off-site*. This approach is used in the *ship-building* industry when standard units (e.g., pipe-holding brackets) are assembled on a nearby assembly line (a product-oriented facility). Some ship-buildings are also experimenting with group technology to group components.

Advantages

- very easy and cheap to arrange.
- can be easily changed if product design is changed.
- since the worker work at one place, the supervision is easy.
- Cost of transporting heavy materials is reduced.
- Responsibility for quality is easily fixed on the worker or group of workers which make the assembly.

Limitations

- such components which need only small and portable tools can be made by this method.
- skilled workers, complicated jigs and fixtures are required.

3.5.2 Process-oriented or Functional Layout

It is a layout that deals with low-volume, high-variety production. In this type, all the machines and equipment of the same type are grouped together in one section or area or department. For example, all welding equipment are kept in one section; all drilling machines in other; all lathes in third section, and so on. It is used in intermittent (discontinuous) type of production. Figure 3.5 shows the movements of two different jobs through different departments according to their sequence of operations. It is most efficient when making products with different requirements or when handling customers, patients, or clients with different needs.

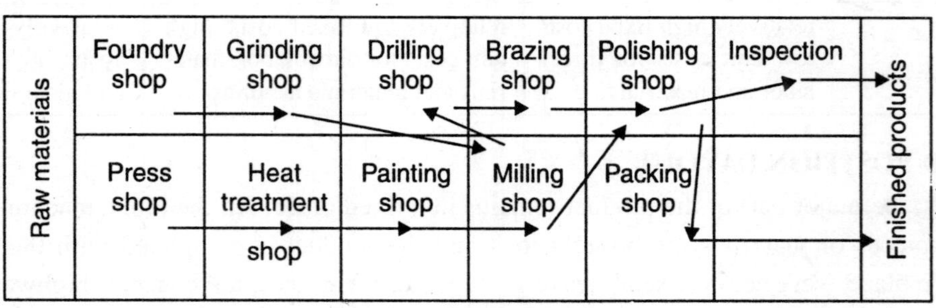

Figure 3.5. Process layout.

In this job-shop environment, each product or each small group of products undergoes a different sequence of operations. A good example of process layout is a *hospital or clinic*. Patients with their own needs, requires routing through admissions, laboratories, operating rooms, radiology, pharmacies, nursing beds, and so on. Equipment, skills, and supervisions are organized around these processes.

Advantages

- different products can be made on the same machine, so the number of machines needed is reduced. This gives lots of flexibility with less capital needed.

- When one machine goes out of order, the job can be done on other similar machines.
- When a worker is absent, another worker of the same section can do the job.
- A worker becomes more skilled and can earn more money by working harder on his machine.
- Varieties of job make the work more interesting for the workers.
- Layout is flexible with respect to the rate of production, design and methods of production.

Limitations

- General purpose equipment requires high labor skills, and WIP inventories are higher because of imbalances in the production processes.
- This layout needs more space.
- Automation of material handling is extremely difficult.
- Completion of a product takes more time due to difficult scheduling, changing setups, and unique material handling. Total production cycle time is more also due to long distances and waiting time.
- Raw material has to travel longer distances, thus the material handling cost is high.
- Needs more inspection and coordination.

3.5.2.1 Approach to Process Layout

When designing a process layout, the most common tactic is to arrange departments or work centers so that the costs of material handling is minimum. For this, departments with large flows of parts or people between them should be placed next to one another. Material handling costs in this approach depend on:

- The number of loads or people to be moved between two departments during some period of time, and
- The distance linked costs of moving loads or people between departments. Cost is considered to be a function of distance between departments.

The **objective function** can be written as follows:

$$\text{Minimize cost} = \sum_{i=1}^{n} \sum_{j=1}^{n} X_{ij} C_{ij} \qquad (3.1)$$

where n = total number of work centers or departments

i, j = individual departments

X_{ij} = number of loads moved from department i to department j

C_{ij} = cost to move a load between department i to department j.

The term C_{ij} combines distance and other costs into one factor. We thereby assume that the difficulty of movement is equal and the pickup and setdown costs are constant. The steps in this approach can be understood by the following example.

Example 3.1. A company management wants to arrange the six departments of its factory in a way that will minimize interdepartmental material handling costs. They make an initial assumption (to simplify the problem) that each department is 20 × 20 feet and that the building is 60 feet long and 40 feet wide. The process layout procedure that they follow involves six steps:

Step-1: Construct a *'from-to-matrix'* showing the flow of parts or materials from department to department (Table 3.4).

Table 3.4

Department	*Assembly*	*Painting*	*Machine shop*	*Receiving*	*Shopping*	*Testing*
Assembly (1)	α	50	100	0	0	20
Painting (2)		α	30	50	10	0
Machine shop (3)			α	20	0	100
Receiving (4)				α	50	0
Shopping (5)					α	0
Testing (6)						α

Step-2: Determine the *space requirements* for each department (Figure-3.5 shows the available plant space).

Step-3: Develop an *initial schematic diagram* showing the sequence of departments through which parts must move. Try to place departments with a heavy flow of materials or parts next to one another (Figure-3.6).

Step-4: Determine the cost of this layout by using the material handling cost equation:

$$\text{Cost} = \sum_{i=1}^{n} \sum_{j=1}^{n} X_{ij} C_{ij}$$

For this problem, the company assumes that a forklift carries all interdepartmental loads. The cost of moving one load between adjacent departments is estimated to be \$1. Moving a load between nonadjacent departments costs \$2. Thus, looking at Table 3.4, we see that the handling cost between departments 1 and 2 is \$50 (i.e., \$1 × 50 loads), the handling cost between departments 1 and 3 is \$200 (i.e., \$2x100 loads), and the handling cost between departments 1 and 6 is \$40 (i.e., \$2 × 20 loads), and so on. The total cost for this layout is shown in Table 3.5.

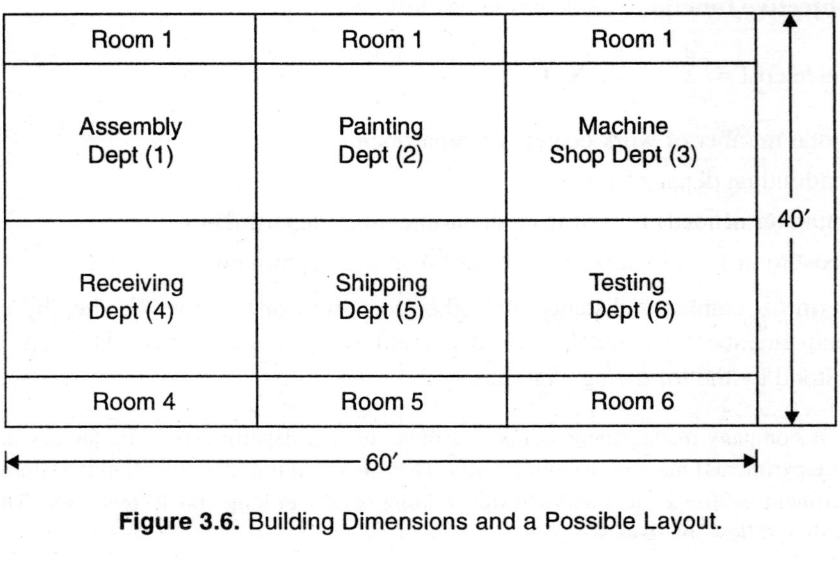

Figure 3.6. Building Dimensions and a Possible Layout.

Table 3.5

Movement Route	*Cost for route ($)*
1-2	1 × 50 = 50
1-3	2 × 100 = 200
1-6	2 × 20 = 40
2-3	1 × 30 = 30
2-4	1 × 50 = 50
2-5	1 × 10 = 10
3-4	2 × 20 = 40
3-6	1 × 100 = 100
4-5	1 × 50 = 50
Total cost	570

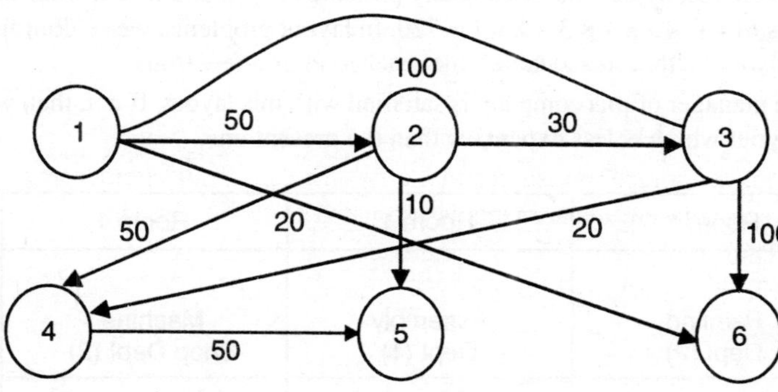

Figure 3.7. Interdepartmental flow graph with number of loads per week.

Step-5: By trial and error, try to improve the layout shown in Figure-3.6 to establish a reasonably good arrangement of departments.

By looking at both the flow graph (Figure 3.7) and the cost calculations, it is obvious that placing departments 1 and 3 together seem desirable. They are presently nonadjacent, and due to the high volume of flow between them the material handling cost is high. One possibility is to exchange the position of 1 and 2. Doing this will change the cost which is shown in Table 3.6.

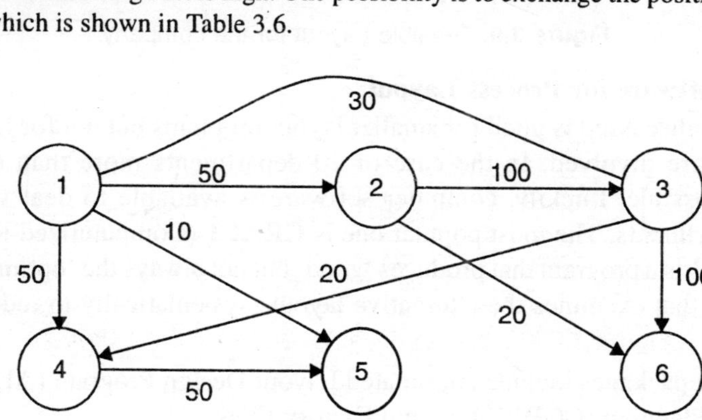

Figure 3.8. Second flow graph with number of loads per week.

Table 3.6

Movement Route	*Cost for route ($)*
1-2	1 × 50 = 50
1-3	1 × 100 = 100
1-6	1 × 20 = 20
2-3	2 × 30 = 60
2-4	1 × 50 = 50
2-5	1 × 10 = 10
3-4	2 × 20 = 40
3-6	1 × 100 = 100
4-5	1 × 50 = 50
Total cost	480

This change, of course, is just one of the many possible combinations. For a six-department problem, the possible combination is $6! = 6 \times 5 \times 4 \times 3 \times 2 \times 1 = 720$. In layout problems, we seldom find the optimal solution and will have to be satisfied with a 'reasonable' one reached after a few trials.

I wonder, if the manager of this company is satisfied with this layout. If not, then we will have to try a few steps more to find a layout which is less expensive than the present one.

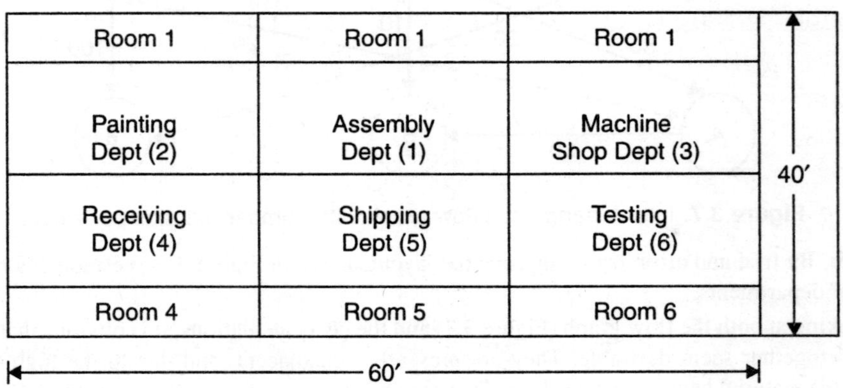

Figure 3.9. Feasible Layout for the company.

3.5.2.2 Computer Software for Process Layout

The graphic approach discussed is good for smaller layout problems but not for larger problems where say 20 departments are involved. In the case of 20 departments more than 600 trillion different configurations are possible. Luckily, computer software is available to deal with layout problems consisting of 40 departments. The most popular one is **CRAFT** (Computerized Relative Allocation of Facilities Technique). It's a program that produces 'good' but not always the 'optimal' solutions. CRAFT is a search technique that examines the alternative layouts systematically to reduce the total material handling cost.

Other software packages include Automated Layout Design Program (ALDEP), Computerized Relationship Layout Planning (CORELAP), and Factory Flow.

3.5.3 REPETITIVE AND PRODUCT-ORIENTED LAYOUT

This is also called assembly line layout because it was first used for assembling automobiles in the USA. This layout is organized around products or families of similar high-volume, low-variety products. In this type of layout, one product or one type of product is produced in a given area. This is used in case of repetitive and continuous production or mass production type industries.

The machines and equipment are arranged in the order in which they are needed to perform operations on a product. The raw material is taken at one end of the line and goes from one operation to the next very rapidly with little material handling required.

This layout **assumes** that:

- Volume of production is adequate for high equipment utilization.
- Product demand is stable enough to justify high investment in specialized equipment.
- Product is standardized or approaching a phase of its life cycle that justifies investment in specialized equipment.
- Supplies of raw materials and components are adequate and of uniform quality (adequately standardized) to ensure that they will work with the specialized equipment.

Advantages

- Material handling cost is minimum.
- Labor does the same type of operations always, so he becomes specialized and does the job very quickly.
- Since the labor has to do only one type of job, he can be easily trained.
- Control of product becomes very easy.
- Reduced WIP inventories, so cost of storage of materials between operations is less.
- Less space is required.
- Smooth and continuous work flow.
- Rapid throughput or product completion time is less.

Limitations

- Not good if the product is changed, no flexibility.
- Difficult to have load balance.
- Very costly because separate machines are needed to do the same operation on different products.
- If one machine in the line fails or if one operator in the line is absent then the output is immediately affected.
- Specialized and strict supervision.

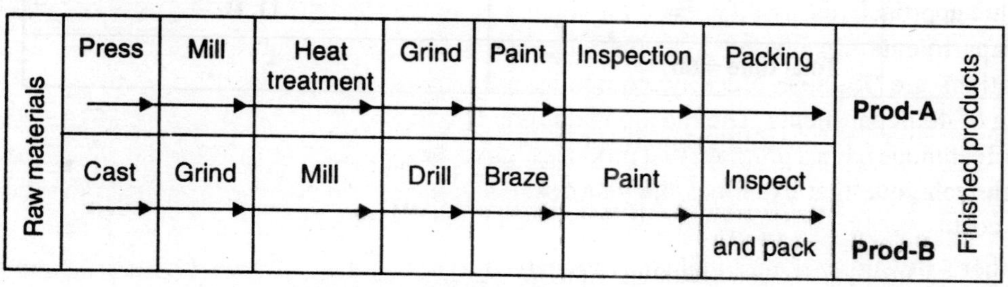

Figure 3.6. Product Layout.

Two types of product layout are **fabrication** and **assembly lines**. The *fabrication line* builds components (viz. car tires, parts of a refrigerator, etc.) on a series of machines. An *assembly line* puts the fabricated parts together at a series of workstations. Both are repetitive processes, and in both cases, the line must be 'balanced'- that is, ***the time spent to perform work on one machine must equal or 'balance' the time spent to perform work on the next machine in the fabrication line.***

Assembly lines can be balanced by moving tasks from one individual to another. The central problem then in product layout planning, is to balance the output at each workstation on the production line so that it is nearly the same, while obtaining the desires amount of output. A well-balanced assembly line has the advantage of high personnel and facility utilization and equity between employees' work loads.

3.5.3.1 Assembly-line Balancing

Line-balancing is done to minimize imbalance between machines or personnel while meeting a required output from the line. For this, the management must know the tools, equipment, and work methods used. Then the time needed for each assembly task (e.g. drilling a hole, tightening a nut, or painting a part) must be determined. Management also needs to know the *precedence* relationship among the activities (i.e. the sequence in which different tasks must be performed). Example-3.2 shows how to turn these task data into a precedence diagram.

Example 3.2. We want to develop a precedence diagram for an electrostatic copier that requires a total assembly time of 66 minutes. Table 3.7 and Figure 3.7 give the tasks, assembly times, and sequence requirements for the copier.

Table 3.7. Precedence data

Task	*Performance time (minutes)*	*Preceding activity*
A	10	—
B	11	A means B cannot be done before A.
C	5	B
D	4	B
E	12	A
F	3	C, D
G	7	F
H	11	E
I	3	G, H
	Total time = 66	

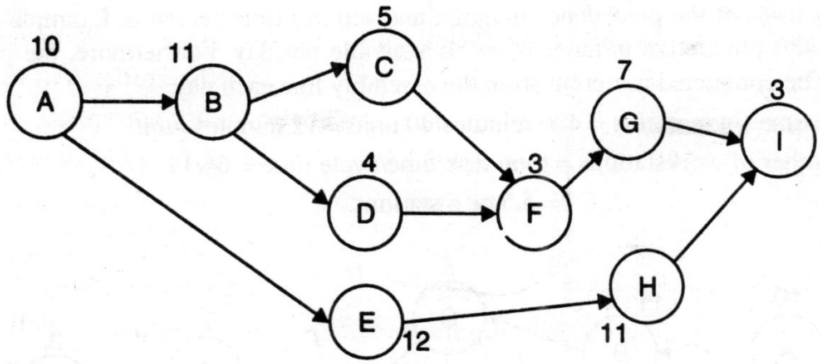

Figure 3.7

Once we have constructed a precedence chart summarizing the sequences and performance times, we will concentrate on grouping tasks into job stations so that we can meet the specified production rate. This will consist of the following steps:

- Calculate the **cycle time** - the maximum time that the product is available at each workstation if the production rate is to be achieved.

  Cycle time = (Production time available per day/Units required per day)
- Compute the **minimum number of workstations.**

  minimum number of workstations = $\sum_{i=1}^{n}$ Time for task i / Cycle time (3.2)

  where n = number of assembly tasks.
- Balance the line by assigning specific assembly tasks to each workstation. An efficient balance is one that will complete the required assembly, follow the specified sequence, and keep the idle time at each workstation to a minimum. A formal method to do this is:
  - Identify a master list of tasks.
  - Eliminate the tasks that have been assigned.
  - Eliminate the tasks whose precedence relationship has not been satisfied.
  - Eliminate the tasks for which inadequate time is available at the workstation.
  - Use one of the line-balancing heuristics described in Table 3.8. The five choices are: (*i*) longest task time, (*ii*) most following tasks, (*iii*) ranked positional weight, (*iv*) shortest time task, and (*v*) least number of following tasks. It is to be noted that **heuristics** provide solutions, but they do not guarantee an optimal solution.

Table 3.8. Layout Heuristics for Assembly-line Balancing

(*i*) Longest task time,	From the available tasks, choose the one with the largest time.
(*ii*) Most following tasks,	From the available tasks, choose the one with the largest number of following tasks.
(*iii*) Ranked positional weight,	From the available tasks, choose the one for which the sum of the times for each following task is longest. From *example 3.3,* we see that the ranked positional weight of task C = 5(C) + 3(F) + 7(G) + 3(I) = 18; task D = 4(D) + 3(F) + 7(G) + 3(I) = 17. Therefore, C would be selected first.
(*iv*) Shortest time task, and	From the available tasks, choose the one with the shortest task time.
(*v*) Least number of following tasks.	From the available tasks, choose the one with the least number of subsequent tasks.

Example 3.3. On the basis of the precedence diagram and activity times given in Example-3.2, the firm determines that there are 480 productive minutes of work available per day. Furthermore, the production schedule requires that 40 units be completed as output from the assembly line each day.

Thus: Cycle time (in minutes) = 480 minutes/40 units =12 minutes /unit

Minimum number of workstations = total task time/cycle time = 66/12

= 5.5 or 6 stations.

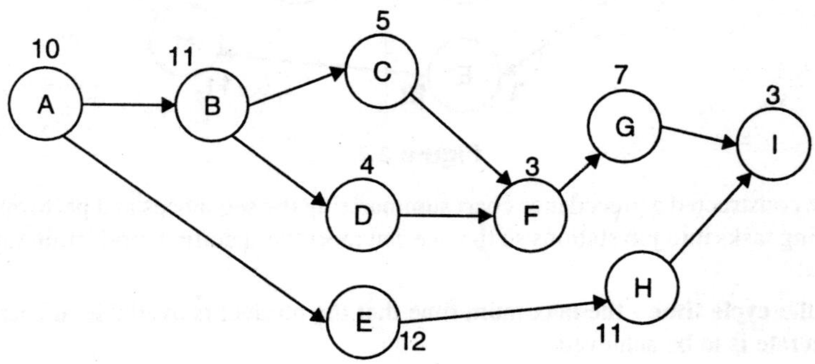

Figure 3.8

Use the *most following tasks heuristic* to assign to workstations.

Figure 3.8 shows one solution that does not violate the sequence requirements and that group tasks into six stations shown by *six different colors*. To obtain this solution, activities with the most following tasks were moved into workstations to use as much of the available cycle time of 12 minutes as possible.

Workstation	*Tasks included in the workstation*	*Time (minutes)*
1	A	10
2	B	11
3	E	12
4	C, D, F	12
5	H	11
6	G, I	10

- The first workstation consumes 10 minutes and has an idle time of 2 minutes.
- The second workstation uses 11 minutes, and the third consumes the full 12 minutes.
- The fourth workstation groups three small tasks and balances perfectly at 12 minutes.
- The fifth has 1 minute of idle time, and the sixth (consisting of tasks G and I) has 2 minutes of idle time per cycle.

Total idle time for this solution is 6 minutes per cycle.

We can calculate the balance efficiency for Example 3.3 as follows:

Efficiency = Σ task times/(actual no. of workstations) $\times$ (assigned cycle time) (3.3)

Efficiency = 66 minutes/(6 stations $\times$ 12 minutes) = 66/72 = 91.7 %

If we open a seventh workstation (for whatever reason), will decrease the efficiency of the balance to 78.6%.

Efficiency = 66 minutes/(7 stations $\times$ 12 minutes) = 66/84 = 78.6 %

3.5.4 OFFICE LAYOUT

The main difference between **office and factory layouts** is the importance placed on information. However, in some office environments, just in manufacturing, production relies on the flow of material. *Office layout deals with grouping of workers, their equipment, and spaces/offices to provide for comfort, safety, and movement of information.*

We should note two major trends in case of office layout. First, *technology*, such as cellular phones, beepers, faxes, the Internet, home offices, laptop computers, and PDAs, allows increasing layout flexibility by moving information electronically. The technological change is altering the way offices function. Second, *virtual companies* create dynamic needs for space and services. These two changes require fewer office employees on-site.

Even though the movement of information is increasingly electronic, analysis of office layouts still requires a task-based approach. Managers, therefore, examine both electronic and conventional communication patterns, separation needs, and other conditions affecting employee effectiveness by using a tool called *relationship chart* shown in Figure 3.9.

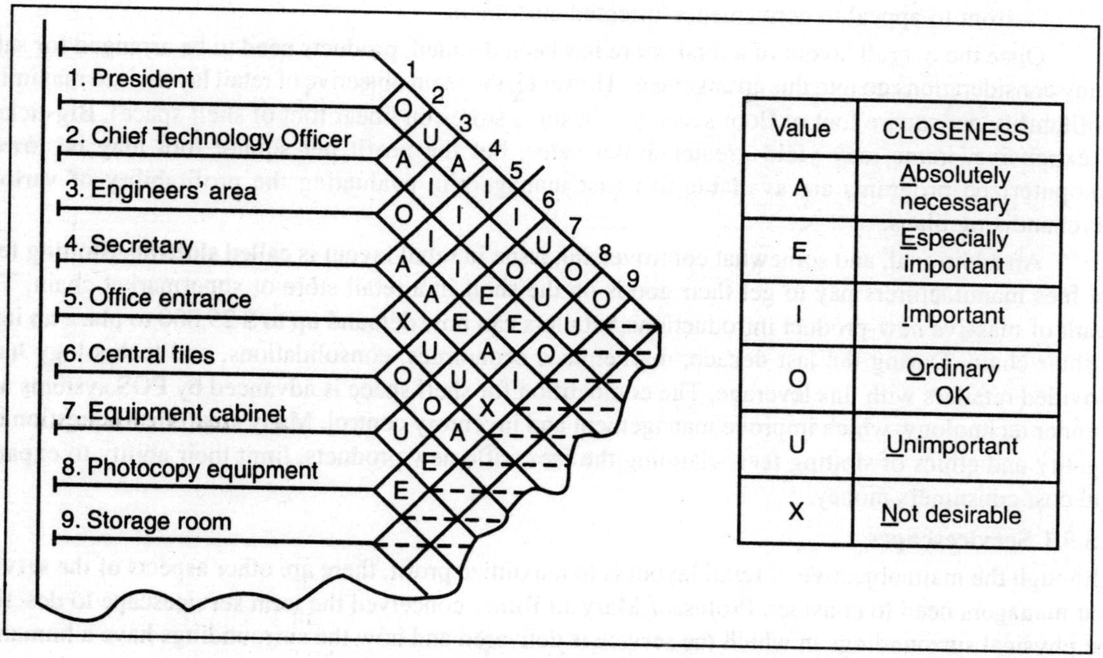

Figure 3.9. Office Relationship Chart.

This chart, prepared for an office of software engineers, indicates that the chief technology officer must be (1) near the engineers' area, (2) less near the secretary and central files, and (3) not at all near the photocopy or storage room.

General office-area guidelines allot an average of about 100 square feet per person (including corridors). A major executive is allotted about 400 square feet, and a conference room area is based on 25 square feet per person, up to 30 people. By making effective use of the vertical dimension in a workstation, some office designers expand upward instead of outward. This keeps each workstation unit (what designers call the 'footprint') as small as possible [Heizer and Render].

3.5.5 RETAIL LAYOUT

Retail layouts are based on the idea that sales and profitability vary directly with customer exposure to products. Thus, most retail managers try to expose customers to as many products as possible. Studies show that the greater the rate of exposure, the greater the sales and the higher the return on investment. The following ideas are helpful for determining the overall arrangement of many stores:

- Locate the high-draw items around the periphery of the store. Thus, we tend to find dairy products on one side of a supermarket and bread and bakery products on another.
- Use prominent locations for high-impulse and high-margin items such as house-wares, beauty aids, and shampoos.
- Distribute what are known in the trade as 'power items'—items that may dominate a purchasing trip— to both sides of an aisle, and disperse them to increase the viewing of other items.
- Use end aisle locations because they have a very high exposure rate.
- Convey the mission of the store by careful selection in the positioning of the lead-off department. For instance, if prepared foods are part of the mission, position the bakery up front to appeal to convenience-oriented customers.

Once the overall layout of a retail store has been decided, products need to be arranged for sale. Many considerations go into this arrangement. However, the main objective of retail layout is to maximize profitability per square foot of floor space (or, in some stores on linear foot of shelf space). Big-ticket, or expensive, items may yield greater dollar sales, but the profit per square foot may be lower. Computerized programs are available to assist managers in evaluating the profitability of various merchandising plans.

An additional, and somewhat controversial, issue in retail layout is called **slotting**. Slotting fees are fees manufacturers pay to get their goods on the shelf in a retail store or supermarket chain. The result of massive new-product introductions, retailers can now demand up to $ 25,000 to place an item in their chain. During the last decade, marketplace economics, consolidations, and technology have provided retailers with this leverage. The competition for shelf space is advanced by POS systems and scanner technology, which improve management and inventory control. Many small firms question the legality and ethics of slotting fees, claiming the fees stifle new products, limit their ability to expand, and cost consumers money.

3.5.5.1 Servicescapes

Although the main objective of retail layout is to maximize profit, there are other aspects of the service that managers need to consider. Professor Mary Jo Bitner conceived the term servicescape to describe the physical surroundings in which the service is delivered and how the surroundings have a humanistic effect on customers and employees. She believes that in order to provide a good service layout, a firm must consider these three elements:

- *Ambient conditions*, such as lighting, sound, smell, and temperature. All of these affect workers and customers and can affect how much is spent and how long a person stays in the building. For example, fine-dinning restaurant with linen tablecloths, candlelit atmosphere, and light music.
- *Spatial layout and functionality*, which involve customer circulation path planning, aisle characteristics (such as width, direction, angle, and shelf-spacing), and product grouping.
- *Signs, symbols, and artifacts* encourage shoppers to slow down and browse. For example, greeter at the door, flower vases at the approach to the office.

3.5.6 WAREHOUSING AND STORAGE LAYOUTS

The objective of warehouse layout is to find the optimum trade-off between handling cost and costs of warehouse space. So, the management's task is to maximize the utilization of the 'cubic space' of the warehouse—that is, utilize its full volume while maintaining low material handling costs, which is defined as all the *costs related to the incoming transport, storage, and outgoing transport of materials to be warehoused. The cost also includes equipment, people, material, supervision, insurance, and depreciation.* Effective warehouse layouts also minimize the damage and spoilage of material within the warehouse.

The variety of items stored and the number of items 'picked' affect the optimum layout. A warehouse storing a few items leads itself to higher density than a warehouse storing a variety of items. Modern warehousing management uses automated storage and retrieval systems (ASRS). It can improve the productivity by an estimated 500% over manual methods.

An important component of warehouse layout is the relationship between the receiving/unloading area and the shipping/loading area. Facility design depends on the type of supplies unloaded, what they are unloaded from (trucks, rail cars, barges, etc), and where they are unloaded.

3.5.6.1 Cross-Docking

Cross-docking means to avoid placing materials or supplies in storage by processing them as they are received. In a manufacturing facility, product is received directly to the assembly line (JIT). In a distribution center, labeled and presorted loads arrive at the shipping dock for immediate rerouting, thereby avoiding formal receiving, stocking/storing, and order-selection activities. Because these activities do not add any value to the product, their elimination is 100% cost savings. Although, cross-docking reduces product handling, inventory, and facility costs, it requires both (i) tight scheduling and (ii) that shipments received include accurate product identification, usually with bar codes so that they can be quickly moved to the proper shipping dock (Heizer and Render).

3.5.7 COMBINATION LAYOUT

Now a days it's difficult to find any one form of layout in its 100 percent purity. In factories, where first the products are manufactured and then assembled, this method is mostly used. Often a combination of layouts must be used. Typically, a process layout is combined with a product layout.

3.6 MATERIAL HANDLING

Material Handling is an inseparable part of plant layout. Methods study, plant layout, and material handling are all components of the design of a production facility. There are more than 430 different types of material handling equipment, and each type is represented by 6 to 10 major manufacturers.

Material Handling (MH) is the handling of materials. The extent of MH activity in a company depends on the type of company, its product, the size of the company, the value of the product, the relative importance of handling to the enterprise, etc.

According to Material Handling Society, MH is the art and science involving the movement, packaging and storing of substances in any form.

In industries, various products are manufactured. During manufacture, materials move from

- one operation to another
- one machine to another

- one department to another
- one workstation to another
- stores to workstation
- workstation to stores, and so on.

Although, MH is an unproductive work, it is an essential and unavoidable activity in an industrial environment. MH cost is an overhead cost which must be kept as low as possible to get the maximum profit. MH cost can vary from 20 to 60 % of the total production cost. A component may be handled 50 times or more before it becomes part of the final product. it is also estimated that 35 to 40 % of the plant accidents are due to bad method of material handling.

3.6.1 PRINCIPLES OF MATERIAL HANDLING

These are narrated as follows:

1. *Orientation principle*: Study the problem thoroughly before preliminary planning to identify existing methods and problems, physical and economic constraints, and to establish future requirements and goals.

2. *Planning principle*: Establish a plan to include basic requirements, desirable options, and the consideration of contingencies for all material handling and storage activities.

3. *Systems principle*: Integrate those handling and storage activities that are economically viable into a coordinated system of operations, including receiving, inspection, storage, production, assembly, packaging, warehousing, shipping, and transportation.

4. *Unit load principle*: Handle product in as large a unit load as possible.

5. *Space utilization principle*: Make effective utilization of all cubic space.

6. *Standardization principle*: Standardize handling methods and equipment wherever possible.

7. *Ergonomic principle*: Recognize human capabilities and limitations by designing material handling equipment and procedures for effective interaction with the people using the system.

8. *Energy principle*: Include energy consumption of the material handling systems and material handling procedures when making comparisons or preparing economic justifications.

9. *Ecology principle*: Use material handling equipment and procedures that minimize adverse effects on the environment.

10. *Mechanization principle*: Mechanize the handling process where feasible to increase efficiency and economy in the handling of materials.

11. *Flexibility principle*: Use methods and equipment that can perform a variety of tasks under a variety of operating conditions.

12. *Simplification principle*: Simplify handling by eliminating, reducing, or combining unnecessary movements and/or equipment.

13. *Gravity principle*: Utilize gravity to move material wherever possible, while respecting limitations concerning safety, product damage, and loss.

14. *Safety principle*: Provide safe material handling equipment and methods that follow existing safety codes and regulations in addition to accrued experience.

15. *Computerization principle*: Consider computerization in material handling and storage systems, when circumstances warrant, for improved material and information control.

16. *System flow principle*: Integrate data flow with physical material flow in handling and storage.

17. *Layout principle*: Prepare an operation sequence and equipment layout for all viable system solutions, then select the alternative system that best integrates efficiency and effectiveness.

18. *Cost principle*: Compare the economic justification of alternative solutions in equipment and methods on the basis of economic effectiveness as measured by expense per unit handled.

19. *Maintenance principle*: Prepare a plan for preventive maintenance and scheduled repairs on all material handling equipment.

20. *Obsolescence principle*: Prepare a long-range and economically sound policy for replacement of obsolete equipment and methods with special consideration to after-tax lifecycle costs.

3.6.2 SIMPLIFIED VERSION OF PRINCIPLES OF MATERIAL HANDLING

1. Eliminate material handling as much as possible by proper layout.
2. Make accurate and complete analysis of the present and future costs of MH.
3. Use various techniques to develop the MH system in plant.
4. Avoid handling of materials by the direct labor specially skilled ones.
5. Avoid using handling equipment below its capacity.
6. Move materials in containerized units (e.g., small milk tins in a box, small cups and plates in a tray, or soft drink bottles in a crate) rather than as a single item.
7. Move materials at a higher speeds and in larger quantity.
8. Use the space effectively for storing and moving materials.
9. Use gravity flow of materials wherever possible.
10. Reduce the distance traveled by materials by proper layout.
11. Avoid backtracking of materials.
12. Avoid rehandling of materials which may spoil the quality (like non-sticking utensils, etc).
13. Choose the right type of MH equipment:
    - For small items (soaps, tea bags, tooth pastes, etc.) - Use boxes.
    - For medium size items (boxes, cartons, tins, etc.) - Use hand trucks.
    - For large size items (lathe machine components, auto parts, etc) - Use overhead cranes.
14. Standardize the MH equipment.
15. Combine the movement and storage of materials.
16. Combine the movement and operations to be performed on materials.
17. Provide safety in the plant while handling materials.
18. Avoid unnecessary mixing of materials.
19. Maintain the MH equipment regularly to avoid breakdowns.
20. Keep gangway clean.
21. Create a separate organization for MH.
22. Train the operators in MH.
23. Plan MH for overall economy.

3.6.3 MATERIAL HANDLING EQUIPMENT

1. **Conveyors**
    - Belt conveyors—airport baggage handling
    - Chain/cable conveyors—coal mines
    - Gravity roller conveyors—power plant coal handling system

- Live roller conveyors—Petroleum companies
- Elevating conveyors—fertilizer factories
- Screw/spiral conveyors—cement factories
- Pipeline conveyors
- Chutes

2. Cranes

- Fixed cranes—steel factory
- Travelling cranes—turbine shop
- Electric hoist—automobile factories
- Winches and capstans

3. Mobile

- Industrial vehicles
  - Fixed platform type
  - Lift platform type—to transport bricks, books, etc.
  - Fork lift trucks
- Motor vehicles or trucks—to transport petroleum products
- Rail road cars or goods train—to transport coal, ores, sheet, rods, etc.
- Cargo ships—to carry oil, food supply, etc.
- Cargo planes—to transport passengers' baggage, equipment, etc.

3.6.4 RELATIONSHIP BETWEEN MATERIAL HANDLING AND FACTORY BUILDING DESIGN OR LAYOUT

- MH and plant layout are very closely related. An effective layout involves least material handling and less costly MH equipment. It also allows material handling without any loss of time, with minimum delays and least back-tracking.
- The total number of movements and the distances moved in one step are also reduced considerably in a properly designed plant layout.
- In a poorly planned layout, the width of aisle or sub-aisle, and ceiling heights may be inadequate to accommodate MH equipment.
- In a well designed plant layout, MH is minimized. Space requirements are considerably reduced. Material movements are much faster and more economical. Bottlenecks and points of congestion are reduced. Machines and workers do not remain idle due to lack of materials. Production line flow becomes smooth.
- For minimum MH, the location of store rooms, tool rooms, lavatories, offices, test floors, shipping, wrapping centers, etc should be judiciously made.

In making equipment layout, the following points should be taken into account:

- Provide aisles (passages) wide enough to accommodate the latest types of mobile MH equipment.
- Keep work at a convenient working level.
- To conserve floor space, use overhead means of conveying and storage.
- Plan first operations nearer to the point of receiving.
- Use yard storage if materials do not need protection from weather.

- Provide proper lights and ventilation in MH area.
- Consider mechanical assistance when workmen
    - Must lift more than 36 kgs, or a female worker has to lift more than 18 kgs of load.
    - Must handle the same materials for more than 30 minutes.
    - Must move materials for a distance of over 50 feet.
    - Are exposed to unusual safety hazards.

REFERENCE

1. H B Maynard Industrial Engineering Hand Book.
2. Philip E. Hicks, Industrial Engineering and Management: A New Perspective, McGraw-Hill International Editions, 1994.

4

Purchasing Systems and Vendor Rating

4.0 INTRODUCTION

Most manufacturing organisations spend more than 60% of their money for materials, i.e., materials soak up a substantial portion of the capital invested in an industrial concern. This emphasizes the need for adequate materials management and control because even a small saving in materials can reduce the production cost to a significant extent and thus add to the profits. *Materials Management may be thought of as an integrated functioning of the different sections of a company dealing with the supply of materials and other related activities so as to obtain maximum co-ordination and optimum expenditure on materials etc., used in an industrial concern.*

4.1 FUNCTIONS OF MATERIAL MANAGEMENT

The material management functions consist of the following:

- Materials planning.
- Procurement or purchasing of materials.
- Receiving and warehousing.
- Storage and store-administration.
- Inventory control.
- Standardization, Simplification and Value-analysis.
- External transportation (i.e., traffic shipping, etc.) and material handling (i.e., internal transportation).
- Disposal of scrap surplus and obsolete materials.

4.2 OBJECTIVES OF MATERIALS MANAGEMENT

The main objectives of material management are:

- To minimize materials cost.
- To procure and provide materials of desired quality when required ,at the lowest possible overall cost of the concern.

- To reduce investment tied in inventories for for use in other productive purposes and to develop high inventory turnover ratios.
- To purchase, receive, transport (i.e., handle) and store materials efficiently and to reduce the related costs.
- To trace new sources of supply and to develop cordial relations with them in order to ensure continuous material supply at reasonable rates.
- To cut down costs through simplification, standardization, value analysis, import substitution, etc.
- To report changes in market conditions and other factors affecting the concern, to the concern.
- To modify paper work procedure in order to minimize delays in procuring materials.
- To conduct studies in areas such as quality, consumption and cost of materials so as to minimize cost of production.
- To train personnel in the field of materials management in order to increase operational efficiency.

4.3 PURCHASING OR PROCUREMENT FUNCTION

The purchasing department occupies a vital and unique position in the organisation of an industrial concern because purchasing is key to the success of a modern manufacturing concern.

- Mass production industries, since they rely upon a continuous flow of right materials, demand for an efficient purchasing division.
- The purchasing function is a liaison agency which operates between the factory organisation and the outside vendors on all matters of procurement.
- *Purchasing implies—procuring materials, supplies, machinery and services needed for production and maintenance of the concern.*

4.3.1 OBJECTIVES OF PURCHASING DEPARTMENT

The objectives of purchasing department are:

- To procure right material
- To procure material in right quantities.
- To procure material of right quality.
- To procure from right and reliable source and vendor.
- To procure material economically, i.e., at right or reasonable price.
- To receive and deliver materials
  - At right place, and
  - At right time

4.3.2 ACTIVITIES, DUTIES AND FUNCTIONS OF PURCHASING DEPARTMENT

They are enumerated as follows:

- Keep records-indicating possible materials and their substitutes.
- Maintain records of reliable sources of supply and price of materials.
- Review material specifications with an idea of simplifying and standardizing them.
- Making contacts with right sources of supply.

- Procure and analyze quotations.
- Place and follow up purchase orders.
- Maintain records of all purchases.
- To make sure through inspection that right kind (i.e., quantity, quality, etc.) of materials
- To act as liaison between the vendors and different departments of the concern such as production, quality control, finance, maintenance, etc.
- To check if the material has been purchased at right time and at economical rates.
- To keep an uninterrupted supply of materials so that production continues with least capital tied inventories.
- To prepare purchasing budget.
- To prepare and update the list of materials required by different departments of the organization within a specified span of time.
- To handle subcontracts at the time of high business activity.
- To ensure that prompt payments are made to the vendors in the interest of good public relations.

4.3.3 CENTRALIZED AND DECENTRALIZED PURCHASING ORGANIZATIONS

The problem of centralizing or decentralizing the purchase activities arises in large organizations—particularly in multi-plant industries.

4.3.3.1 Advantages of Centralized Purchasing

The centralization of purchasing

- Almost invariably makes for more efficient ordering of materials
- Forms a basis to gin bargaining advantage
- Eliminates duplication of efforts
- Helps procuring uniform and consistent materials
- Simplifies purchasing procedure
- Simplifies the payment of invoices; and
- Permits a degree of specialization among buyers.
- Disadvantages of Centralized Purchasing
- Centralized purchasing is little slower and more cumbersome than decentralized purchasing.

4.3.3.1.1 Applications of Centralized Purchasing

- For concerns using few materials whose quality and availability are vital to the success of the concern.
- For purchasing small items of fairly high value such as tool bits, grinding wheels, dial gauges, etc., as well as those for which bigger quantity discounts can be obtained.

4.3.3.2 Advantages of Decentralized Purchasing

- Improved efficiency.
- Faster procurement of materials.
- Control over purchases is no longer remote.
- Decentralized operations are more flexible.

4.3.3.2.1 Disadvantages of Decentralized Purchasing

- Where different plants of a large organisation require quite different types of materials.

- Where branch plants require heavy and bulky items such as oil products, fuels, paints, etc.
- Where purchases are to be made within the local community to promote better public relations.

4.4 MODES OF PURCHASING MATERIALS

Purchase of materials can be done by one of the following methods:

4.4.1 SPOT QUOTATIONS

In this method, the purchaser can go to the market, collect at least three quotations (for purchasing one material) from different suppliers, and based on the price and other terms and conditions take a spot decision to go for the purchase deal. Then he can pay the cash and buy the material or commodity. In this method, the vendor quoting the least price generally gets the attention of the buyer.

4.4.2 FLOATING THE LIMITED INQUIRY:

- In this method, the purchaser sends letters to some of his known or registered vendors to supply the price and other details of the items to be purchased.
- After getting replies from vendors, the quotations are opened and a comparative statement is prepared. This helps the decision maker to have a glance before taking the final decision.
- Comparative statement is analyzed in the light of the following factors:
  - Price of the item or material
  - Material specifications and quality
  - Place of delivery
  - Delivery period
  - Taxes, etc.
  - Terms of payment
  - Validity of tender
  - Guarantee period.

4.4.3 TENDER

A tender or bid or quotation is in the form of a written letter or published document in the newspapers. The aim is to find the price for procuring some items or materials or to get a work done within the desired period within certain specified conditions.

4.4.3.1 TYPES OF TENDER

The tenders may be of the following three types:

Single tender: Here, the tender is invited from one reliable supplier only. Single tender is called under the following cases:

- proprietary items
- high quality items
- C-class items such as rulers, clips, pins, pencils, erasers, etc.

Open tender: This is also called *press tender* because it is generally published in Newspapers, trade journals, etc. for the purchase of desired materials.

- it is open to everybody, any vendor can furnish the quotations.
- Open tender can catch the attention of a large number of vendors.

- A vendor is supposed to deposit an earnest money along with the tender information. This is required to ensure that the vendor does not back out from the rates quoted by them.

Closed tender: It is where the contract can only be awarded to one single supplier or consortium of suppliers

4.5 STEPS IN ONE COMPLETE PURCHASING CYCLE

These steps are:

1. Recognition of need, receipt and analysis of purchase requisition.
2. Selection of potential sources of supply.
3. Making request for quotations.
4. Receipt and analysis of quotations.
5. Selection of right source of supply.
6. Issuing the purchase order.
7. Follow-up and expediting the order.
8. Analyzing receiving reports and processing discrepancies and rejections.
9. Checking and approving vendor's invoices for payment.
10. Closing completed orders.
11. Maintenance of records and files.

4.5.1 SOME QUESTIONS RELATED TO PURCHASE

What are the different tender notice types?

The tender notices have different 'document types'. These document types are determined by the procedure that should be followed before a contract can be awarded. The most common notice types are listed below:

Invitation to Tender Notice—*Open procedure*: This applies when a purchase authority has a procedure in place which will definitely lead to the award of a contract. The procedure is *open* because all interested parties are invited to tender.

Invitation to Tender Notice—*Restricted procedure*: This applies when a purchase authority has a procedure in place which will definitely lead to the award of a contract. The procedure is *restricted* because suppliers are first invited to express an interest and tenders are only invited from those firms that have qualified against certain criteria.

Invitation to Tender Notice—*Negotiated procedure*: This applies when a purchase authority has a procedure in place which will definitely lead to the award of a contract. The procedure is *negotiated* because the purchase authority may only consult suppliers of their choice and negotiate the terms of the contract with one or more of them. The negotiated procedure should only be used in exceptional circumstances, for example, in extreme urgency or perhaps in situations where it is difficult to define exact requirements.

Prior-information Notice: These are released by public sector organizations only. They give prior information about requirements that are expected to be awarded in future. Normally an Invitation to Tender Notice relating to any of the requirements listed will be published at a later date. However it is clear that not all awarding authorities follow the proper procedures so the Tenderers Direct advise that interested suppliers should contact the purchase authority regardless of the type of tender notice published.

Periodic Indicative Notice: These are published by utilities as opposed to public sector organizations. They come in two main forms: (*a*) With call for competition or (*b*) Without call for competition. The former invites interested suppliers to contact the purchase authority and enter into a competitive process. The second acts rather like the Prior Information Notice above, merely informing the marketplace of expected future requirements.

Qualification Notice: These are published only by Utilities as opposed to public sector organizations. They invite potential suppliers to pre qualify under certain criteria to enable them to be invited to bid for contracts at a future date.

Contract Award Notice: This is published by the purchase authority after the award of a contract. It provides the date the contract was awarding, the name of the successful supplier(s) and the value of the contract (unless omitted for reasons of confidentiality).

Earnest Money: It is demanded from the supplier who quotes the tender to prevent him from backing out from his promised rates for the supply of the materials.

Security Deposit: Once a vendor is selected on the basis of his quotation, he is asked to make a *security deposit* so that if he fails to supply the items in time or of inferior quality, the security deposit can be forfeited.

4.5.2 TENDER PROCEDURE

The tender procedure varies from one nation to another in a small way. We have taken three examples to illustrate this fact.

EXAMPLE 1: The *European Agency for Reconstruction* uses standard EC procedures concerning tenders. Here are the basic steps:

1. For each of the Republic of Serbia, Kosovo, and the Republic of Montenegro—and for the former Yugoslav Republic of Macedonia (fYROM)—the Agency devises an annual program outlining its general strategy and work program in the different sectors (energy, agriculture etc.).
2. This program is submitted to the European Commission for approval, and then to the Agency's Governing Board.
3. The Agency then prepares detailed Financing Proposals for each of the key sectors of operation, presenting the work to be undertaken in each sector and setting a budget.
4. These Financing Proposals are submitted to the European Commission, to the Governing Board and also to the 'CARDS' Committee for approval.
5. The Agency then prepares Terms of Reference for each individual project to be implemented in the framework of the Financing Proposal.
6. Once the Terms of Reference (TOR) for a project are ready, (depending on its financial value) the Agency puts it out for tender, by publishing an announcement on the Europeaid site and in the printed version of the Official Journal of the European Communities.
7. The Agency tenders for three categories of contracts: Service, Supply and Works.
8. There are several types of tender procedures: international open tender, restricted international tender, open local tender and simplified procedure. What type of tender is announced is dependent on the value of the contract. This will be stated clearly on the relevant page of the Europeaid site, along with instructions as to how to participate in the tender.
9. Throughout the project's implementation, and after its completion, the Agency carries out regular project evaluation and monitoring.

4.5.3 EXAMPLE 2: PURCHASE PROCEDURE IN OSAKA GAS CO., JAPAN READS AS FOLLOWS:

1. Preliminary Procedure. If you wish to supply products to Osaka Gas for the first time, please apply to the Purchasing Department. In doing so, please describe your company's financial status, the product(s) you wish to provide us and the terms of supply. These details should be provided by using a brochure or company profile statements explaining the company's financial position, and brochures on the product(s) and technical data. It is important that you can explain the advantage of your products to Osaka Gas in the light of our basic purchase policies, and the benefits that a business relationship with your company could bring to Osaka Gas. You may be required by Osaka Gas to submit Japanese translation of the foregoing documents if such documents are not prepared in Japanese. Information and data on your company and your product(s) will be stored and managed in our files as "Products and Suppliers". The information will be used for selecting the companies to which we ask to submit estimates.

Should it be the first time you wish to supply materials or equipment for which Osaka Gas has clearly defined purchase conditions, such as delivery time and product specifications, we conduct a preliminary examination of your company and the product(s) you wish to supply, and make a comprehensive evaluation based on the following criteria:

- Necessity of the product(s).
- Whether the product(s) can satisfy the standards set by Osaka Gas regarding quality, performance, reliability, safety, price, delivery reliability, and compatibility with existing facilities, as well as the company's financial condition, supply capacity, facility capacity, technological capacity, maintenance and service systems. The merit of establishing a business relationship with the new supplier will also be considered.
- Information for the preliminary examination can be in any format as long as it provides sufficient data for evaluating the above criteria. However, if deemed necessary, Osaka Gas may request additional information, product samples and/or explanation. After passing the preliminary examination, the information and data on your company and products will be stored and managed in our files as 'Companies from Which Estimates Can Be Requested', to be used in selecting those companies to which we ask to submit estimates. The results of the preliminary examination are available upon request, although any information considered confidential by Osaka Gas will be excluded.

2. Details of purchasing procedure. The specifications and number/quantity and delivery of equipment, devices and materials are determined by the department(s) that will be using the product(s) or materials. The Purchasing Department conducts purchase activities based on purchase requests submitted by the/these department(s).

The Purchasing Department, at its sole discretion, selects companies from which estimates will be sought. Suppliers are selected from the files of "Companies with Previously Established Business Relationships", "Companies from Which Estimates Can Be Requested" and "Products and Suppliers". Selection is made by comprehensivly evaluating such factors as the quality and performance of the equipment, device(s) or materials to be purchased, compatibility with existing facilities, degree of reliability, product requirements including safety, delivery time, the scale of the order, after-sale service and the company's previous business record. As a rule, Osaka Gas asks several companies to submit estimates. However, only one company may be specified for estimate submission in such special cases as those concerned with industrial property rights, those requiring maximum levels of safety that only one specific supplier can ensure, cases where only one specific supplier can assure compatibility with existing facilities, or in case of urgency.

As a rule, when requesting an estimate from a company that it has selected, Osaka Gas will set out a specification from listing Osaka Gas's requirements in respects of quality, performance standard, size, inspection and method of inspection. The selected companies will be asked to submit cost estimates and specifications to Osaka Gas prior to a specified date.

Specification sheets submitted by potential suppliers at their own expense are checked by the Purchasing Department and the department(s) that will be using the product(s), in order to determine whether the required standards are met by the product(s). All products must pass this examination. During this process, Osaka Gas may request additions or changes to the specifications.

After valid cost estimates and specifications have been comprehensively evaluated in respect of price, technical requirements, etc. Osaka Gas will commence negotiation with the company with the most attractive proposal to discuss the amount of the contract and other terms and conditions. The selection of such a company shall be made by Osaka Gas at its sole discretion. Contract terms and conditions will be decided upon mutual agreement.

The business will be established upon conclusion of a contract, in the form of a written document if necessary. The obligations and liabilities of Osaka Gas arise only when such contract is concluded.

Delivery dates specified in the contract must be strictly observed. Precise details of the delivery schedule will be agreed between the supplier and the relevant department(s) of Osaka Gas. Delivered equipment, device(s) or materials must pass inspections conducted by the relevant department(s) of Osaka Gas. When deemed significant, an interim inspection may be conducted during the manufacturing process.

Payment will be made according to the payment terms specified in the contract.

3. Other information. (*i*) This "Guide to Business Transactions with Osaka Gas" explains the basic policies of the purchasing activities by Osaka Gas and does not have any legally binding power. The legal obligations of Osaka Gas arise only when a valid purchasing contract is concluded between a supplier and Osaka Gas and the terms and conditions of such a contract supersede the statements made hereunder in case of conflict.

(*ii*) Osaka Gas and the supplier shall keep information made available through business under strict control and neither party shall reveal any confidential information to a third party, without the other party's written consent.

(*iii*) If the delivery of equipment, device(s) or materials is made later than the date specified in the contract, Osaka Gas may demand indemnity for the damages or losses incurred.

(*iv*) The contract between a supplier and Osaka Gas shall be governed by the laws of Japan and in the event a dispute arises in respect of the contract or any other matter, it shall be determined in accordance with Japanese law.

(*v*) Each Supplier, who concluded a contract with Osaka Gas, shall be responsible for observing all of the governmental regulations applicable to it or the transaction with Osaka Gas and shall indemnify and hold harmless Osaka Gas from and against any liability, damage, loss, cost, expense, suit or proceeding incurred by Osaka Gas in connection with such supplier's breach of the foregoing governmental regulations.

4.5.4 EXAMPLE 3 (PURCHASE PROCEDURE IN MAHARASHTRA STATE ELECTRICITY BOARD), INDIA FOLLOWS THE FOLLOWING PROCEDURES

1. Purchases are made by inviting Public/Global Tenders.

2. Tender Advertisement:

(*a*) Advertisement of Tender Notices are published for wide publicity in English News paper in following areas: Mumbai/Pune/Ahmedabad, Delhi/Calcutta, Madras.

(*b*) It is also given in Regional News Papers as below:

Area	Language
Mumbai	Gujarati
Nagpur	Hindi
Nasik/Aurangabad	Marathi

(*c*) Tender Document: It is a standard document and consists of:

- Instruction to Tenderers.
- General Terms & Conditions of Tender.
- Special Terms & Conditions
- Schedule of requirement, prices and break up of prices.
- Questionnaire to Tenderer.
- Technical Specification, if applicable.
- Price Variation Formula, if applicable.

(*d*) Following important information is given in Advertisement.

- Tender No.
- Description of Material.
- Estimated Amount.
- Tender Fee.
- Due date & Time (Hrs.) for submission of tender.
- Due date & Time (Hrs.) for opening of tender.
- The aspects like reservation of item for SSI Sector and material requirement with ISI mark are indicated.
- The tender documents are supplied in triplicate.

(*e*) The address for issue, receipt and opening of tender is:

Office of the Technical Director (Stores)
Maharashtra State Electricity Board,
1st floor, Prakashgad,
Prof. Kanekar Marg,
Bandra (E), Mumbai - 400 051

3. Opening of Tenders:

(*i*) The tenders are opened in presence of the representatives of the tenderers and MSEB (Maharashtra State Electricity Board) Officers. The details like prices, delivery period and terms and conditions related to the evaluation of offers such as Excise duty, Sales tax etc. are read out at the item of tender opening.

(*ii*) Annexure "C" regarding acceptance of matching with lowest acceptable rate submitted along with officers is read out.

4. Opening of Annexure B "C" (Regarding Matching Rate):

Confirmation for acceptance of the order at the lowest acceptable rate in Annexure "C" (forrn enclosed with the tender documents) is required to be submitted in a separate sealed cover duly

Superscribing Tender No. and Due date and Time of submission on or before 3 p.m. on the same date of the next month of tender opening or earlier as prescribed in the tender document when required.

5. Evaluation of Tenders:

(*i*) Distribution of Material—The offer not in conformity with standardized terms and conditions of the tender in toto are not evaluated.

Compliance of qualifying requirements wherever specified is also checked. No correspondence is made with the tenderer about deviations in their offer.

(*ii*) EHV and Generation Material, Post Tender negotiation with tenderers for withdrawal of Technical/Commercial deviations in offer are permitted without affecting original prices and ranking of tenderers.

After receipt of technical evaluation report form indenting department the purchase Proposal is prepared and submitted to Competent authority for decision.

Factory of New Tenderers are inspected by our Inspection Wing.

After receipt of decision purchase orders are placed by respective Purchase Groups,

IMPORTANT GENERAL TERMS AND CONDITIONS

A. Earnest Money Deposit (EMD):

1. The Tenderer should pay E.M.D. along with Tender.
2. The Tender without payment of E.M.D. are summarily rejected unless
   - Tenderer is having a valid Permanent Bank Guarantee of Rs. Five Lakh (Rs. 500,000) with Central Purchase Agency of the Board,
   - Tenderer is exempted on account of statutory directives as below:
     (*a*) All Government and Semi Government Institutions under Government of Maharashtra and Zilla Parishad in Maharashtra and fully owned undertaking of any State Government and Government of India (for the item manufactured by such institutions/units).
     (*b*) SSI Unit permanently registered with the Directorate of Industries, Maharashtra only for the items mentioned in their Permanent Registration Certificate.
     (*c*) SSI Unit registered with National Small Industries Corporation (NSIC) and Small Industries Services Institute of Government of India only for the items manufactured by them.
3. If exempted from payment of E.M.D., Documentary evidence should be produced. New firms should get the B.G. approved from Bank. Guarantee Section before due date of submission of Tender, in prescribed form of the Board.
4. E.M.D. should be 3% of the offered value upto Rs. 1,75,000/- and thereafter, 1% of the balance offered value. The maximum E.M.D. payable against the tender shall be limited to Rs. Five lakhs.

B. Security Deposit. The tenderer should agree for payment of Security Deposit. The supplier shall pay Security Deposit within 15 days from the date of receipt of order at the rate for 10% of the value of the order unless having valid permanent Bank Guarantee of Rs. 5 Lakhs with MSEB. For SSI units in Maharashtra Security Deposit applicable is 3% of the order value subject to maximum of Rs. 50000/-. For orders value upto Rs. 50000/- in case of by SSI units and Rs. 25000/- in case of Register suppliers on the list of Development Commissioner (Industry) and Stores Purchase Officer no security deposit is payable. SSI Units having industries outside of Maharashtra State are not eligible for exemption in Security deposit.

C. Prices: The prices should be quoted only on FOR Destination basis for supplies at various places in Maharashtra inclusive excise duty, sales tax, Risk in transit, freight and other charges if any showing the break up.

D. Validity: The tenderer should keep the offer valid for acceptance upto and including last date of calendar month, covering the date of completion of 180 days from the date of opening of tender and shall also agree to extend the period of validity required by the Board.

E. Payment: The tenderer should accept Boards prescribed payment terms of 100% payment within 60 days from the date of receipt of entire lot by A/C payee cheque.

F. Liquidated Damages: Tenderer should accept Board's terms for liquidated damages for late delivery. In case the materials are not delivered within the period stipulated in the order liquidated damages @1/2% per week or part of week on the price subject to a maximum of Cumulative ceiling of 10% on the contract value.

G. Delivery period: It is mandatory on the part of the tenderer to quote the delivery on the monthly basis. The offer shall be rejected if the commencement period and rate of delivery per month are not indicated by the tenderer. Delivery period is reckoned from the date if issue of Letter of Award.

H. Sample: Wherever applicable/ required as per tender details sample should be submitted with the offer failing offer is rejected.

I. Post Tender Deviations: In case of EHV and Generation material post Tender negotiation with Tenderers for withdrawal of Technical and Commercial deviations in the offer are permitted without affecting original prices and ranking of the tenderer.

ALERTS

- Postponement of due date of submission and opening
- Change in Technical Specification
- Deleted Items
- Added Items
- Short Tender Notice
- Change in Quantity
- Cancellation of Tender
- Prepone of due date of submission of Annexure "C"
- Corrigendum
- Validity extension desired upto__________

PRICE VARIATION

Payment to the suppliers are made as per rates accepted in the order. However, to account for changes in Market conditions, exchange rates in currencies, Basic prices of some metals etc., concept of payment on Price Variation basis has seen accepted by M.S.E.B. for this purpose price variation formula is introduced for some of the items like Oil, Salt, Conductor, Cables, Transformers, Switchgears etc.

Sample P.V. formulae are enclosed in Annexure 'A'.

1. Weather proof Cable
2. H.T. and L.T. Stay Sets
3. G.I. Pins
4. XLPE Aluminum Cables

5. PVC insulated cables
6. Power Transformers of rating above 8 MVA for voltages upto and including 245KV
7. Auto Transformers above 8 MVA and 245 KV
8. Switchgear and Control Gear
9. Transformer Oil

Technical specifications: While procuring the material detailed specifications of the items is given separately alongwith Tender Documents. However, some Guaranteed Technical Specifications in case of some important items are enclosed in Annexure "B".

1. Transformers
2. Isolators
3. Insulators
4. A.C.S.R. Conductor
5. Item Rates

Items purchased by the C.P.A. are required to be dispatched to our Major Stores/Stores Centers spread all over Maharashtra. However in few cases some of the items (400 KV material) are directly required to be dispatched to sub station/Power Station sites. The stores section is working under Deputy Chief Engineer (Store Management), Dharavi, Mumbai.

4.6 VENDOR RATING

A supplier or vendor rating system is a continuous management process, designed to measure, evaluate and improve supplier performance, enabling companies to make informed future sourcing decisions.

In plain terms, the Vendor Rating system checks to what extent a supplier does what he agreed to do like quality, delivery reliability, flexibility and the price.

As to Quality it compares the delivery to the agreed requirements (specifications). Quality problems may appear at incoming inspection or at any later stage. It would be helpful to develop a Quality Index, which lays down the relative number of quality problems a supplier has, in relation to the total number of deliveries he makes.

In effect, a supplier or vendor rating system will allow a company to benchmark their supplier's performance against the performance of similar suppliers serving the company.

Often online, the process can also be used to provide extremely important and useful feedback to suppliers in order to identify action plans and improvement opportunities.

Rating systems are often designed to meet the specific objectives and priorities of the business with suppliers being measured against a standardized and weighted points scale.

To establish Delivery Reliability, the date, a delivery is made should be checked against the agreed date. Once again the number of problematic deliveries in relation to the total number, could be expressed in an index namely the **Delivery Reliability Index.**

Flexibility as we define it here, measures how good the supplier is at shortening the agreed lead time when asked. For instance, if the company requires a supplier to deliver a week earlier than initially agreed, is he flexible enough to accommodate the company? Of course a supplier with a 6 week lead time can more easily nudge off one week than another one who has already brought down his lead time to 10 days. Therefore, in any calculation of flexibility, the lead-time itself plays an important part. A measure for flexibility could be the **Flexibility Index**.

4.7 WHAT IS EXPECTED OF A BETTER BUYER

You're expected to solicit bids ... negotiate for lower costs and better service ... know exactly what should be included in contracts ... and come up with innovative cost-cutting ideas.

But, probably the toughest part of your job is trying to squeeze the hours you need out of your busy schedule to keep up with the changes in the purchasing industry.

There's no question that it's time consuming to explore new avenues for finding the best vendors and suppliers ... to keep abreast of the most up-to-date value analysis (VA) techniques ... and to check out current cost-saving ideas.

4.8 SOME WORKING DEFINITIONS

Every company has its own culture and a technical vocabulary. Technical vocabularies tend to differ somewhat from one company to another. However, for the purpose of calculating the above mentioned Indices and in order to avoid misunderstandings, we should define exactly what we mean by the technical terms used in the definitions and equations. These definitions should be properly conveyed to the concerned vendor so as to make sure that the company and the vendor are talking about the same things. Some of the technical vocabularies are given below:

Schedule is the agreed quantity of a commodity that has to be delivered by an agreed date.

Creation Date is the date on which a schedule is entered into the company's Procurement Management System.

Vendor Lead Time (VLT) is the previously agreed fixed period between the date the supplier receives the order and delivery.

Agreement Date is the date, on which the supplier has agreed to deliver, mentioned on the purchase order.

Promise Date is the date on which the supplier promises to deliver.

Receiving Date is the date on which the company actually receives the goods.

First Price is the price quoted by the vendor for the first purchase of the current evaluation period or for the last purchase of the previous evaluation period. (per product family)

Last Price is the price quoted by the vendor for the last purchase of the current evaluation period. (per product family)

Average Price is the average price quoted by the vendor for all the purchases during the current evaluation period. (per product family)

Lowest Price is the lowest price quoted by any vendor for products supplied during the current evaluation period.(per product family)

The **purchase order** should mention the agreement date, adjusted for transport time according to the local conditions. The supplier should confirm this date by sending back an order confirmation.

On-Time Delivery is when the Receiving Date = the Promise Date = the Agreement Date.

4.8.1 QUALITY INDEX (QI)

The QI is calculated on a monthly basis, *per supplier and per product family* for all commodities received in the course of that particular month. It reflects the results of inspection, re-inspection and complaint handling.

$$QI = 1000 - (R_1 + R_2) * 500$$

where, R_1 = (the number of problematic schedules) / (the total number of schedules) Problematic schedules are:

- Schedules refused at income inspections,
- Items refused at re-inspections,
- Complaints formulated by internal or external customers. The problematic schedules are only taken into account for as far as the supplier can be held accountable for the problem. (decision of the Quality Manager)

  R_2 = A monthly average of the rejection ratios

  = (the number of initially rejected items in schedule)/(the total number of items in that schedule)

For schedules up for re-inspection and for complaints, the rejection ratio would always be 1 by definition. Depending on how delivered schedules are grouped and entered into the formula, the monthly index can be calculated *per supplier or per product family or per department.*

EVALUATION

Once the quality performance is measured and the index calculated over a certain period (monthly, quarterly) it has to be assessed in terms of what the company's internal customers expect from this relationship. The QI is evaluated as:

Quality Index	*Assessment relationship*
QI at least 995	Excellent
QI from 990 to 994	Very Good
QI from 950 to 989	Good
QI from 900 to 949	Reasonable
QI less than 900	Poor

4.8.2 DELIVERY RELIABILITY INDEX (DRI)

DRI is calculated on a monthly basis, *per supplier and per product family*, for all commodities received during that month.

Three Dates play important role in the calculation of the index: the initial *Agreement Date* mentioned on the purchase order, the possibly altered *Promise Date* and the actual *Receiving Date* of the goods.

At the time when the order is placed, Agreement Date and Promise Date are identical, as the supplier promises to deliver on the agreed date.

When the supplier notifies that he won't be able to make the Agreement Date, he will propose a new Promise Date. The Promise Date is no longer identical to the Agreement Date. It is possible however that the new Promise Date is caused by a change in specifications, or that it benefits our internal customer. In that case the Agreement Date is changed along with the Promise Date.

DRI = (Rating * Factor)/100

where, Rating = the quantified difference between the Promise Date and the Receiving Date.

Factor = the quantified difference between the Promise Date and the Agreement Date.

Quantifying the differences consists in attributing a number of points in function of the number of days that separate the different dates. The maximum of points i.e. 100 is attributed to a Just-In-Time (JIT) delivery.

The *RATING* is the average number of points for all deliveries made in that particular month. The quantification is as follows: (notice that early delivery is penalized only a trifle less gravely than late).

RATING	**EARLY**				**JIT**	**LATE**			
Difference in days	< 35	– 21 to – 34	– 14 to – 20	– 7 to – 13	– 6 to + 6	+ 7 to + 13	+ 14 to + 20	+ 21 to + 34	> 35
Points	1	10	70	90	100	80	50	10	1

The *FACTOR* is the average number of points for all deliveries made in that particular month. The quantification is as follows:

FACTOR	**EARLY**				**JIT**	**LATE**			
Diff. in days	< 35	– 21 to – 34	– 14 to – 20	– 7 to – 13	– 6 to + 6	+ 7 to +13	+ 14 to + 20	+ 21 to	>35
Points	100	100	100	100	100	80	50	10	1

EVALUATION

Once the delivery reliability is quantified and the index calculated over a certain period (monthly, quarterly) it has to be assessed in terms of what the company's internal customers expect from the relationship.

The DRI is evaluated as:

Delivery Reliability Index	*Assessment relationship*
DRI = 100	Excellent
DRI from 95 to 99	Very Good
DRI from 90 to 94	Good
DRI from 80 to 89	Reasonable
DRI less than 80	Poor

4.8.3 FLEXIBILITY INDEX (FI)

The FI is calculated on a monthly basis, *per supplier and per product family* for all commodities received in the course of that particular month. It reflects the flexibility contained in short lead-times and the ability to perform even faster.

$$FI = FI_1 + FI_2$$

where, FI_1 = (number of schedules requested and delivered faster than VLT * X) /(number of schedules received)

X being 10 in case the VLT is 1 week.

X being 20 in case the VLT is more than one week.

FI_2 quantifies the VLT for all the schedules delivered by a supplier in a certain period (different commodities often having different VLTs) according to the matrix below and takes the average.

Average VLT in weeks	0	1	2	3	4	5
FI_2	100	90	80	70	60	50
Average VLT in weeks	6	7	8	9	>=9	
FI_2	40	30	20	10	0	

EVALUATION

Once the average VLT is quantified and the "faster than VLT" deliveries registered, the Flexibility Index for a certain period is known. It has to be assessed in terms of what the company's internal customers expect from this relationship. The FI is evaluated as:

Flexibility Reliability Index	*Assessment relationship*
FI at least 80	Excellent
FI from 60 to 79	Very Good
FI from 40 to 59	Good
FI from 20 to 39	Reasonable
FI less than 20	Poor

4.8.4 PRICE PERFORMANCE INDEX (PPI)

PI is calculated on a monthly basis, *per supplier and per product family*, for all commodities received during that month.

Four Prices play an important role in the calculation of the index: the initial *First Price*, the *Final Price*, the *Lowest Price* and the *Average Price* of the goods.

CALCULATION

$$PPI = (P_1 * P_2) * 100$$

where, P_1 = ratio of Lowest Price to the Average Price

P_2 = ratio of First Price to the Final Price

EVALUATION

Once the price performance is quantified and the index calculated over a certain period (monthly, quarterly) it has to be assessed in terms of what the company's internal customers expect from the relationship.

The PI is evaluated as:

Price Performance Index	*Assessment relationship*
PPI ≥ 125	Excellent
PPI from 110 to 124	Very Good
PPI from 100 to 109	Good
PPI from 85 to 99	Reasonable
PPI less than 85	Poor

4.8.5 FREQUENCY OF RATING

If the company has a very diverse and large vendor base, it might not be possible to rate each and every vendor on a monthly basis. In such a case the company is presented with two options. Firstly the company can increase the duration of the evaluation period; with staggered evaluations for different vendors. Secondly the company can classify the vendors on some criterion into three classes and the rate vendors in each of the class on different frequencies. The first method is more suited when the company does not want to keep continuous monitoring of its vendors, whereas the second method is more suited when the company would like to track vendor performance on a preferential basis.

Frequency of Rating Matrix

	Monthly	*Quarterly*	*Half Yearly*	*Yearly*
Class A Items	ü			
Class B Items		ü		
Class C Items			ü	

4.8.6 USE OF THE INDICES

To monitor progress and to identify problem areas, an overall survey of indexes could be plotted out on a monthly basis. Buyers and Suppliers can look into performance surveys, grouped *per supplier and per product family*. Each purchasing officer/executive gets a survey of the performance of suppliers in his/her area, prompting him / her to undertake corrective action where necessary. Corrective action may either focus internally on the company itself (fine-tune agreements, revise specifications) or externally on the supplier (audit his quality system, compare notes with other units of the company, search for alternative sources) or on both (initiate improvement plans together).

When assessing suppliers, all indices should be taken into account and compared to the performances of other suppliers within the same product family i.e. the *BENCHMARKING REPORT*. Hence, after Vendor Rating ***Benchmarking*** is the next step.

http://www.indiainfoline.com/bisc/omvr8.html

4.9 STORES AND MATERIAL CONTROL

Materials and supplies constitute the most important assets in most of the business enterprises. The success of the business, besides other factors, depends to a great extent on the efficient storage and material control.

- Material pilferage, deterioration of materials and careless handling of stores lead to reduced profits.
- Even losses can be incurred by concerns in which the store-room is available to all employees without check as to the qualities and purpose for which materials are to be used.

4.9.1 REQUIREMENTS OF A MATERIAL CONTROL SYSTEM

- Proper coordination of departments such as purchase, receiving, testing, storage, accounting, etc.
- Making economy in purchase and use of materials.
- Operating an internal check to verify all transactions involving materials, supplies, equipment, etc.
- Storing materials and supplies properly in a safe place.
- Operating a system of perpetual inventory to find at any time the amount and value of each kind of material in stock.
- Setting of quantity standards.
- Operating a system to see that right material is available to department at the time of its need.
- Keeping proper records of all material transactions.

4.10 STORES MANAGEMENT

Stores management ensures:

- That the required material never goes out of stock ;
- That no material is available in (much) excess than required
- To purchase materials on the principle of economic order quantity so that the associated costs can be minimized; and
- To protect stores against damage, theft, etc.

This can be achieved by the following:

- A proper purchasing practice (i.e., when to order materials).
- An adequate procedure of receipt and issue of materials.
- Proper methods of storing materials.
- An effective system of physical control of materials.
- A proper method of keeping store records.

4.10.1 FUNCTIONS OF STORES DEPARTMENT AND THE DUTIES OF THE STORE-KEEPER

They are given as follows:

- To receive materials, goods and equipment, and to check them for identification.
- To receive parts and components which have been processed in the factory.
- To record the receipt of goods.
- To correct positioning of all materials and supplies in the store.
- To maintain stocks safely and in good condition by taking all precautions to ensure that they do not suffer from damage, pilfering or deterioration.
- To issue items to the users only on the receipt of authorized stores requisitions.

- To record and update receipts and issue of materials.
- To check the bin card balances with the physical quantities in the bins.
- To make sure that stores are kept clean and in good order.
- To prevent unauthorized persons from entering the stores.
- To make sure that materials are issued promptly to the users.
- To plan store for optimum utilization of the cubic space (i.e., length, breadth and height).
- To ensure that the required materials are located easily.
- To initiate purchasing cycle at the appropriate time so that the materials required are never out of stock.
- To coordinate and cooperate to the full extent with the purchasing, manufacturing, inspection and production planning and control departments.

4.10.2 LOCATION AND LAYOUT OF STORES

Following points need to be taken care of:

- Location of the stores should be carefully decided and planned so as to ensure maximum efficiency.
- The best location of stores is one that minimizes total handling costs and other costs related to stores operation and at the same time provides the needed protection for stored items and materials.
- Store location depends upon the nature and value of the items to be stored and the frequency with which the items are received and issued.
- In general, stores are located close to the point of use. Raw materials are stored near the first operation, in-process materials close to the next operation, finished goods near the shipping area and tools and supplies in location central to the personnel and equipment served.
- All departments should have easy access to the stores and especially those which require heavy and bulky materials should have stores located nearby.
- In big industries having many departments, stores department possibly cannot be situated where it is convenient to deliver materials to all departments and at the same time be near the receiving department ; thus it becomes often necessary to set up sub-stores conveniently situated to serve different departments. This leads to the concept of decentralized stores.
- In decentralized stores system, each section of the industry (e.g., foundry, machine shop, forging, etc.) has separate store attached with it; whereas in centralized stores system, the main store located centrally fulfills the needs for each and every department.

4.10.3 ADVANTAGES OF CENTRALIZATION OF STORES

Centralized store results into the following benefits:

- Better supervision and control.
- It requires less personnel to manage and thus involves reduced related costs.
- Better layout of stores.
- Inventory checks facilitated.
- Optimum (minimum) stores can be maintained.
- Fewer obsolete items.
- Better security arrangements can be made.

4.10.4 ADVANTAGES OF DECENTRALIZATION OF STORES

- Reduced material handling and the associated cost.
- Convenient for every department to draw materials, etc.
- Less risk by fire or theft.
- Less chances of production stoppages owing to easy and prompt availability of materials, etc.
- An idea about the disadvantages of centralized and decentralized stores can be had from the advantages of decentralized and centralized stores.

5

Operations Planning and Control

5.0 INTRODUCTION

Production is an organized activity of converting raw materials (RM) into useful products. Production activity takes place in a wide range of *manufacturing* and *service* sectors. Production system requires the optimal utilization of natural resources like men (labor), money, machine, materials, and time. Thus, it is essential that before starting the work of actual production, production planning is done in order to anticipate possible difficulties, and decide in advance as to how the production should be carried out in a best and economical way.

Operation and Production are sometimes used as synonyms but in reality *operation* is a more comprehensive term, whereas *production* is a special type of operation in industrial context. Operation could be a fighting a war or a literacy drive among masses or poverty eradication from society and so on. Here is a couple of definitions of *Operations Planning and Control* (OPC).

Production, or *Operations Planning and Control* (OPC) is concerned with implementing the plans, i.e., the detailed scheduling of jobs, assigning of workloads to machines (and people), and the actual flow of work through the system.

Operations Planning and Control (OPC) philosophy is: *"First plan your work, then work your plan"*. Before starting any work, planning is necessary for the effective utilization of available resources. *Planning* is the determination phase of production management.

Operations planning is concerned with the determination, acquisition and arrangement of all facilities necessary for the future operations, whereas *Operations control* is concerned with the implementation of a predetermined operations plan or policy and the control of all aspects of operations according to such a plan or policy. It is also called 'Production Planning and Control (PPC)' in manufacturing sector.

Formally OPC or PPC can be defined as the process of planning the production in advance, setting the exact route of each item, fixing the starting and finishing date for each item, giving production orders to shop and lastly following up the progress of products according to orders. It is also called the 'nerve center' of the factory.

5.1 BENEFITS OF BETTER OPERATIONS PLANNING AND CONTROL

The benefits of a better OPC are summarized in three groups as follows:

(*i*) **Benefits to Consumers/Investors.** Better planning leads to increased productivity in the firm, efficient deliveries of the products at proper time, more products available to the consumers at cheaper price, and better quality. This means more values for the consumers' money and more satisfaction from the products. This also means lots of profit margin to the investors who in turn can recycle more money back to the production system, which will improve the efficiency and productivity of the plant, and thus the cycle may go on.

(*ii*) **Benefits to Producers, Employees, Community and Share-holders.** Better planning means that the firm can earn more money and in turn can pay better wages to its employees. There will not be any interrupted employment as it was in older days, when there used to be none or very little scientific planning. This will lead to job security, improved working conditions and thus increased satisfaction among the employees. This will also keep the employees highly motivated for more productive work.

To the investors or the share-holders there is a security of money and an adequate return in the form of dividends. The Government may get lots of revenue by way of taxes and the community may get more economic and social stability, better infrastructure.

(*iii*) **Benefits to The Nation.** The Nation gains economic, political and social stability, a better image on the global front, and increased say in the global policy. It also brings security and prosperity to the nation.

5.2 MAIN FUNCTIONS OF OPC

The following are the *key functions* of Operations Planning and Control:

(*a*) *Release orders* to the system in accordance with the *priority* plan. *Priority* means control over the status of jobs and work activities by specifying the order in which materials or jobs are assigned to work centers.

(*b*) *Assign jobs* to specific work centers (including machine loading, or shop loading). These activities are also called '*short-run capacity planning*'.

(*c*) Provide *sequencing priorities* to specify the order in which jobs are to be processed. This function may also include the *dispatching function*, which is the actual authorization for the work to begin.

(*d*) Control the *manufacturing lead time* by tracking and expediting jobs if required.

(*e*) Monitor the priority *status of jobs* via summary, scrap, rework, and other reports.

(*f*) Monitor the capacity *status of facilities* via *input/output* reports of workload versus capacity. The input/output controls are also referred to as '*short-run capacity control*'.

The *sequencing, tracking, expediting*, and *status control* activities mentioned in (*c*, *d*, *e*, and *f*) are popularly associated with the term **shop floor controls** [Joseph G. Monks].

Different techniques (such as: graphical, charting, computer algorithms) have been developed to help accomplish the above functions. Some of these techniques will be discussed later in this chapter.

5.2.1 SOME SPECIFIC ACTIVITIES OF OPC

Typical activities in OPC are to

- Forecast the demand for an existing product and find out the demand of a new product. Also estimate in advance the cost of a new product.

- Plan for capacity required to meet production needs. Ensure utilization of capacity, equipment and other facilities.
- Schedule production activities with respect to the resources like labor, machines, working hours, etc. Fix the starting and finishing dates for each item.
- *Plan for materials (to be available in right time and in right quantity). Maintain appropriate inventories in the correct location.*
- Prepare route sheet, and schedules for production and machine loading.
- Issue orders for various activities to be performed.
- Simplify the activities and standardize the methods.
- Track materials, labor, machines, customer orders and other resources. Direct and coordinate the company's resources towards the achievement of desired goals in the most efficient manner.
- Communicate with customers and suppliers on specific issues. Respond when things go wrong and unexpected problems arrive.
- Meet customers' requirements in a dynamic environment.
- Give production orders to shops, and
- Follow up the progress of products according to orders.

5.3 DETAILED FUNCTIONS OF OPC

These are being discussed in a detailed manner under the following titles. These functions consist of the following: *Planning, Routing, Scheduling, Dispatching, Follow up, and Inspection.*

5.3.1 PLANNING PHASES

Planning is affected by type of product - larger or smaller size, seasonal, analytical or synthetic, type of manufacturing systems - continuous, job shop, or batch production. Planning phase consists of the following:

- Investigation about the complete details and requirements of the product to be manufactured.
- Estimation of future demand (forecasting)
- Planning the design, quality and quantity of the product to be manufactured, and the sequence of operations
- Determination of material requirement, its quantity and quality, equipment and its capacity, manpower need, and transportation needs
- Detailed drawing of components and their assemblies
- Information about the stores and delivery times
- Information about the equipment, their capacity and specifications
- Information regarding standard times for the product
- Information about the market conditions
- Type of workers employed and their salaries

5.3.2 ROUTING OR SEQUENCING

Sequencing procedures seek to determine the best order for processing a set of jobs through a set of facilities. Two types of problems can be identified. First, the static case, in which all jobs to be processed are known and are available, and in which no additional jobs arrive in the queue during the exercise. Second, the dynamic case, which allows for the continuous arrival of jobs in the queue. Associated with these two cases are certain objectives. In the static case the problem is merely to order a given queue of jobs through a given numbers of facilities, each job passing through the facilities in the required order and spending the necessary amount of time at each. The objective in such a case is usually to minimize the total time required to process all jobs: the throughput time. In the dynamic case the objective might be to minimize facility idle time, to minimize work in progress or to achieve the required completion or delivery dates for each job. Sequencing procedures are relevant primarily for static cases.

Several simple techniques have been developed for solving simple sequencing problems, for example the sequencing of jobs through two facilities, where each job must visit each facility in the same order. Fairly complex mathematical procedures are available to deal with more realistic problems, but in all cases either a static case is assumed or some other simplifying assumptions are made. Route or sequencing depends on the nature and type of industries as discussed below:

5.3.2.1 Continuous Industry

In this type of industry, once the route is decided in the beginning, generally no further control over the route is needed. The raw material enters the plant, moves through different processes automatically till it gets final shape, e.g. soft drink bottling plant, brewery, food processing unit, etc.

5.3.2.2 Assembly Industry

Such industries need various components to be assembled at a particular time. So, it is necessary that no component should fail to reach at the proper time and proper place in required quantity, otherwise the production line will be held up, resulting in wastage of time and production delay (e.g. assembly of bike, scooter, car, radio, type writer, watch, etc). If all batches visit the same sequence of workstations, the system is called a **flow shop**.

In these industries much attention is paid for routing. A work-flow sheet for every component is prepared which gives full information about the processes, machines and the sequence in which parts will reach at the particular place and time. This type of routing needs a good technical knowledge, so the staff of the production control department must be qualified and experienced one.

5.3.2.3 Job-shop Industry

This is also called sequencing and *scheduling situation with many products*. The general job shop problem is to schedule production times for N jobs on M machines. At time 0, we have a set of N jobs. For each job we have knowledge of the sequence of machines required by the job and the processing time on each of those machines. Due dates may also be known. The objective may be to minimize the makespan for completion of all jobs, minimizing the number of tardy jobs or average tardiness, minimizing the average flow time, or achieving some weighted combination of these criteria.

This problem is very complex and difficult to solve. On each of the M machines there are N! possible job orderings making a total of (N!)M possible solutions. For just 10 jobs on 5 machines there are over 6x1031 choices. Some techniques of optimization like *Dynamic programming, and Branch and bound* have been attempted to do scheduling in random or job shop environment. However, we will try to look at some other options with some examples.

Since such industries always handle different types of products, so after receiving the manufacturing orders, the planning dept has to prepare each time the detailed drawing and planning. This will indicate the proper sequence of routes for the job. In a job shop, each part type has its own route. These individual routes may be carefully planned by an experienced process planner. So, in such industries the PPC dept should be an expert in massive planning work. Because of the variety of product requirements, job shops must be designed for higher flexibility. Batches must be free to move between any pair of workstations, and normally should be processed in any order. Individual workstations must be capable of performing a wide variety of tasks. Expertise should be process related rather than product related. Job shops tend to be based on process layout.

It is observed that in a job shop, jobs spend 95 percent of their time in nonproductive activity. Much of this time is spent waiting in the queue. The remaining 5 percent is divided between lot setup and processing. Many facilities do not produce high enough volumes of a particular parts to justify products layout. Random batch arrival rates and processing times mean variability in resource requirements through time.

The complexities of scheduling and engineering change orders in this environment aggravate the problem. One solution could be to use the group technology (GT) approach to classify product similarities that will allow medium volume/variety facilities to implement multiple product layouts. However, this approach will not be of much use in case of highly customized job shop, where each customer needs a specific feature in the product. Thus, even though the job shop production system is less efficient, it has a place in the existing environment.

5.3.3 LOADING OR ASSIGNMENT

It means assignment of job to a facility, viz: machine, men, dept, etc. Assigning a subject to a teacher is loading. Loading should be done at the higher level. Frequently, when attempting to decide how orders are to be scheduled onto available facilities, one is faced with various alternative solutions. For example, many different facilities may be capable of performing the operations required on one customer or item. Operations management must then decide which jobs are to be scheduled onto which facilities in order to achieve some objective, such as minimum cost or minimum throughput time. One simple, rapid, but approximate method of facility/job assignment is best described by means of an example shown in Figure 5.1.

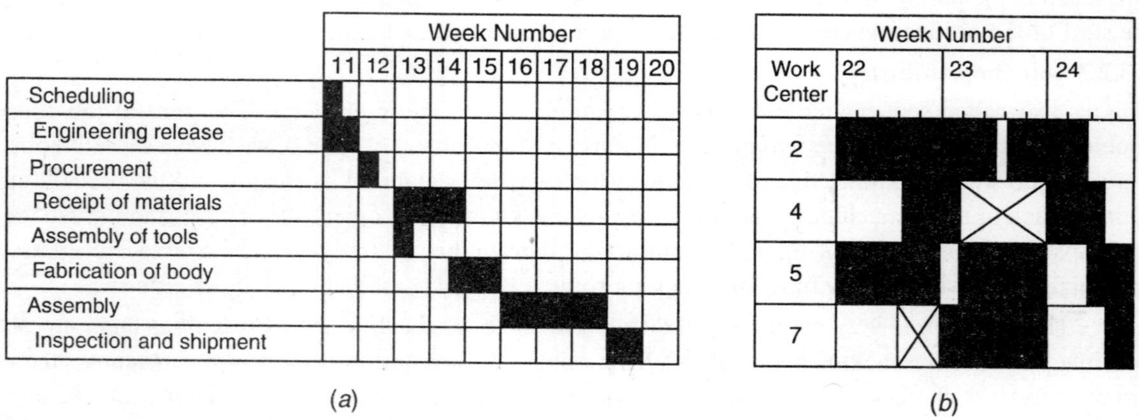

Figure 5.1

Example 5.1. A company must complete five orders during a particular period. Each order consists of several identical products and each can be made on one of several facilities. Table-5.1 gives the operation time for each product on each of the available facilities. The available capacity for these facilities for the period in question is: A = 100 hours, B = 80 hours, and C = 150 hours.

Table 5.1. Operation Time Per Item on Each facility

Order No (i)	No. of Items per order, Q_i	Operation time per item on facility j (hours)								
		A	OPT	I_j	B	OPT	I_j	C	OPT	I_j
1	30	5.0	150	1.0	4.0	120	0.60	2.5	75 **J1**	0
2	25	1.5	37.5	0	2.5	62.5 **J2**	0.67	4.0	100	1.67
3	45	2.0	90 **J3**	0	4.0	180	1.00	4.5	202.5	1.25
4	15	3.0	45	0.2	2.5	37.5	0	3.5	52.5 **J4**	0.40
5	10	4.0	40	1.0	3.5	35	0.75	2.0	20 **J5**	0
Capacity (hr)			100			80			150	
% use			90			78			98	

OPT—Order Processing Time (hour)

The index number for a facility is a measure of the cost disadvantage of using that facility for processing, and is obtained by using this formula:

$$I_j = (X_{ij} - X_{imin}) / X_{imin}$$

where I_j = Index number for facility j

X_{ij} = Operation time for item i on facility j

X_{imin} = Minimum operation time for item i

For order 1: IA = (5.0 – 2.5)/2.5 = 1.0

IB = (4.0 – 2.5)/2.5 = 0.6

IC = (2.5 – 2.5)/2.5 = 0

Table 5.2 shows the index numbers for all facilities and orders. Using Table 5.2 and remembering that the *index number is a measure of the cost disadvantage of using that facility,* we can now allocate orders to facilities.

- The best facility for order 1 is C (IC = 0); the processing time for that order (75 hours) is less than the available capacity. We can therefore schedule the processing of this order on this facility.
- Facility A is the best facility for order 2, but also the best for order 3. Both cannot be accommodated because of limitations on available capacity, so we must consider the possibility of allocating one of the orders to another facility. The next best facility for order 2 is facility B (IB = 0.67) and for order 3 the next best facility is also facility B (IB = 1). Because the cost disadvantage on B is less for order 2, allocate order 2 to B and 3 to A as shown in the table.
- The best facility for order 4 is B but there is now insufficient capacity available on this facility. The alternatives now are to reallocate order 2 to another facility or to allocate order 4 elsewhere. In the circumstances it is better to allocate order 4 to facility C.
- Finally order 5 can be allocated to its best facility, namely, facility C.

Example 5.3. Suppose there are three machines and 6 jobs need operation on them. All machines are capable of doing the operation but the time of operation varies from machine to machine. Assign the jobs so that (*i*) the overall operation time is minimum, (*ii*) the capacity of each machine is not exceeded.

Table 5.2

Job no	*Operation time on machine (hours)*					
	Machine-1	I_j	*Machine-2*	I_j	*Machine-3*	I_j
1	10 **J1**	0	12	0.2	15	.50
2	8 **J2**	0	16	1.0	10	.25
3	12 **J3**	0	15	0.25	17	.42
4	15	0	17 **J4**	0.13	20	.33
5	12	0	15	0.25	14 **J5**	.16
6	11	0	13 **J6**	0.18		.36
Capacity (hr)	30 (30)	0	30 (30)		30 (14)	
% Use	100		100	46		

The solution is superimposed on the Table 5.2.

Index no = (Time for non-optimal machine)/Time for the best machine

Example 5.4. A piece of mining equipment requires the manufacturing times shown in Table 5.3. Each of the activities must be done sequentially, except that steel fabrication can begin 2 weeks after purchasing begins, and the hydraulics and electrical activities can be done concurrently. Construct a Gantt chart for this job.

Table 5.3

Activity	*Weeks*	*Activity*	*Weeks*
Engineering	3	Electrical	4
Purchasing	3	Control	1
Steel fabrication	1	Field test	2
Hydraulics	2	Packaging	1

Solution: The Gantt Chart is drawn in Table 5.4. The chart shows the different activities along with their respective durations.

Table 5.4

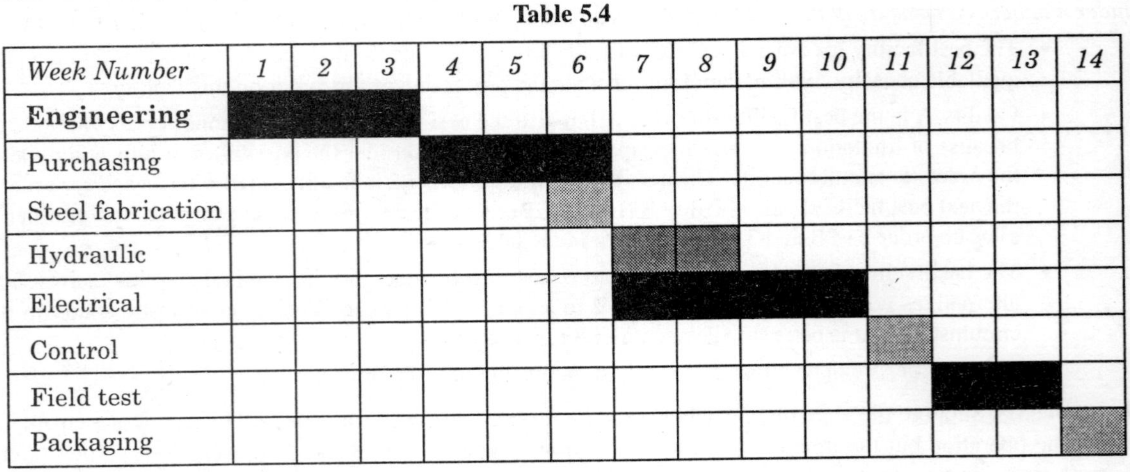

5.3.4 SCHEDULING

It is the time phase of loading. It is assignment of job to a facility specifying the particular sequence of the work and the time of actual performance. Examples of scheduling include: railway time-table, examination schedule, the time table for teaching various subjects. Scheduling should be done at relatively lower level of the organization.

Scheduling activities are highly dependent on the type of the production system and the output volume delivered by the system. Scheduling activities differ in

(*a*) High-volume system

(*b*) Intermediate-volume system, and

(*c*) Low-volume Systems

High-Volume (flow) Systems

They make use of specialized equipment that routes work on a continuous basis through the same fixed path of operations, generally at a rapid rate. The problems of order release, dispatching, and monitoring are less complex than in low-volume, make-to-order systems. However, material flows must be well coordinated, inventories carefully controlled, and extra care taken to avoid equipment breakdowns, material shortages, etc. to avoid production-line downtime.

Intermediate-volume (flow and batch) Systems

They utilize a mixture of equipment and similar processes to produce an intermittent flow of similar products on the same facilities. The sequencing of jobs and production-run lengths are of significant concern to schedulers, as they attempt to balance the costs of changeover time against those of inventory accumulations.

Low-Volume (batch or single job) Systems

They use general-purpose equipment that must route orders individually through a unique combination of work centers. The variable work-flow paths and processing time generates queues, work-in-process inventories, and capacity utilization concerns that can require more day-to-day attention than in the high- or intermediate-volume systems.

Figure 5.2 gives a summary of some of the important characteristics of high-, intermediate-, and low-volume systems. There may be some overlapping in classifications. For example, some intermittent operations are much like job shops, whereas some low-volume operations are done in batches. And job shops often exist within continuous systems. The table also gives some comparative data for projects.

	High Volume	Intermediate Volume	Low Volume	
Type of prduction system	Continuous (flow operations)	Intermittent (flow and batch operations)	Job Shop (batch or single jobs)	Project (single jobs)
Key characteristics	• Sepecialized equipment • Same sequence of operations unless guided by microprocessors and robots	• Mixture of equipment • Similar sequence for each batch	• General-purpose equipment • Unique sequence for each job	• Mixture of equipment Unique sequence and location for each job
Design concerns	• Line balancing • Changeover time and cost	• Line and worker-machine balance • Changeover time and cost	• Worker-machine balance • Capacity utilization	• Allocating resources to minimize time and cost
Operational concerns	• Material shortages • Equipment breakdowns • Quality problems • Product mix and volume	• Material and equipment problems • Set-up costs and run lengths • Inventory accumulations (run-out times)	• Job sequencing • Work-center loading • Work flow and work in process	• Meeting time schedule • Meeting budgeted costs • Resource utilization

Figure 5.2. Characteristics of Scheduling Systems.

5.3.4.1 Scheduling Strategies

Scheduling Strategies vary among firms and range from very detailed scheduling to no scheduling at all. A cumulative schedule of total workload is useful for long-range planning of approximate capacity needs. However, detailed scheduling of specific jobs on specific equipment at times far in future is often impractical—because of inevitable changes.

For *continuous systems*, detailed schedules (production rates) can often be firmed as the master schedule is implemented.

For *job shop operations*, schedules may be planned based on the estimated labor and equipment (standard hour) requirements per week at key work centers. When detailed scheduling is desirable, capacity is sometimes allocated to specific jobs as late as a week, or a few days, before the actual work is to be performed. One of the goals of agile manufacturing activities is to enhance the system's ability to respond very quickly to such customer needs. However, detailed scheduling is not always used; some firms simply rely on priority decision rules like *first come, first served.*

Order Release

Order release converts a need from a planned-order status to a real order in the shop or with a vendor by assigning it either a shop order or purchase order number. Well-designed scheduling and control systems release work at a reasonable rate that keeps unnecessary backlogs from the production floor. *Releasing all available jobs as soon as they are received from customers is a common cause of increased manufacturing lead times and excess work in process (WIP).* Figure 5.3 illustrates how the *order release* function creates a *scheduled receipt*. As the shop day and current calendar day coincide, the planned-order release takes place. The order quantity is deleted (from the MRP planned-order release row), and a shop order for that amount is added to the dispatch list, along with a start and due date priority. The order quantity is then reentered (on the MRP form) as a scheduled receipt on the listed due date.

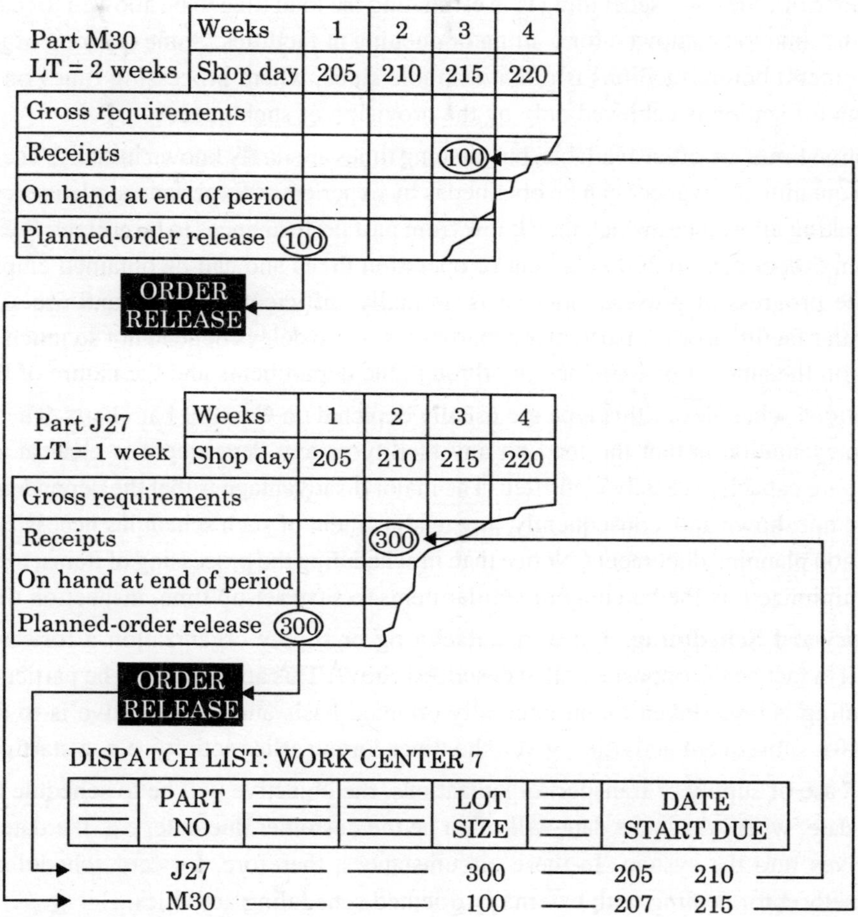

Figure 5.3. Relationship between planned-order releases and dispatch list.

5.3.4.2 Techniques of Scheduling

(*a*) **Master Scheduling (MS):** It shows the dates on which important production items are to be completed. It's a weekly or monthly break-up of the production requirements for each product. Whenever any order is received, it is accommodated first in the MS considering the availability of the machine and labor.

It helps production manager for advance planning & to have check over the production rate and efficiency.

(*b*) **Shop Manufacturing Schedule:** After preparing the MS, shops schedules (SS) are prepared. It assigns a definite period of time to a particular shop for manufacturing products in required quantity. It shows how many products are to be made, and on what day or week.

(*c*) **Backward or Reverse Scheduling:** External due date considerations will directly influence activity scheduling in certain structures. The approach adopted in scheduling activities in such cases will often involve a form of reverse scheduling with the use of bar or Gantt charts. A major problem with such reverse or 'due date' scheduling is in estimating the total time to be allowed for each operation, in particular the time to be allowed for waiting or queuing at facilities. Some queuing of jobs (whether items or customers) before facilities is often desirable since, where processing times on facilities are uncertain, high utilization is achieved only by the provision of such queues.

Operation times are often available, but queuing times are rarely known initially, The only realistic way in which queuing allowances can be obtained is by experience. Experienced planners will schedule operations, making allowances which they know from past performances to be correct. Such allowances may vary from 50 per cent to 2000 per cent of operation times and can be obtained empirically or by analysis of the progress of previous jobs. It is normally sufficient to obtain and use allowances for groups of similar facilities or for particular departments, since delays depend not so much on the nature of the job, as on the amount of work passing through the departments and the nature of the facilities.

Operations schedules of this type are usually depicted on Gantt or bar charts. The advantage of this type of presentation is that the load on any facility or any department is clear at a glance, and available or spare capacity is easily identified. The major disadvantage is that the dependencies between operations are not shown and, consequently, any readjustment of such schedules necessitates reference back to operation planning documents. Notice that, in scheduling the processing of items, total throughput time can be minimized by the batching of similar items to save set-up time, inspection time, etc.

(*d*) **Forward Scheduling:** For a manufacturing or supply organization a forward scheduling procedure will in fact be the opposite of that described above. This approach will be particularly relevant where scheduling is undertaken on an internally oriented basis and the objective is to determine the date or times for subsequent activities, given the times loran earlier activity, e.g. a starting time.

In the case of supply or transport organizations, the objective will be to schedule forward from a given start date, where that start date will often be the customer due date, e.g. the date at which the customer arrives into the system. In these circumstances, therefore, forward scheduling will be an appropriate method for dealing with externally oriented scheduling activities.

Example 5.5. A job is due to be delivered at the end of 12th week. It requires a lead time of 2 weeks for material acquisition, 1 week of run time for operation-1, 2 weeks for operation-2, and 1 week for final assembly. Allow 1 week of transit time prior to each operation. Illustrate the completion schedule under (*a*) forward, and (*b*) backward scheduling methods.

Solution: The solution is shown in Figure 5.4.

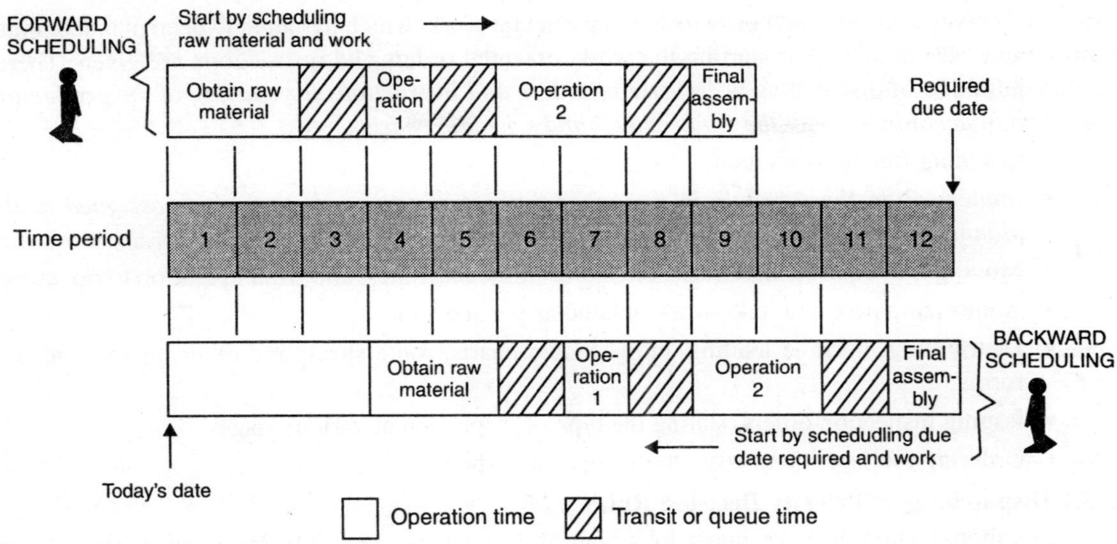

Figure 5.4. Forward and Backward Scheduling.

(*e*) **Optimized Production Technique (OPT):** OPT was developed in Israel. It recognizes the existence of bottlenecks through which the flow gets restricted. It consists of modules that contain data on products, customer orders, work center capacities, etc., as well as algorithms to do the actual scheduling. A key feature of the program is to simulate the load on the system, identify *bottleneck* (as well as other) operations, and develop alternative production schedule.

OPT is guided by the following rules:

- Balance flow, not capacity.
- The level of utilization of a non-bottleneck is not determined by its own potential but some other constraint in the system.
- An hour lost at a bottle-neck is an hour lost for the total system.
- An hour saved at a non-bottle-neck is a mirage.
- Bottlenecks govern both throughput and inventories.
- The transfer batch may not, and often should not , be equal to the process batch.
- The process batch should be variable, not fixed.
- Move material as quickly as possible through the non-bottleneck work center till it reaches the bottle-necks, where the work is scheduled for maximum efficiency (large batches), thereafter the work moves faster.
- Batch is of two types: transfer batch should be as small as possible (ideally 1), and the Process batch is larger.

OPT has some similarities with materials requirement planning (MRP). It can be considered an extension of MRP: MRP can be used to form the basis of a system for computer-aided scheduling and inventory control, to which can be added the OPT approach for the identification of bottlenecks and the maximization of throughputs.

5.3.5 SEQUENCING AND DISPATCHING PHASE

Sequencing activities are closely identified with detailed scheduling, as they specify the order in which jobs are to be processed at the various work centers. *Dispatching* is concerned with starting the processes. It gives necessary authority to start a particular work, which has already been planned under 'routing' and 'scheduling'. For starting the work, essential orders and instructions are given. Therefore, the definition of dispatching is *'release of orders and instructions for starting of the production for an item in accordance with the 'route sheet' and schedule charts'.*

Dispatching functions include:

- *Implementing the schedule in a manner that retains any order priorities assigned at the planning phase.*
- Moving the required materials from stores to the machines, and from operation to operation.
- Authorizing people to take work in hand as per schedule
- Distributing machine loading and schedule charts, route sheet, and other instructions and forms.
- Issuing inspection orders, stating the type of inspection at various stages.
- Ordering tool-section to issue tools, jigs and fixtures.

5.3.5.1 Dispatching or Priority Decision Rules

Job shops generally have many jobs waiting to be processed. The principal method of job dispatching is by means of *priority rules*, which are simplified guidelines (heuristics) to determine the sequence in which jobs will be processed. The use of priority rule dispatching is an attempt to formalize the decisions of the experienced human dispatcher. Most of the simple priority rules that have been suggested are listed in Table 5.6. Some of the rules used job assignment are: first come, first served (FCFS), earliest due date (EDD), longest processing time (LPT), and preferred customer order (PCO). These rules can be classified as: **Static** or **Dynamic.**

Static rules do not incorporate an updating feature. They have priority indices that stay constant as jobs travel through the plant, whereas *dynamic* rules change with time and queue characteristics.

Table 5.6. Standard Dispatching Rules

Rule	*Full form*	*Description of the rule*
SPT	Shortest processing time	Select a job with minimum processing time.
EDD	Earlier Due Date	Select a job which is due first.
FCFS	First Come, First Served	Select a job that has been in workstations queue the longest.
FISFS	First in System, First Served	Select a job that has been on the shop floor the longest.
S/RO	Slack per Remaining Operation	Select a job with the smallest ratio of *slack to operations remaining* to be performed.
Covert		Order jobs based on ratio-based priority to processing time.
LTWK	Least Total Work	Select a job with smallest total processing time (SPT).
LWKR	Least Work Remaining	Select a job with smallest total processing time for unfinished operations.
MOPNR	Most Operations Remaining	Select a job with the most operations remaining in its processing sequence.

MWKR	Most Work Remaining	Select a job with the most total processing time remaining.
RANDOM	Random	Select a job at random.
WINQ	Work in Next Queue .	Select a job whose subsequent machine currently has the shortest queue.

LTWK and EDD (assuming due dates are fixed) are *static* rules. LWKR is *dynamic*, since the remaining processing time decreases as the job progresses through the shop, i.e. through time. Slack-based rules are also dynamic.

Slack = due date – current time – remaining work

Rules can also be classified as **myopic** or **global**. Myopic rules look only at the individual machine, whereas global rules look at the entire shop. SPT is myopic whereas WINQ is global.

1. *Job slack* (S): This is the amount of contingency or free time, over and above the expected processing time, available before the job is completed at a predetermined date (to), i.e. $S = t_o - t_1 - \Sigma a_j$, where t_i = present date (e.g. day or week number, where $t_i < t_o$), Σa_j = sum of remaining processing times. Where delays are associated with each operation, e.g. delays caused by inter-facility transport, this rule is less suitable, hence the following rule may be used.
2. *Job slack per operation*, i.e. S/N, where N = number of remaining operations. Therefore where S is the same for two or more jobs, the job having the most remaining operations is processed first.
3. *Job slack ratio*, or the ratio of the remaining slack time to the total remaining time, i.e. $S/(t_0 - t_1)$. In all the above cases, where the priority index is negative the job cannot be completed by the requisite date. The rule will therefore be to process first those jobs having negative indices.
4. *Shortest imminent operation* (SIO), i.e. process first the job with the shortest processing times.
5. *Longest imminent operation* (LIO). This is the converse of SIO.
6. *Scheduled start date*. This is perhaps the most frequently used rule. The date at which operations must be started in order that a job will meet a required completion date is calculated, usually by employing reverse scheduling from the completion date, e.g.

$$X_i = t_0 - \Sigma a_j$$

or, $$X_i = t_o - \Sigma(a_i + f_i)$$

where, X_i = scheduled start date for an operation,

f_i = delay or contingency allowance.

Usually some other rule is also used, e.g. first come, first served, to decide priorities between jobs having equal X_i values.

7. *Earliest due date*, i.e. process first the job required first.
8. *Subsequent processing times*. Process first the job that has the longest remaining process times, i.e. Σa_i or, in modified form, $\Sigma(a_i + f_i)$.

9. *Value.* To reduce work in progress inventory cost, process first the job which has the highest value.
10. *Minimum total float.* This rule is the one usually adopted when scheduling by network techniques.
11. *Subsequent operation.* Look ahead to see where the job will go after this operation has been completed and process first the job which goes to a 'critical' queue, that is a facility having a small queue of available work, thus minimizing the possibility of facility idle time.
12. *First come, first served* (FCFS).
13. *Random* (e.g. in order of job number, etc.).

Rules 12 and 13 are random since, unlike the others, neither one depends directly on job characteristics such as length of operation or value.

Priority rules can be classified further as follows:

1. Local rules depend solely on data relating to jobs in the queue at any particular facility.

2. General rules depend on data relating to jobs in the queue at any particular facility and/or data for jobs in queues at other facilities.

Local rules, because of the smaller amount of information used, are easier and cheaper to calculate than general (sometimes called global) rules. All of the above rules with the exception of rule 11 are local rules.

One further classification of rules is as follows:

- Static rules are those in which the priority index for a job does not change with the passage of time, during waiting in anyone queue.
- Dynamic rules are those in which the priority index IS a function of the present time.

Rules 4, 5, 6, 7, 8, 9, 10, 11, 12 and 13 are all **static**, whereas the remainders are **dynamic.** Perhaps the most effective rule according to present research is the SIO rule, and, lore particularly, the various extensions of this rule. Massive simulation studies have shown that, of all 'local' rules, those based on the SIO rule are perhaps the most effective, certainly when considered against criteria such as minimizing the number of Jobs in the system, the mean of the 'completion distribution' and the throughput time. be SIO rule appears to be particularly effective in reducing throughput time, the 'truncated SIO' and the 'two-class SIO' rules being perhaps the most effective derivatives, having the additional advantage of reducing throughput time variance and lateness.

The 'first come, first served' priority rule has been shown to be particularly beneficial in reducing average lateness, whereas the 'scheduled start date and total float' rule has been proved effective where jobs are of the network type.

Example 5.6. Let the current time is 10. Machine B has just finished a job, and it is time to select its next job. Table 5.7 provides information on the four jobs available. For each of the dispatching rules discussed in Table 5.6, determine the corresponding sequence.

Table 5.7. Available Jobs for Example 5.5

				Operation (machine, p_{ij})		
Job	*Arrival to system*	*Arrival at B*	*Due Date*	*1*	*2*	*3*
1	10	10	30	**(B, 5)**	(A, 1)	(D, 6)
2	0	5	20	(A, 5)	**(B, 3)**	(C, 2)
3	0	9	10	(C, 3)	(D, 2)	**(B, 2)**
4	0	8	25	(E, 6)	**(B, 4)**	(C, 4)

Solution: p_{ij} = processing time for job i on machine j

SPT: Looking at machine B, we find that jobs (1, 2, 3, 4) have processing times of (5, 3, 2, 4). Placing jobs in increasing order of processing time results in the job sequence {3, 2, 4, 1}. So load job 3 on machine B.

EDD: Jobs (1, 2, 3, 4) have due dates (30, 20, 10, 25) respectively. Arranging in increasing order of the due dates, we have the job sequence (3, 2, 4, 1), which means job 3 should be loaded next on machine B.

FCFS: Jobs arrived at machine B at times (10, 5, 9, 8). Placing earliest arrivals first, we obtain the job sequence (2, 3, 4, 1).

Example 5.7. (*i*) Sequence the jobs given in Table 5.7 by the following priority rules:

(*a*) FCFS (First Come First Served), (*b*) EDD (Earliest Due Date), (*c*) LS (Least Slack), (*d*) SPT (Shortest Processing Time), and (*e*) LPT (Longest Processing Time).

(*ii*) Compare the effectiveness of FCFS and SPT rules in terms of (*a*) Average completion time, (*b*) Average job lateness, (*c*) Average no. of jobs at work centers

Table 5.7a

Job	*Due dates (DD) (days)*	*Process time (PT) (days)*	*LS = DD – PT*
A	8	7	1
B	3	4	– 1
C	7	5	2
D	9	2	7
E	6	6	0

Solution: The solution is shown in Tables 5.7*a*, 5.7*b*, and 5.7*c* below.

Tables 5.7b

Job	*FCFS*	*EDD*	*LS = EDD – PT*	*SPT*	*LPT*
1st	A = 8	B = 3	B = -1	D = 2	A = 7
2nd	B = 3	E = 6	E = 0	B = 4	E = 6
3rd	C = 7	C = 7	A = 1	C = 5	C = 5
4th	D = 9	A = 8	C = 2	E = 6	B = 4
5th	E = 6	D = 9	D = 7	A = 7	D = 2

Tables 5.7c. Sequencing of Jobs as per Different Rules

FCFS Priority rule									
Job sequence	*PT*	*Flow time (FT) = cumulative time*	*Due date (DD)*	*Days late = FT – DD*	*Job sequence*	*PT*	*Flow time (FT) =*	*Due date (DD)*	*Days late = FT – DD*
A	7	7	8	0	D	2	2	9	0
B	4	11	3	8	B	4	6	3	3
C	5	16	7	9	C	5	11	7	6
D	2	18	9	9	E	6	17	6	11
E	6	24	6	18	A	7	24	8	16
	24	76		44		24	60		36

Tables 5.7d. Effectiveness of FCFS and SPT

	Average completion time (days)	*Average lateness (days)*	*Average no. of jobs at WC = ΣFT/ΣPT*	*Remark*
FCFS	76/5 = 15.2	44/5 = 5.8	76/24 = 3.2 jobs	SPT is better than FCFS
SPT	60/5 = 12	36/5 = 7.2	60/24 = 2.5 jobs	

5.3.5.2 Forms Used in Dispatching

Work orders: are issued to departments to commence the desired lot of products.

Time card: is given to each operator in which the time taken by each operation and other necessary operations are given.

Inspection tickets: are sent to the inspection department, which shows the quality of the work required, and stages at which inspection is to be carried out. Afterwards these are returned with the inspection report and quantity rejected.

Move tickets: are used for authorizing the movement of the material from store to shops, and from operation to operation.

Tool and equipment tickets: authorizes the tool department that new tools, jigs, fixtures and other equipment may be issued to shops.

5.3.6 CONTROLLING OR FOLLOW-UP PHASE

After dispatching production orders to various shops, it is necessary to regulate the progress of job through various processes. For this purpose, a follow up section is formed.

The function of follow-up section is to report daily the progress of work in each shop in a prescribed format and to investigate the causes of deviation from the planned performance. This section sees that production is being performed as per schedule and tries to expedite it.

5.3.6.1 Purpose of Controlling

Material: should reach the shop in required time so that production could be started as per schedule.

Job progress: the follow up section sees that a particular product is passing through all its operation from raw material to final shape as per schedule.

Assembly: follow up section sees that all the parts should be ready for assembly purpose in actual quantities at required time.

Causes of delay includes:

- Error in routing, scheduling and dispatching
- Shortage and delay of material supply
- Equipment breakdown
- Lack of proper tools, gauges, jigs and fixtures, etc.

UNSOLVED PROBLEMS

1. Shown below are due dates (number of days until due) and process time remaining (number of days) for five jobs that were assigned a letter as they arrived. Sequence the jobs by priority rules: (*i*) FCFS, (*ii*) EDD (earliest due date), (*iii*) LS (least slack), (*iv*) SPT (shortest processing time), and (*v*) LPT (longest processing time).

Job	*Due date (days)*	*Process time (days)*
A	9	6
B	8	5
C	5	8
D	7	9
E	3	7

6

Inventory Control

6.0 INTRODUCTION

An inventory is a list of items or goods. Inventory and stock control are used interchangeably in business circle. There are various types of inventory depending upon the context or situations. For example, inventory in a library means the list of books, journals, periodicals, furniture, fans, etc. A typical firm carries different kinds of inventories such as: raw materials and purchased parts; partially completed goods called work-in-process (WIP); finished-goods or merchandise in retail stores; replacement parts, tools, and supplies; and goods-in-transit to warehouses or customers (called pipeline inventory). Generally a firm has about 30 percent of its current assets and as much as 90 percent of its working capital invested in inventory. Because inventories may represent a significant portion of total assets, a reduction of inventories can result in a significant increase in return on investment (ROI)—a ratio of profit after taxes to total assets. In this chapter we will discuss the purpose of inventories, basic requirements of inventory management, different models of inventory control, and other related issues.

6.1 PURPOSE OF INVENTORIES

Before discussing different issues related to inventory control, we should discuss: what is the purpose of holding stocks in the first place? *Inventories serve the following purposes:*

To meet anticipated demand. These inventories are referred to as *anticipation stocks* because they are held to satisfy expected demand. Examples of this type of demand are stereo systems, tools, or clothing.

To smooth production requirements. Firms that experience seasonal patterns in demand often build up inventories during off-season periods to meet overly high requirements during certain seasonal periods. These inventories are aptly named *seasonal inventories.* Companies that process fresh fruits and vegetables deal with seasonal inventories. So do stores that sell greeting cards, skis, snowmobiles, or Christmas trees.

To decouple components of the production-distribution system. The inventory buffers permit other operations to continue temporarily while machine breakdowns are resolved. Similarly, buffers of raw materials are used to insulate production from disruptions in deliveries from suppliers. Finished good inventories are used to buffer sales operations from manufacturing disruptions. By recognizing the cost and space needed, companies start to realize the elimination of disruptions can greatly decrease the need for the inventory buffers decoupling operations.

To protect against stock-outs. Delayed deliveries and unexpected increases in demand increase the risk of shortages. Delay can occur because of weather conditions, traffic congestion, supplier stock-outs, deliveries of wrong materials, quality problems, and so on. The risk of shortage can be reduced by holding *safety or buffer stock*, which are stocks in excess of average demand to compensate for *variability* in demand and lead time. Lead time is the time elapsed between the placement of order and its delivery.

To take advantage of order cycles. Inventory storage enables a firm to buy and produce in *economic lot size* in order to minimize purchasing and inventory costs without having to try to match purchase or production with demand requirements in the short run. This results in *periodic* orders, or order *cycles*. The resulting stock is known as *cycle stock*. In some cases, it is also practical or economical to group orders and/or to order at fixed intervals.

To hedge against price increases or to take advantage of quantity discounts. Materials purchased in larger quantities may be cheaper due to discounts and lower transport cost. Paper work and inspection of incoming goods are often simplified when larger quantities are ordered. However, the downside to this is that a huge sum of money is tied up in dormant goods, more space is occupied, more material handling cost is involved, and losses due to deterioration and obsolescence can occur [Samuel Eilon].

To ensure against scarcity of materials and permit operations. Work-in-process and pipeline inventories allow the smooth operations throughout a production-distribution system.

6.2 OBJECTIVE OF INVENTORY MANAGEMENT

The overall objective of inventory management is to achieve satisfactory levels of customer service while keeping inventory costs within reasonable limits. In this context, a decision maker must make two fundamental decisions: the *timing of the order* and *size* of *orders* (i.e., when to order and how much to order).

The performance of inventory management can be measured in the following terms:

Customer satisfaction: This is measured by the number and quantity of backorders and/or customer complaints. If the customers' complaints are less then the customer satisfaction is high and vice-versa.

Inventory turnover: This is the ratio of annual cost of goods sold to average inventory investment. It is a widely used measure. The *turnover ratio* indicates how many times a year the inventory is sold. The higher the ratio, the better, because that implies more efficient use of inventory. It can be used to compare companies in the same industry.

Days of inventory on hand: The expected number of days of sales that can be supplied from existing inventory. A balance is desirable: a higher number of days might imply excess inventory, while a lower number might imply a *risk of running out of stock.*

6.2.1 REQUIREMENTS FOR EFFECTIVE INVENTORY MANAGEMENT

These requirements are:

- A system to keep track of the inventory on hand and on order. That is to find out how much we have, and how much we should have based on stock-level fluctuations, rate of demands, etc. Then take steps to close the gap between the two.

- A reliable forecast of demand that includes an indication of possible forecast error.
- Knowledge of lead times and lead time variability.
- Reasonable estimates of inventory holding costs, ordering costs, and shortage costs.
- A classification system for inventory items.

To answer these issues, we will discuss some common stock control systems in the subsequent sections.

6.2.2 INVENTORY COUNTING SYSTEMS

Inventory counting systems can be periodic or perpetual. Under a **periodic inventory system**, a physical count of items in inventory is made at periodic intervals (e.g., weekly, monthly) in order to decide how much to order for each item. Examples are small retailers. This system allows placing orders for many items at the same time. However, there is a lack of control between reviews and there is a need to protect against shortage between review periods by carrying extra stock.

6.2.3 A PERPETUAL INVENTORY SYSTEM

It is also known as a *continual* system which keeps track of removals from inventory on a continuous basis. When the amount on hand reaches a predefined minimum, a fixed quantity Q is ordered. The system provides continuous monitoring of inventory withdrawals and the setting of optimal order quantity. However, there is an added cost for record keeping and physical count is still needed to verify inventory records. Discrepancy could occur due to errors, pilferage, spoilage, and other factors. Examples are bank transactions, supermarkets, discount stores, and department stores. Perpetual systems range from a very simple one **(e.g., two-bin system)** to a very sophisticated one.

6.2.3.1 A Two-Bin System

A **two-bin system** is a very elementary and most commonly used system. It is also called the *min-max system*. The items are divided into two bins: the first one is for satisfying the current demand, while the second one is to satisfy the demand during the replenishment period. Items are withdrawn from the first bin until its contents are exhausted. It is then time to reorder by using the order card placed at the bottom of the first bin. The second bin contains enough stock to satisfy expected demand until the order is filled, plus an extra cushion of stock that will reduce the chance of stock-out if the order is late or if usage is greater than expected.

When the ordered batch arrives, the level of the second bin is restored to its original high value, and the balance is put in the first bin from which the current demand is fulfilled again. This division into bins may be either physical or just on the paper.

Advantages:

- It is simple, reliable, and easy to explain and operate,
- There is no need to record each withdrawal from inventory.

Disadvantages:

- The reorder card may not be turned in for a variety of reasons (e.g., misplaced, the person responsible forgets to turn it in),

- Absence of adequate data on stock levels and consumption rates. This affects the evaluation of batch sizes for orders.

All these problems can be reduced by suitable classification of items into slow, medium, and fast moving.

Perpetual systems can be either *batch* or *on-line* based. In batch systems, inventory records are collected periodically and entered into the system. In on-line system, the transactions are recorded immediately. The advantage of on-line systems is that they are always up-to-date. In batch systems, a sudden surge in demand could result in reducing the amount of inventory below the reorder point between the periodic read-ins. Frequent batch collections can reduce the problem.

These days, most firms use computerized checkout systems that reads a **universal product code** (UPC), or *bar code*, printed on an item tag or on package. A typical UPC or bar code has 11 or 12 digits. A zero on the left identifies an item as a grocery item. The next five digits indicate the manufacturer. The last five digits identify the item. Small packaged items, like candy and gum, have six digits for identifying the item.

0 14800 23208

Figure 6.1. Bar Code.

Other usage of bar code includes the printout of price and quantity, part counting and monitoring, and for the automation of routing, scheduling, sorting, and packaging.

6.2.4 ORDERING CYCLE SYSTEM

It is based on periodic reordering of all items. With every cycle the stock of each item is brought up to its level, which is dependent on the length of the cycle, the replenishment period, and the consumption rate. When the replenishment period and demand rate do not change, the reorder quantity obviously increases with the cycle time, so that short cycles are required if rapid turnover of stock is desirable [Samuel Eilon].

Advantages over Two Bin System

- All orders for replenishment are issued at the same time.
- Ordering mechanism is regular and not subject to sporadic arrivals of warning signals from the store.

Disadvantage:

- Usually more stock is held when this system is adopted than with the 2-bin system.

Following **variations** of ordering cycle system are possible:

(*i*) **All items one cycle**

- All the items are replenished in every cycle. This is useful when the number of items is not too large, and the differences in demand are not very significant.

- However, in this system the average stock level tends to increase with the number of items.

(*ii*) **Multicycles**

- The items are divided into groups and each group has its own ordering cycle, independent of the other groups. The groups are formed either by selecting goods that to be ordered from the same vendor or by taking items with similar demand characteristics.
- The system is adopted when the stores have to deal with a large number of items.

6.2.5 DEMAND FORECASTS AND LEAD-TIME INFORMATION

Inventories are used to satisfy demand requirements, so it is essential to have reliable estimates of demand and the lead time (the time between submitting an order and receiving it). The greater the potential variability, the greater the need for additional stock to reduce the risk of shortage between deliveries. Knowledge of actual sales from **point-of-sales (POS) systems** can greatly enhance forecasting and inventory management in real time.

6.2.6 INVENTORY COST INFORMATION

Three basic costs associated with inventory management are: *holding or inventory carrying cost, ordering or set-up cost, and shortage cost.*

Holding or **carrying costs** relate to having the items physically in storage. Costs include the cost due to interest, insurance, taxes, depreciation, obsolescence, deterioration, spoilage, pilferage, breakage, and warehousing costs (heat, light, rent, security). They also include opportunity costs associated with having funds which could be used elsewhere tied up in inventory. Note that it is the *variable* portion of these costs that is pertinent.

The significance of the various components of holding cost depends on the type of item involved, although taxes, interest, and insurance are generally based on the dollar value of the inventory. Items that are easily concealed (e.g., pocket cameras, transistor radios, calculators) or fairly expensive (cars, TVs) are prone to theft. Fresh seafood, vegetables, meats and poultry products, and baked goods are subject to rapid deterioration and spoilage. Dairy products, salad dressings, medications, batteries, and film also have limited shelf lives.

Holding costs are stated in either of the two ways: as a percentage of unit price or as a dollar amount per unit. In any case, typical annual holding costs range from 20 percent to 40 percent of the value of an item. In other words, to hold a $100 item for one year could cost from $20 to $40.

Ordering costs are the costs of ordering and receiving inventory. They are the costs that vary with the actual placement of an order. These include determining how much is needed, preparing invoices, shipping costs, inspecting goods upon arrival for quality and quantity, and moving the goods to temporary storage. Ordering costs are generally expressed as a fixed dollar amount per order, regardless of order size.

When a firm produces its own inventory instead of ordering it from a supplier, the costs of machine setup (e.g., preparing equipment for the job by adjusting the machine, changing cutting tools) are analogous to ordering costs; that is, they are expressed as a fixed charge per production run or set-up cost, regardless of the size of the run.

Shortage costs result when demand exceeds the supply of inventory on hand. These costs can include the opportunity cost of not making a sale, loss of customer good will, late charges, and similar costs. Furthermore, if the shortage occurs in an item carried for internal use (e.g., to supply an assembly line), the cost of lost production or downtime is considered a shortage cost. Such cost can easily run into hundreds of dollars a minute or more. Shortage costs are sometimes difficult to measure, and they may be subjectively estimated.

6.3 TYPES OF INVENTORY CONTROL TECHNIQUES

Inventory can be controlled by these two techniques: (*a*) Qualitative techniques, (*b*) Quantitative techniques.

6.3.1 QUALITATIVE TECHNIQUES

They consist of selective control methods based on Pareto 80-20 principle, which states that *there are a critical few and trivial many.* According to this all the items of an industry are classified into some broad groups on certain basis and the attention is paid to their control accordingly. It is not practical to monitor inexpensive items with the same intensity of care as very expensive items. Some of the popular classifications selective control techniques are as follows:

- **ABC classification**
- **FSN classification**
- **VED classification**

6.3.1.1 ABC classification

ABC stands for '*always better control*'. The items on hand are classified into A, B, and C types on the basis of the **value in terms of capital** or **annual dollar usage** (i.e., dollar value per unit multiplied by annual usage rate), and then allocates control efforts accordingly. Thus, the items with *high value and low volume* are kept in A-type, items with *low value and high volume* are kept in C-type, and the items with *moderate value and moderate volumes* belong to the B-type. A-type items are given the maximum attention while ordering for purchase, and C-type the least. B-type gets the moderate attention. Typically, three classes of items are called: A (very important), B (moderately important), and C (least important).

The actual number of categories varies from organization to organization, depending on the extent to which a firm wants to differentiate the control efforts. With three classes of items, A items generally account for about 15 to 20 percent of the number of items in inventory but about 60 to 70 percent of the dollar usage. At the other end of the scale, C items might account for about 60 percent of the number of items but only about 10 percent of the dollar usage of an inventory. The distribution of these three types are shown in Figure 6.2.

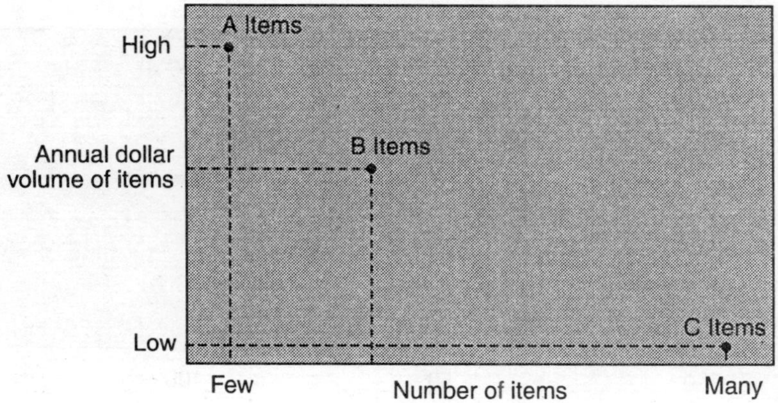

Figure 6.2. Classification of Items.

A type items should receive close attention through frequent reviews of amounts on hand and control over withdrawals to make sure that customer service levels are attained. The C type items should receive lesser control (e.g. two-bin systems, bulk orders), and the B type items should have controls that lie between the two extremes.

Example 6.1. ABC Analysis. A computer hardware company has organized its 10 items on an annual dollar-volume basis. Details like item numbers, their annual demand, unit cost, annual dollar volume, and percentage of the total represented by each item are shown in Table 6.1.

Solution: The items are classified as A, B, and C In the Table 6.1 and the same is shown graphically in the accompanied figure.

Table 6.1. ABC Analysis of 10 Items

Item no. (1)	*% of no. of items stocked* (2)	*Annual volume (Units)* (3)	*Unit cost ($)* (4)	*Annual $ volume = (3) × (4)*	*% of annual Dollar volume*	*Combined %*	*Class*
1	20%	1000	90.00	90,000	38.8%	72%	A
2		500	154.00	77,000	33.2%		A
3	30%	1550	17.00	26,350	11.3%	23%	B
4		350	42.86	15,001	6.4%		B
5		1000	12.50	12,500	5.4%		B
6	50%	600	14.17	8,502	3.7%	5%	C
7		2000	0.60	1,200	0.5 %		C
8		100	8.50	850	0.4 %		C
9		1200	0.42	504	0.2 %		C
10		250	0.60	150	0.1 %		C
		8550		$232,057	100%		

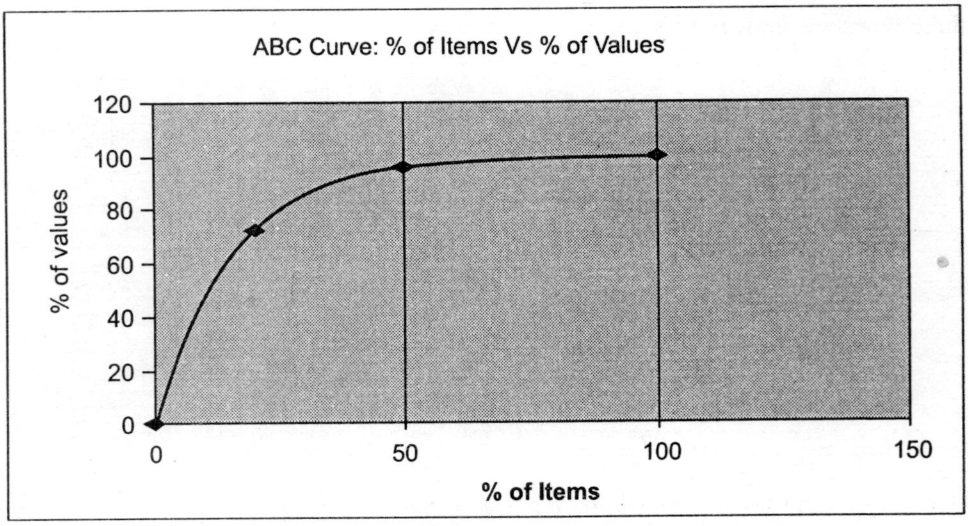

Note that C type items are not necessarily unimportant; incurring a stock-out of C items such as the nuts and bolts used to assemble manufactured goods can result in a costly shutdown of an assembly line. However, due to the low annual dollar volume of C items, there may not be much additional cost incurred by ordering larger quantities of some items, or ordering them a bit earlier.

6.3.1.2 FSN Classification

In this method, the items are classified according to the **rate of consumption**. Thus, the materials can be fast (F), slow (S) and non-moving types (N). F-type materials get the maximum attention, and the N-type the minimum for their control and procurement. Let us apply this concept in our kitchen as they say *charity begins at home*. Let the different items in our home be: rice, pulses, salt, sugar, tea, vegetables, fruits, medicine, cosmetics, shaving blades, wound plasters, and dry-fruits. According to FSN, they can be classified as

F = Rice, pulse, salt, sugar, tea are consumed almost daily at relatively faster rate and they need more attention to avoid stock-out situation in the house specially if some unexpected guests happen to drop in from somewhere.

S = Fruit, dry fruits are consumed at a moderate speed and need moderate attention.

N = Medicine, shaving blades, wound plasters, cosmetics are consumed at a very negligible rate and need less attention. They can be bought once and can be consumed leisurely when need arises.

The same concept can be extended to industrial or war situation. For example, the bullets are fast moving items but a nuclear bomb is almost a non-moving item. In fact it may never be used but it consumes lot of revenue. Such items are sometimes called insurance items as they ensure a kind of deterrent and may prevent a war between two nations just by their presence.

6.3.1.3 VED Classification

The materials are classified according to its **criticality in the production system.** Thus, materials can be vital (V), essential (E) and desirable (D) types. Maximum attention is paid to the procurement and control of vital items and less to the desirable ones. It is so because the lack of vital items can bring the production of the plant down and the plant will run into losses. For example, based on VED classification, the 1000 items of a steel plant can be classified as

V = 200—Much attention is given to the vital items.

E = 300—Moderate attention is given to these items.

D = 500—Less attention is given to these items.

The three broad techniques discussed above can be extended to have the following classifications as shown in Tables 6.2*a* and 6.2*b*.

Table 6.2a. Combination of ABC and FSN

	F	S	N
A	**AF**	**AS**	AN
B	**BF**	BS	BN
C	CF	CS	CN

Table 6.2b. Combination of part of Table 6.2a and VED

	V	E	D
AF	**AFV**	**AFE**	**AFD**
AS	**ASV**	**ASE**	ASD
BF	**BFV**	BFE	BFD

The types shown in bold fonts need more attention than the others in the above two Tables.

6.3.2 QUANTITATIVE TECHNIQUES OR MODELS

They can be split into two types depending on the demand rate and the nature of demand as shown in Table 6.3.

- Deterministic models, and
- Probabilistic or non-deterministic models.

6.3.2.1 Deterministic Models

In this the demand of an item is known and fixed, but in **probabilistic models** the demand of an item is not known (stochastic). Under the **deterministic situation**, we have the following models of inventory control:

Table 6.3. Types of Inventory Models

		DEMAND RATE	
		Same for each period	**Varies from one period to another**
NATURE OF DEMAND	**Known, constant**	Static Deterministic	Dynamic Deterministic
	Random variable having probability distribution	Static Probabilistic	Dynamic Probabilistic

6.3.2.1.1 Basic EOQ Model

The materials can be either produced or purchased. In both situations, however, one needs to know the following:

- *How much to produce in one time?*
- *How much to procure (order) in one time?*

The answer to this depends on the total-cost of production or total cost of purchase of items:

- *What are the cost of production or purchase them?*

There are three types of costs in purchasing: Material cost, Order placement cost or set up cost in production situation, Inventory carrying cost (it includes the cost of insurance, transportation, taxes, storage, obsolescence, etc).

In this basic model we have the situation where:

The company orders from an outside supplier. The outside supplier delivers to the purchasing plant precisely the quantity it asks for; and it passes that stock onto its customers (either external customers, or internal customers within the same company (e.g. if ordering raw materials for use in the production process). This model makes the following **assumptions**:

- Stock is used up at a constant rate (R units per year).
- Fixed set-up cost Co for each order—often called the order cost.
- No lead time between placing an order and arrival of the order (instantaneous replenishment).
- Variable stock holding cost C_h per unit per year.
- No safety stock is maintained.

Then we need to decide Q, the amount to order each time, often called the economic order quantity (EOQ) or *lot* size.

With these assumptions the graph of stock level over time takes the form shown in Figure 6.3.

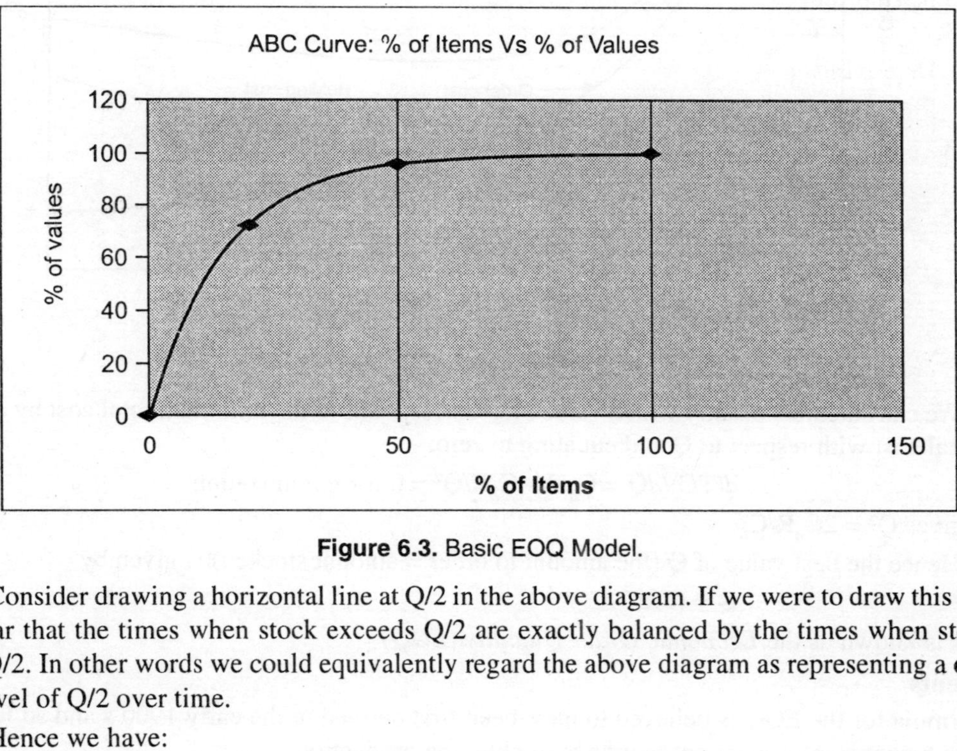

Figure 6.3. Basic EOQ Model.

Consider drawing a horizontal line at Q/2 in the above diagram. If we were to draw this line then it is clear that the times when stock exceeds Q/2 are exactly balanced by the times when stock falls below Q/2. In other words we could equivalently regard the above diagram as representing a **constant** stock level of Q/2 over time.

Hence we have:

Annual holding cost $= C_h(Q/2)$ (6.1)

where Q/2 is the average (constant) inventory level

Annual order cost $= C_o(R/Q)$ (6.2)

where (R/Q) is the number of orders per year

So total annual cost, $TC = C_h(Q/2) + C_o(R/Q)$ (6.3)

Total annual cost is the function that we want to *minimize* by choosing an appropriate value of Q.

Note here that, obviously, there is a purchase cost associated with the R units per year. However this is just a constant as R is fixed so we can ignore it here.

The diagram in Figure 6.4 illustrates how these two components (annual holding cost and annual order cost) change as Q, the quantity ordered, changes. As Q increases holding cost increases but order cost decreases. Hence the total annual cost curve is as shown below - somewhere on that curve lies a value of Q that corresponds to the minimum total cost.

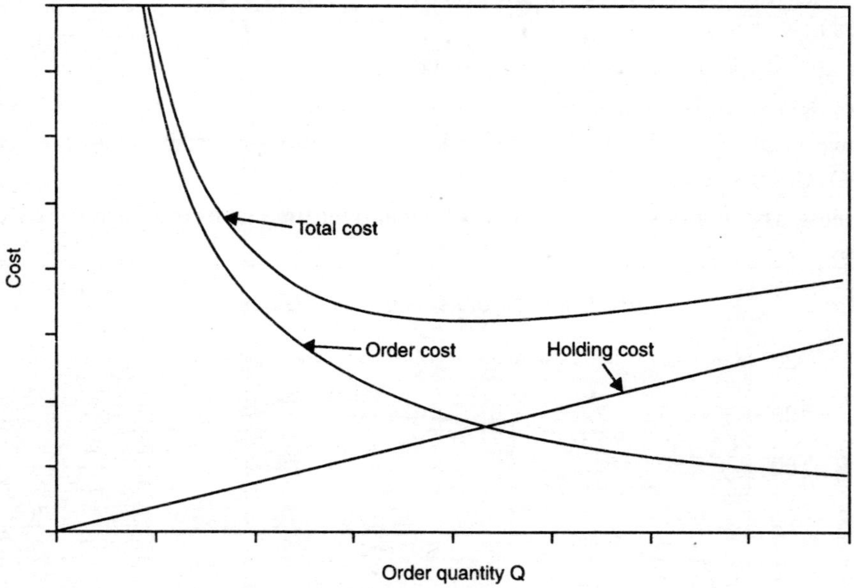

Figure 6.4. Variation of Costs With Q.

We can calculate exactly which value of Q corresponds to the minimum total cost by differentiating total cost with respect to Q and equating to zero.

$$d(TC)/dQ = C_h/2 - C_oR/Q^2 = 0 \text{ for minimization}$$

which gives $Q^2 = 2C_oR/C_h$

Hence the best value of Q (the amount to order = amount stocked) is given by

$$Q = (2RC_o/C_h)^{0.5} \quad (6.4)$$

and this is known as the *Economic Order Quantity (EOQ)*

Comments

This formula for the EOQ is believed to have been first derived in the early 1900's and so EOQ dates from the beginnings of mass production/assembly line production.

To get the *total annual cost associated with the EOQ* we have from Eq. 6.3 that

$$\text{Total annual cost} = C_h(Q/2) + C_o(R/Q)$$

so putting Q = (2RCo/Ch)0.5 into this we get the total annual cost as

$$TC = C_h((2RC_o/C_h)^{0.5}/2) + C_o(R/(2RC_o/C_h)^{0.5})$$

$$= (RC_o\, C_h/2)^{0.5} + (RC_o\, C_h/2)^{0.5}$$

$$TC = (2RC_oC_h)^{0.5} \quad (6.5)$$

Hence total annual cost is $(2RC_oC_h)^{0.5}$ which means that when ordering the optimal (EOQ) quantity we have that total cost is proportional to the square root of any of the factors (R, C_o and C_h) involved.

So, if we were to reduce C_o by a factor of 4 we would reduce total cost by a factor of 2 (note the EOQ would change as well). This, in fact, is the basis of **Just-in-Time (JIT),** to reduce (continuously) C_o and C_h so as to drive down total cost.

To return to the issue of management costs being ignored for a moment the basic justification for this is that if we consider the total cost curve shown above, then assuming we are not operating a policy with a very low Q (JIT) or a very high Q—we could argue that the management costs are effectively fixed for a fairly wide range of Q values. If this is so then such costs would not influence the decision as to what order quantity Q to adopt. Moreover if we wanted to adopt a more quantitative approach we would need some function that captures the relationship between the management costs we incur and our order quantity Q—estimating this function would certainly be a non-trivial task.

Example 6.2. A retailer expects to sell about 200 units of a product per year. The storage space taken up in his premises by one unit of this product cost at \$20 per year. If the cost associated with ordering is \$35 per order what is the economic order quantity given that interest rates are expected to remain close to 10% per year and the total cost of one unit is \$100.

Solution: We use the EOQ formula, $EOQ = (2RC_o/C_h)^{0.5}$

Here R = 200 units, C_o = \$ 35 and the holding cost Ch is given by

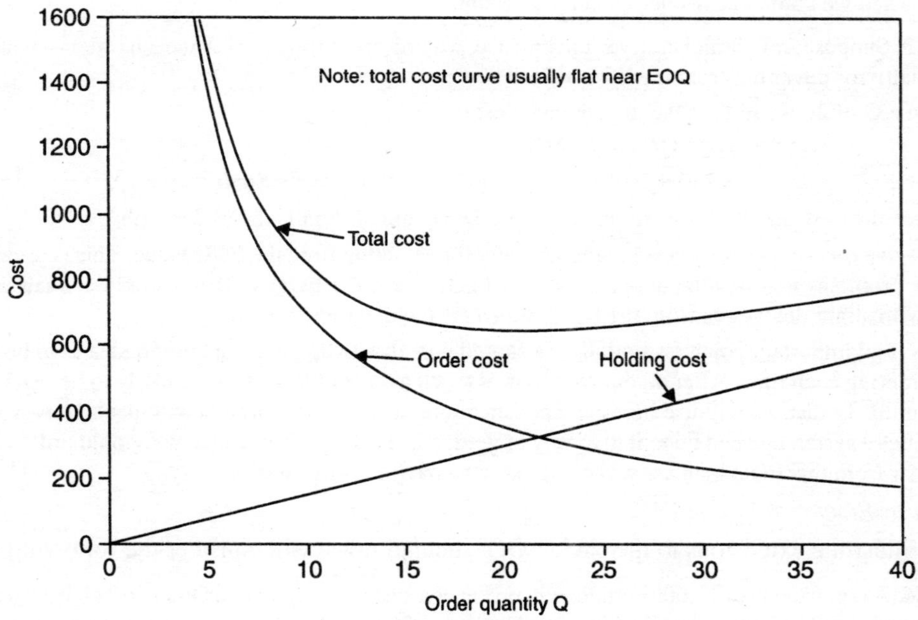

Figure 6.5. Variation of Costs With Q.

C_h = \$20 (direct storage cost per unit per year) + \$100 × 0.10 (this term indicates the money interest lost if one unit sits in stock for one year)

i.e. C_h = \$30 per unit per year

Hence $EOQ = (2RC_o/C_h)^{0.5} = (2 \times 200 \times 35/30)^{0.5} = 21.602$ units

But as we must order a whole number of units we have: **EOQ = 22**

We can illustrate this calculation by reference to the Fig - 6.5 which shows order cost, holding cost and total cost for this example.

With this EOQ we can calculate our total annual cost from the equation

Total annual cost = $C_h(Q/2) + C_o(R/Q)$

Hence for this example we have that

Total annual cost = $(30 \times 22/2) + (35 \times 200/22) = 330 + 318.2 = \$\ 648.2$

Note: If we had used the exact Q value given by the EOQ formula (i.e. Q = 21.602) we would have had that the two terms relating to annual holding cost and annual order cost would have been exactly equal to each other i.e. holding cost = ordering cost at EOQ point (or, referring to the diagram above, the EOQ quantity is at the point associated with the Holding Cost curve and the Order Cost curve intersecting).

i.e. $(C_hQ/2) = (C_oR/Q)$ so that $Q = (2RC_o/C_h)^{0.5}$

In other words, as in fact might seem natural from the shape of the Holding Cost and Order Cost curves, the optimal order quantity coincides with the order quantity that exactly balances Holding Cost and Ordering Cost.

Note however that this result only applies to certain simple situations. It is not true (in general) that the best order quantity corresponds to the quantity where holding cost and ordering cost are in balance.

Note the appearance here of the figure of 20,000 relating to material cost. This is calculated from using 200 units a year at a unit cost of £100 each. Strictly, this cost term should have been added to the total annual cost equation $[C_h(Q/2) + C_o(R/Q)]$ we gave above. We neglected it above as it was a constant term for this example and hence did not affect the calculation of the optimal value of Q. However, we will need to remember to include this term below when we come to consider quantity discounts.

Example 6.3. Suppose, for administrative convenience, we ordered 20 and not 22 at each order —what would be our cost penalty for deviating from the EOQ value?

With a Q of 20 we look at the total annual cost

$$= (C_hQ/2) + (C_oR/Q)$$

$$= (30 \times 20)/2 + (35 \times 200/20) = 300 + 350 = \$650$$

Hence the cost penalty for deviating from the EOQ value is \$650 – \$648.2 = \$1.8

Note that this is, relatively, a very small penalty for deviating from the EOQ value. This is usually the case in inventory problems i.e. the total annual cost curve is flat near the EOQ so there is only a small cost penalty associated with slight deviations from the EOQ value (see the diagram above).

This is an important point. Essentially we should note that EOQ gives us a rough idea as to how many we should be ordering each time. After all our cost figures (such as cost of an order) are likely to be inaccurate. Also it is highly unlikely that we will use items at a constant rate (as the EOQ formula assumes). However, the EOQ model provides a systematic and quantitative way of getting an idea as to how much we should order each time. If we deviate far from this EOQ then we will most likely be paying a large cost penalty.

Extensions to EOQ

In order to illustrate extensions to the basic EOQ calculation we will consider the following examples:

Example 6.4. A company uses 12,000 components a year at a cost of 5 cents each. Order costs have been estimated to be \$5 per order and inventory holding cost is estimated at 20% of the cost of a component per year. Note here that this is the sort of cheap item that is a typical non-JIT item. **What is the EOQ ?**

Solution: Here R = 12,000 units, C_o = \$ 5 and as the inventory holding cost is 20% per year the annual holding cost per unit C_h = cost per unit × 20% = \$0.05 × 0.2 per unit per year = 0.01.

Hence EOQ = $(2RC_o/C_h)^{0.5} = (2 \times 12000 \times 5/0.01)^{0.5}$ = 3464 units.

Example 6.5. If orders must be made for 1, 2, 3, 4, 6 or 12 monthly batches what order size would you recommend and when would you order?

Solution: Here we do not have an unrestricted choice of order quantity (as the EOQ formula assumes) but a restricted choice as explained below.

This is an *important* point—the EOQ calculation gives us a *quantity* to order, but often people are better at ordering on a *time* basis e.g. once every month. *In other words we need to move from a quantity basis to a time basis.*

For example the EOQ quantity of 3464 has an order interval of (3464/12000) = 0.289 years, i.e. we order once every 52(0.289) = 15 weeks. Would you prefer to order once every 15 weeks or every 4 months? Recall here that we saw before that small deviations from the EOQ quantity lead to only small cost changes.

Hence if orders must be made for 1, 2, 3, 4, 6 or 12 monthly batches the best order size to use can be determined as follows.

Obviously when we order a batch we need only order sufficient to cover the number of components we are going to use until the next batch is ordered - if we order less than this we will run out of components and if we order more than this we will incur inventory holding costs unnecessarily. Hence for each possible batch size we automatically know the order quantity (e.g. for the 1- monthly batch the order quantity is the number of components used per month = R/12 = 12000/12 = 1000).

As we know the order quantity we can work out the total annual cost of each of the different options and choose the cheapest option. The total annual cost (with an order quantity of Q) is given by $(C_hQ/2) + (C_o R/Q)$ as shown in Table 6.4.

Table 6.4. Total Annual Cost

Batch size option	*Order quantity Q*	*Total annual cost*
Monthly	1000	65
2-monthly	2000	40
3-monthly	3000	35
4-monthly	4000	35
6-monthly	6000	40
12-monthly	12000	65

The least cost option therefore is to choose either the 3-monthly or the 4-monthly batch.

In fact we need not have examined all the options. As we knew that the EOQ was 3464 (associated with the minimum total annual cost) we have that the least cost option must be one of the two options that have order quantities *nearest* to 3464 (one order quantity above 3464, the other below 3464) i.e. *either* the 3-monthly (Q = 3000) *or* the 4-monthly (Q = 4000) options. This can be seen from the shape of the total annual cost curve in Figure 6.6. The total annual cost for these two options could then be calculated to find which was the cheapest option.

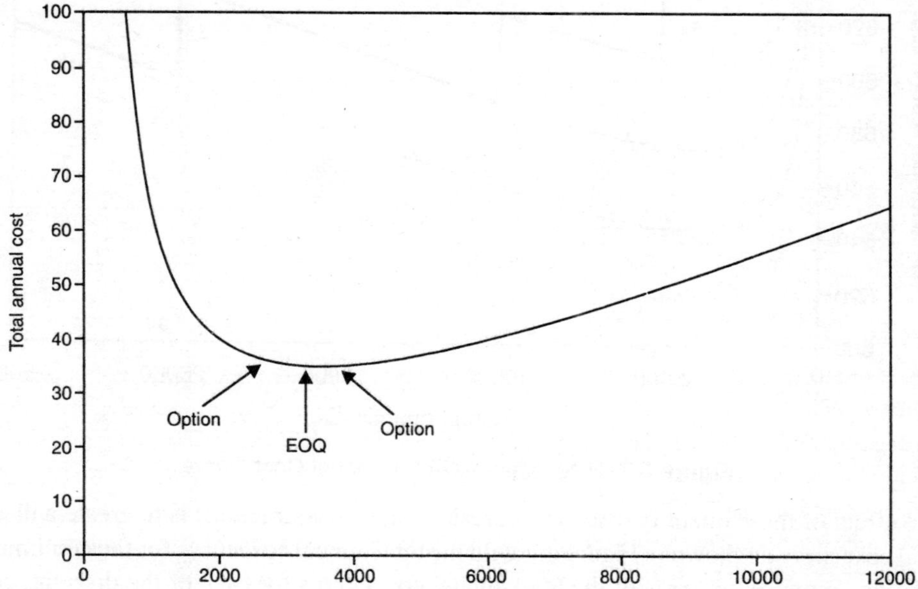

Figure 6.6. Total Annual Cost Curve.

Example 6.6. If the supplier offers the following quantity discount structure what effect will this have on the order quantity?

Order quantity	*Cost (per unit)*
0 — 4,999	\$0.05
5,000—9,999	\$0.05 less 5%
10,000—19,999	\$0.05 less 10%
20,000 and above	\$0.05 less 15%

For example, if we were to order 6000 units we would only pay 0.95(0.05) for each of the 6000 units, i.e. the discount would be given on the entire order.

Solution: Here, as mentioned above, we need to remember to add to the total annual cost equation $[C_h(Q/2) + C_o(R/Q)]$ a term relating to R multiplied by the unit cost, as the cost of a unit is now no longer fixed but variable (unit cost = a function $f(Q)$ of the order quantity Q).

Hence our total annual cost equation is

$$C_h(Q/2) + C_o(R/Q) + R[f(Q)]$$

It is instructive to consider what changes in this equation as we change the order quantity Q. Obviously R and Co remain unchanged, however, Q and $f(Q)$ change. So what about C_h? Well, it can remain constant or it can change. You need to look back to how you calculated C_h. If it included money tied up then, as the unit cost $f(Q)$ alters with Q, so too does the money tied up.

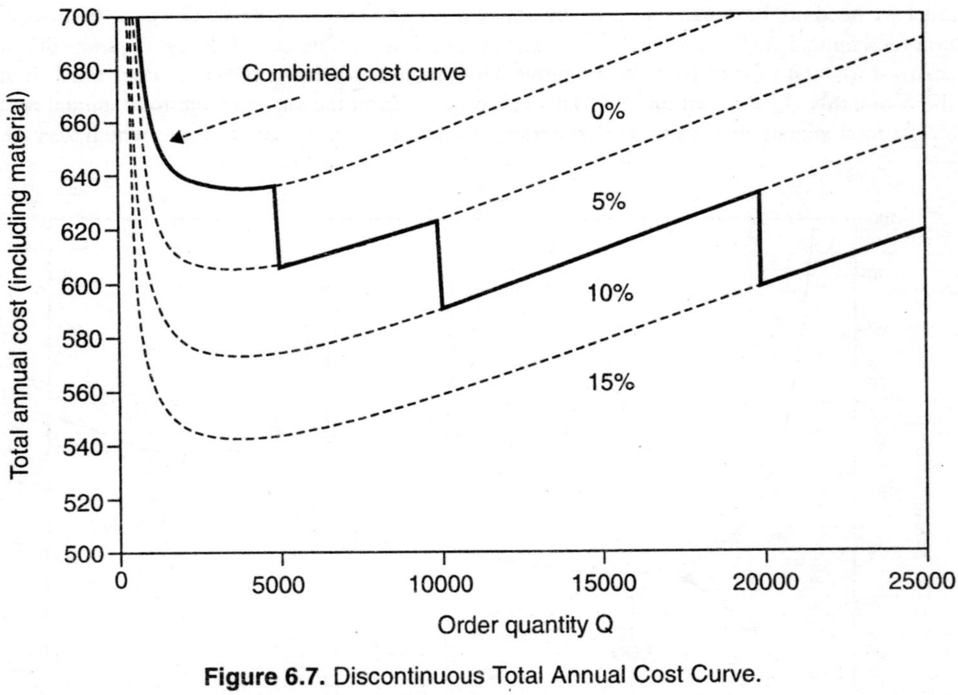

Figure 6.7. Discontinuous Total Annual Cost Curve.

The effect of these quantity discounts (breaks in the cost structure) is to create a discontinuous total annual cost curve as shown in Figure 6.7 with the total annual cost curve for the combined discount structure being composed of parts of the total annual cost curves for each of the discount costs.

The order quantity which provides the lowest overall cost will be the lowest point on the Combined Cost Curve shown in the diagram above. We can precisely calculate this point as it corresponds to:

- Either an EOQ for one of the discount curves considered separately (note that in some cases the EOQ for a particular discount curve may not lie within the range covered by that discount and hence will be infeasible);
- or one of the breakpoints between the individual discount curves on the total annual cost curve for the combined discount structure.

We merely have to work out the total annual cost for each of these types of points and choose the cheapest.

First the EOQ's:

Discount	*Cost Cost*	C_h *Cost*	*EOQ Cost*	*Inventory*	*Material*	*Total*
0	0.05	0.01	3464	34.64	600	634.64
5%	0.0475	0.0095	3554	Infeasible		
10%	0.045	0.009	3651	Infeasible		
15%	0.0425	0.0085	3757	Infeasible		

Note here that we now include *material (purchase)* cost in total annual cost. The effect of the discount is to reduce the cost, and hence Ch the inventory holding cost per unit per year - all other terms in the EOQ formula (R and Co) remain the same. Of the EOQ's only one, the first, lies within the range covered by the discount rate.

For the breakpoints we have:

Order quantity	*Cost*	C_h	*Inventory cost*	*Material cost*	*Total cost*
5,000	0.0475	0.0095	35.75	570	605.75
10,000	0.0450	0.0090	51	540	591
20,000	0.0425	0.0085	88	510	598

From these figures we can see that the economic order quantity associated with minimum total annual cost is 10,000 with a total annual cost of 591.

Note that this situation illustrates the point we made before when we considered the simple EOQ model, namely that it is not true (in general) that the best order quantity corresponds to the quantity where holding cost and ordering cost are in balance. This is because the holding cost associated with Q =10,000 is $C_h(Q/2) = 0.009(10000/2) = 45$, whilst the ordering cost is $C_o(R/Q) = 5(12000/10000) = 6$.

6.3.2.1.2 EOQ Model with Reorder Point

In the basic model, we discussed '*how much should be ordered*'? In this model we will discuss '*when to order*'? The determinant of when to order in a continuous inventory system is the *reorder point*, the inventory level at which a new order is placed. The following ordering policies are followed:

Periodic Review. An ordering policy that requires reviewing the inventory level at fixed points in time to determine how much to order on the basis of the amount of inventory on hand at that time.

Continuous Review. An ordering policy that requires reviewing the inventory continuously to determine when the recorder point is reached.

Economic-Order-Quantity (EOQ) Inventory Model

It assumes that the inventory pertains to one and only one item. The inventory is replenished in batches rather than being replaced continuously over time. The demand is deterministic and occurs at a known rate of R units per time period. The lead time L is deterministic and known. Shortages are not allowed. That is, there must always be enough inventory on hand to meet the demand. Ordering occurs in a fixed quantity Q when the inventory reaches a certain reorder point R_o.

Implementing this reorder policy therefore requires monitoring the inventory regularly to determine when level R_o is reached. The appropriate values of both Q and R_o are chosen to achieve an overall minimum total cost on the following components:

A fixed ordering cost of \$ C_o per order. A purchase cost of \$C per unit regardless of the number of units ordered (no quantity discounts). A carrying rate of *i* (that is, the holding cost, $C_h = {}_iC$ for each unit in inventory per time period). Shortage costs are irrelevant because shortages are not allowed. Let's explain this model with Example 6.6.

Example 6.7. Determine how and when to place orders for X-ray film for a **City Hospital** to ensure that the hospital never runs out of stock while keeping the total cost as low as possible.

Characteristics of the system:

Only one item is being considered: X-ray film. This film is replaced in batches ordered from an out-of-town supplier. Past records indicate that demand has been relatively constant at 1500 films per month and so can be considered deterministic. The supplier has committed to meet orders in 1 week (L = 1 week). Shortages are not allowed, as specified by hospital management.

Cost data:

A fixed ordering cost of \$100 to cover the costs of placing each order, paying delivery charges , etc. A purchase cost of \$20 per film with no quantity discount. A carrying rate of 30% per year (i = 0.30) to reflect the cost of storing the film in a special area as well as the opportunity cost of the money invested in the idle inventory.

Solution:

Annual demand (R or D)

$$R = (1500 \text{ films/month}) (12 \text{ months/year}) = 18{,}000 \text{ films per year}$$

Lead Time (L)

$$L = 1 \text{ week} = 1/52 \text{ of a year}$$

Annual Carrying Rate $i = 0.30$

Ordering Cost $C_o = \$100$ per order

Purchase Cost $C = \$20$ per film

Annual Holding Cost (C_h)

$$C_h = i\,C = 0.30(20) = \$6 \text{ per film per year}$$

Total Cost Function

(*a*) Total Cost = (Ordering Cost) + (Purchasing Cost) + (Holding Cost)

$$= (C_o\, R/Q) + (C\, R) + (Q\, C_h)/2$$

Computing the Optimal Order Quantity

$$Q = (2RC_o/C_h)^{0.5} = (2 \times 18000 \times 100/6)^{0.5} = 774.60 \text{ units}$$

Annual Cost when Q = 774

Total Annual Cost $= (C_o\, R/Q) + (C\, R) + (Q\, C_h)/2$

$$= (100 * 18000)/(774) + (20 * 18000) + (774 * 6)/2$$

$$= 364{,}647.58$$

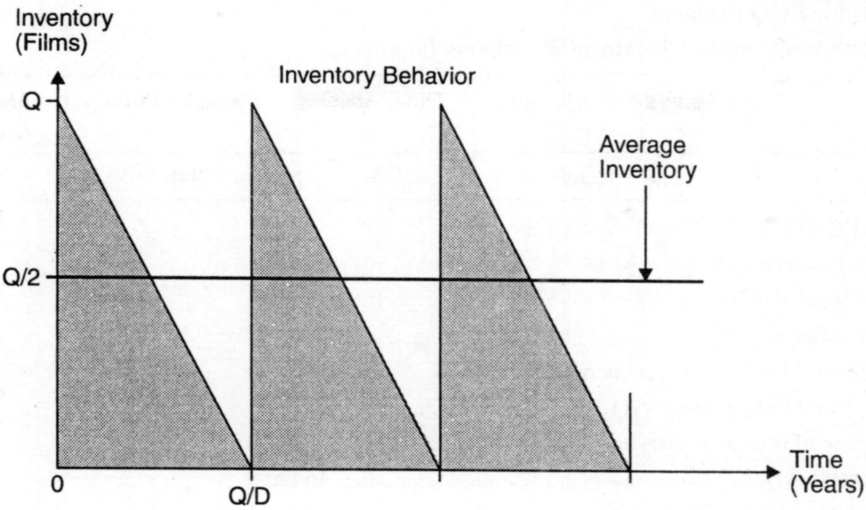

Figure 6.8

Annual Cost when Q = 775

Total Annual Cost $= (C_o\ R/Q) + (C\ R) + (Q\ C_h)/2$

$= (100 * 18000)/(775) + (20 * 18000) + (775 * 6)/2$

$= 364{,}647.58$

(*b*) Average number of orders per period = (demand per period)/(order quantity) = R/Q

(*c*) Time between orders = (order quantity)/(demand per period) = Q/R

(*d*) **Determining the Reorder Point**

Reorder Point (R_o) = demand during the lead time = R L = 18000*(1/52) = 346

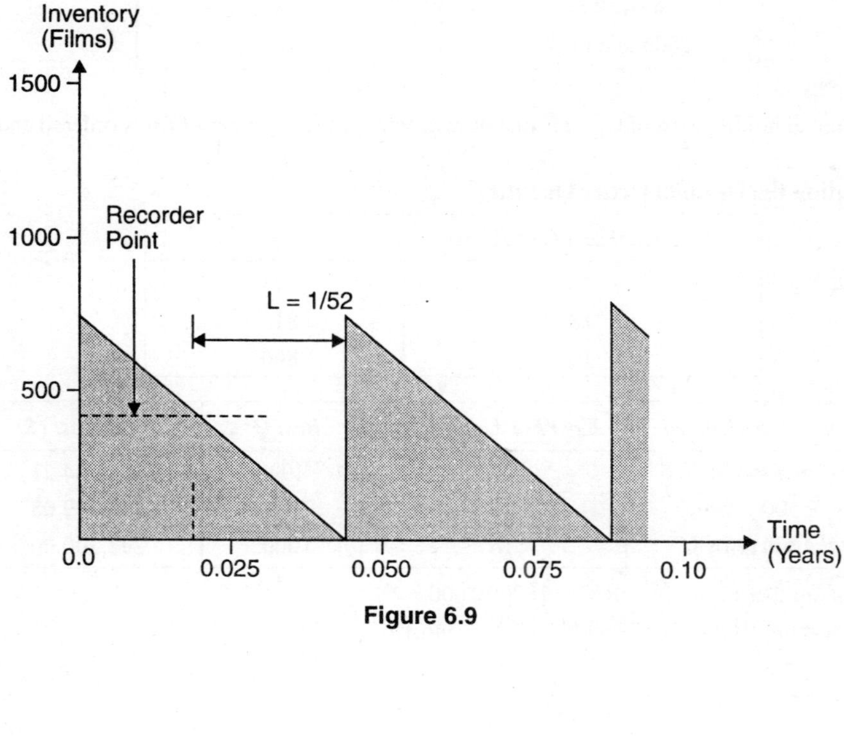

Figure 6.9

Results for EOQ Problem

The EOQ Model of the **City Hospital** Ordering Information

Item Name	*Item ID*	*Orders/Setups*	*Order Size*	*Recorder Point*	*Max Orders Outstanding*
X-RAY FILM	1	23.2	775	346	1

AGGREGATE INVENTORY VALUES

Inventory carrying charge = 30 %

Service level = 95 %

Total number of items 1

Average working stock investment ($) 750.00

Cost to order EOQ items ($/yr) 2322.58

Average working stock carrying cost ($/yr) 2325.00

Total cost ($/yr) 4647.58

Number of orders of EOQ item 23

Example 6.8 (The EOQ Model with Quantity Discounts). The data related to the City Hospital Problem with Quantity Discounts are as follows:

An annual demand of R = 18,000 films per year

A lead time of 1 week L = 1/52 year

An annual carrying rate of i = 0.30 per year.

A fixed ordering cost of C_o = $100 per order

A purchase cost C based on the number of films ordered as follows:

Number Ordered	*Cost Per Unit ($)*
1—499	20
500—999	18
1000 and over	16

Find the EOQ.

Solution: An annual holding cost of $C_h = i\,C$ that now depends on the number of films ordered and the associated unit cost (C).

Computing the Optimal Order Quantity

Purchase Cost C ($ /Unit)	*Q*
20	775
18	816
16	866

Number Ordered	*Cost Per Unit ($C)*	*Best Q*	*Total Cost ($)*
1—499	20	499	365,104.21
500—999	18	816	328,409.08
1000 & over	16	1000	292,200.00

Average number of orders = R/Q = 18000/1000 = 18

Recorder point (R_o) = RL = 18000*(1/52) = 346.15.

Reorder point (ROP)

It is the inventory balance at which a new order is placed. The ROP is reached when the inventory balance = (Expected demand during LT + the safety stock needed to protect against possible excess demand over that expected during the LT)

There can be two policies to deal with the reordering issues:

(*i*) **Fix the size of the orders**, and let the ordering frequency (or the length of time between orders) vary to take care of the fluctuation of the demand.

Two bin system: It is used for spare parts management. It is based on fixed order size. In this method, the individual inventories are under constant watch. The stock is physically segregated into two bins. Stock is drawn from one bin until it is empty. When the first bin is empty, a reorder is placed; thereafter the stock is drawn from the second bin. The system is simple to operate and needs a minimum record keeping.

(*ii*) **Fix the ordering frequency**, and let the size of the orders vary with the demand.

In either case, a safety stock must be carried over to meet the unexpected variation in demand during lead time (i.e., between placing and receiving the orders).

Safety Stock (SS) in a Fixed Order System

Under this system, a fixed quantity of material (fixed lot size) is always ordered. However, the time an order is placed is allowed to *vary* with fluctuation in usage. The situation is depicted in Figure 6.10.

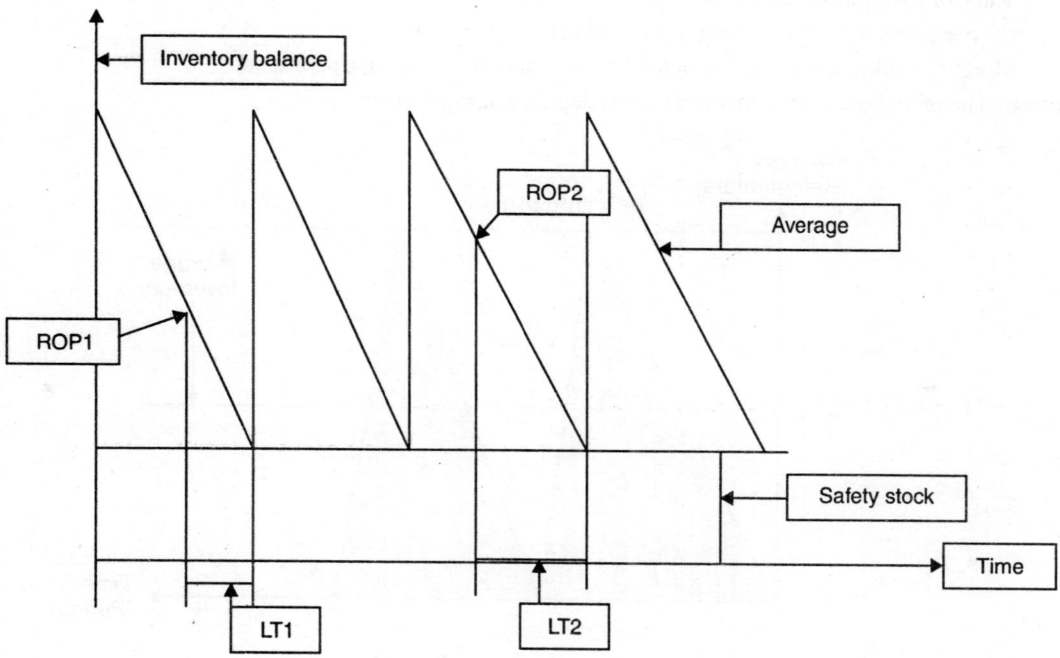

Figure 6.10. Fixed Order System.

- Expected inventory balance (I) = (SS + Q/2) = (S + Q/2)
- The amount of stock on hand and on order is the maximum amount that will be available for use during the lead time.
- A reorder is placed when (Inv. on hand + Orders placed but not received) = (forecast demand over LT + SS over the LT).

Example 6.9. Let C_o = \$10, C_h = \$1, R = 5 units, C_1 = \$2, C_2 = \$1, and q = 15

First compute $Q = (2R\ C_o/C_h)^{0.5} = (2*5*10/1)^{0.5} = 10$

Since, $Q < q$, it is necessary to check whether q is less than q_1. The value of q_1 is computed as follows:

$$TC_1\,(Q) = TC_2\,(q_1)$$

$$RC_1 + R\,C_o/Q + C_h\,Q/2 = RC_2 + R\,C_o/q_1 + C_h\,q_1/2$$

$$\Rightarrow \quad 5*2 + (5*10)/10 + (1*10)/2 = 5*1 + (5*10)/q_1 + (1*\,q_1)/2$$

$$\Rightarrow \quad q_{12} - 30\,q_1 + 100 = 0$$

$$\Rightarrow \quad q_1 = 26.18 \text{ or } 3.82$$

By definition, q_1 is selected as the larger value. Since $q_1 > q$, it follows that $Q = q = 15$, and

$$\mathbf{TC(Q)} = T\,C_2\,(15) = RC_2 + R\,C_o/15 + C_h\,Q/2 = 5*1 + (5*10)/15 + (1*15)/2 = \$15.83.$$

Example 6.10. Production-Order-Quantity (POQ) Inventory Model. A Refrigerator manufacturing Company wants to determine how many and when to produce refrigerators to meet an anticipated demand of 6000 per year at the least total cost. The other details are given below:

Production rate of refrigerators, P = 800 refrigerators per month

Annual demand of refrigerators, R or D = (6000 units/year) /(12 months/year)
= 500 refrigerators per month

Lead time, L = 1 week = 1/52 year = 12/52 month = 0.231 month

Setup cost of C_o = \$1000 per production run

Value of each refrigerator, C = \$250

Carrying rate, i = 0.24 per year = 0.24 /12 per month = 0.02

Monthly holding cost, $C_h = i\,C$ = 0.02 * 250 = \$5 per refrigerator per month.

Solution: The model relevant to this situation is depicted in Figure 6.11.

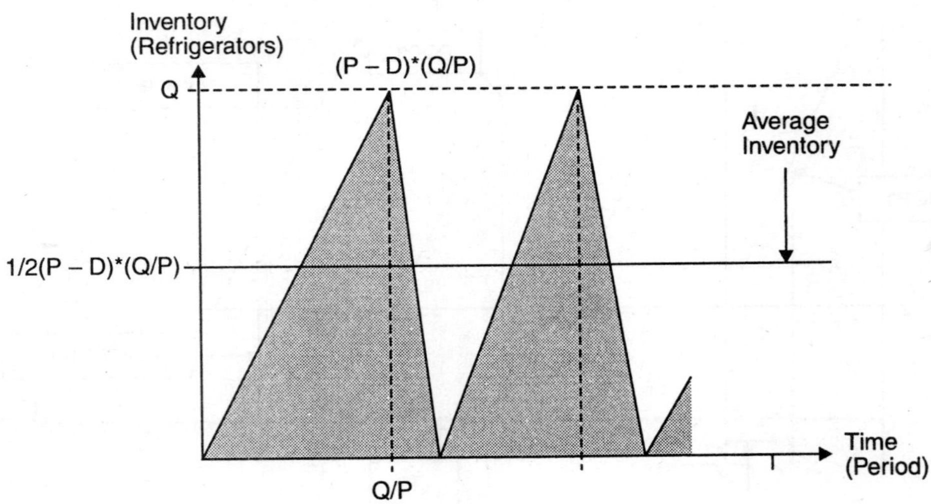

Figure 6.11. POQ Inventory Model.

$$Q = \left(\frac{2RC_o}{(C_h)(P - R)/R}\right)^{0.5} = \{(2 \times 500 \times 1000/\{6(800 - 500)/800\}]^{0.5} = 730.30 \text{ units}$$

Average number of orders per period = (demand per period)/(order quantity)
= R/Q

Determining the Reorder Point

Cycle Time (T) = Time at which the number of units from the production run is used up

$$T = Q/R = 730/500 = 1.46 \text{ month}$$

t = time at which the previous production is finished

$t = Q/P = 730/800 = 0.9125$ month

Reorder point (R_o) = demand of refrigerators during the lead time

$$R_o = LR = (0.231 \text{ month})(500 \text{ units/month}) = 115.5 \text{ units} = 116 \text{ units}$$

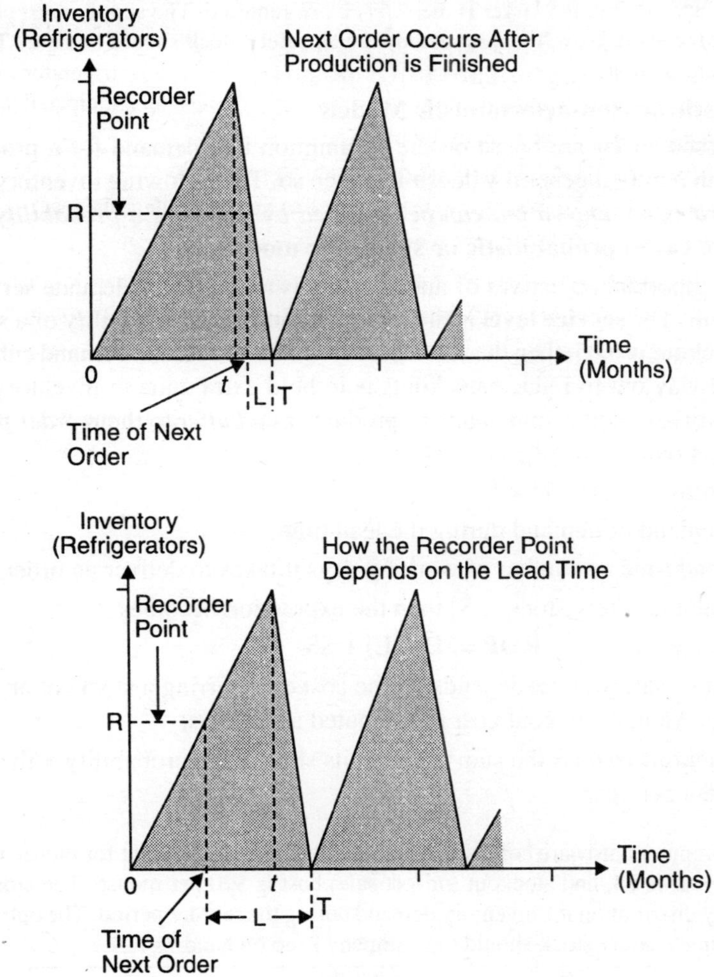

Figure 6.12

Computer Output for POQ Problem

POQ for Home Appliances

ORDERING INFORMATION

Item Name	*Item ID*	*Orders/Setups*	*Order Size*	*Recorder Point*	*Max Orders Outstanding*
Refrigerator	1	8.2	730	116	1

AGGREGATE INVENTORY VALUES

Inventory carrying charge = 24 %

Total number of items 1

Average working stock investment ($) 34218.75

Cost to order POQ items ($ / yr) 8219.18

Safety stock

Safety stock is needed to meet (*i*) Variation in demand, (*ii*) Variation in lead time or (*iii*) Both. The greater the degree of variability present, the larger is the *safety stock* required. The supply must come in when the stock reaches the safety stock level. Now, the issue is how much safety stock should be held? This situation has been discussed in a separate section.

6.3.2.2 Probabilistic or Non-deterministic Models

The models discussed so far are based on the assumption that demand for a product is constant and certain. However, in reality it generally doesn't happen so. The following inventory models apply when *the product demand is not known but can be specified by means of a probability distribution.* These types of models are called **probabilistic or stochastic models.**

One of the important objectives of management is to maintain adequate service level in the face of uncertain demand. The **service level** is the **complement** of the probability of a stockout. Thus, if the probability of a stockout is 0.05, then the service level is 0.95. Uncertain demand enhances the possibility of a stockout. One way out to reduce stockouts is to hold extra units in inventory which is known as **safety stock**. It involves adding some units of products as *a buffer* to the *reorder point.* We know from the previous discussion:

Reorder point = ROP = D × L

where D = daily demand or demand during the lead time

L = order lead time or number of working days it takes to deliver an order.

If we include the safety stock (SS) then the expression becomes

ROP = (D × L) + SS

The amount of safety stock depends on the cost of incurring a stockout and the cost of holding the extra inventory. Annual stockout cost is computed as follows:

Annual stockout costs = the sum of the units short × the probability × the stockout cost/unit x the number of orders per year.

Example 6.11. A computer hardware company has found that its reorder point for mouse is 60 units. Its carrying cost per mouse per year is $3, and stockout (or lost sale) cost is $20 per mouse. The store has experienced the following probability distribution for inventory demand during the reorder period. The optimum number of orders per year is 5. How much safety stock should the company keep on hand ?

Number of Units	*Probability*
30	.15
40	.10
50	.20
60 (ROP)	.25
70	.25
80	.05

Solution: Given, reorder point = ROP1 = 60 = DL

Here the goal is to decide the amount of safety stock that minimizes the sum of the additional inventory holding costs and stockout costs.

Annual holding cost = holding cost per unit x units added to the ROP

Thus, a safety stock of 20 mice means the new ROP2 = 60 + 20 = 80 units.

Change in holding cost = \$ 3 × 20 = \$ 60

Now let us compute the stockout cost. For any safety stock level, stockout cost is the expected cost of stocking out. We can compute this by the following equation

Annual stockout costs = the sum of the units short x the probability of demand at that level × the stockout cost/unit × the number of times per year the stockout can occur (which is the number of orders per year). Then we add stockout costs for each possible stockout level for a given ROP.

If SS = 0, and demand during LT = 70, then number of units short = 70 – 60 = 10

If SS = 0, and demand during LT = 80, then number of units short = 80 – 60 = 20

Thus the stockout costs for SS = 0 are

= (10 units short)(.25)(\$20 per stockout)(5 possible stockouts per year)
+ (20 units short)(.05)(\$20 per stockout)(5 possible stockouts per year)

= \$250 + \$100 = \$350

The following table shows the computations:

Safety stock	*New ROP*	*Additional holding cost*	*Stockout cost for possible demands of 70 and 80 units.*	*Total cost*
20	80 units	\$3 × 20 = \$ 60	\$ 0	\$ 60
10	70 units	\$3 × 10 = \$ 30	(10)(.05)(\$20)(5) = \$ 50	\$ 80
0	60 units	\$3 × 0 = \$ 0	(10)(.25)(\$20)(5) + (20)(.05)(\$20)(5) = \$ 350	\$ 350

So, the safety stock with the lowest total cost is 20 units of mice. Therefore, this safety stock alters the ROP to 60 + 20 = 80 units.

Note: when it is difficult to find the cost of stockout, then a manager may decide a policy to keep enough safety stock on hand to meet a prescribed customer service level. The service level, for example, could be to meet 95% of the demand (which means allowing stockouts only 5% of the time). If the demand during lead time is assumed to follow a normal distribution curve, then only mean (μ), and standard deviation (σ) are needed to define the inventory requirements for any given service level. We will use the following formula:

$$ROP = \text{expected demand during LT} + Z\sigma$$

where Z = number of standard deviation

σ = standard deviation of demand during LT.

Example 6.12. Let the average demand of an item is 300 units/year, or 6 items/week, and the lead time (LT) to procure it from the vendor is 8 weeks. Then

- The consumption during LT = demand during lead time × Lead time
  = 8 × 6 = 48 units.
- If demand during LT < 48 units, then the stock level will be more than safety stock (SS).
- If demand during LT > 48 units, then stock level will be less than safety stock (SS).
- If for some reason, the demand during LT > (48 units + SS), then a stock out occurs.

The optimum level of SS is that for which the sum of annual costs of stock holding and stock out is minimum.

Example 6.13. A Hospital stocks a respiratory kit that whose demand during the reorder period is normally distributed. The average demand during the reorder period is 350 kits, and the standard deviation is 10 kits. The hospital management wants to allow stockouts only 5 % of the time.

(*i*) What is the appropriate value of Z?

(*ii*) How much safety stock should the hospital maintain?

(*iii*) What reorder point should be used?

The Figure 6.13 helps in understanding the situation graphically.

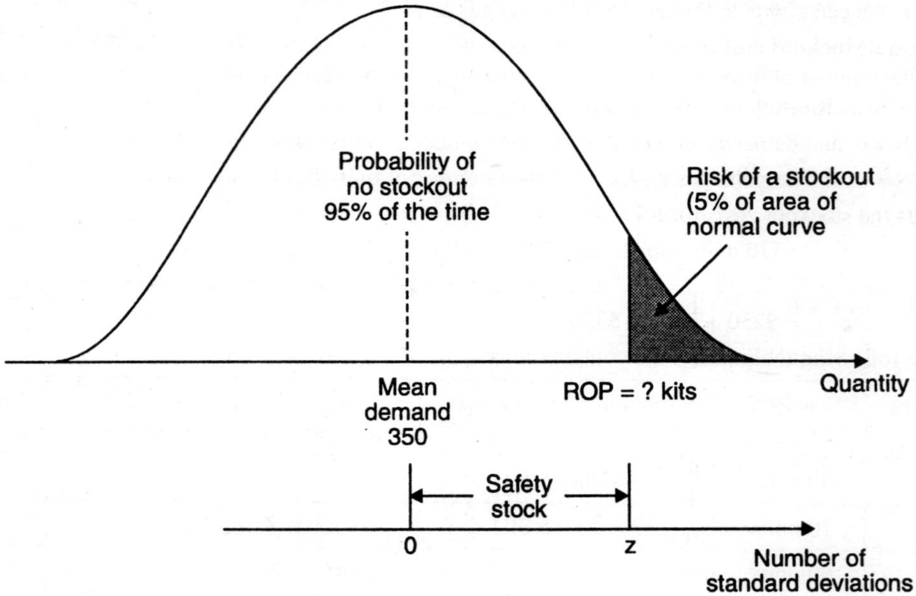

Figure 6.13. Normal Distribution Curve.

Solution: μ = mean demand = 350 kits

σ = standard deviation of demand during LT = 10 kits

Z = number of standard normal deviates

(*i*) we use the properties of a standard normal distribution curve to find a Z value for an area under the curve of .95 (i.e. 1 – .05). Using a normal Table (see Appendix 2), we find a Z value of 1.65 standard deviation from the mean.

(*ii*) Safety stock = $(X - \mu)$

We know that $Z = (X - \mu)/s$

Or, the safety stock = $(X - \mu) = Z\sigma = 1.65 \times 10 = 16.5$ units

(*iii*) ROP = expected demand during LT + Zs

= 350 kits + 16.5 kits of safety stock

= 366.5 or 367 kits

Extension

The formulas used above assume that an estimate of expected demand during lead times and its standard deviation are available. When data on lead time demand are not available, these formulas cannot be used (Heizer). In that case we need to determine if:

(*a*) Demand (D) is variable and lead time is constant, then

ROP = (average daily demand × Lead time in days) + ZsDLT

Where σ_{DLT} = standard deviation of demand per day = $(\text{Lead time} \times \sigma_D)^{0.5}$

(*b*) Only lead time (LT) is variable, then

$$ROP = (\text{daily demand} \times \text{average Lead time in days}) + ZD\sigma_{LT}$$

(*c*) Both demand and lead time are variable, then

$$ROP = (\text{average daily demand} \times \text{average Lead time in days}) + Z[(\text{average Lead time} \times \sigma^2_D) + (\text{average D})^2\, \sigma^2_{LT}]^{0.5}$$

Example 6.14 (Unsolved). 1. A manufacturer gets an order of 24000 units of one of his products for a year. The supply should be instantaneous. The customer does not maintain any buffer stock, so he will not tolerate any shortage in supply. The inventory holding cost is 10% of unit cost and the set up cost of machine, fixture, etc is $ 350 per run.

(*a*) Find the optimum size of production lot for minimum total cost.

(*b*) How many runs will be required for this and the duration of each run?

(*c*) What is the cycle time?

Assume the capacity of the equipment as 3000 units per month. Each unit costs $5.

6.4 STOCKING OF PERISHABLES

Stocking and replenishment of perishables, when the reordering cycle is used, can present some special problems. At the beginning of a period, the store is stocked to a certain level, and during this period consumption takes place. If we run out of stock before the end of the period, any subsequent demand in that period can obviously not be satisfied. If we stock too much, we run the risk of having a residue in stock at the end of the period. This residue may, in some cases, be a total loss, for example, in cases of newspapers, journals, foodstuff, certain chemicals, pharmaceutical goods, and photographic material. These products are called *perishables*. They carry their full value throughout the cycle but become virtually worthless beyond a certain deadline.

Some products lose a significant part of, but not all, their value when they are carried over the deadline. These may be termed '*semi-perishables*'. Products of this kind may be certain kinds of books, style goods, consumer goods such as household appliances, automobiles, computers, and spare parts. An automobile, for example, will get its full price as long as newer models are not introduced into the market, but after they appear, it becomes 'an old model' and has to be sold at a reduced price.

Example 6.15. A newspaper can be sold for the full price for one day only. The next day, its news has become stale, and although it carries many features and articles that maintain their value for several days to come, the paper as an article for sale has become valueless.

Suppose that a news agent had a full record of the demand (= actual sales + demand that he could not meet) of a certain paper, as shown in Table 6.5; the frequency of the demand could be plotted as in Figure 6.14. The distribution is quite close to the normal one. The average demand was found to be 80 papers a day with a maximum recorded daily demand of 95 and a minimum of 64 papers. Suppose the news agent sells each paper for 10 cents and has to pay 7 cents for each that he orders. Assuming that he cannot return unsold papers, the news agent makes 3 cents on every paper that he sells, he misses an opportunity to gain 3 cents on each paper that he cannot supply, and loses 7 cents on each paper he is unable to sell. How many papers, then, should he order, assuming no periodical demand fluctuations occur?

Table 6.5. Demand Record for a Daily Newspaper

Number of papers	*Frequency of demand*	*Total number required*
64	1	64
65	0	0
66	1	66
67	3	201
68	3	204
69	3	207
70	5	350
71	10	710
72	13	936
73	17	1241
74	22	1628
75	30	2250
76	35	2660
77	44	3388
78	48	3744
79	47	3713
80	50	4000
81	48	3888
82	45	3690
83	44	3652
84	38	3192
85	32	2720
86	24	2064
87	14	1218
88	14	1232
89	12	1068
90	6	540
91	4	364
92	1	92
93	2	186
94	1	94
95	1	95
Total	618	49457

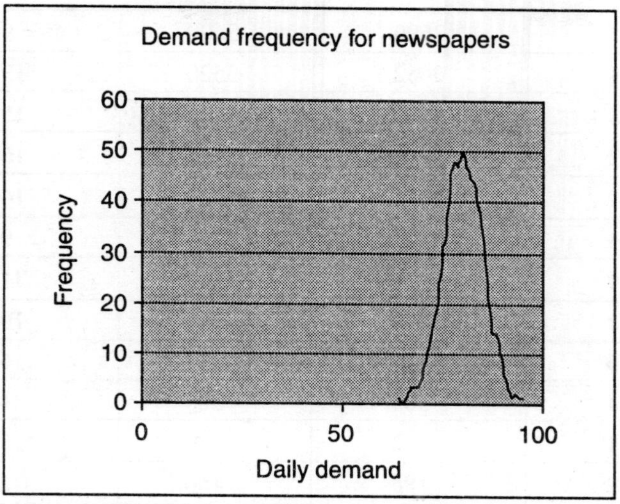

Figure 6.14. Demand Frequency For Newspapers.

Solution: Suppose he decided to take the average demand (i.e., 80 papers per day) as his order quantity. Based on this demand, we can analyze the situation as shown in Table 6.6.

Table 6.6 Profit and Losses when the order of papers = 80 per day

Demand of papers	*Frequency of demand*	*Total Number required*	*Total number sold*	*Number not supplied*	*Leftovers*
64	1	64	64	0	(80 – 64) × 1 =16
65	0	0	0	0	0
66	1	66	66	0	14
67	3	201	201	0	39
68	3	204	204	0	36
69	3	207	207	0	33
70	5	350	350	0	50
71	10	710	710	0	90
72	13	936	936	0	104
73	17	1241	1241	0	119
74	22	1628	1628	0	132
75	30	2250	2250	0	150
76	35	2660	2660	0	140
77	44	3388	3388	0	132
78	48	3744	3744	0	96
79	47	3713	3713	0	47
80	50	4000	4000	0	0
81	48	3888	3840	1 × 48 = 48	0

82	45	3690	3600	2 × 45 = 90	0
83	44	3652	3520	132	0
84	38	3192	3040	152	0
85	32	2720	2560	160	0
86	24	2064	1920	144	0
87	14	1218	1120	98	0
88	14	1232	1120	112	0
89	12	1068	960	108	0
90	6	540	480	60	0
91	4	364	320	44	0
92	1	92	80	12	0
93	2	186	160	26	0
94	1	94	80	14	0
95	1	95	80	15	0
			48242	1215	1198

Summary of policy 1

No. of papers sold = 48,242

Loss due to unsatisfied demand of 1215 papers = 1215 × 0.03 = $36.45

Loss due to 1198 papers = 1198 × 0.07 = $ 83.36

Profit made on the sales = 48,242 × (0.10 – 0.07)= 48,242 × 0.03 = $ 1447.26

Table 6.7. Profit and Losses when the order of papers = 76 per day

Demand of papers	*Frequency of demand*	*Total Number required*	*Total number sold*	*Number not supplied*	*Leftovers*
64	1	64	64	0	(76 – 64) × 1 = 12
65	0	0	0	0	0
66	1	66	66	0	10
67	3	201	201	0	27
68	3	204	204	0	24
69	3	207	207	0	21
70	5	350	350	0	30
71	10	710	710	0	50
72	13	936	936	0	52
73	17	1241	1241	0	51
74	22	1628	1628	0	44
75	30	2250	2250	0	30
76	35	2660	2660	0	0
77	44	3388	3344	44	0

78	48	3744	3648	96	0
79	47	3713	3572	141	0
80	50	4000	3800	200	0
81	48	3888	3648	240	0
82	45	3690	3420	270	0
83	44	3652	3344	308	0
84	38	3192	2888	304	0
85	32	2720	2432	288	0
86	24	2064	1824	240	0
87	14	1218	1064	154	0
88	14	1232	1064	168	0
89	12	1068	912	156	0
90	6	540	456	84	0
91	4	364	304	60	0
92	1	92	76	16	0
93	2	186	152	34	0
94	1	94	76	18	0
95	1	95	76	19	0
			46617	2840	351

Summary of policy 2

No. of papers sold = 46,617

Loss due to unsatisfied demand of 2840 papers = 2840 × 0.03 = \$85.20

Loss due to 351 papers = 351 × 0.07 = \$ 24.57

Profit made on the sales = 46,617 × (0.10 – 0.07)= 46,617 × 0.03 = \$ 1398.51

The example shows how the news agent could affect the total profit by adjusting his order quantity level.

7

Material Requirement Planning

7.0 INTRODUCTION

The inventory model discussed in Chapter-6 presumed that the demand for one item was independent of the demand for another item. For example, EOQ model assumes that the demand of car parts is independent of the demand of car itself. However, in reality the demand for one item may be related to the demand for another item. For example, demand for tires and radiators depends on the number of cars to be produced. For each car to be manufactured, five tires (four plus one standby) are needed. These are situations with 'dependent demand items'. Materials requirement planning (MRP) deals with this kind of situation effectively.

MRP has become a centerpiece for all manufacturing systems. The key to successful production and operations management in a manufacturing company is the balancing of requirements and capacities. It's that simple and yet very challenging.

MRP is a computer based technique to determine the quantity and timing for the acquisition of dependent demand items needed to satisfy the master production schedule (MPS) requirement. It is used for lumpy or erratic demands. Since the control of purchasing depends on the order for the finished products, the technique is said to be one of '*dependent demand*'.

7.1 NEED FOR MATERIALS PLANNING

Based on the manner the materials managers react to inventory situation, there could be two types of inventory systems: **reactive** and **planning**. MRP systems have replaced the *reactive inventory* systems in many organization. Managers using reactive systems ask, 'what should I do now ?', whereas managers using planning systems look ahead and ask, 'what will I be needing in the future ? How much and when ?'

Reactive systems are simpler to manage in many respects but have serious drawbacks like high inventory costs and unreliable delivery performance. The *planning system* is more complex to manage, but it offers numerous advantages. It reduces inventories and their associated costs because it carries only those items and components that are needed—no more and no less.

Demand dependency is an important consideration in choosing between reactive and planning systems. It is the degree to which the demand for some item is associated with the demand for another item. In case of *independent demand* situation, demand for one item is unrelated to the demand for others. whereas, in *dependent demand* situation, if we know the demand for one item, we can deduce the demand for one or more related items. We don't need to have large safety stocks for dependent demand items because we usually know exactly how many will be needed.

7.1.1 TERMS USED IN MRP

Gross Requirement

It is the projected needs for raw materials, components, subassemblies, or finished goods by the end of the period shown. Gross requirement comes from the master schedule (for end items) or from the combined needs of other items. But in MRP it is the quantity of item that will have to be disbursed, i.e. issued to support a parent order (or orders), rather than the total quantity of the end product

Scheduled Receipts

They are materials already on order from a vendor or in-house shop due to be received at the beginning of the period. Put differently, they are open orders scheduled to arrive from vendors or elsewhere in the pipeline.

On Hand or Available

The expected amount of inventory that will be on hand at the beginning of each time period. This includes amount available from previous period *plus* planned order receipts and scheduled receipts *less* gross requirements.

On Hand = Scheduled receipt + Available from previous period – GR

Net requirement: The actual amount needed in each time period.

Net requirement = gross requirement – total scheduled receipt – on hand

$$NR = (GR - SR - OH)$$

Planned order receipt

The quantity expected to be received by the beginning of the period in which it is shown under lot-for-lot ordering; this quantity will equal net requirement. Any excess is added to available inventory in next time period.

Planned order release

It indicates a planned amount to order in each time period; equals planned-order receipts offset by lead time. This amount generates gross requirements at the next level in the assembly or production chain. When an order is executed it is removed from the "planned order-receipt" and planned-order-release row and entered in the "scheduled receipt" row.

7.2 BASIC MRP CONCEPTS

Material requirement planning is based on several basic concepts, which are implicitly defined. These concepts are

- Independent versus dependent demand
- Lumpy demand
- Lead time
- Common use item
- Time phasing.

7.2.1 INDEPENDENT DEMAND

It exists when a demand for a particular item is unrelated to a demand for other item or when it is not a function of demand of other inventory item. Independent demands are not derivable or calculable from the demand of something else hence they must be forecast.

7.2.2 DEPENDENT DEMAND

It is defined as dependent if the demand of an item is directly related to, or derived from the demand of another item or product. This dependency may be "vertical" such as when the component is needed in order to build a subassembly or product, or "horizontal" as in the case of an attachment or owner's manual shipped with the product in most manufacturing businesses, the bulk of the total inventory is in raw materials, component parts, and subassemblies, all largely subjected to dependent demand. Since such demand can be calculated, and precisely determined from the demand for those items that are its sole causes, it need not and should not, be forecast.

The demand for the end product may have to be forecast. But none of the component items, including the raw materials, need be forecast separately. An example can be given for a certain wagon or rail coach manufacturing company. It may have to forecast how many wagons it can sell, and when. Having done that, however, the manufacturing company need not forecast the number of wheels, since each wagon needs four sets of wheels.

In dependent demand, there is a material conversion stage, which creates the relationship between raw materials, semi-finished parts, component parts, subassemblies and assemblies. Each of which carries a unique identity (part number) and as such represents an inventory item in its own right that must be planned and controlled. Demand for all these inventory items is being created internally, as a function of the next conversion stage to take place. If one of the assemblies of a gear box is taken as an example. A sheet steel is made into a forging blank which, in turn, is machined into a gear which then becomes one of a number of components used in assembling the gear box - a major component of a transmission. The transmission will be required for the building of some end-product (vehicle), which is also an assembly. MRP is the appropriate technique for determining quantities of dependent demand item.

7.2.3 LUMPY DEMAND

Manufacturing is frequently done on an intermittent basis in lots, or models, of one type or another. The components of a finished product are needed only when the product is being manufactured. Thus, there may be large demands on inventory at some times and none at other times, making the demand **'lumpy'.** When the demand occurs in large steps, it is referred to as "lumpy demand." MRP is an appropriate approach for dealing with inventory situations characterized by lumpy demand.

7.2.4 LEAD TIME OF ITEM

The lead-time for a certain job is the time that must be allowed to complete the job from start to finish. In manufacturing, lead-time is divided into ordering lead-time and manufacturing lead-time. An ordering lead time for an item is the time required from initiation of the purchase requisition to receipt of the item from the vendor. In this case if the item is raw material that is stocked by the vendor, the ordering lead time should be relatively short. If the item must be fabricated by the vendor, the lead time may be substantial, perhaps several months.

Manufacturing lead time is the time needed to process the part through the sequence of machines specified on the route sheet. It includes not only the operation time but also the non-productive time that must be allowed. In MRP, lead times are used to determine starting dates for assembling final products and sub-assemblies, for producing component parts and for ordering raw materials.

The different individual lead times of inventory item that makes up the product is also another factor that affect material requirements. Because the component item order must be completed before the parent item order that will consume it can be started, the back-to-back lead times of order that the four items consume in the following example may be added up to find the cumulative lead time.

If the manufacturing lead times for the four items of a truck are

Transmission	A	1 weeks
Gearbox	B	2 weeks
Gear	C	6 weeks
Forging blank	D	3 weeks
Cumulative lead-time		12 weeks

7.2.5 COMMON USE ITEMS

In manufacturing, one raw material is often used to produce more than one component type. And a component type may be used on more than one final product. For example if the product structure in Fig-7.1 is used to manufacture a product X, a component A is required, which needs another component B. Component B also requires other three components among which C requires D and component D requires the other end component E which may be a raw material. It is clearly seen from the other branch of the tree that the end item E is also required to manufacture N, S and T. Hence E is required to manufacture two different components of the finished product X. Similar relations can be shown between the component P and X. *MRP collects these common use items from different products to effect economies in ordering the raw materials and manufacturing the components.*

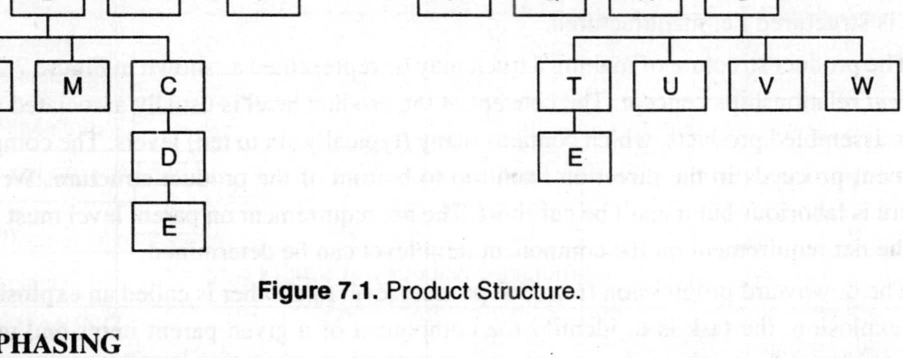

Figure 7.1. Product Structure.

7.2.6 TIME PHASING

Time phasing means adding the time dimension to inventory status data by recording and storing the information on either specific dates or planning periods with which the respective quantities are associated.

The inventory status information was expanded by adding data on requirements (demand) and "availability" (the difference between the quantity required and the sum of on-hand and on-order quantities). Using the classic inventory status equation we can write

$$a + b - c = x$$

where a = quantity on hand
b = quantity on order
c = quantity required
x = quantity available (for future requirements)

The quantity required (c) would be derived from customer orders or a forecast, or a calculation of dependent demand. The quantity available (x) has to be calculated. Negative availability signifies lack of coverage and the need to place a new order.

Generally, time phasing means developing the information on timing to provide answers to questions like:

- *When is the quantity on order due to come in, and is it a single order or are there more than one?*
- *When will the stock run out?*
- *When should the replenishment order be completed?*
- *When should it be released?*

MRP calculates item demand and time-phases for all inventory.

7.3 FACTOR AFFECTING THE COMPUTATION OF MRP

The computation of material requirement is affected by the following six factors:

7.3.1 PRODUCT STRUCTURE

Product structure imposes the principal constraint on the computation of requirements, due to its content of several manufacturing levels of materials, component parts, and subassemblies. This computation, while arithmetically very simple, requires that a rather involved procedure be followed. A procedure which clearly identifies the structure of the product by using a bill of material with different levels or using parent-child relationship. The product level or manufacturing level is related to the way the product is structured i.e. manufactured.

The product structure of making a truck may be represented as shown in Figure 7.2 using *parent-component* relationships concept. The concept of the product level is usually associated with relatively complex assembled products, which contains many (typically six to ten) levels. The computation of net requirement proceeds in the direction from top to bottom of the product structure. We note that this procedure is laborious but it can't be cut short. The net requirement on parent level must be determined before the net requirement on the component item level can be determined.

The downward progression from one product level to another is called an **explosion**. In executing the explosion, the task is to identify the component of a given parent items and to ascertain the location (address) from where they may be retrieved and processed.

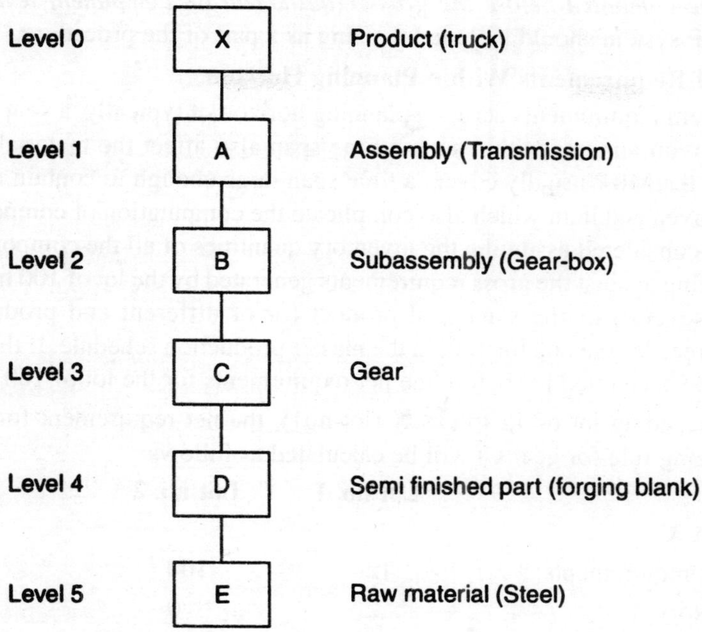

Figure 7.2. Product Structure for a Truck.

7.3.2 LOT SIZING

It is the ordering of inventory items in quantities exceeding net requirements, for the reason of economy, or convenience. In the example given above the parent items A, B, and C have been assumed to be ordered in quantities equal to the respective net requirements for these items. But in reality, the lot sizing, whereever employed, would invalidate this assumption. It is because the gross requirement for a component derives directly from the (planned) order quantity of its **parent(s).**

To illustrate this concept, let us modify the example such that gear C be produced with an order quantities that must be a multiple of 5 (because of some consideration in the gear machining process), the net requirement of 76 will have to be covered by a planned order for 80. This will increase the gross requirement for the forging blank D correspondingly. This computation is illustrated below:

Gear C (Parent)

Net requirement = 76

Planned-ordered release = 80

which is (76 + 4) to satisfy the condition that the order quantity should be a multiple of 5.

Forging (Component)

Gross requirement = 80

Inventory = 46

Net requirement = 34

Lot sizing is a particular technique used to determine the order quantities for a given inventory item. The general rule of MRP logic states that: *The mutual parent-component relationship of items on contiguous product levels dictates that the net requirement on the parent level, as well as its coverage by planned order, be computed before the gross requirement on component level can be correctly determined.* An MRP system should include lot sizing as a part of the procedure.

7.3.3 Recurrence of Requirements Within Planning Horizon

The timing of end-item requirements across a planning horizon of typically, a year span or longer, and recurrence of these requirements within such a time span also affect the material requirements. The planning horizon of the MRP usually covers a time span large enough to contain multiple (recurring) requirements for a given end item which also complicate the computation of component requirements. For the truck that is considered assuming the inventory quantities of all the component items involved are available for netting against the gross requirements generated by the lot of 100 trucks, but there may be another lot (or several) of the same end product (or of different end product using the same transmission) that precedes the one for 100, in the master production schedule. If that is the case, its net requirements must be accounted for before the net requirements for the lot of 100 can be determined.

If there is preceding lot of 12 trucks X (lot no1), the net requirement for the respective lots (retaining the lot-sizing rule for gear C) will be calculated as follows:

	Lot no. 1	Lot no. 2	
Transmission **A**			
Gross requirements:	12	100	
Inventory	2	0	
Net requirements	10	100	
Gear box **B**			
Gross requirements:	10	100	
Inventory	15	5	⟵ (available for no.2)
Net requirements:	– 5	95	
Gear **C**			
Gross requirements:	0	95	
Inventory	0	7	
Net requirements:	0	88	
Planned order	0	90	
Forging blank **D**			
Gross requirement	0	90	
Inventory	0	46	
Net requirement	0	44	

As can be seen, the existence of a preceding lot of 12 has changed the net requirements for a lot of 100. The net requirements for the forging blank, for instance, have increased from 34 (that we have seen in derivation of gross requirement) to 44. Due to lot-sizing this increase of 10 doesn't coincide with the increase of 12 in the end-product requirements (order in multiple of 5).

Example 7.1. An assembly of the end product, truck X with its product structure in Figure 7.2 was scheduled for week 50, component-order release dates and completion date could be calculated by successively subtracting the lead time values from 50 as shown below:

Complete order for item A	Week 50
Minus lead time of item A	01
Release order for item	49

Complete order for item B 49
Minus lead time of item B 02
Release order for item 47
Complete order for item C 47
Minus lead time of item C **06**
Release order for item 41
Complete order for item D 41
Minus lead time of item D 03
Release order for item .... Week 38

Lead time values (or procedure for determining these values based on order quantity) must be supplied to the MRP system, which stores them for use in establishing a proper alignment of requirements and planned-order data in the course of the requirements explosion. Subtracting the lead time from the date of the net requirement, i.e. positioning the planned-order release forward of the timing of the net requirement it covers is called offsetting for lead time.

7.4 OBJECTIVES OF MRP SYSTEM

The primary objective of this system is to determine gross and net requirements, i.e., discrete period-demand for each item of inventory, so as to be able to generate information needed for correct inventory order action—an action of new type or a revision of previous action in procurement and shop orders. The essential data elements accompanying this action are:

- Item identity (part number)
- Order quantity
- Date of order release
- Date of order completion (due date)

Taking the above data, an analysis is made by MRP system for action that effect the system such as

- Increase in order quantity
- Decrease in order quantity
- Order cancellation
- Advancement of order due date
- Deferment of order due date
- Order suspension (indefinite deferment).

In any manufacturing operation, the questions of what materials and components are needed, in what quantities, and when-and the answer to these questions are vital. An MRP system is designed to provide just these answers. MRP provides the following:

- *Inventory reduction*: MRP determines how many of components are needed and when, in order to meet the master schedule.
- *Reduction in production and delivery lead time*: MRP identifies materials and components quantities, timings, availabilities, and procurement and production actions required to meet delivery deadlines. By coordinating inventories, procurement, and production decisions. MRP

helps avoid delays in production.. It prioritizes production activities by putting due dates on customer job orders.

- *Realistic commitments*: Realistic delivery promises can enhance customer satisfaction.
- *Increased efficiency*: MRP provides close coordination among various work centers as products progress through them.

7.5 PREREQUISITES AND ASSUMPTIONS OF MRP

The main prerequisites and assumptions that are implied by MRP system are discussed below:

7.5.1 PREREQUISITES

(*a*) **A master production schedule exists and can be stated in bill of material terms:** How many end items are to be produced and when? MRP systems presuppose that the master production schedule can, in its entirety, be stated in bill of material terms.

(*b*) **All inventory Items are uniquely identified**: Each inventory item should be unambiguously identified through a unit code or part number.

(*c*) **A bill of material exists at planning time**: The bill of material must not merely list all the components of a given product, but must be so structured as to reflect the way the product is actually made, in steps from raw material to component part to subassembly to end item.

(*d*) **Inventory records containing data** on the status of every item are available.

7.5.2 ASSUMPTIONS

(*a*) **File data integrity:** File data must be accurate, complete, and upto date, if the MRP system is to prove successful or even useful.

(*b*) **Individual item lead times are known**: An MRP system presupposes that lead times for all inventory items are known and can be supplied to the system, at least as estimates.

(*c*) **Every inventory item goes into and out of stock**: An MRP system assumes that every inventory item under its control goes into and out of stock, i.e. there will be reportable receipts following which the item will be in an "on-hand' state and will eventually be disbursed to support an order for an item. Or in short the progression of the manufacturing process from one stage to the next will be monitored.

(*d*) **All components of an assembly are needed at the time of assembly order release:** In determining the timing of item gross requirements planning procedure assumes that all components of an assembly must be available at the time an order for that assembly is to be released to the factory.

(*e*) **Discrete disbursement and usage of component material:** for instance, if fifty units of an item are required for a given (fabrication or subassembly) order, MRP logic expects that exactly fifty units will be consumed. Materials that come in continuous form (rolls of sheet metals, coils of wire, etc) do not meet this expectation cleanly and therefore require that standard planning procedures be modified and the system adopted to handle such inventory items properly.

(*f*) **Process in dependence of manufacturing items**: This means that a manufacturing order for any given inventory item can be started and completed on its own and not be contingent on the existence, or progress, of some other order for purpose of completing the process.

7.6 INPUTS TO MRP

As described in preceding discussion, MRP is a processor which processes inputs (relating data) to give a time phased detailed schedule for raw materials and components. These inputs are shown in Figure 7.3.

- Master production schedule (MPS)
- Bill of material (BOM)
- Inventory status file (ISF) which provides the information such as: Inventory status, Replenishment lead times, and Manufacturing lead time.

7.6.1 MASTER PRODUCTION SCHEDULE (MPS)

One of the three principal inputs of MRP system, the master production schedule, is a list of what end products are to be produced, how many of each product is to be produced, and when the products are to be ready for shipment. A master production schedule (Figure 7.4) is to MRP system what a program is to a computer. It is a driving input which an MRP system depends for its real effectiveness and usefulness because it is the determinant of future load, inventory investment, production, and delivery service.

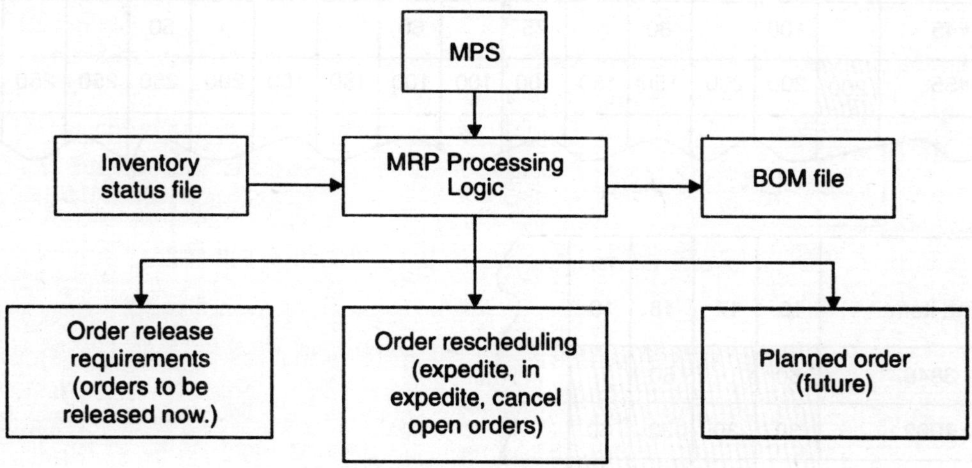

Figure 7.3. MRP System.

Product demand that makes up the master schedule can be separated into three categories. The first consists of firm **customer order for** specific products. These orders usually include a specific delivery date, which has been promised to the customer by the sales department. The second category is **forecasted demand.** Based on statistical techniques applied to past demand, estimates provided by the sales staff, and other sources, the firm will generate a forecast of demand for its various product lines. The third category is **demand for individual component parts**, which will be used as repair parts and are stocked by the firm's service department. The third category is excluded from the master schedule because it doesn't represent demands for end products.

For the purpose of material requirements planning, the time periods of the master production schedule must be identical to those on which the MRP system is based. The sales forecast and the master production schedule that management and the marketing organization use are often, however, developed and stated in terms of months or quarters. They are also stated in terms of product models. The MPS must then be broken down and restated in terms of weeks and specific end-item numbers. The period of time that the master production spans is the planning horizon which may be divided into a firm portion and a tentative portion. The firm portion is determined by the cumulative (procurement and manufacturing) lead time. Taking some samples by considering the previous example of a tractor producing company, the planning horizon, the broken down of the master production schedule can be shown as follows:

Planning horizon

Firm | Tentative

Product	A	M	J	J	A	S	O	N	D	J	F	M	A	M	J
Hoist #35	50			50			50			60			60		
Hoist #45		100		80		75		60				50			
Hoist #55	200	200	200	150	150	100	100	100	150	150	200	250	250	250	250

End item	16	17	18	19
Motor 3848	60		60	
Motor 4002	30	30	30	30
Drum 12-305	25	50		

Figure 7.4. A Master Production Schedule.

7.6.2 BILL OF MATERIAL (BOM)

Computation of the raw material and component requirements for end products listed in the master schedule, is done by the product structure. The product structure is specified by the bill of materials, which is a listing of component parts and subassemblies that make up each product. A file which lists all assemblies together is the bill-of-materials file.

The structure of an assembled product can be pictured by taking a simple product in which a group of individual components make up two subassemblies, which in turn make up the product (Figure 7.5). The product structure is in the form of a pyramid in which lower level feeding into the levels above the items at each successively higher level are called the parents of the items in the level directly below. For example, subassembly S_1 is the parent of components C_1, C_2 and C_3. Product P_1 is the parent of subassemblies S_1 and S_2. In the product structure, the amount (number) of each item required for the parent item is specified. This is indicated by a number in parentheses to the right and below each block.

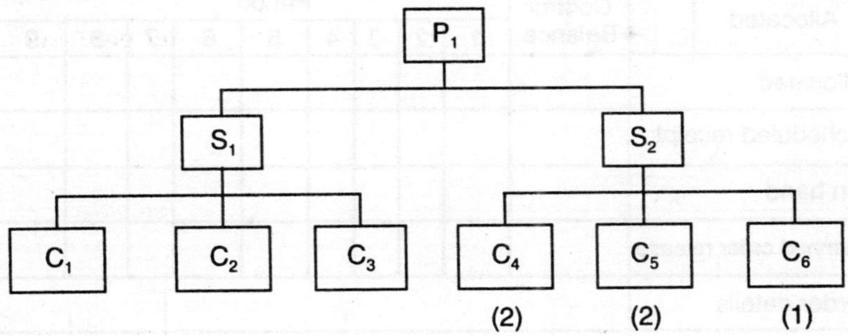

Figure 7.5. Product Structure for Product P_1.

For example subassembly S_2 contains two of each components C_4 and C_5 and one of components C_6. The other information contained in the bill-of-material file are the part number, child parent numbers, the date each child is to become effective or to be removed from use in the bill (effective date control for schedule engineering changes), dropout and yield percentages, shop floor delivery des'ination, and engineering revision level.

7.6.3 INVENTORY RECORD FILE

It comprises the individual item inventory records containing the status data required for the determination of net requirements. This file is kept update by the position of inventory transactions which reflect the various inventory events taking place. Each transaction (stock receipt, disbursement, scrap, etc) changes the status of the respective inventory item.

In addition to the status data, the inventory records also contain so-called planning factors used principally for the size and timing of planned orders. Planning factors include item lead time, safety stock (if any), scrap allowance, lot-sizing algorithms, etc. The item lead time for raw materials, components and assemblies must be established in the inventory record file in which the ordering lead time can be determined from purchasing records and the manufacturing lead time can be determined from the process route sheets (or routing file).

MRP depends on accurate inventory records to perform its planning function. This is accomplished by utilizing a computerized inventory system which maintains the inventory record file or item master file. The types of data contained in the record for a given item would typically include the categories shown in Figure 7.6. The file contains three segments:

1. Item master data segment
2. Inventory status segment
3. Subsidiary data segment.

Segment													
Item master Data Segment	Part no	Description	Lead time	Std cost	Safety stock								
	Order Qty	Set up	Cycle	Last year's usage	Class								
	Scrap allowance	Cutting data	Pointers	Etc									
	Allocated		Control Balance	Period 1	2	3	4	5	6	7	8	9	Total
Item master Status Segment	Allocated												
	Scheduled receipt												
	On hand												
	Planned order release												
Subsidiary Data Segment	Order details												
	Pending action												
	Counters												
	Keeping track												

Figure 7.6. Inventory Record File.

7.6.3.1 The item master data segment

It gives the item identification (by part numbers) and other data such as lead time, cost, and order quantity.

7.6.3.2 Inventory status segment

It provides a time-purchased record of inventory status. In MRP it is important to know not only the current level of inventory, but also the future change that will occur against the inventory status. Therefore the inventory status segment lists the gross requirements for the item, scheduled receipts, on-hand status, and planned—order release.

7.6.3.3 Subsidiary data segment

It contains miscellaneous information pertaining to purchase orders, scrap or rejects, engineering change actions, and so on.

Generally the three segments in the inventory record file consists of **Item master data segment** which has

- Item identity
- Item characteristics
- Planning factors
- Safety stocks
- Pointer to other files.

7.7 MRP OUTPUTS

The MRP program (system) generates a variety of outputs that can be used in planning and management of the plant operation. The outputs of MRP system can be divided into two main parts.

(*i*) *Primary output,* (*ii*) *Secondary output*

7.7.1 PRIMARY OUTPUTS

The primary outputs of the MRP system are the following:

- **Order-release notice:** calling for the planned orders.
- **Rescheduled notice:** calling for changes in open-ordered due dates.
- **Reports:** showing planned orders to be released in future periods.
- **Cancellation notices,** including cancellation of open order because of changes in the master schedule.
- **Reports** on inventory status.

7.7.2 SECONDARY OUTPUTS

The other type of output report that can be generated by MRP system is the secondary output. It includes

- **Performance reports of various** types, indicating cost, item-usage, actual versus planned lead time, and other measures of performance.
- **Exception reports,** showing deviations from schedule, orders that are overdue, scrap, and so on.

7.7.3 INVENTORY FORECASTS

It indicating projected inventory levels (both aggregate inventories and item inventory) in future periods. The MRP inputs and outputs are summarized in Table 7.1 for ready reference.

Table 7.1. MRP Inputs and Outputs

Inputs	*Outputs*
MPS of end items required.	Order release data to capacity requirement planning (CRP) for load profiles.
Inventory status file of on-hand and on-order items, lot sizes, lead times, etc.	Orders to purchasing and in-house production shops.
Product structure (BOM) file of what components and subassemblies go into each end product.	Rescheduling data to MPS.
	Management reports and inventory updates.

7.8 MRP LOGIC IN BRIEF

The MRP program (a computer software) calculates the number of each subassemblies and components required to produce a specified number of end products. It does this by **exploding** the end product into successively lower levels in the product structure. It calculates for each item in each product structure and for each time period (typically one week) in the planning horizon how many of that item are needed (gross requirement), how many units from inventory are already available, the net quantity that must be planned on receiving in new shipments (planned order receipts or order due), when orders for the new shipments must be placed (planned order releases) so that all materials arrive just when needed. If

GR = Gross Requirement (the overall quantity of an item needed during a time period to meet planned output levels).

OD = Order Due (Scheduled receipt) or inventory in pipeline (the quantity of an item that will be received at the beginning of a time period from suppliers as a result of orders that have already been placed).

OH = On Hand stock or available quantity (the quantity of an item expected to be available at the end of a time period for meeting requirements in succeeding periods).

OH = scheduled receipts + planned order receipts – GR + amounts available from the previous period.

SS = Safety Stock, then

NR = Net Requirement = [GR – OD – OH + SS]

POR = Planned Order Release

7.8.1 A SAMPLE OF MANAGEMENT INFORMATION (OUTPUT) FROM MRP

MRP output includes a report similar to the sample shown in Table-7.2 for each item in the product structure. The sample report shows that 400 units of this item are needed (GR) in week 4 and another 500 are needed in week 8. No outstanding orders were previously placed, so there are no units of this item scheduled for receipt as of this time. There are, however, 50 uncommitted units of the item already available in inventory, and these will go toward meeting the week 4 requirement. Consequently, net requirements are 350 units for week 4 and 500 units for week 8. Thus we should plan on receiving 350 units in week 4 and 500 units in week 8. Since this item has a 3 week procurement lead time, the first order must be placed (released) in week 1 and the second order in week 5.

Table 7.2. An MRP report for one item

Item identification: #3201—Mounting bracket

Lead time: 3 weeks, Report date: Week 0

Week	1	2	3	4	5	6	7	8
Gross requirement				400				500
Scheduled receipts								
Available for next period: 50	50	50	50					
Net requirements				350				500
Planned order receipts				350				500
Planned order releases (POR)	350				500			

This report identifies the procurement actions required to keep production on schedule. It also gives suppliers advanced notification of the demands soon to be placed on them. Weekly updating will revise schedules to reflect that an order must be received earlier (expedited), can be received later (de-expedited), or can even be cancelled. This information system is especially important when there are many end items with hundreds or thousands of related subcomponents that must be coordinated among numerous suppliers and work centers.

Example 7.2. A company makes kitchen chairs called model H. It requires two subassemblies F and G, one for the seat and the front legs and another for the backrest and rear legs (see Figure 7.7). To assemble the seat to the front legs, a worker needs four fasteners. Similarly, two assemble the backrest to the rear legs, a worker needs 4 more fasteners. The two subassemblies are then attached to each other with four more fasteners. When the two subassemblies are combined, the chair is complete.

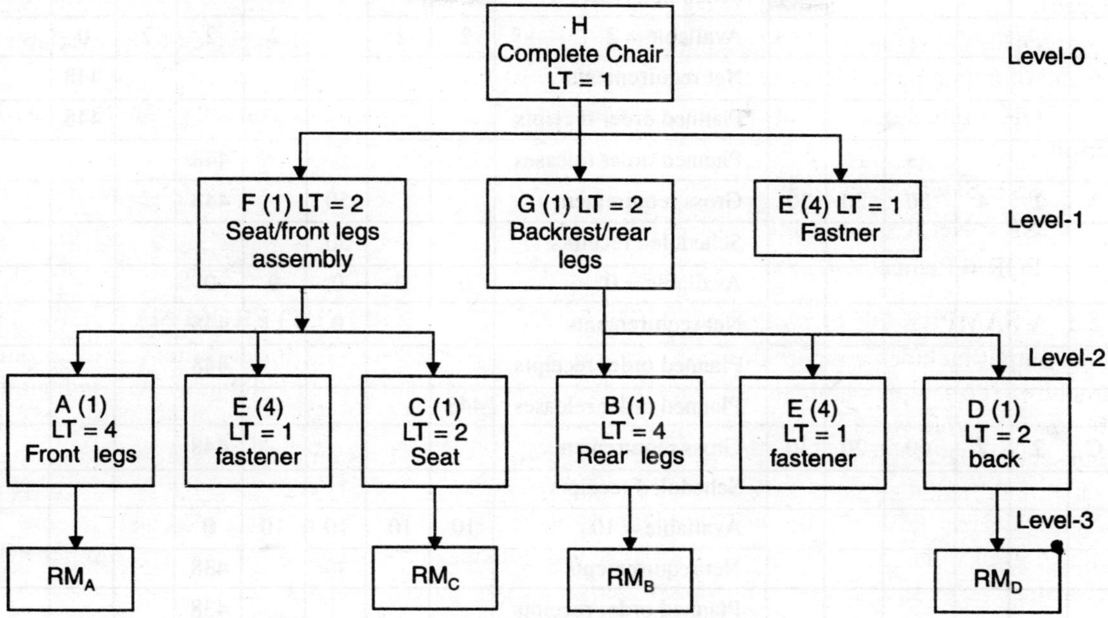

Figure 7.7. Product Structure Tree and Item information.

Solution: The solution is shown in Table 7.3 below. The steps are self explanatory.

Table 7.3. Material Requirements Plan

Item ID	*Level code*	*Lead time (weeks)*	*On hand*	*Safety-stock*	*Allocated*	*Assume Lot-for-lot ordering*	*Week 1*	*Week 2*	*Week 3*	*Week 4*	*Week 5*	*Week 6*	*Week 7*	*Week 8*
H	0	1	100	50	0	Gross requirement	1	2	3	4	5	6	7	500
						Scheduled receipts								
						Available = 50	50	50	50	50	50	50	50	0
						Net requirements								450
						Planned order receipts								450
						Planned order releases							450	
G	1	2	200	30	60	Gross requirement							450	
						Scheduled receipts								
						Available = 110	110	110	110	110	110	110	0	
						Net requirements							340	
						Planned order receipts							340	
						Planned order releases					340			

F	1	2	52	30	20	Gross requirement							450	
						Scheduled receipts								
						Available = 2	2	2	2	2	2	2	0	
						Net requirements							448	
						Planned order receipts							448	
						Planned order releases					448			
A	2	4	50	20	30	Gross requirement			50		448			
						Scheduled receipts			50					
						Available = 0	0	0	0	0	0			
						Net requirements			0		448			
						Planned order receipts					448			
						Planned order releases	448							
C	2	2	60	20	30	Gross requirement					448			
						Scheduled receipts								
						Available = 10	10	10	10	10	0			
						Net requirements					438			
						Planned order receipts					438			
						Planned order releases			438					
B	2	4	150	20	30	Gross requirement					340			
						Scheduled receipts								
						Available = 100	100	100	100	100	0			
						Net requirements					240			
						Planned order receipts					240			
						Planned order releases	240							
D	2	2	52	20	30	Gross requirement			50		340			
						Scheduled receipts								
						Available = 2	2	2	0		0			
						Net requirements			48		340			
						Planned order receipts			48		340			
						Planned order releases	48		340					
E	2	1	500	300	150	Gross requirement					3152		1800	
						Scheduled receipts								
						Available = 50	50	50	50	50	0	0	0	
						Net requirements					3102		1800	
						Planned order receipts					3102		1800	
						Planned order releases				3102		1800		

Example 7.3. If the MPS specifies 200 units of Product P1 in week 17. Number in the parenthesis indicates the no. of units of that item required to produce 1 unit of the item at the next higher level. For example, 4 C1 are required to produce 1 unit of SA1, and 2SA1s are required to produce I unit of P1. 716 units of C5 are already in the inventory. C4 is a purchased item and that 75 units of C4 are scheduled to arrive in week 12.

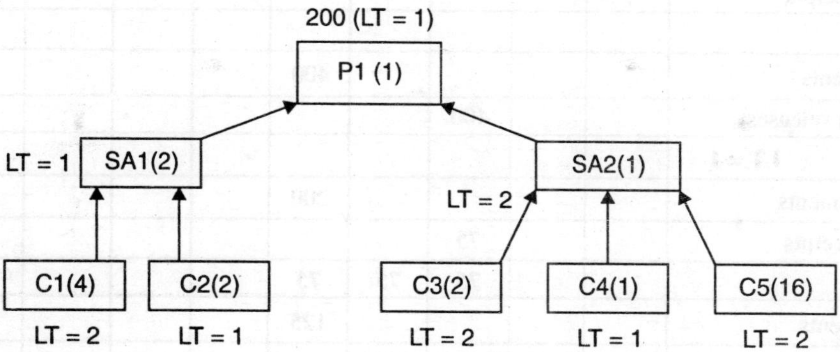

Figure 7.8. Product Structure.

- Then from the given product structure in Figure 7.8, we can calculate the required no. of units of each subassembly and each component as follows:
  SA1 = 400, SA2 = 200, C1 = 1600, C2 = 800, C3 = 400, C4 = 200, C5 = 3200
- We must consider the lead times required for each item. P1 has a lead time of 1 week. This means that 400 units of SA1 and 200 units of SA2 must be available at the end of week 16. The LT for SA2 is 2 weeks. This means that 400 units of C3, 200 units of C4, and 3200 units of C5 must be ready no later than the end of week 12.
- These calculated requirements for each item is the gross no. of units needed to satisfy the MPS. If some of these items are already in inventory or if an order is scheduled for delivery in the near future, then these must be subtracted from the GR to determine the net requirements (NR) for satisfying the MPS. Since 716 units of C5 are already in the inventory, the NR for C5 = 3200 – 716 = 2484 units.

75 units of C4 are scheduled to arrive in week 12. Our GR for C4 were calculated earlier as 200 units to be available at the end of week 14. So, the NR for C4 = 200-75 = 125 units.

- These are shown in the following Table 7.4.

Table 7.4

Period	10	11	12	13	14	15	16	17	18	19
Item: P1 LT = 1								200		
Gross requirements										
Scheduled receipts										
On hand = 0										
Net requirements								200		
Planned order releases							200			
Item: SA2 LT = 2										
Gross requirements							200			
Scheduled receipts										
On hand = 0										
Net requirements							200			

Planned order releases					200					
Item: C3 LT = 2										
Gross requirements					400					
Scheduled receipts										
On hand = 0										
Net requirements					400					
Planned order releases			400							
Item: C4 LT = 1										
Gross requirements					200					
Scheduled receipts			75							
On hand = 0			75	75	75					
Net requirements					125					
Planned order releases				125						
Item: C5 LT = 2										
Gross requirements					3200					
Scheduled receipts										
On hand = 716	716	716	716	716	716					
Net requirements					2484					
Planned order releases			2484							

Example 7.4. A firm produces a maintenance and repair parts cart (MRP cart) for use in a warehouse. The cart product structure is shown below. The firm has 2 axles (number 2005) and 1 wheel assembly (number 2006) in stock. They have an order for 3 carts in period 10. Use an MRP format with lot-for-lot ordering (i.e. order the exact number of units required), and determine the order size and order-release period for all components.

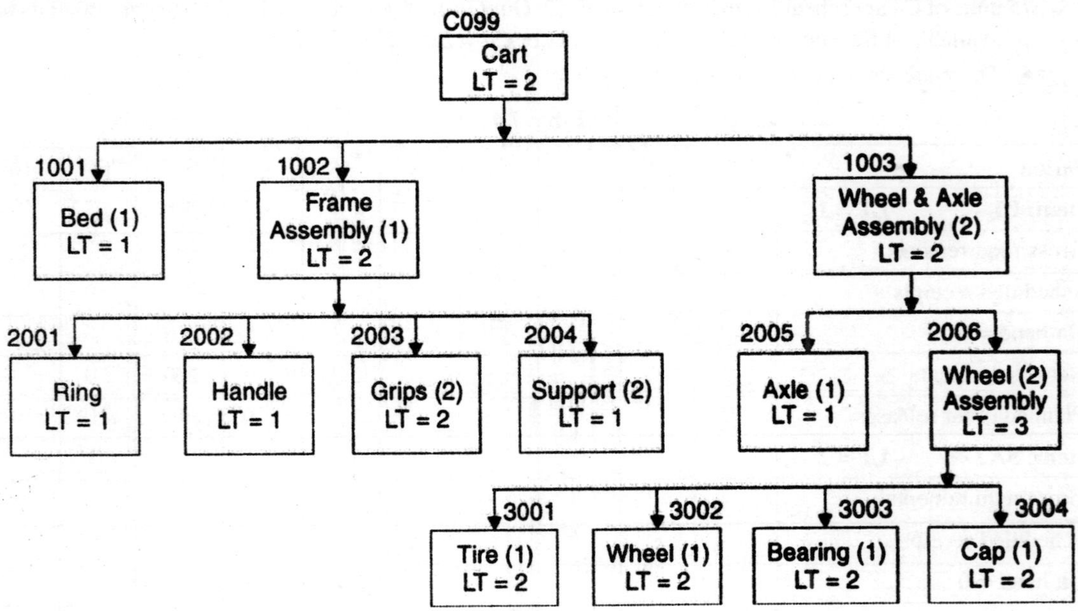

Figure 7.9. Product Structure.

Solution: The solution steps are shown in Table 7.5.

Table 7.5

Period (Weeks)	1	2	3	4	5	6	7	8	9	10
Requirement										3
Item = Cart; Code No = C099; Quantity = 1: Lead Time = 2; Lot-for-Lot; Safety Stock = 0										
Gross Requirement	0	0	0	0	0	0	0	0	0	3
Scheduled Receipt	0	0	0	0	0	0	0	0	0	0
On Hand Quantity	0	0	0	0	0	0	0	0	0	0
Net Requirement	0	0	0	0	0	0	0	0	0	3
Planned Order Receipt										3
Planned Order Release								3		
Item = Bed; Code No = 1001; Quantity/Assembly = 1: Lead Time = 1; Lot-for-Lot; Safety Stock = 0										
Gross Requirement	0	0	0	0	0	0	0	3	0	0
Scheduled Receipt	0	0	0	0	0	0	0	0	0	0
On Hand Quantity	0	0	0	0	0	0	0	0	0	0
Net Requirement	0	0	0	0	0	0	0	3	0	0
Planned Order Receipt								3		
Planned Order Release							3			
Item = Frame; Code No = 1002, Quantity/Assembly = 1: Lead Time = 2; Lot-for-Lot; Safety Stock = 0										
Gross Requirement	0	0	0	0	0	0	0	3	0	0
Scheduled Receipt	0	0	0	0	0	0	0	0	0	0
On Hand Quantity	0	0	0	0	0	0	0	0	0	0
Net Requirement	0	0	0	0	0	0	0	3	0	0
Planned Order Receipt								3		0
Planned Order Release						3				
Item = Wheel & Axle Assembly; Code No = 1003; Quantity/Assembly = 2: Lead Time = 2; Lot-for-Lot; Safety Stock = 0										
Gross Requirement	0	0	0	0	0	0	0	6	0	0
Scheduled Receipt	0	0	0	0	0	0	0	0	0	0
On Hand Quantity	0	0	0	0	0	0	0	0	0	0
Net Requirement	0	0	0	0	0	0	0	6	0	0
Planned Order Receipt								6		
Planned Order Release						6				

Item = Ring; Code No = 2001; Quantity/Assembly = 1; Lead Time = 1; Lot-for-Lot; Safety Stock = 0										
Gross Requirement	0	0	0	0	0	3	0	0	0	0
Scheduled Receipt	0	0	0	0	0	0	0	0	0	0
On Hand Quantity	0	0	0	0	0	0	0	0	0	0
Net Requirement	0	0	0	0	0	3	0	0	0	0
Planned Order Receipt						3				0
Planned Order Release					3					

Item = Handle; Code No = 2002; Quantity/Assembly = 1 Lead Time = 1; Lot-for-Lot; Safety Stock = 0										
Gross Requirement	0	0	0	0	0	3	0	0	0	0
Scheduled Receipt	0	0	0	0	0	0	0	0	0	0
On Hand Quantity	0	0	0	0	0	0	0	0	0	0
Net Requirement	0	0	0	0	0	3	0	0	0	0
Planned Order Receipt						3				0
Planned Order Release					3					

Item = Grips; Code No = 2003; Quantity/Assembly = 2: Lead Time = 2; Lot-for-Lot; Safety Stock = 0										
Gross Requirement	0	0	0	0	0	6	0	0	0	0
Scheduled Receipt	0	0	0	0	0	0	0	0	0	0
On Hand Quantity	0	0	0	0	0	0	0	0	0	0
Net Requirement	0	0	0	0	0	6	0	0	0	0
Planned Order Receipt						6				
Planned Order Release				6						

Item = Support; Code No = 2004; Quantity/Assembly = 2: Lead Time = 1; Lot-for-Lot; Safety Stock = 0										
Gross Requirement	0	0	0	0	0	6	0	0	0	0
Scheduled Receipt	0	0	0	0	0	0	0	0	0	0
On Hand Quantity	0	0	0	0	0	0	0	0	0	0
Net Requirement	0	0	0	0	0	6	0	0	0	0
Planned Order Receipt						6				
Planned Order Release					6					

Item = Axle; Code No = 2005; Quantity/Assembly = 1: Lead Time = 1; Lot-for-Lot; Safety Stock = 0										
Gross Requirement	0	0	0	0	0	6	0	0	0	0
Scheduled Receipt	0	0	0	0	0	0	0	0	0	0
On Hand Quantity = 2	2	2	2	2	2	2	0	0	0	0
Net Requirement	0	0	0	0	0	4	0	0	0	0
Planned Order Receipt						4				
Planned Order Release					4					

Item = Wheel Assembly; Code No = 2006; Quantity/Assembly = 2: Lead Time = 3; Lot-for-Lot; Safety Stock = 0										
Gross Requirement	0	0	0	0	0	12	0	0	0	3
Scheduled Receipt	0	0	0	0	0	0	0	0	0	0
On Hand Quantity = 1	1	1	1	1	1	1	0	0	0	0
Net Requirement	0	0	0	0	0	11	0	0	0	3
Planned Order Receipt						11				3
Planned Order Release			11						3	
Item = Tire; Code No = 3001; Quantity/Assembly = 1: Lead Time = 2; Lot-for-Lot; Safety Stock = 0										
Gross Requirement	0	0	11	0	0	0	0	0	0	0
Scheduled Receipt	0	0	0	0	0	0	0	0	0	0
On Hand Quantity	0	0	0	0	0	0	0	0	0	0
Net Requirement	0	0	11	0	0	0	0	0	0	0
Planned Order Receipt			11							
Planned Order Release	11									
Item = Wheel; Code No = 3002; Quantity/Assembly = 1: Lead Time = 2; Lot-for-Lot; SStock = 0										
Gross Requirement	0	0	11	0	0	0	0	0	0	0
Scheduled Receipt	0	0	0	0	0	0	0	0	0	0
On Hand Quantity	0	0	0	0	0	0	0	0	0	0
Net Requirement	0	0	11	0	0	0	0	0	0	0
Planned Order Receipt			11							
Planned Order Release	11									
Item = Bearing; Code No = 3003; Quantity/Assembly = 1: Lead Time = 2; Lot-for-Lot; SStock = 0										
Gross Requirement	0	0	11	0	0	0	0	0	0	0
Scheduled Receipt	0	0	0	0	0	0	0	0	0	0
On Hand Quantity	0	0	0	0	0	0	0	0	0	0
Net Requirement	0	0	11	0	0	0	0	0	0	0
Planned Order Receipt			11							
Planned Order Release	11									
Item = Cap; Code No = 3004; Quantity/Assembly = 1: Lead Time = 2; Lot-for-Lot; Safety Stock = 0										
Gross Requirement	0	0	11	0	0	0	0	0	0	0
Scheduled Receipt	0	0	0	0	0	0	0	0	0	0
On Hand Quantity	0	0	0	0	0	0	0	0	0	0
Net Requirement	0	0	11	0	0	0	0	0	0	0
Planned Order Receipt			11							
Planned Order Release	11									

Summary

Item Description	*Code Number*	*Quantity Required*	*Release Date*
Cart	C099	3	Week 8
Bed	1001	3	Week 7
Frame	1002	3	Week 6
Wheel & Axle Assembly	1003	6	Week 6
Ring	2001	3	Week 5
Handle	2002	3	Week 5
Grip	2003	6	Week 4
Support	2004	6	Week 5
Axle	2005	4	Week 5
Wheel Assembly	2006	11	Week 3
Tire	3001	11	Week 1
Wheel	3002	11	Week 1
Bearing	3003	11	Week 1
Cap	3004	11	Week 1

7.8.2 LIMITATIONS AND ADVANTAGES OF MRP

An MRP system provides tight and accurate control over the many complex and interdependent activities of the plant. All activities are synchronized such that parts are being manufactured (or received from vendors, if purchased) exactly when they are needed for the next stage of production. This system avoids the problems of excess work-in-process (WIP) inventory, unavailability of components when needed, grossly uneven utilization of resources, and so on.

7.9 MANUFACTURING RESOURCE PLANNING (MRP II)

MRP-II has not replaced MRP, nor is it an improved version of MRP; rather, it represents an effort to expand the scope of production resource planning, and to involve other functional areas of the firm in the planning process. When the concepts of MRP are extended to the entire range of manufacturing operations, and when corrective action is incorporated into the system, the result is a 'closed-loop MRP system'. In this, the various functions of 'operations planning and control (forecasting, operations planning, inventory management, MRP calculations, dispatching, and progress control)' have been integrated into one unified system. It also provides for feedback from vendors (delayed order deliveries, etc) and from customers (changes in orders, models, etc). Further, extension to the MRP concept can be made by linking the closed loop MRP system to the financial function of the organization. This type of structure is called **M**anufacturing **R**esource **P**lanning or **MRP-II.**

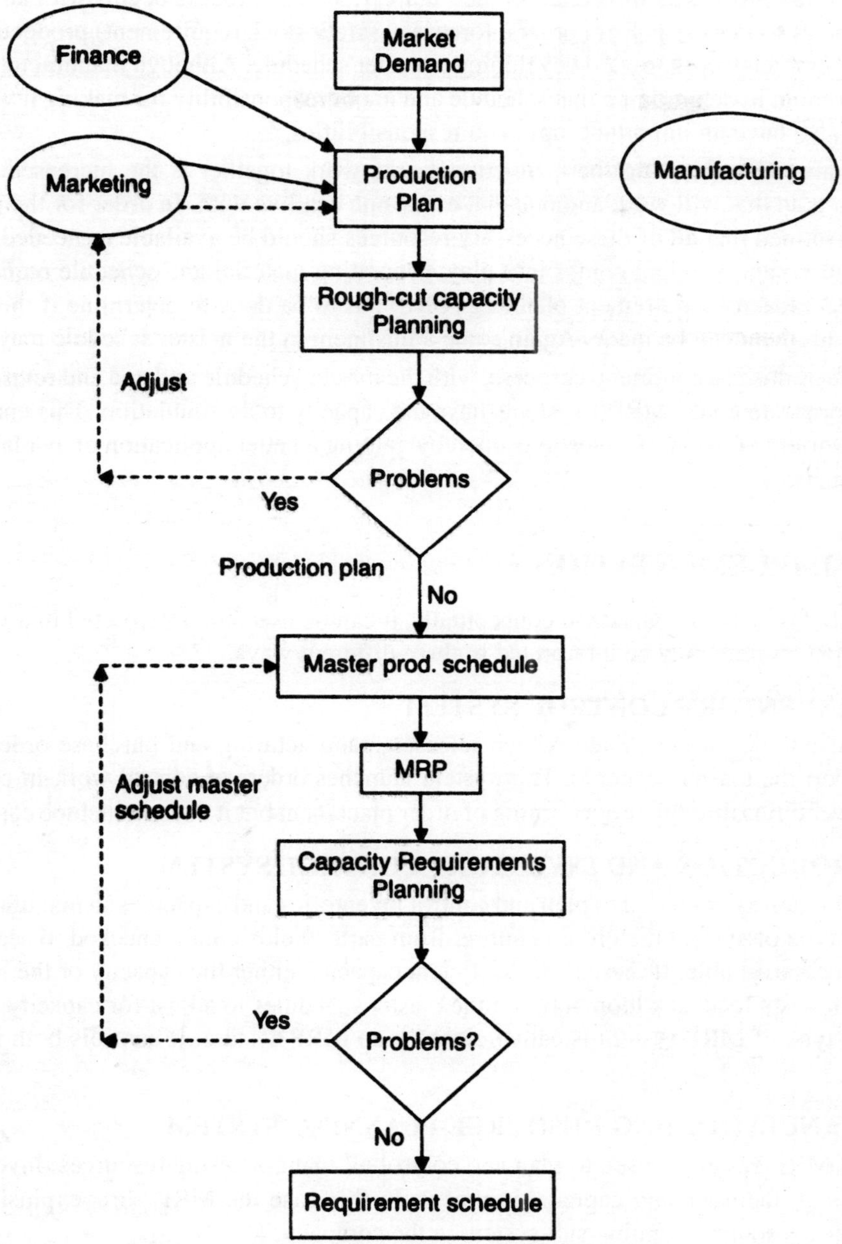

Figure 7.10. Overview of MRP II.

MRP-II software package includes a simulation capability. This allows the manager to explore various 'what if' questions. For example, if a particular customer requests that its order for 500 units be delivered 3 weeks earlier than original contract date, the simulator allows the manager to determine whether this request can be granted without an adverse effect on other customer orders.

The major purpose of MRP-II is to integrate the primary functions (marketing and finance) as well as other functions such us personnel, engineering, and purchasing in the planning process. MRP is at the heart of the process as illustrated in the Figure 7.10. The process begins with an aggregation of demand from all sources (e.g. Firm orders, forecasts, safety stock requirement) production, marketing, and finance personnel work toward developing a master schedule. Although manufacturing people will have a major input in determining that schedule and major responsibility for making it work, marketing and finance also have an important input and responsibilities.

The rationale of having these functional area work together is the increased likely hood of developing a plan that will work and one that every one can live with. In order for the plan to work, it must be determined that all of these necessary resources should be available as needed. After this, the material requirement planning comes into play, generating material and schedule requirements. Then more detailed capacity requirement planning (CRP) has to be done to determine if this more specific capacity requirement can be made. Again some adjustment in the master schedule may be required.

In effect, this is a continuous process, with the master schedule updated and revised as necessary to achieve corporate goals. MRPII systems have the capacity to do simulation. This enables managers to answer a variety of "what if" questions, thereby gaining a better application of available options and their consequences.

7.10 MRP IMPLEMENTATION

Although MRP is easy to understand conceptually, it can be used and interpreted in a variety of ways. Generally MRP system may be interpreted in three different ways.

7.10.1 AN INVENTORY CONTROL SYSTEM

An inventory control system which releases manufacturing and purchase orders for the right time to support the master schedule. This system launches orders to control work-in-process and raw materials inventories through proper timing of order placement but it doesn't include capacity planning.

7.10.2 A PRODUCTION AND INVENTORY CONTROL SYSTEM

It is an information system used to plan and control inventories and capacities in manufacturing companies. In this type of system the order resulting from parts explosion are checked to see whether sufficient capacity is available. If there is not sufficient capacity, either the capacity or the master schedule is changed. It has a feedback loop between the master schedules to adjust for capacity availability. As a result this type of MRP system is called closed loop MRP system. It controls both inventories and capacity.

7.10.3 A MANUFACTURING RESOURCE PLANNING SYSTEM

This type of MRP system is used to plan and control all manufacturing resources: inventory capacity, cash, personnel, facilities and capital equipment. In this case the MRP parts-explosion system also drives all other resource-planning sub-system in the company.

It takes a great deal of effort to make MRP successful. As a matter of fact, researches indicate that five elements are essential for successful implementation of MRP:

- Implementation planning
- Adequate computer support
- Accurate data
- Management support
- User knowledge

7.10.3.1 Implementation planning

The main pre-requisite for any MRP effort is implementation planning. Unfortunately, too many companies jump in and start implementing MRP without adequate preparation. Later, confusion and misunderstanding occur as problems arise. Implementation planning can help smooth out implementation efforts by advance planning and problem prevention efforts such as: Education of senior management, selection of project manager, appointment of an implementation team representing all parts of the company, preparation of objectives, identification of expected benefits and costs and detailed plan.

7.10.3.2 An Adequate computer support

One of the essential elements to implement MRP is adequate computer system. Nowadays, there are about 100 MRP software packages available in market. Many companies use these standard packages rather than writing their own computer program.

7.10.3.3 Accurate data

An MRP system requires accurate data when decisions are made from information supplied by the computer. A company that doesn't install an MRP system will need to create accurate bill of materials as a first step. Once the BOMs are accurate, a system will be needed to keep them that way. This will require an engineering charge coordinator who is in change of all changes to the BOM.

Inventory records must also be accurate to support the MRP system. A system of cycle counting is the best way to improve and maintain the accuracy of inventory records. All other MRP system data such as shop routings, shop floor status, and costs-must be initially screened for errors and then maintained in an acceptable state of accuracy.

7.10.3.4 Management support

Many studies have shown that top-management support is the key to successful implementation of MRP. Top managers must be actively involved in installing and operating the MRP system. They must give their time and they must change the way they operate the company.

7.10.3.5 User knowledge

An MRP system requires an entirely new approach to manufacturing. All company employees must understand how they will be affected and grasp their new roles and responsibilities. When MRP is first being installed only a few key managers need to be educated. But as the system begins to be used, all supervisors, middle managers, and top managers need to understand MRP, including managers inside and outside of manufacturing.

If an MRP system is installed according to the above guidelines, it will have great benefits to the company by:

- Reduction of inventory
- Improving customer service
- Having a good response to changes
- Change in demand
- Change in master schedule
- Giving a better productivity
- Better utilization of machines
- Providing future data on an item-by item basis.

Because of its focus on timing, MRP can do what none of its predecessors could, i.e. generate outputs that serve as valid inputs to other manufacturing logistics programs including purchasing, shop scheduling, dispatching and activity control, and capacity requirement planning. Sound MRP constitutes a solid basis for other computer applications in production and inventory control.

MRP has the ability to suggest ordering, at the right time, the right item in the right quantities for delivery on the right date. It issues action calls according to a detailed time-phased plan that it develops. It keeps this plan up-to-date by reevaluating and revising it periodically in response to changes in the environment.

7.11 HOW CAN INDUSTRY BENEFIT FROM MRP?

Most manufacturing companies can benefit from MRP system if it is properly installed and utilized. Successful companies range from the small plant to the large plant. While some companies may benefit from a very elaborate MRP system, others may need only a simple system. Each company should determine the scope of MRP system needed on the basis of the incremental costs and benefits. Starting with a minimum system, a company can add features and determine whether the additional cost is justified by the additional benefits. By using this approach, each company can arrive at the type of MRP system, which is best suited to its needs.

Having a fixed master schedule and fixed lead times are not the obligatory requisite for a company to install MRP, because MRP system doesn't get spoilt by change in its capacity due to adjusting changes. However, those companies that have a fixed master schedule or fixed lead times can operate their MRP systems with less inventory than those that must add safety lead time or safety stock to cover uncertainties in supply or demand. Users of MRP system can be classified by the type of BOM they have as shown in Figure 7.11.

- Process industry
- Assembly only
- Assembly and fabrication

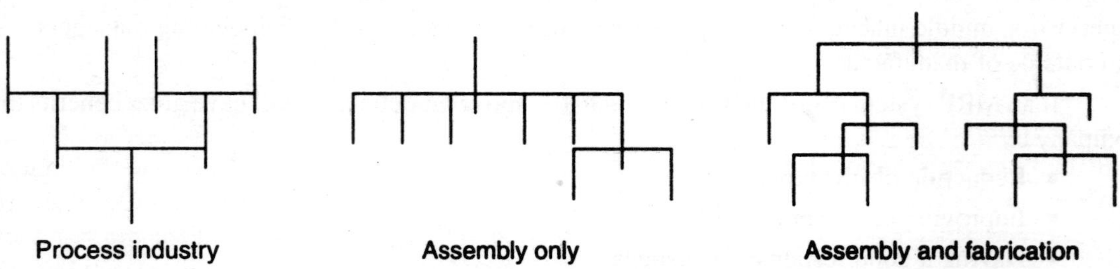

Figure 7.11. Types of BOM.

Process industry

A given input is split into several different outputs. For example: cracking and distillation of petroleum company, food processing industry, etc.

Assembly only

In these companies, all parts are purchased, and the company is not vertically integrated.

Assembly and Fabrication

It is a company which has a BOM of both assembly and fabrication operations. This company-which might be a machinery or appliance manufacturer-is vertically integrated through all stages of manufacturing.

Generally, the most benefit from MRP is achieved by companies of the third type, which have the most complex bills of materials.

There is tremendous room for the application of MRP concepts in the service industry. If a bill of materials is replaced by a bill of labor or a bill of activities, one can explode the master schedule of output into all the activities and personnel required to deliver a particular mix of services. Some service operations will also require a bill of materials where materials are important part of the goods-services bundle. As an example, The Ethiopian Airlines uses this system for maintenance system.

Pure Repetitive Manufacturing

In this manufacturing situation, the master schedule is the same from day-to-day and level loaded. In this case, a pull system such as JIT, work very well. Since there are no changes in the end products being made from day to day, the component parts needed each day are the same. The only uncertainty is breakdowns in the production process. These disruptions are handled by a pull system, since production will stop when using work centers stop. There is no need for MRP system to predict future production requirements with its more complicated, and expensive, computerized elements. The JIT system is adjusted for major events by the MRP system.

Batch Manufacturing

A batch process might utilize a hybrid of MRP-II and JIT type of system, particularly when the batches are somewhat repetitive in nature. In this case the master schedule will not be identical from day-to-day but will have some repetitive elements. MRP II is used to push material in to the factory and to plan capacity, while the JIT (pull system) is used for execution on the shop floor. This makes it possible to eliminate the shop-floor control element of MRP II with its substantial work-in-process tracking.

The hybrid system works particularly well when batch production has been organized in to cells so that MRP can provide shop orders to the cells rather than to each machine type JIT is used to pull material though each of the cell.

Job shop manufacturing

A job shop process which is batch oriented and not repetitive must use MRP II to plan and control production. An extreme example of this situation is where the factory makes only to order and each order is different like that of AMCE Company in Ethiopia. In this system a pull system will not work. Different types of structure of engines must be pushed in to the company to meet customer's demand that are different for each order. A capacity planning and shop-floor control system is needed to regulate the flow of material through production. Even in this case however, certain elements of JIT such as reduction of setup times, multifunction workers, problem solving by workers and managers, and supplier partnerships can be used except kanban system.

As can be seen, there are various situations which are best suited to a pure JIT or pure MRP control systems and there are many opportunities for both too.

Example 7.5. Given the product structure below, compute the net requirements to produce 100 units of subassembly A. No stock is on hand or on order.

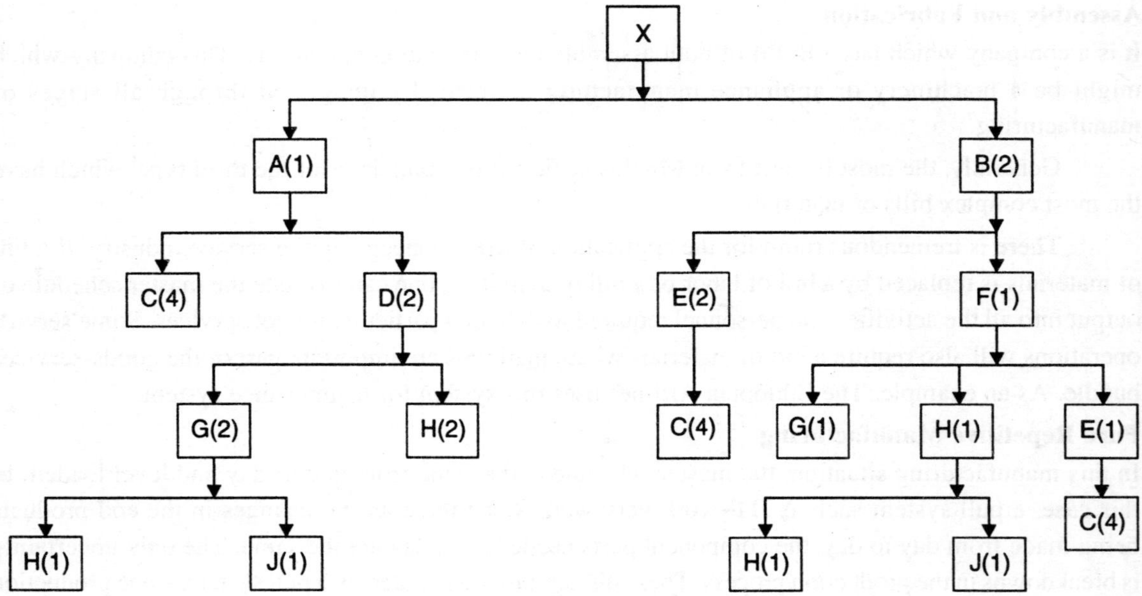

Figure 7.12

Example 7.6. A furniture company wants to make 200 chairs for its customers in the 5th week of August 2005. You have been asked to prepare an MRP (materials requirement planning) for the required components with the product structure shown in Figure 7.13, and BOM (bill of materials) in Table 7.6.

Table 7.6

Items	*Inventory*	*Lead time (weeks)*
Chairs	120	1
Leg assembly	55	2
Back assembly	30	1
Seats	45	3
Rails	110	1
Legs	140	2
Tops	30	2
Spindles	80	2

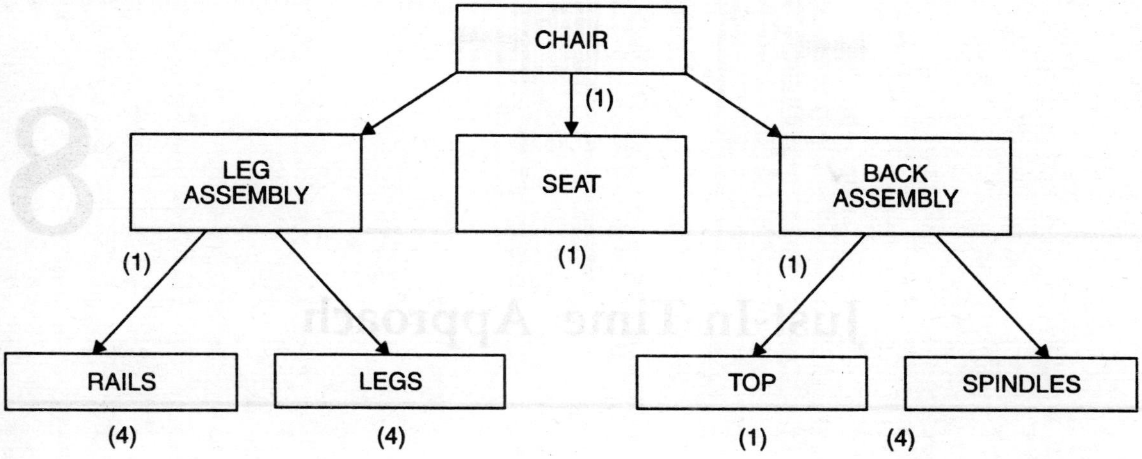
CHAIR
(1)
LEG ASSEMBLY
SEAT
BACK ASSEMBLY
(1)
(1)
(1)
RAILS
LEGS
TOP
SPINDLES
(4)
(4)
(1)
(4)

Figure 7.9

8

Just-In-Time Approach

8.0 INTRODUCTION

Just-In-Time (JIT) originated in Japan. It is recognized as technique/philosophy/way of working and is generally associated with the Toyota motor company. In fact JIT was initially known as the 'Toyota Production System'. Within Toyota Taiichi Ohno, a Mechanical Engineer & Manager by profession is credited as the originator of this way of working. The beginnings of this production system are rooted in the historical situation that Toyota faced. After the Second World War the president of Toyota said 'Catch up with America in three years, otherwise the automobile industry of Japan will not survive'. At that time one American worker produced approximately nine times as much as a Japanese worker. Taiichi Ohno found that American manufacturers made great use of economic order quantities-the idea that it is best to make a 'lot' or 'batch' of an item (such as a particular model of car or a particular component) before switching to a new item. They also made use of economic order quantities in terms of ordering and stocking the many parts needed to assemble a car.

Ohno felt that such methods would not work in Japan - total domestic demand was low and the domestic market demanded production of small quantities of many different models. Accordingly, Ohno devised a new system of production based on the elimination of waste. In his system waste was eliminated by:

- **Just-In-Time.** Items only move through the production system as and when they are needed
- **Autonomation.** Automating the production system so as to include inspection - human attention only being needed when a defect is automatically detected whereupon the system will stop and not proceed until the problem has been solved.

Ohno identified a number of sources of waste that he felt should be eliminated:

- **Overproduction.** Waste from producing more than is needed.
- **Time spent waiting.** Waste such as that associated with a worker being idle whilst waiting for another worker to pass him an item he needs (this may occur in a sequential line production process).
- **Transportation/movement.** Waste such as that associated with transporting items around a factory.
- **Processing time.** Waste such as that associated with spending more time than is necessary processing an item on a machine.

- **Inventory.** Waste associated with keeping stocks.
- **Defects.** Waste associated with defective items.

At that time, the car prices in the USA were typically set using *selling price = cost + profit* mark-up. However in Japan, low demand meant that manufacturers faced price resistance, so if the selling price is fixed, how can one increase the profit mark-up? Obviously by reducing costs and hence a large focus of the system that Toyota implemented was to do with cost reduction.

To aid in cost reduction Toyota instituted production leveling-eliminating unevenness in the flow of items. So, if a component which required assembly had an associated requirement of 100 during a 25 day working month then 4 were assembled per day, one every two hours in an eight hour working day. Leveling also applied to the flow of finished goods out of the factory and to the flow of raw materials into the factory.

Toyota changed their factory layout. Previously all machines of the same type, e.g. presses, were together in the same area of the factory. This meant that items had to be transported back and forth as they needed processing on different machines. To eliminate this transportation different machines were clustered together so items could move smoothly from one machine to another as they were processed. This meant that workers had to become skilled on more than one machine - previously workers were skilled at operating just one type of machine. Although this initially met resistance from the workforce it was eventually overcome.

8.1 HISTORY OF RELATIONS BETWEEN MANAGEMENT AND WORKERS

Whilst we may think today that Japan has harmonious industrial relations with management and workers working together for the common good, the fact is that, in the past, this has not been true. In the immediate post Second World War period, for example, Japan had one of the worst strike records in the world. In 1953, the car maker Nissan suffered a four month strike - involving a lockout and barbed wire barricades to prevent workers returning to work. That dispute ended with the formation of a company backed union, formed initially by members of the Nissan accounting department. Striking workers who joined this new union received payment for the time spent on strike, a powerful financial incentive to leave their old union during such a long dispute. The slogan of this new union was *'Those who truly love their union love their company'*.

8.1.1 ADAPTATION TO NEW PRODUCTION ENVIRONMENT

In order to help the workforce to adapt to what was a very different production environment Ohno introduced the analogy of teamwork in a baton relay race. As you are probably aware typically in such races four runners pass a baton between themselves and the winning team is the one that crosses the finishing line first carrying the baton and having made valid baton exchanges between runners. Within the newly rearranged factory floor workers were encouraged to think of themselves as members of a team - passing the baton (processed items) between themselves with the goal of reaching the finishing line appropriately. If one worker flagged (*e.g.* had an off day) then the other workers could help him, perhaps setting a machine up for him so that the team output was unaffected.

8.1.2 THE KANBAN CONTROL

In order to have a method of controlling production (the flow of items) in this new environment Toyota introduced the kanban. The kanban is essentially information as to what has to be done. Within Toyota the most common form of kanban was a rectangular piece of paper within a transparent vinyl envelope.

The information listed on the paper basically tells a worker what to do - which items to collect or which items to produce. In Toyota two types of kanban are distinguished for controlling the flow of items:

- **A withdrawal kanban.** Which details the items that should be withdrawn from the preceding step in the process.
- **A production ordering kanban.** Which details the items to be produced.

All movement throughout the factory is controlled by these kanbans—in addition since the kanbans specify item quantities precisely no defects can be tolerated—*e.g.* if a defective component is found when processing a production ordering kanban then obviously the quantity specified on the kanban cannot be produced. Hence, the importance of autonomation (as referred to above) the system must detect and highlight defective items so that the problem that caused the defect can be resolved.

Another aspect of the Toyota Production System is the reduction of **setup time**. Machines and processes must be re-engineered so as to reduce the setup time required before processing of a new item can start.

In the Western world, JIT only began to impact on manufacturing in the late 1970's and early 1980's. Even then it went under a variety of names—*e.g.* Hewlett Packard called it 'stockless production'. Such adaptation by Western industry was based on informal analysis of the systems being used in Japanese companies. Books by Japanese authors (such as Ohno himself) detailing the development of JIT in Japan were not published in the West until the late 1980's.

8.1.3 JIT TODAY

Just-In-Time (JIT) is a very popular term these days among the managers of various industries. No conference on *Operations Management* is seen complete unless some topics or papers are included in the deliberation. It is seen in various ways by the practitioners in manufacturing, services and administrative sectors. JIT is a system, a concept, a philosophy, a set of tools, a way of life and so on. No two JIT are same—they vary according to the places and conditions in which they are being applied.

JIT is both a philosophy and a set of methods for manufacturing. JIT emphasizes waste reduction, total quality control, and devotion to the customer. It strives to eliminate sources of manufacturing waste by producing the right part in the right place at the right time. Waste results from any activity that adds cost without adding value, such as moving and storing of an item. It tries to provide the right part at the right place and at the right time.

JIT is also known as lean production or stockless production system. It should improve profits and return on investment by reducing inventory levels (or increasing the inventory turnover rate), improving product quality, reducing production and delivery lead times, and reducing other costs (such as those associated with machine setup and equipment breakdown). In a JIT system, underutilized (or excess) capacity is used instead of buffer inventories to hedge against problems that may arise. JIT applies primarily to repetitive manufacturing processes in which the same products and components are produced over and over again. The general idea is to establish flow processes (even when the facility uses a jobbing or batch process layout) by linking work centers so that there is an even, balanced flow of materials throughout the entire production process, similar to that found in an assembly line. To accomplish this, an attempt is made to reach the goals of driving all queues toward zero and achieving the ideal lot size of one unit.

JIT is a manufacturing system whose goal is to optimize processes and procedures by continuously pursuing waste reduction.

8.1.4 JIT APPLICATION PROFILE

Just-In-Time (JIT) has assumed a kind of mystique of an oriental philosophy. Much of it is plain common sense-as more American and European companies are discovering to their benefit. General Motors, IBM, Hewlett-Packard, General Electric, and Black and Decker are among the big US companies that have adopted JIT production methods. European companies are joining them, Britain's state owned Rover Group is the latest recruit. Its car division has announced that 'preferred suppliers' will get long-term contracts to prove the bids which make up more than half of its production costs.

One misconception of JIT is that it is limited to the flow line/large-batch environment of the automotive industry. Once the automotive company has started along the JIT route, there seems to be no area which does not benefit from JIT principles like the elimination of waste. JIT applies very well to the tool-room (job-shop) as it does to the assembly line. Techniques for eliminating waste can be applied to good effect outside manufacturing as well, such as in sales and distribution.

The following Figure 8.1 illustrates the suitability of JIT for a range of process choice environments [Alan Harrison]. Those at the *center* of the diagram are prime candidates for JIT manufacturing. Those at the *top left* or *bottom right* will be suitable for selected applications. In the case of job-shops, such applications may include total quality, workforce flexibility, and the promotion of flow in manufacture.

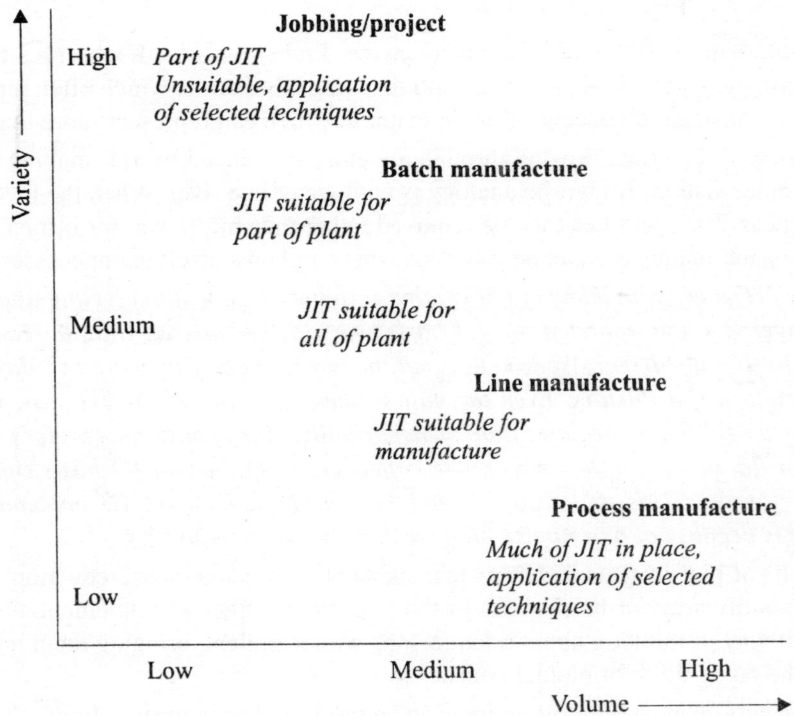

Figure 8.1. JIT and Choice of Process.

Most successful JIT applications have been in repetitive manufacturing, where batches of standard products are produced at high speeds and high volumes. Smaller, less complex job shops have used JIT, but operations have been changed so that they behave somewhat like repetitive manufacturing [Jack Byrd et al].

JIT concepts, which started in manufacture, have spread to all functions of a business. In Japan, JIT has developed into a total management system from marketing to delivery. It has diffused through suppliers and distributors. It has provided Japanese companies with a formidable competitive advantage over their Western rivals. If we are competing against a Japanese company, we are competing against JIT.

Putting this concept into practice means a reversal of the traditional thinking process. In conventional production processes, units are transported to the next production stage as soon as they are ready. In JIT, each stage is required to go back to the previous stage to pick up the exact number of units needed [Marc L. Songini].

A close relationship with suppliers-often called co-manufacturing-is one of about 40 JIT techniques, not all of which are made-in-Japan. *Marks and Spencer*, a successful British retailing group, has been closely tied to its suppliers since the 1920s, when it recognized that mass manufacturing and mass retailing had somehow to be linked together.

Toyota is accredited with systematizing JIT. The Japanese carmaker defines it as *the 'reduction of cost through the elimination of waste'*. It spreads throughout Japan in the 1970s as a logical way to manage a large flow of materials. Materials do not increase in value unless they are being processed. So profits are increased when inventory and safety stocks are reduced or replaced by small, frequent deliveries.

Unlike automation, JIT is not capital intensive. Prof. Voss of UK observes that the average manufacturing company put 75% of its effort into reducing labor costs, which often represent about 10 % of its total costs, instead of concentrating on material which can represent more than half its costs.

The volume of materials flowing through a factory is reduced by JIT, making bottlenecks and other problems more visible. A favorite analogy is with water in a river. When the level of water falls, rocks start to appear. The rocks can then be removed rather than hit. It can, for instance, become plain that it is pointless automating a warehouse because the warehouse itself is unnecessary.

We apply JIT concept in many of our routine activities even without feeling about it. We get the newspapers delivered to our doorsteps on JIT basis everyday because we want to read them when the news items are fresh and current. We won't accept the newspapers if they are two days old - after all who wants to read them as history. Even the nature likes many things the JIT way. We are supplied oxygen by nature on JIT basis. We don't store them normally. Many consumers prefer to have their food items (chapati or flat bread, pizzas, burger, tea, coffee, etc.) supplied on JIT basis right at the time of need - not before or after. This means there is an inbuilt desire to have the JIT implemented in our day to day life but it is because of our mindset that we don't do so in industries.

The **results of just-in-time** inventory management are apparent: cost reduction, increased speed to market and identification of bottlenecks in the workflow. Effective implementation, however, requires a different way of thinking about relationships with suppliers, bringing them into a cooperative endeavor with the recognition of mutual goals.

Corporate culture must promote an inquiring attitude and an interest in finding better ways to do things through communication and cooperation. The Ford and Toyota examples illustrate a final important point for knowledge management: Some of the best ideas for process improvement can come from tapping the brains of those closest to the situation.

Generally JIT manufacturing system is:

- To have only required inventory when needed,
- To improve quality to zero defects,

- To reduce lead times by reducing setup times,
- To incrementally revise operations themselves,
- To accomplish these things at a minimum cost.

It is insufficient for firms just to be *high-quality* and *low-cost* producers. Today, they must also be first in getting products and services to customer fast. To compete in this new environment, order-to-delivery cycle must be drastically reduced. JIT is weapon of choice today to reduce elapsed time of this cycle.

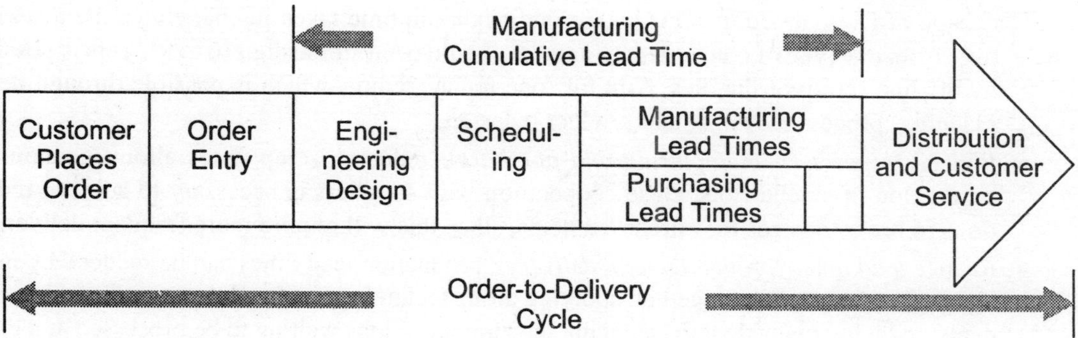

Figure 8.2. Order-to-Delivery Cycle.

A JIT company adds value with every activity where JIT has been introduced; there have been dramatic increases in the proportion of the actual value-adding time to the total cycle time, often more than 70%. Since non-JIT companies usually report about 15%, JIT improves operating efficiency significantly [John Y. Lee et al]. By eliminating non-value added costs, such as defective materials, in-process inventories, and delays; JIT simplifies the entire manufacturing system and improves long-term productivity.

Recently, the business strategy commonly refereed to as just-in-time has become more and more dominant in many aspects of business. Many corporations have begun to use the system to improve efficiency and customer service. Although the system has been criticized as a lofty idea or a theory rather than an attainable business practice, the company that have implemented the idea have profited from it [Padraic Gurdon].

JIT has been found to be so effective that it increases productivity, work performance and product quality, while saving costs and it helps companies spotlight those areas that are falling behind and need improvement [John Y. Lee et al]. It also slashes inventory, free up space on the factory floor and shine a blinding spotlight on the delivery and quality performance of parts suppliers. Therefore, the result of JIT was smaller inventories of both parts and final products with smaller inventories, billions of dollars were freed up for investment purposes [Mike Whittenberg]. This protects companies during the lean years when demand may exceed production.

8.2 KEYS TO SUCCESSFUL JIT IMPLEMENTATION

There are some prerequisites for successful JIT implementation. Industries need to do the following:

- *Stabilize and level the Master Production Schedule (MPS) with uniform plant loading*: create a uniform load on all work centers through constant daily production (establish freeze windows to prevent changes in the production plan for some period of time) and mixed model assembly (produce roughly the same mix of products each day, using a repeating sequence if several products are produced on the same line). Meet demand fluctuations through end-item inventory rather than through fluctuations in production level.

- *Reduce or eliminate setup times*: The process of JIT is to produce parts in a lot size of 1. In many cases this is not economically feasible because of the cost of set up compared with inventory carrying cost. The JIT solution to this problem is to reduce the setup time as much as possible ideally to zero. Bringing down the set up time for machine is the key factor to implement JIT system. This concept is popularly known by the name 'Single Minute Exchange of Dies (SMED)'. This means the maximum time taken in changing a die to switch over from one type of component to another should be in single digit (0 to 9). This is possible by off-line set up of the dies. Aim for 'one-touch' setup - which is possible through better planning, process redesign, and product redesign.
- *Reduce lot sizes (manufacturing and purchase):* reducing setup times allows economical production of smaller lots; close cooperation with suppliers is necessary to achieve reductions in order lot sizes for purchased items, since this will require more frequent deliveries.
- *Reduce lead times (production and delivery)*: production lead times can be reduced by moving work stations closer together, applying group technology and cellular manufacturing concepts, reducing queue length (reducing the number of jobs waiting to be processed at a given machine), and improving the coordination and cooperation between successive processes; delivery lead times can be reduced through close cooperation with suppliers, possibly by inducing suppliers to locate closer to the factory.
- *Preventive maintenance*: use machine and worker idle time to maintain equipment and prevent breakdowns.
- *Flexible work force*: workers should be trained to operate several machines, to perform maintenance tasks, and to perform quality inspections. In general, the attitude of respect for people leads to giving workers more responsibility for their own work.
- *Require supplier quality assurance and implement a zero defects quality program*: errors leading to defective items must be eliminated, since there are no buffers of excess parts. A quality at the source (jidoka) program must be implemented to give workers the personal responsibility for the quality of the work they do, and the authority to stop production when something goes wrong. Techniques such as "JIT lights" (to indicate line slowdowns or stoppages) and "tally boards" (to record and analyze causes of production stoppages and slowdowns to facilitate correcting them later) may be used.
- *Small-lot (single unit) conveyance*: use a control system such as a kanban (card) system to convey parts between work stations in small quantities (ideally, one unit at a time). In its largest sense, JIT is not the same thing as a kanban system, and a kanban system is not required to implement JIT (some companies have instituted a JIT program along with a MRP system), although JIT is required to implement a kanban system and the two concepts are frequently equated with one another.

8.2.1 THE KANBAN SYSTEM

The Kanban system was developed by Toyota in the early stages of JIT improvement campaign. The particular feature of a Kanban system is that it short-circuits normal ordering procedures: as supplies of a Kanban-controlled material are used up, new supplies are requested simply by releasing a re-order card which is sent direct to the supply point (*i.e.* the manufacturer or stock lists). It is often described as a 'pull' system, in contrast with traditional ordering procedures, which 'push' orders into the system.

The term 'Kanban' simply means 'card'. To explain the Kanban concept, consider the case of an assembler who is drawing a particular component from a pallet which, when full, contains 100 pieces. As the last piece is drawn, the assembler takes an identifying card from the empty pallet and sends it back down the line to the earlier work center where that part (among others) is made. On receiving the Kanban card, the work center responsible for supplying the component makes a new batch of 100 and sends it to the assembly post (so that the assembler isn't kept waiting, there will probably be an extra pallet in the system to maintain the supply while the new batch is being made). This means that there is a minimum of paperwork, and the order cycle is generated on a 'pull' basis, the components only being made when there is an immediate need for them, thus keeping work-in-progress to a minimum. If you are familiar with the 'two-bin' method of stock control you will recognize the similarity.

Due to a lack of space and lack of natural resource, the Japanese have developed an aversion for waste by viewing scrap and rework as waste and thus strive for perfect quality. They also believe that inventory storage wastes space and ties up valuable capital and materials.

JIT uses a simple part withdrawal kanban (Figure 8.3) to pull parts from one work center to the next. Parts are kept in small containers, and only a specific number of these containers are provided. When all containers are filled, the machines are shut off, and no more parts are produced until the subsequent work center provides another empty container. Thus the work-in-process inventory is limited to available containers, and parts are provided only when needed.

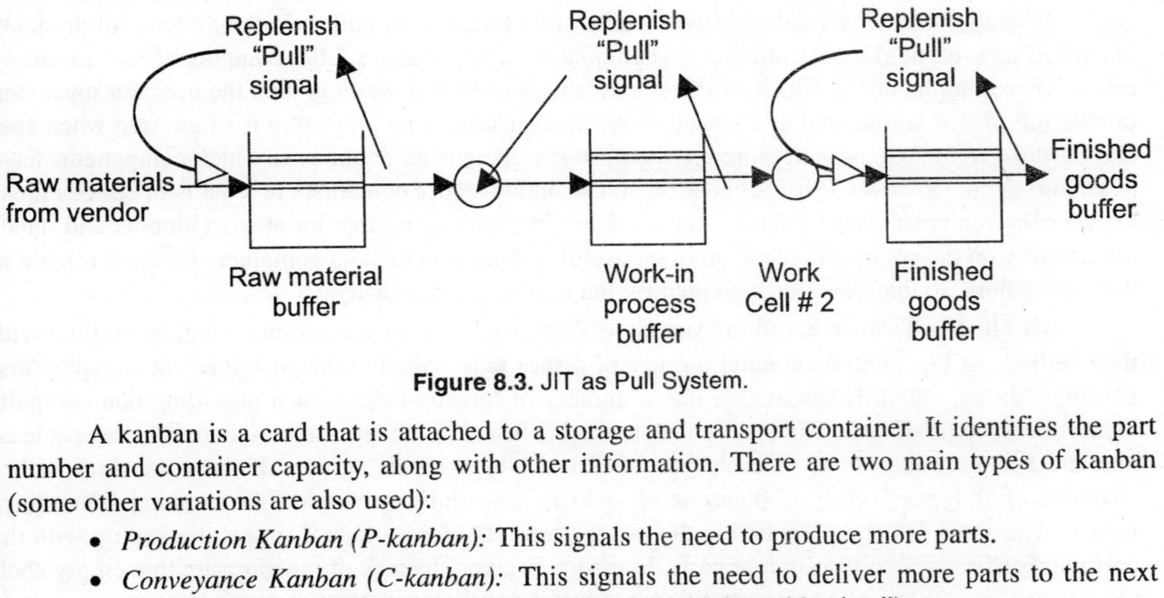

Figure 8.3. JIT as Pull System.

A kanban is a card that is attached to a storage and transport container. It identifies the part number and container capacity, along with other information. There are two main types of kanban (some other variations are also used):

- *Production Kanban (P-kanban):* This signals the need to produce more parts.
- *Conveyance Kanban (C-kanban):* This signals the need to deliver more parts to the next work center (also called a "move kanban" or a "withdrawal kanban").

A kanban system is a pull-system, in which the kanban is used to pull parts to the next production stage when they are needed; a MRP system (or any schedule-based system) is a push system, in which a detailed production schedule for each part is used to push parts to the next production stage when scheduled. The weakness of a push system (MRP) is that customer demand must be forecast and production lead times must be estimated. Bad guesses (forecasts or estimates) result in excess inventory, and the longer the lead time, the more room for error. The weakness of a pull system (kanban) is that following the JIT production philosophy is essential, especially concerning the elements of short setup times and small lot sizes.

(*a*) **Two Card Kanban (Double Kanban).** This is the original Toyota method, developed at a time when replenishment supplies were routed through a component or parts store (though it can also be used when no stores intervention is involved). The card released by the user authorizes the stores to 'move' a replenishment supply to the user. When they do so, a second card, which is found on the pallet they are about to supply, is removed and sent to the component supplier as authority to 'produce' another standard quantity.

Dual-Card Kanban Rules

- No parts to be made unless P-kanban authorizes production.
- Exactly one P-kanban and one C-kanban should be there for each container (the number of containers per part number is a management decision).
- Only standard containers are used, and they are always filled with the prescribed (small) quantity.

(*b*) **The 1 Card Kanban.** Similar to the 2-card system, but a single card acts as both 'move' and 'produce' authority. This method is typically used where the supply point is close to the user point, so that the supply and user operatives move the empty and full pallets between the two work centers themselves without the intervention of a stores function. It is also commonly used where the movement of pallets is automated.

(*c*) **The Container-Based Kanban.** In this variant the Kanban card is dispensed with altogether. Instead, there are a predetermined number of containers or pallets in the system, all uniquely identified to a particular part number or component: if the maker of the component has an empty container waiting he or she fills it; if there is no empty container waiting, then the operator must stop production of that component and switch to some other task. This procedure is often used when special-purpose containers or pallets are provided, so that there is no doubt as to which components have to go into them. However, it is also possible to use multipurpose containers in what is in effect a cross between the container-based and the 1 card systems, by painting the appropriate part number and standard quantity on the containers itself. Another useful technique is to paint containers for similar parts in different colors, so that operators can identify the right container easily.

(*d*) **The Shelf-space Kanban.** Anyone who has used a motorway cafeteria will be familiar with this method. At the cafeteria counter a range of dishes is provided to the customer via a display/dispensing cabinet, which is subdivided into a number of 'pigeon-holes', each providing one compartment for each type of dish. The instructions to the kitchen staff are 'ensure that there is always at least one and not more than three of each type of dish available in the cabinet. If there are three dishes available of all types of dish, stop producing and find something else to do (like cleaning your equipment)'. The same principle, applied to the factory, takes the form of shelf spaces marked up with the part number/description of different parts. Someone is given the task of making sure that empty shelf places are filled. When all spaces are filled, production of the item stops.

(*e*) **The Floor Grid Kanban.** Exactly the same as a shelf-space Kanban, but typically used for bulky or heavy components which are unsuitable for putting on shelves.

Summary

In all the above examples of Kanban, an essential feature of the system is that the number of containers or locations is systematically reduced by management to the point where supply is kept just in balance with the rate of use, so that the replenishment supply arrives 'just-in-time' for the user. The usual way of doing this is to keep taking away one more container each day (or week) until you reach the point where production is interrupted because the next full container doesn't arrive in time (i.e. it's 'just-too-late'!); replacing one container should then bring the supply back into balance with the rate of use. If you use this method, make sure you keep one or two full containers somewhere out of sight, ready to slip into the line quickly so that the interruption to production doesn't cause a problem. This trial and error method of finding out how many Kanban containers are needed is popular because in practice Kanban are usually introduced gradually, in parallel with the old method of supply; if the same containers are used as previously, some will become surplus to requirements anyway when the faster Kanban supply is implemented, so you might as well take advantage of this to reduce the number in use gradually, in the way described.

If this trial and error method worries you, or if you've decided to buy a new type of container for your Kanbans, there is a way of working out in advance exactly how many containers will be needed; using a 'simulation' model will enable you to test the effects of different demand levels and a different mix of production with a high degree of confidence.

From the above you will realize that Kanban is not just another name for just-in-time: it is only part of a JIT implementation. The 'true' Kanban system is normally only suitable for high turnover components, which are in regular use, and you should generally avoid using Kanbans on high-cost components. However, you can get some of the benefits of a Kanban system, even with high-cost components, by using the shelf-space or floor grid method.

If you decide to use the Kanban concept in your own factory, don't constrain yourself by trying to conform too rigidly to what I have referred to as the 'true' Kanban system. Be flexible: adapt the basic concept to your own circumstances in whatever way you think appropriate, remembering that the prime considerations are minimizing material and work-in-progress stocks, simplifying re-ordering paperwork, and empowering the actual users of the material to call for supplies as and when they need them.

In the sections to follow, we will discuss some more features of JIT:

8.3 JAPANESE VS AMERICAN MANAGEMENT

William Ouchi listed some of the distinguishing features [William O. Ouchi] of **Japanese organization** as: *Life time employment, slow evaluation and promotion, non-specialized career paths, implicit control mechanisms, collective decision making, collective responsibility, and holistic concern for employees.* In contrast, qualities inherent in American organizations include *short-term employment, rapid evaluation and promotion, specialized career paths, explicit control mechanisms, individual decision making, individual responsibility, and more segmented concern for workers [J. Bernard Keys et al].* Ouchi offered a new American approach, called Theory Z which is a synthesis of the best aspects of both approaches. It synthesizes traditional American and current Japanese methods, and stresses the contribution of every employee in solving problems through group consensus.

8.3.1 DOWNSIDES OF JAPANESE MANAGEMENT

Some of the drawbacks [Alan D. Hansen] of Japanese system of management are as follows:

- Women are often not considered part of the permanent work force. They are encouraged to quit work when they get in the family way.

- Companies carry out extensive background checks on prospective employees, including interviews with family members, neighbors and teachers, and genealogical research to ensure that the candidate has the proper ancestry.
- Lifetime employment is not available to women; even for men the lifetime ends, in many cases, with mandatory retirement at age 55.
- Employees are strongly socialized to conform to company norms, which often discourage religious or social activities.
- The Japanese govt. subsidizes industry through tax breaks and incentives, and provides barriers to protect Japanese industry.

8.3.2 JIT MANUFACTURING SYSTEM OVERVIEW

The main idea behind the principle of JIT is to exclude the roots of manufacturing waste by getting just the right quantity of raw materials and generating just the right quantity of products in the right place at the right time. In other words JIT is a process aimed at increasing value added and eliminating waste by providing the environment to perfect and simplify the processes.

JIT works as a pull system and applies to generally every level in a multi-level production system. A *pull system* is actually "the subsequent process that pulls its requirements from the preceding processes in question". One useful and effective way to implement this "pull" production is a kanban system [Cralg Felder].

Companies are beginning to turn to internet based technologies to communicate with their suppliers, making the JIT ordering and delivering process speedier and more flexible. Although applied mostly to manufacturing, the concepts are not limited to this area of the business. Indeed JIT concepts are always applied to non-manufacturing areas in the same way as in manufacturing areas in the excellent company.

The philosophy of JIT is a continuous improvement that puts emphasis on prevention rather than correction, and demands a company wide focus on quality [Matt Schemidt]. It is about developing competence and simplification in the way we do things by squeezing out waste every step of the way. But there are no short cuts to excellence. We can learn from, and so avoid the pitfalls of, companies which have already embarked on the JIT journey. It is not necessary to make the same mistakes[S.M Thacker].

The requirement of JIT is that equipment, resources and labor are made available only in the amount required and at the time required to do the job. It is based on producing only the necessary units in the necessary quantities at the necessary time by bringing production rates exactly in line with market demand [Marc L. Songini]. In short, JIT means making what the market wants, when it wants it, while using a minimum of facilities, equipment, materials, and human resources.

The relationship of JIT to manufacturing strategy development can be considered in terms of both its impact on customer needs and of matching or improving or competitor activities. Table-8.1 shows how JIT benefits can be used to provide different forms of competitive advantage. For example, an improvement in *flexibility* helps to make the facility more *responsive* to changes to customer demand, and shortens lead time.

Table 8.1. JIT and Competitive Advantage

JIT capability	Competitive advantage derived from JIT capability
WIP reduction	Lower-cost manufacture
Increased flexibility	Responsive to customer demands: volume, short lead time, product change
Raw materials reduction	Lower-cost manufacture
Increased quality	Higher-quality products Lower-cost manufacture
Increased productivity	Lower-cost manufacture
Reduced space requirements	Lower-cost manufacture
Lower overheads	Lower-cost manufacture

A JIT system is designed to expose errors (Figure 8.4) and get them corrected rather than covering them up with inventory because a perfect quality is required for the successful functioning of a JIT system. A company implementing the JIT system must attend to several important details such as:

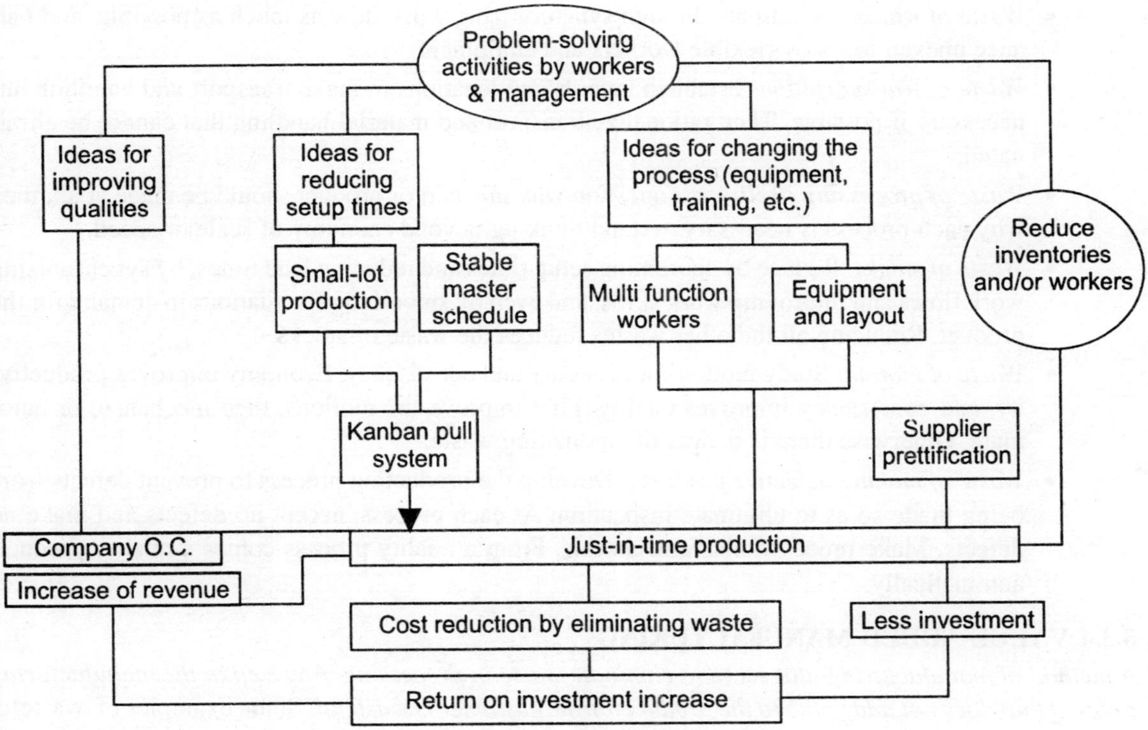

Figure 8.4. JIT System.

Smooth material flow-simplify material flow patterns: Requires a total rearrangement of the production lines and direct access to and from receiving and shipping docks. By doing this, uninterrupted material flow from receipt, directly through each production stage, than to delivery is possible.

Reduction of setup times-prior to JIT: Many discrete part manufacturing had machine setups that sometimes required several hours that is intolerable in a JIT system.

Reduction of vendor lead Times: Instead of receiving large shipments of purchased parts every 2 or 3 months, under JIT we want to receive parts "Just in time" for the needed production operation.

Zero-Defect components: A JIT system cannot tolerate defective components, either manufactured or purchased.

Disciplined shop floor control: In a JIT system, it is desired to keep inventories very low and to maintain an 'unclogged,' responsive operation. This requires that strict adherence to precise order release times be adhered to at all times which means that machines and machine operators are sometimes idle.

8.3.3 THE SEVEN WASTES IN JIT

Shigeo Shingo, a recognized JIT authority and engineer at the Toyota Motor Company identifies [*Everette E. Adam et al.*] seven wastes [Hall R.] as being the targets of continuous improvement in production processes.

- *Waste of overproduction*: eliminate by reducing setup times, synchronizing quantities and timing between processes, compacting layout, visibility, and so forth. Make only what is needed now.
- *Waste of waiting:* eliminate through synchronizing work flow as much as possible, and balance uneven loads by flexible workers and equipment.
- *Waste of transportation:* establish layouts and locations to make transport and handling unnecessary if possible. Then rationalize transport and material handling that cannot be eliminated.
- *Waste of processing itself:* First question why this part or product should be made at all, then why each process is necessary. Extend thinking beyond economy of scale or speed.
- *Waste of stocks:* Reduce by shortening setup times and reducing lead times, by synchronizing work flows and improving work skills, and even by smoothing fluctuations in demand for the product. Reducing all the other wastes reduces the waste of stocks.
- *Waste of motion:* Study motion for economy and consistency. Economy improves productivity, and consistency improves quality. First improve the motions, then mechanize or automate. Otherwise there is danger of automating waste.
- *Waste of making defective products:* Develop the production process to prevent defects from being made so as to eliminate inspection. At each process, accept no defects and make no defects. Make process failsafe to do this. From a quality process comes a quality product-automatically.

8.3.4 VALUE-ADDED MANUFACTURING

A method of manufacturing that seeks to eliminate waste in processing. Any step in the manufacturing process that does not add value to the product for the customer is wasteful. Some examples of wasteful steps are: process delays, material transport, storages, work-in-process (WIP) inventories, finished goods inventories, excessive paper processing, etc that do not add value to the product.

Professor Robert W. Hall, Indiana University, suggests these points to the Japanese manufacturing system.

- Produce what the customer desires.
- Produce products only at the rate the customer wants them.
- Produce with perfect quality.
- Produce instantaneously—with zero unnecessary lead time.
- Produce with no waste of labor, material, or equipment; every move has a purpose so there is zero idle inventory.
- Produce by methods that allow people to develop.

JIT system cannot be implemented overnight. It should be a gradual process. It may be practical to have a *hybrid model* in the early phase. According to Shingo, Toyota Motor Company took 20 years [S. Shingo] to implement JIT system. We also need to note the following points:

- Not all Japanese companies practice JIT.
- There are several versions of JIT. Each company that practices the JIT philosophy does so a little differently.
- Variations in cultures account for variations in JIT philosophies and techniques. For example, the kanban card system is natural to the Japanese, who generally enjoy playing cards. In USA, the cards are often spurned and kanban squares, kanban lights, or yelling ' Hey, Jack! Send me some more materials!' are used instead.
- JIT is less a set of techniques and more an umbrella encompassing several techniques such as the total quality control, total employee involvement, kanban, setup time reduction, zero inventories, and pull coordination.

8.4 HOW JAPANESE MANUFACTURING IDEALLY WORKS?

Ideally the Japanese approach to manufacturing would be as follows:

- First, identify the customers' needs. Find out what customers require in terms of quantity, quality, and schedule.
- Second, obtain the exact amount of material needed for today and process it piece by piece. The first person in the manufacturing process must perform their job and hand the piece to the next person. The piece must be correct to avoid delays down the line. If there is an error and the next person cannot use the piece, it should be handed back with admonishment. However, there is a willingness to help solve any problems so this will not happen again.
- There is no in-process inventory. Everything currently being made is needed by the customer, so no finished goods inventory exists.
- Quality is perfect. Waste cannot be hidden-poor products that are 2, 3, or 4 % defective cannot be made and put in storage to be sorted later.
- Finally, everyone is involved to simplify the job, and management strives to aid all employees accomplish this goal. Cooperation, teamwork, and a consensus in all decisions are foremost in management's mind.

8.4.1 STOCKLESS PRODUCTION

Everything is made as ordered, and delivered only as needed. Production is 'Just-in-time'. The results of stockless production programs in Japan based on 1981 data collected by Professor Jinichiro Nakane, Waseda University, Tokyo, is shown in Table 8.2.

Table 8.2. Results.of stockless production programs in Japan

Company	*Duration of programs (in years)*	*Inventory reduction (% of the original value)*	*Throughput time reduction (% of original value)*	*Labor productivity (% increase)*
A	3	45	40	50
B	3	16	20	80
C	4	30	25	60
D	2	20	50	50

8.5 COMPARISON OF MRP AND JIT

MRP and JIT are compatible and can be used together in certain situations. There are three situations to be considered in comparing MRP and JIT.

- Pure repetitive manufacturing
- Batch manufacturing
- Job shop manufacturing

8.5.1 PUSH VS PULL SYSTEM

The terms push and pull are used to describe two different systems for moving work through a production process.

8.5.1.1 Push System

When work is finished at a workstation, the output is pushed to the next station; or, in the case of the final operation, it is pushed on to final inventory. In this system work is pushed on as it is completed, with no regard for whether the next station is ready for the work. In a totally predictable environment, demand forecasts would always be realized; bill of materials will be absolutely accurate; suppliers would ship on time and with total accuracy; nothing would be misplaced or miscounted; machines would never fail; all personnel would be present when expected; and all intervals in the process would be totally predictable. In such an environment, all manufacturing activities may be scheduled using the push MRP system.

Table 8.3. Push Vs Pull Systems

	Push System	**Pull System**
Signal to produce more	Schedule or plan	Customer signal
Timing of signal	Advance of the need	At the time of the need
Type of signal	Paper or computer	Container, square, cart, or paper
Information scope	Global	Local only
Planning horizon	Fairly long	Very short

Level demand needed	No	Generally yes
Standard parts/products	Not necessary	Generally necessary
Large queues possible	Yes	No
Negatives	Too much inventory Not visual. Long planned lead times. Requires more information.	Does not plan ahead. Missed customer demand at the beginning of the product lifecycle and too much inventory at the end.
Best for	Non-repetitive, batch. Seasonal demand, short product lifecycles. Long lead time purchasing.	Repetitive, high-volume manufacturing. Stable demand.
Problem visibility	Not visible	Visible
Stress to improve	Little	Much
Problems found from	Computer reports	Shop floor

Source: Professor Arthur V. Hill

8.5.1.2 Pull system

Control of moving the work rests with the following operation; each work station pulls the output from the preceding station as it is needed. Output of the final operation is pulled by customer demand or the master schedule. Thus in pull system, work is moved in response to demand from the next stage in the process.

There is yet another theory called TOC or Theory of Constraints which is not as popular as JIT. Some of its features are being discussed in the next section for the readers.

8.6 REQUIREMENTS FOR SUCCESSFUL IMPLEMENTATION OF JIT

For JIT to be successful the following requirements must be met:

1. The environment has to support it.
2. The most appropriate way to implement JIT is to do it step by step.
3. A hybrid model (traditional + JIT) is the most appropriate. If JIT fails, the traditional model will be used as a fallback position.
4. A flexible management system is essential. The private sector is usually more compatible.
5. Key elements of the JIT system must be in place. They are:
   (*i*) Close ties with few reliable suppliers.
   (*ii*) Low inventories of raw materials, work-in-process inventories and finished goods.
   (*iii*) Appropriate material handling system, so that there won't be work-in-process inventories.
   (*iv*) Small lot sizes with shorter lead times.
   (*v*) Low cost set-up times.

8.7 GOALS OF JIT MANUFACTURING SYSTEM

JIT is about doing the simple things well, and gradually doing them better and it is about developing competence and simplification in the way we do things. In addition to this, it is also about squeezing out waste every step of the way. Generally, JIT manufacturing seeks to achieve the following goals:

1. To produce the required quality or zero defects. In manufacturing, traditionally people thought that zero defects producing was not possible because of the fact that people thought that at some level of production it would be no longer be possible to produce without defects. Also despite there were defects, the product did reach customers expectation. With the aim of JIT there will be no longer any cause of a defect and therefore all products will meet more than the expectations. This is also related to a part of quality management.

An approach to quality control that starts from the premise that if quality cannot be built into the process, then the only way to ensure that no defective products are passed on to the customer (downstream process) is to inspect every part made.

In a Just-in-time environment where waiting for an inspector would be intolerable, the alternatives are self-inspection and error proofing. Inspection at source also improves the likelihood of discovering the root cause of the problem so it can be eliminated.

Each individual and function involved in the manufacturing system must, therefore, accept the responsibility for the quality level of its products. Traditional companies believe quality is costly, defects are caused by workers, and the minimum level of quality that can satisfy the customer is enough. Companies practicing the JIT believe quality leads to lower costs, than systems cause most defects, and that quality can be improved within the Kaizen framework. This concept introduces the correction of the problem before many other defective units have been completed.

2. Zero set-up time. Reducing the set-up times leads to a more predictable production. No set-up time also leads to a shorter production time/production cycle, and less inventories.

To effectively implement a low inventory system, the common practice of lot sizing through the economic order quantity model must be forgotten. Therefore, the time to set up for a different product in the line needed to be significantly reduced. Innovative designs and changeover techniques are critical.

3. To produce the required items or zero inventories. Inventories, including work-in-progress, finished goods and sub-assemblies, have to be reduced to zero. There will be no sub-assemblies, no work-in-progress and no finished goods. This means a different view than in traditional manufacturing, where inventories are seen as a buffer against a fluctuating demand, or as a buffer against non-reliable suppliers. Also, in traditional manufacturing inventory was built up to make sure expensive machines were running for full capacity, because only then the hourly costs were as low as possible.

In JIT, the inventory is minimized and thus, throughput and cycle times improved significantly. Also, through elimination of large inventories, huge space savings are realized because there is no need for large warehouses.

4. Zero handling. Zero handling in JIT means eliminating all non-value adding activities. So, zero-handling means reducing (by redesigning) non-value adding activities.

5. Zero lead-time. Lead time is the time between ordering a product and receiving it. The time taken to process orders, order parts, manufacture goods, store, pick and dispatch goods all impact the customer lead-time.

Zero lead-time is a result of the usage of small lots and increases the flexibility of the system. When there are no lead times, the possibility to make planning which do not rely on forecasts becomes bigger and bigger. The JIT philosophy recognizes that in some markets it is impossible to have zero lead-times, but makes clear that when a firm focuses on reducing lead-times, this firm can manufacture in the same market.

6. Enable Productivity in Diversified Small-Quantity Production. With every customer desiring a customized product, diversity is extremely important. Many product variations can be made on a single line, with short changeover times.

7. Reducing Manufacturing Cost. Designing products that facilitate and ease manufacturing processes. This will help to reduce the cost of manufacturing and building the product to specifications. One aspect in designing products for manufacturability is the need to establish a good employer and employee relationship. This is to cultivate and tap the resources of the production experts (production floor employee), and the line employees to develop cost saving solutions. Participatory quality programs utilize employee knowledge about their job functions and review the department performance, encouraging with rewards for suggested cost saving solutions.

8. Jidohka (automation with a human touch). Technological advancements needed to be taken advantage of along with improving worker skill level, without sacrificing employee morale.

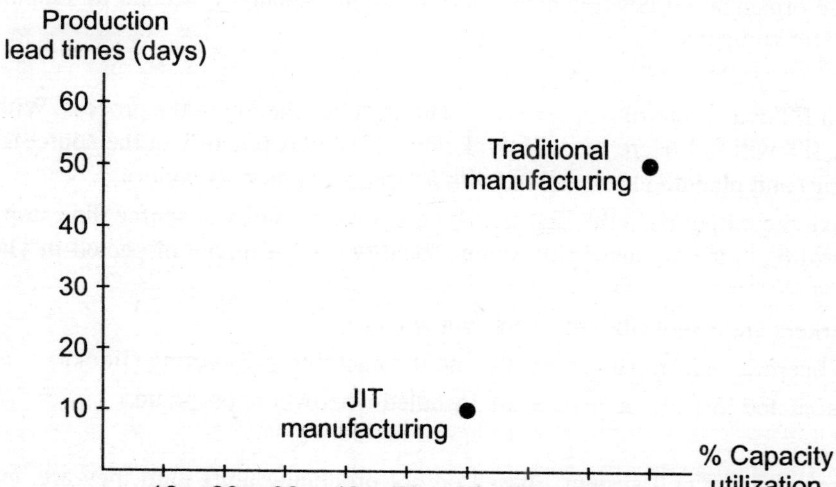

Figure 8.5. Relationship between Traditional and JIT Manufacturing.

Increasing production capacity reduces manufacturing lead times. Only slight increases in production capacities can lead to:

- Significant reduction of manufacturing lead times
- Significant reduction of work-in-process inventory

Generally, today's manufacturing environment requires greatly increased product diversity, reduced product life cycles and greatly enhanced customer expectations in terms of quality and delivery lead time. Therefore, production managers need to look at product lead times and seeking to reduce them to the absolute minimum.

8.7.1 IMPORTANT ASPECTS IN JIT MANUFACTURING

People

JIT has influence in ordering, scheduling and producing sides of a manufacturing firm. This influence in the manufacturing firm depends on employees, suppliers or customers. They are the ones on which the JIT-principle is relying. This results in a well known quote: "It is the people that make JIT work" [Roger B. Brooks]. Manufacturers put a large element of training in the JIT to reach to the following goals:

- **Mutual trust and team work**: When managers and workers see each other as equal, committed to the organization and its success, they are more willing to cooperate with each other in order to find the problems and solve these problems.
- **Empowerment of the workers:** A firm which empowers its workers gives its workers the authority to solve problems on their own. When this is done, workers have the authority to stop production to solve problems instead of first waiting for guidance from the above. The objective of worker empowerment is having workers involved in problem solving at the shop floor level.

JIT is a *total* system, which means that all company members work towards improvement goals. If only some of the members are involved, then only some of the problems will be solved. It is on this aspect of JIT that another Japanese idea - total quality - most closely impacts. Total quality is used here to describe the organization development (OD), or culture changes, needed to support development into the excellent company.

Quality

Quality within JIT-manufacturing is necessary and must be inherent in the process. Without high quality standards, JIT will fail. Here we will think about JIDOKA (Quality at the source), POKA YOKE (Error proofing) and plan do check action, with its statistical process control.

To make the output right the first time by employing quality at source, line stop and fool proof devices. According to the Japanese philosophy, "quality is built-in, not inspected-in"[Jack Byrd et al]. Therefore,

- Workers are responsible for their own works.
- An operator can stop an assembly line if something goes wrong (Jidoka).
- Automated inspection devices are installed wherever appropriate.

Techniques

The JIT-technique is a "pull system", based on not producing units until they are needed. The well known kanban card is used as a signal to produce. A number of core techniques are used to attack waste across a broad front. It is the combined effect of applying these techniques which makes JIT such a formidable competitive weapon. The whole is greater than the parts.

JIT manufacturing techniques include using the smallest possible machine, putting away everything that is not needed, arranging things in the best possible way, and *jidoka*, the stopping of the production line when abnormal conditions occur.

Integration

Integrated Process Control (IPC) achieves the goals of **JIT** manufacturing by optimizing production to meet both manufacturer and customer requirements. In IPC, two concepts control the process of continual improvement. They are:

- First, the process of continual improvement is directed toward producing product of quality at low cost.
- The second concept is that customers needs have to be continually monitored since they change regularly.

The development of an IPC system is based on understanding these two requirements and combining them into a single system.

JIT integration can be found in following points of JIT manufacturing firm:

Management and Labor Responsibilities: Decision-making and communications are generally associated with inefficiencies in a company. Problems with communications include ambiguity in the interpretation of the requirement and failure to specify the requirement. To allow employees to contribute to the decision-making cycle requires changes. IPC reduces the involvement of management but increase the involvement of production line supervision and production workers.

The Role of Other Functions in Process Control (PC): PC is improving the production process by continual improvement. In manufacturing, production would seem to be the function responsible for PC. However, the action or lack of action of functions outside of production can influence production.

The production function: Productions responsibility to a company is to minimize the cost of manufacturing and provide product that meets customer requirements. Integrating quality into production is a priority in a competitive market.

The Engineering Function: Engineering's responsibility in PC is to design for customer requirements and product production requirements. To satisfy a customer's need is just as important as designing a product using top production technology.

The purchasing function: The responsibility of the purchasing function is to ensure that the required materials are available at the proper quality level, on time, and at a fair price. *The sales function* provides most of the information on a customer's needs and requirements that are used by engineers to determine product specification and configuration.

8.7.2 ADVANTAGES AND DISADVANTAGES OF JIT

Advantages of JIT

Advocates of JIT claim it is a revolutionary concept that all manufacturers will have to adopt in order to remain competitive [Marc L. Songini]. JIT encompasses the successful execution of all production activities required to produce a product, from designing to delivery. Its benefits are many:

1. Shortened lead time.
2. Reduced time spent on non-process work.
3. Eliminate waste and rework and consequently reduce requirements for raw materials, person, power and machine capacity
4. It increases worker motivation and teamwork.
5. Reduced inventory. As a result:
   - Frees up working capital for other projects.
   - Less space is needed.
   - Customer responsiveness increases.

6. Reduce or eliminate setup times
7. Reduce lot sizes (manufacturing and purchase): reducing setup times allows economical production of smaller lots; close cooperation with suppliers is necessary to achieve reductions in order lot sizes for purchased items, since this will require more frequent deliveries.
8. Problem clarification.
9. Cost savings
   (*a*) ***Materials Cost Savings*:** Materials cost savings is basically the reduction of costs incorporated with purchasing, receiving, inspection, and stockroom costs. Elements in Materials Cost Saving are:
   - Reduction of Suppliers
   - Long-term Contracts
   - Reduce Order Scheduling
   - Simplify Receiving Systems
   - Eliminate unpacking
   - Eliminate Inspection
   - Eliminate inventory Stocking
   - Eliminate Excess Material.

   (*b*) ***Manufacturing Cost Savings*:** Manufacturing cost savings identifies saving in the engineering, production, and the quality control activities. A major part of manufacturing cost savings is keeping a high level of quality, quality reduces cost and increases revenue.

   (*c*) ***Sales Cost Savings*:** Sales cost saving comes in the form of reducing overlap between the supplier and the customer, which is inspection and testing. The most effective situation that the sales department can establish is finding customers that also use JIT systems.
10. Total product cycle time drops.
11. Product quality improved.
12. Reduced scrap and rework
13. Smoother production flow
14. Less inventory, of raw materials, work-in-progress and finished goods.
15. Higher productivity
16. Higher worker participation
17. More skilled workforce, able and willing to switch roles
18. Reduced space requirement
19. Improved relationships with suppliers

Disadvantages of JIT

There are often a number of barriers that also have to be overcome to achieve the final goal.

- The JIT method demands a much disciplined assembly-line process. The entire factory has to be in sync to successfully exploit its methods. Manufacturers can afford fewer errors in the delivery of the supplier's component; if a part isn't there, the assembly line stops, and that can result in the loss of manpower and cash.

- Changes in production planning, inaccurate forecasting procedures resulting in under or over forecasting of demand, equipment failures creating capacity problems and employee absenteeism all create problems in implementing JIT.
- JIT requires special training and the reorganization of policies and procedures.
- The organizational cultures vary from firm to firm. There are some cultures that tie to JIT success but it is difficult for an organization to change its cultures within a short time.
- Difference in implementation of JIT. Because JIT was originally established in Japan, the benefits may vary.
- Resistance to change. JIT involves a change throughout the whole organization, but human nature resists changing. The most common resistances are emotional resistance and rational resistance. Emotional resistances are those psychological feeling which hinder performance such as anxiety. Rational resistance is the deficient of the needed information for the workers to perform the job well.
- JIT requires workers to be multi-skilled and flexible to change.

Some more modern ideas are discussed in the following section. This new concept is known as the 'Theory of Constraints' or TOC.

8.8 THEORY OF CONSTRAINTS (TOC)

A business book written as a novel, The Goal by Dr. Eliyahu Goldratt explains the principles of the TOC through a series of personal and business scenarios.

8.8.1 SYSTEMS THINKING

Fundamentally, **TOC looks at problems from a system level**, in contrast to some quality methods that are focused on *specific processes.* When improving a system, one *must look at the goal of the system,* and then what *constrains it from achieving the goal.* The goal of a business is to make money, now and in the future. The constraint can be viewed as its weakest link, and a system can have only one weakest link at any given time. TOC helps us find and manage that weakest link. In other words, improvement activity anywhere else does little to improve the overall strength of the system. In fact, strengthening a non-weak link could further strain the weakest link to the point of breaking the system. How's that for focus!.

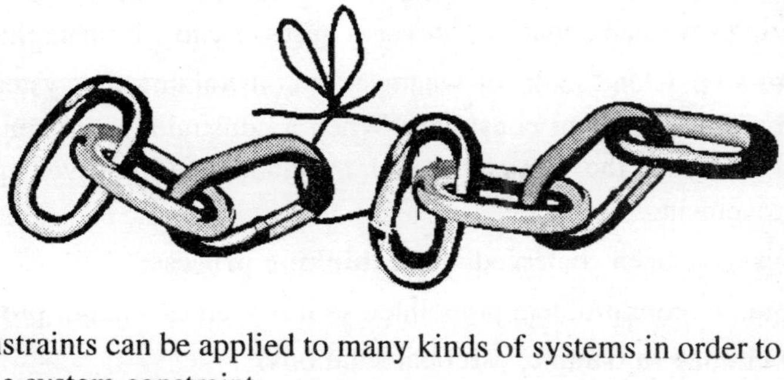

Theory of Constraints can be applied to many kinds of systems in order to uncover and manage the weakest link or the system constraint.

For example, in the following production system, *what is the maximum output per day? Where is the weakest link?*

(*i*) Input ⇒ [18 units/day] ⇒ [20/day] ⇒ [10/day] ⇒ [Market demand 15]

In the system below, *what is the maximum output per day? Where is the weakest link?*

(*ii*) Input ⇒ [18 units/day] ⇒ [20/day] ⇒ [20/day] ⇒ [Market demand 15]

In the first example, *the maximum output per day is 10 units because that is the most Step 3 can produce.* But even if we add a second machine to Step 3 effectively doubling its output, the system can only produce 15 units per day. *The market can only accept 15* units and even though it is now an external constraint, if the goal is to make money, then revenue must be created by selling the finished unit in the market. *If market demand is saturated and the unit goes into finished goods inventory, it has not been converted to money and the goal has not been achieved.* Because each step is subject to interdependence and variability, it is important that the system be stabilized using SPC, and the average output of the non-constraints be kept slightly greater than the average of the weakest link, in order to prevent starving the constraint and losing system throughput.

The system optimum is not the sum of the local optima. *Do not attempt to optimize every step of the system, as this will sub-optimize the whole system.* This is because work-in-process will accumulate, wasting resources like cash flow and floor space. Further, improvements on the weakest link can cause it to shift elsewhere and it may not become visible until something new goes wrong. *The key is to manage the system by having knowledge of the system.*

System constraints can be either physical or policy. Policy constraints are more difficult to identify but managing them can lead to bigger improvements.

8.8.2 FIVE FOCUSING STEPS OF TOC

To concentrate improvement efforts, these steps will have the greatest impact:

1. **Identify the system constraint:** Where is the weakest link? Is it physical or policy?
2. **Decide how to exploit the constraint:** How can we get the most out of the constraint without spending a lot of money? Manage all non-constraints to supply only enough that constraint can use.
3. **Subordinate everything else to the above decision** to reduce their limiting impact. Tune the rest of the system (some steps up, some steps down) to enable the constraint to operate at its maximum effectiveness.
4. **Elevate the constraint:** If steps 2 and 3 have not removed the constraint, consider more substantial improvements to do whatever is necessary to eliminate the constraint.
5. **Go back to step 1**, and look for whatever is constraining the system now. Do not allow inertia to become a system constraint. When a constraint is broken, review policies that came from or caused the former constraint. Standardize improvements and engage in on-going improvement.

These five steps have been coalesced into a **thinking process:**

- **What to change** (core problem pinpointed so it is seen as a major problem)
- **To what to change to** (simple, practical solutions)
- **How to cause the change** (induce appropriate people to invent such solutions)

8.8.3 THE FIVE LAYERS OF RESISTANCE

- We don't have that problem.
- The proposed solution doesn't work.
- There would be negative effects if we did it.
- There are obstacles to implementing it.
- Others must be convinced first (I don't want to be the only one doing it).

8.8.4 QUANTIFYING THE IMPROVEMENT

To measure the effects of improvements on the system, Goldratt uses three measures:

- **Throughput (T):** The rate at which the entire system generates money through sales.
- **Inventory (I):** All the money the system invests in things it intends to sell. This includes materials, equipment (it can be sold later to generate money), but not depreciation.
- **Operating Expense (OE):** The money the system spends converting inventory into throughput. This includes labor, utilities, depreciation, etc.

To know if a local improvement will improve the system, determine if it will increase throughput, or decrease inventory or operating expense without reducing throughput. If it will, then proceed with the improvement. Theoretically, I and OE cannot be reduced below zero, so their long-term contribution to the organization is limited. Throughput, on the other hand, has much more upside potential, being constrained only by how much can be sold in the market. Quality Function Deployment (QFD) is one method to improve market sales by producing better products. New Lanchester Strategy is one method we will study to increase market share.

8.9 TOC TOOLS

We will discuss the following TOC tools in this section:

- *Current Reality Tree (CRT)*
- Conflict Resolution Diagram (CRD)
- Future Reality Tree (FRT)
- Pre-Requisite Tree (PRT)
- Transition Tree (TT)

8.9.1 CURRENT REALITY TREE (CRT)

This tool examines the cause and effect logic behind the undesirable effects (UDE) in our system. It helps identify the system constraint or what to change. It helps people agree on what is the problem. People making CRT must have knowledge of the system.

- Start with 5-10 undesirable effects to ID core problem.
- Select any two and connect with arrow showing which causes which. When multiple causes lead to a result, link their arrows with an ellipse (like an 'AND' gate in logic). No ellipse indicates 'OR'.
- Insufficiency: if needed, add intermediary stages between arrows to clarify.
- Connect other UDEs to tree already created. Add other missing elements. Loops are ok.
- Trace arrows back to root cause. If more than 70% of UDEs connect, it is probably the root cause (as shown in yellow).

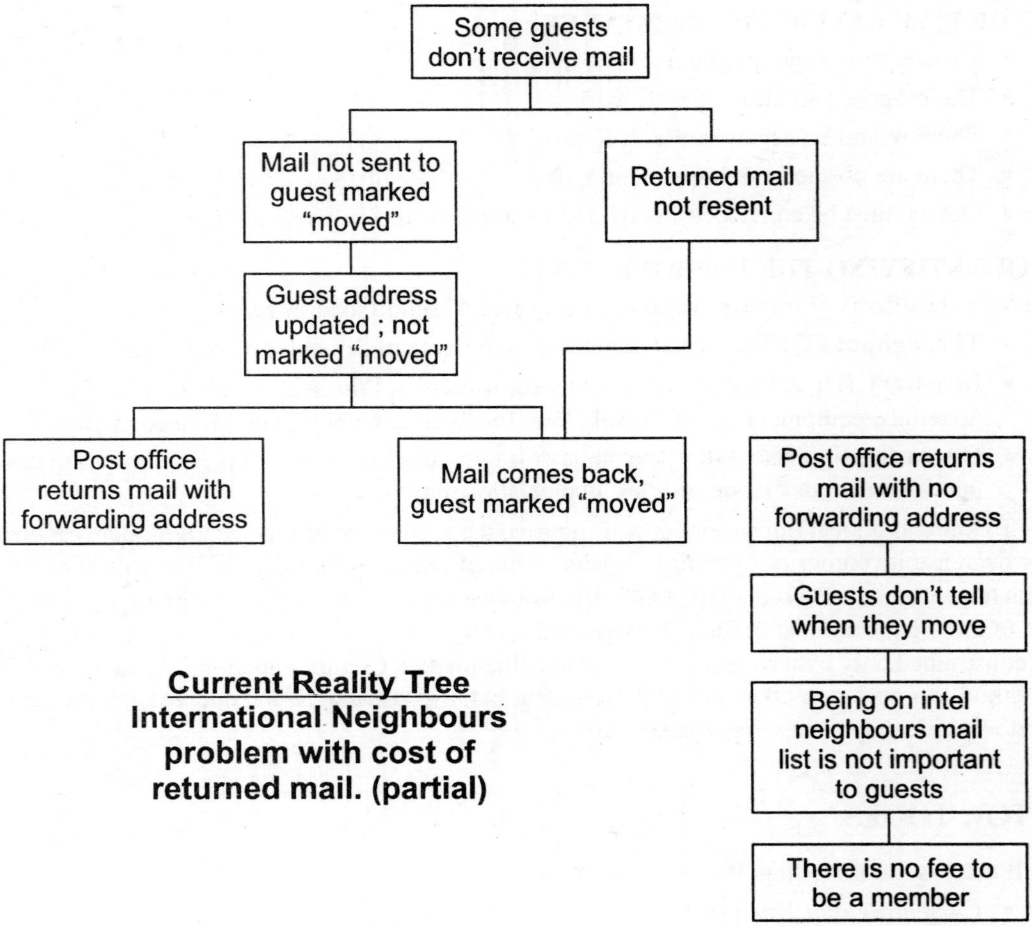

Figure 8.6. Current Reality Tree.

8.9.2 CONFLICT RESOLUTION DIAGRAM (CRD) OR EVAPORATING CLOUD

It reveals hidden conflicts and underlying assumptions behind the UDEs. It can lead to breakthrough solutions. It helps us begin to answer what to change to. This helps people agree on the direction of a solution that will work. Write on sticky-notes. People making CRD must have knowledge of the system.

1. Start with conflicting prerequisites.
2. Identify requirements prerequisites are trying to satisfy.
3. Identify objective of having both requirements.
4. Develop underlying assumptions of all arrows. Because...
5. Create 'injections' or actions to neutralize conflict. Select best one and validate.
6. If objective is clear from the beginning, but implementation is difficult, Steps 1-3 may be reversed.

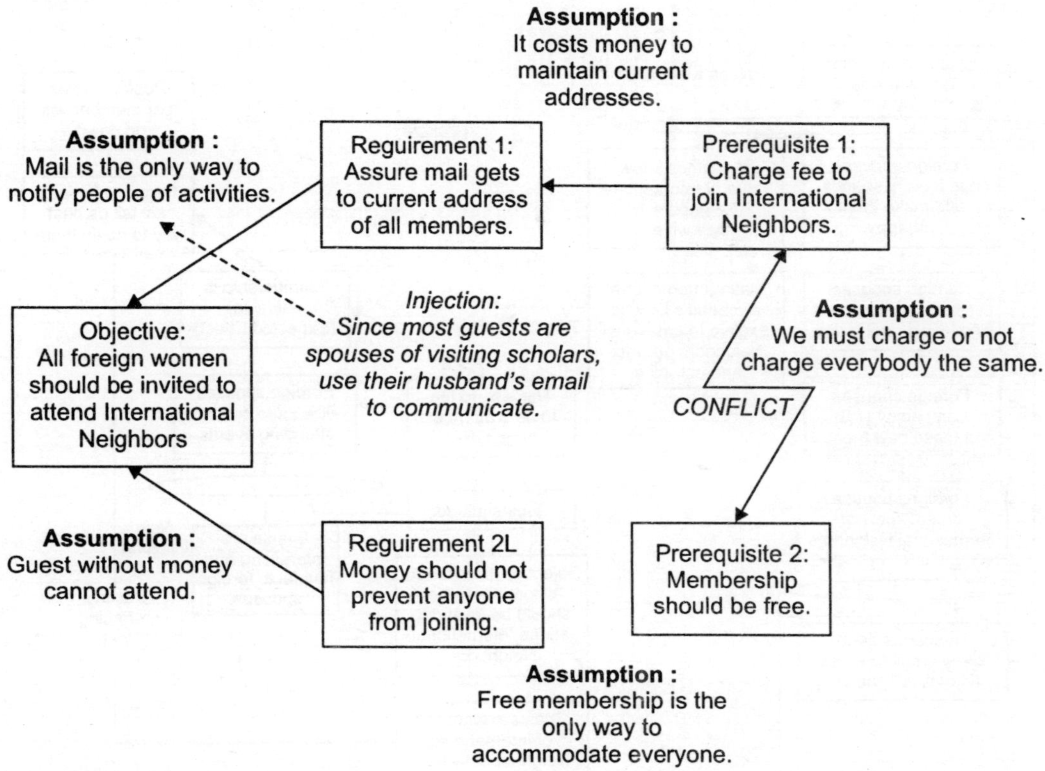

Conflict Resolution Diagram for how to assure notification of International Neighbor events without incurring high mailing costs to keep addresses up-to-date.

Figure 8.7. Conflict Resolution Diagram.

8.9.3 FUTURE REALITY TREE (FRT)

Use this to confirm the solution and to identify potential negative side effects. This finishes the answer to what to change to. This helps remove negative effects and helps people see solution will work. Write on sticky-notes and number. People making FRT must have knowledge of the system:

- Positively rephrase core problem from CRT into Desirable Effect (DE). Place at top.
- Place current reality (top of CRT) and injections from CRD at the bottom and objective from CRD in the middle. Multiple injections are ok.
- Build tree upward from injections to objectives to DEs, adding additional injections and statements to build a logical bridge to objectives.
- Look for Positive Reinforcing Loops.
- Add a Negative Branch, from the original injection to undesirable effects. At point where injection turns negative, look for underlying assumptions and try new injections to "trim" these negative branches.

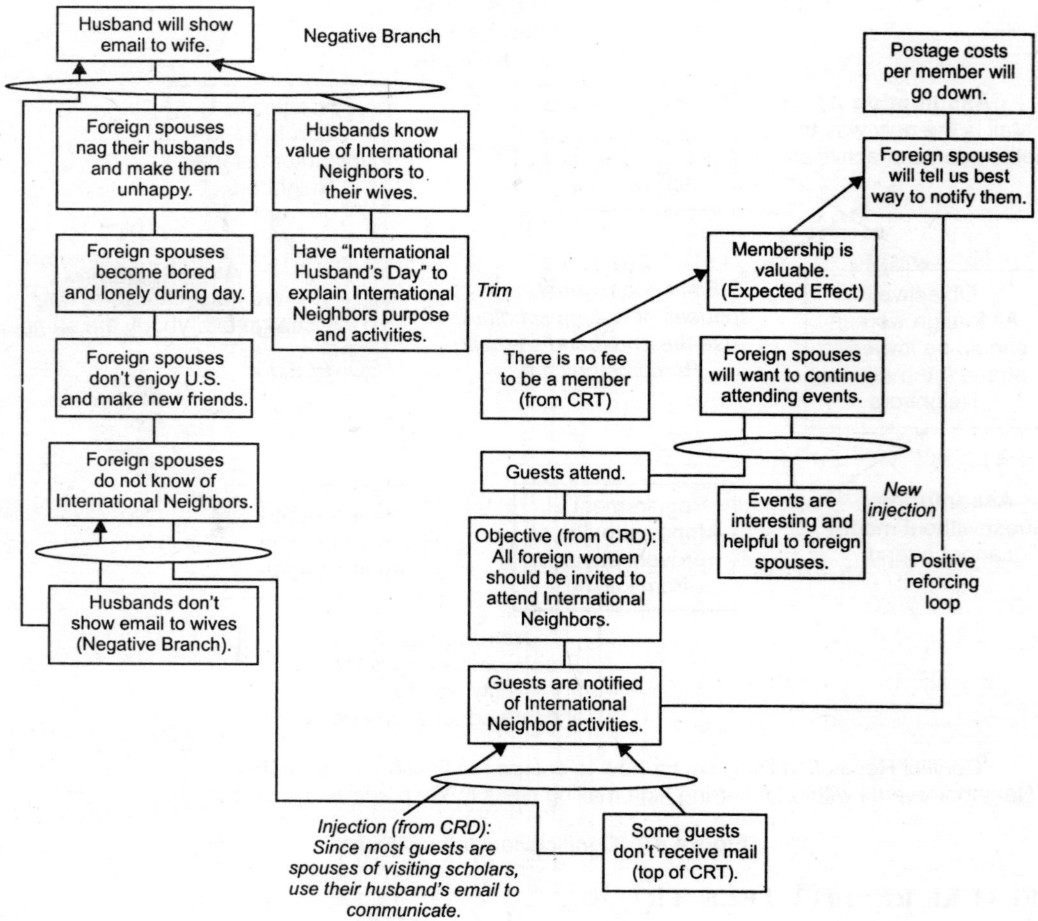

Figure 8.8. Future Reality Tree.

8.9.4 PREREQUISITE TREE (PRT)

This is used to outline how to cause the change. It helps identify obstacles, sequence, and milestones. This helps see obstacles to overcome in implementing the solution. Write on sticky-notes and number. People making PRT must have knowledge of the system.

- Write objective at the top.
- Raise obstacles (OBS) and attach intermediate objectives (IO) to overcome them. (CRD can be used.)
- Arrange obstacles and IOs in time sequence and connect to each other and to objective.
- Arrange so that IOs will remove obstacles to implementation.

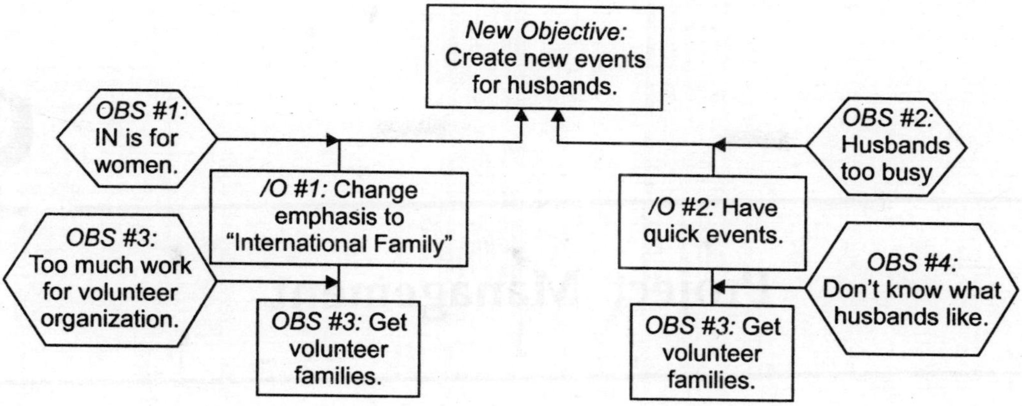

Figure 8.9. Prerequisite Tree.

8.9.5 TRANSITION TREE (TT)

Detailed step-by-step implementation of the solution. This is used to cause the change. This helps see the plan of action for overcoming obstacles and implementing the change. Write on sticky-notes and number. People making TT must have knowledge of the system.

- Place your objective at the top of the page.
- Group each current reality, desired effect, and an action to achieve the effect. Arrange from bottom to top in implementation sequence.
- These three items should lead to the next effect, which is grouped with its current reality and next action.
- Continue upeard until the objective is reached. Continue downward until you get the first action to be taken.

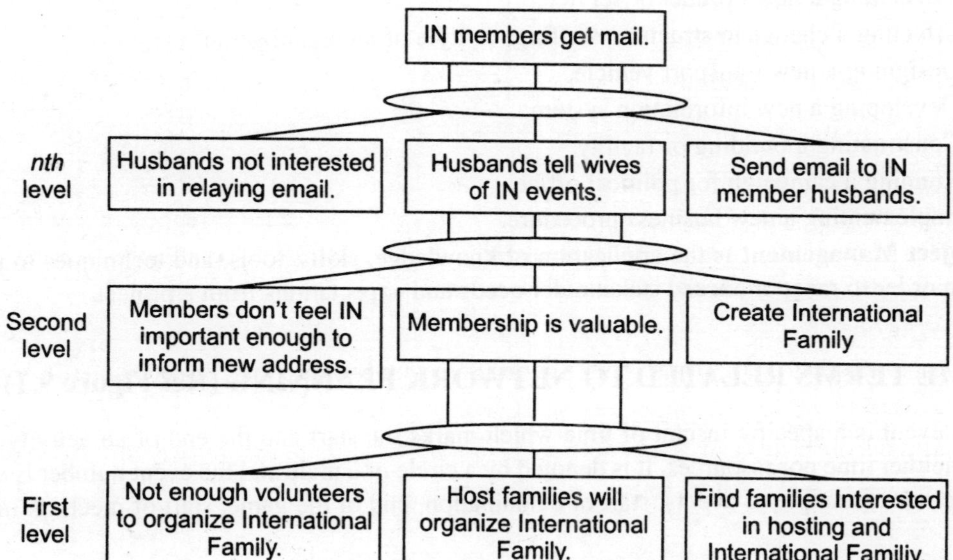

Figure 8.10. Transition tree.

9

Project Management

9.0 INTRODUCTION

A project is a *temporary* endeavor undertaken to create a *unique product* or service. We call it *temporary* because every project has a definite beginning and a definite end. *Temporary* does not necessarily mean short in duration; many projects last for several years. In every case, however, the duration of a project is finite. Projects are not ongoing efforts. In addition, temporary does not generally apply to the product or service created by the project. Most projects create a lasting result. For example, a project to erect a national monument will create a result expected to last for centuries. *Unique* means that the product or service is different in some distinguishing way from all similar products or services. For example, a Professor may be teaching a subject repeatedly for many semesters but every time the students are different, or he may be using a different style of teaching or examples to explain the subject to the students. That way, every time the Professor is facing a new challenge, and a new project in itself. Some **examples of** Projects are:

- Developing a new product or service.
- Effecting a change in structure, staffing, or style of an organization.
- Designing a new transport vehicle.
- Developing a new information system.
- Constructing a building or facility.
- Running a campaign for political office.
- Implementing a new business procedure.

Project Management is the application of knowledge, skills, tools, and techniques to project activities in order to meet or exceed stakeholder needs and expectations from a project.

9.1 SOME TERMS RELATED TO NETWORK PLANNING (Ref Figure 9.1)

Event: An event is a specific instant of time which marks the start and the end of an activity. Event consumes neither time nor resources. It is denoted by a circle or a node and the event number is written within the circle. Example of events: start of examination, end of the game, start of meeting, meeting ended, etc.

Activity: A project consists of different types of tasks or jobs to be performed. These jobs or tasks are called activities. An activity may be a process, a material handling or material procurement cycle. Examples of activities: Laying the foundation of a building, process of writing examination, arranging for bank loans, etc. An activity is shown by an arrow and it begins and ends with an event. Unlike event, an activity consumes time and resources. An activity is denoted by *a*, *b*, *c*, etc. which is marked below the arrow and estimated time to accomplish the activity is written above the arrow.

Dummy activity: When two activities start at the same instant of time (like activities *b* and *c* in Figure 9.1), the head events are joined by a dotted arrow-known as a dummy activity. A dummy activity does not consume time. It may be critical or non-critical. It becomes a critical activity when its earliest start time (EST) is same as its latest finishing time (LFT).

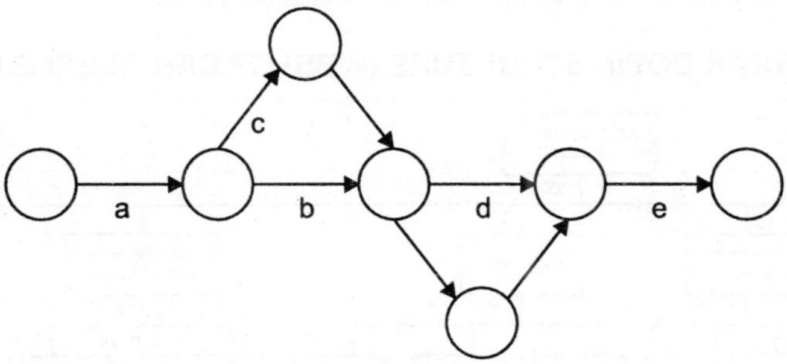

Figure 9.1. An Example of A Network Diagram.

Critical activities: An activity is called critical if its earliest start time plus the time taken by it is equal to the latest finishing time. In a network diagram, critical activities are those which if consume more than their estimated time, the project will be delayed. A critical activity in a network diagram is denoted by a thick arrow to distinguish it from a non-critical activity.

Critical path: Critical path (CP) is formed by critical activities. A CP is the longest path and consumes the maximum time. A CP has zero float. A dummy activity joining two critical activities is also a critical activity. Any amount of delay on CP will delay the entire project by the same amount. So, a CP re.

Subprojects: Projects are frequently divided into more manageable smaller projects which are called subprojects. Subprojects are often contracted out to an external enterprise or to another functional unit in the performing organization. Examples of subprojects include:

- A single project phase.
- The installation of plumbing or electrical fixtures on a construction project.
- Automated resting of computer programs.

Work Breakdown Structure (WBS): WBS represents a systematic and logical breakdown of the project into its component parts. It is constructed by dividing the project into major parts, with each of these being further divided into sub-parts. This is continued till a breakdown is done in terms of manageable units of work for which responsibility can be defined.

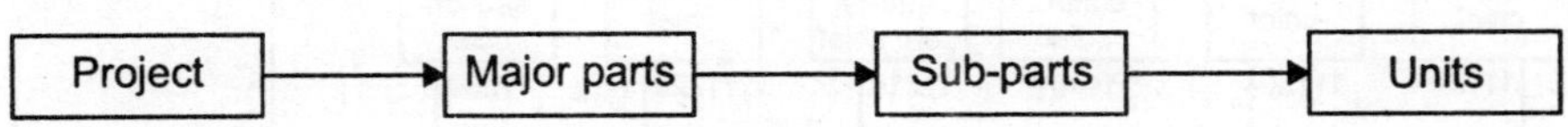

WBS is a *deliverable* oriented grouping of project elements which organizes and defines the total scope of the project. Each descending level represents an increasingly detailed definition of a project component which may be products or services. WBS helps in:

- Effective planning by dividing the work into manageable elements which can be planned, budgeted, and controlled.

- Assignment of responsibility for work elements to project personnel and outside agencies.
- Development of control and information system.

Organization Breakdown Structure (OBS)

OBS represents formally how the project personnel and outside agencies are going to work for the project. To assign responsibility for the tasks mentioned, the WBS has to be integrated with project organization structure or the OBS.

Example 9.1. An industrialist is planning to have a car assembly plant in a remote area of India. He wants you to prepare WBS and OBS to realize the completion of this car assembly project.

WORK BREAK DOWN STRUCTURE (WBS) OF CAR ASSEMBLY PLANT

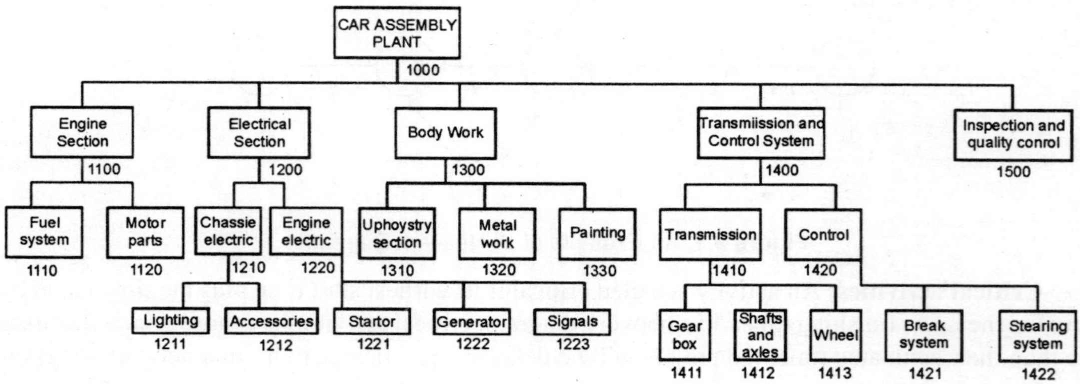

Figure 9.2a. An Example of WBS.

ORGANIZATION BREAKDOWN STRUCTURE (OBS) FOR A CAR ASSEMBLY PLANT

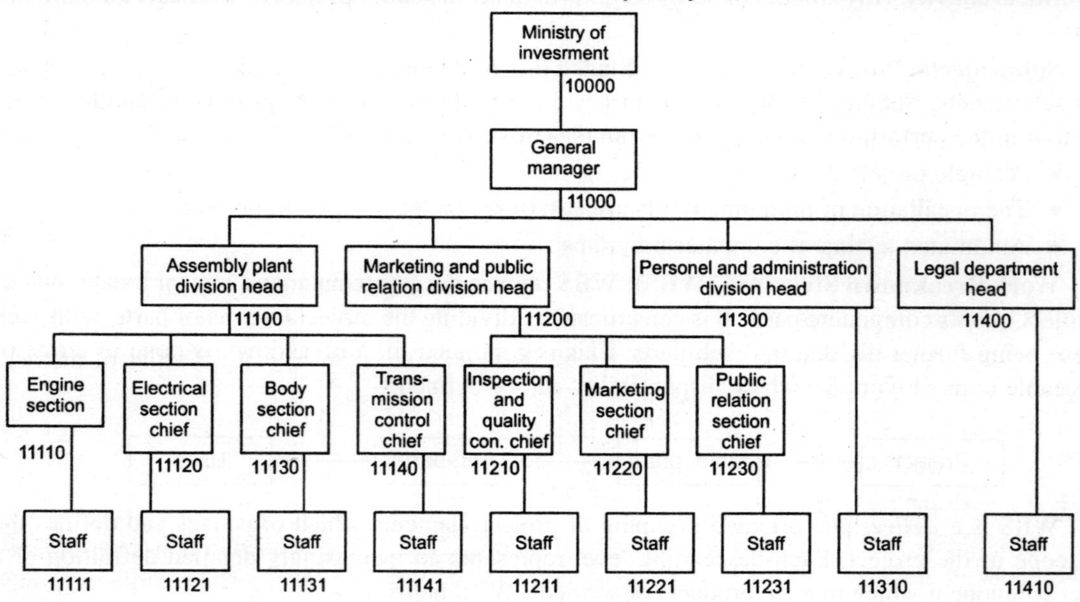

Figure 9.2b. An Example of OBS.

9.2 CPM AND PERT MODEL

Notations: t_p = pessimistic time

t_o = optimistic time

t_m = most likely time

t_e = expected time of an activity

T_e = expected length of the project

σ_t = standard deviation of time

V_t = variance of time

EST = early start time of an event

LFT = late finish time of an event

t_{ij} = time duration needed to complete the job ij

CPM stands for C*ritical Path Method.* It has mostly been used in deterministic situations like construction projects. For the most part, houses, bridges, and skyscrapers use standard materials whose properties are well known. They employ more or less standard components and stable technology. Changes occur mainly in design, size, shapes, and arrangements of different components- rather than in design concepts. CPM takes just one time into account, and it deals with deterministic situation. It is activity oriented and can be used for both large and small projects. It is widely recognized and is the most versatile and potent management planning technique. CPM is used for planning and controlling the most logical and economic sequence of operations for accomplishing a project.

CPM Technique

CPM follows the following steps for accomplishing a project planning:

- Break down the project into various activities systematically.
- Label all activities.
- Arrange all the activities in logical sequence.
- Construct the arrow diagram.
- Number all the nodes (events) and activities.
- Find the time for each activity.
- Mark the activity times on the arrow diagram.
- Calculate early and late, start and finishing times.
- Tabulate various times and mark EST and LFT on the arrow diagram.
- Calculate the total project duration.
- If it is intended to reduce the total project duration. Crash the critical activities of the network.
- Optimize the cost.
- Update the Network.
- Smooth the network resources.

PERT is Program Evaluation and Review Technique. This is mostly used in non-deterministic or probabilistic or stochastic situations such as: space research, R & D projects. These projects (going to Mars, Moon, etc) are relatively new; their technology is rapidly changing, and their products are nonstandard. There is some standard hardware in ICBMs (Inter-continental Ballistic Missiles) and lunar rockets, but much of their design and construction needs new type of materials and technology, and projects are contracted, planned, and scheduled before all technological problems have been solved.

Thus, there is a large amount of uncertainty in design, construction, and configuration of the new weapons systems and spaceships. There is little past history on which to base network construction and time estimates.

PERT was first used in 1957 for the planning and control of the Polaris Missiles program in US navy with a goal to finish the project two years in advance.

- PERT is commonly used to conduct the initial review of a project .It is very useful device to plan the time and resources.
- PERT is used in activity where timings could not be estimated with enough certainty. It can be employed at those places where a project cannot be easily defined in terms of time or resources required.
- However, events can be readily defined which means it is known that, first, part A will be manufactured, only then subassembly S can be built, and so on.
- PERT offers a lot of advantages for non-repetitive type of projects, R & D, prototype production, space research,.defense projects, etc.
- Because of the uncertainty of activity timings, PERT fits into a probabilistic model. Probability concept helps in estimating activity timings. The statistical probability feature of PERT foretells the probability of reaching the specified target dates.
- PERT is mainly concerned with events and is thus seen as an event oriented system.

PERT Techniques

The PERT planning technique consists of the following steps:

- The project is broken down into different activities systematically.
- Activities are arranged in logical sequence.
- The network diagram is drawn. Events and activities are numbered.
- Using three time estimate, the expected time for each activity is calculated.
- Standard deviation and variance for each activity are computed.
- Earliest starting times, and latest finishing times are calculated.
- Expected time, earliest starting time, and latest finishing times are marked on the network diagram.
- Slack is calculated.
- Critical path(s) are identified and marked on the network diagram.
- Length of critical path or total project duration is found out.
- Lastly, the probability that the project will finish at due date is calculated.

9.2.1 TIME ESTIMATES IN PERT

To take care of uncertainty, PERT takes three time estimates into account: *optimistic, most likely, and pessimistic time.* PERT time estimates follow beta distribution.

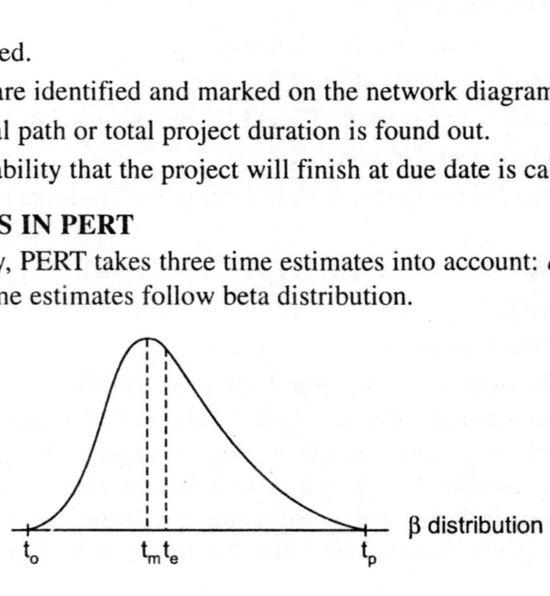

Optimistic time(to): This is the shortest time taken by an activity if everything goes exceptionally well.

Most likely time(tm): It is the time in which the activity is normally expected to complete under normal contingencies.

Pessimistic time (tp): It is the maximum time that would be required to complete the activity if bad luck were encountered at every turn. This does not include catastrophes like earthquakes, floods, fires, etc.

These time estimates are not always easy to prepare, but together they give useful information about the expected uncertainties of an activity. For standard activities, the three time estimates should not vary much from each other. But the greater the uncertainty of an activity, the wider will be the range of the estimated completion times.

PERT calculates the expected value of duration as a weighted average of three time estimates. It assumes that to and tp are equally likely to occur, and tm is four times more likely to occur than the other two. Hence, the expected time

$$t_e = (t_o + 4t_m + t_p)/6$$

The expected time is the time that we would expect if the activity were repeated a large number of times. But in reality, activities do not get repeated many times; they usually occur just once.

9.2.2 ALGORITHM USED IN CALCULATING CRITICAL PATH

There are two methods for computing the critical path. They are:

(*a*) Forward pass, and

(*b*) Backward pass

Algorithms for two are given below:

(*a*) **Forward pass**

S = start time of the project (usually = 0)

ET_i = S for all beginning events

$$ET_j = \max_i \{ ET_i + t_{ij} \},$$

where the maximization is over all the events i that precede event *j*

T = max {ET(all events)}, which is the earliest finish time for the project.

(*b*) **Backward pass**

LT_j = T for all ending events

$$LT_i = \min_j \{ LT_j - t_{ij} \},$$

where the minimization is over all the events *j* that succeed event *i*.

The relationship between activity and event times is summarized as follows:

$$ES_{ij} = ET_i$$
$$EF_{ij} = ET_i + t_{ij}$$
$$LF_{ij} = LT_j$$
$$LS_{ij} = LT_j - t_{ij}$$

$$TS_{ij} = LT_j - ET_i - t_{ij}$$
$$FS_{ij} = ET_j - ET_i - t_i = TS_{ij} - LT_j + ET_j$$

where ES = Earliest start, EF = Earliest first, LS = Latest start, LF = Latest first, TS = Total slack, FS = Free slack.

9.3 VARIABILITY OF ACTIVITY TIMES

If the time required for an activity is highly variable (*i.e.*, if the range of our estimates is very large), then we will be less confident of the average value we calculate than if the range were narrower. *Standard deviation* and variance are commonly used in statistics as measures of variability among the numbers. The variance is the average squared difference of all numbers from their mean value. If the three time estimates are 3, 4, and 8 weeks, then their mean is 5, and **variance** = $\{(3 - 5)^2 + (4 - 5)^2 + (8 - 5)^2\}/3 = 14/3$, and the **standard deviation** is the square root of the variance or about 2.16 weeks in this case.

PERT simplifies the calculation of σ_t and V_t as follows:

$$\sigma_t = (t_p - t_o)/6$$
$$V_t = \{(t_p - t_o)/6\}2$$

The variance of a sum of independent activity times is equal to the sum of their individual variances. Since T_e is the sum of t_e's along the critical path, then the variance of T_e equals the sum of all the variances of these activities.

Example 9.2. Three time estimates for each activity of the network are given in Table 9.1. For this given data do the following: (*a*) Draw the network diagram, (*b*) Find the critical path, and (*c*) the variance of the CP.

Table 9.1

Activity	t_o	t_m	t_p
1-2	2	5	14
1-3	3	12	21
2-4	5	14	17
3-4	2	5	8
4-5	1	4	7
3-5	6	15	30

Solution: The network is drawn below.

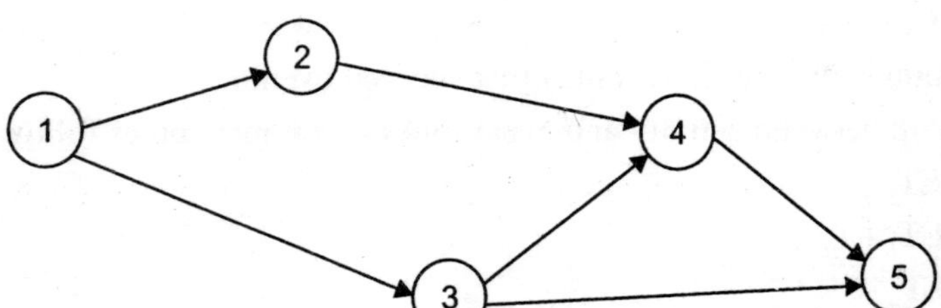

Table 9.2

Activity	t_o	t_m	t_p	t_e	σ_t	V_t
1-2	2	5	14	6	2	4
1-3	3	12	21	**12**	3	**9**
2-4	5	14	17	13	2	4
3-4	2	5	8	5	1	1
4-5	1	4	7	4	1	1
3-5	6	15	30	**16**	4	**16**

$$t_e = (t_o + 4t_m + t_p)/6$$

$$\sigma_t = (t_p - t_o)/6$$

$$V_t = \{(t_p - t_o)/6\}2$$

Critical path (CP), $T_e = 1\text{-}3\text{-}5 = 12 + 16 = 28$

Variance of the CP, $V_t = 9 + 16 = 25$

Hence, the standard deviation $\sigma_T = 5$

Standard deviation of each activity and for the entire project gives the manager additional information about variations in job and project times that he can anticipate.

9.4 PROBABILITY OF COMPLETING A PROJECT BY A GIVEN DATE

We calculated T_e by adding the t_e's along the critical path. Since t_e's are all random variables, then so is T_e. But the interesting result is that T_e does not have the same distribution as the t_e's but follows approximately what is called a normal distribution, the bell-shaped curve. A normal distribution is symmetric with a single peak value, and it is described completely by its mean (μ) and standard deviation (σ). *Two normal curves with the same m and s are always identical.*

We know that 68% of the area under a normal curve is within one s of the average of the distribution. Since, the area under a probability curve corresponds with probability measures, we can state the following conclusion: *A random variable drawn from a normal distribution has a 0.68 probability of being within one s of the distribution average.*

In terms of project duration, the interpretation is similar:

- There is a 68 % chance that the actual project duration will be within one σ of the estimated average length of the project, T_e.
- There is more than 95 % chance that the project duration will be within 2σ of the estimated average, and
- It is almost certain (99.7 %) that the project duration will not be more than 3σ away.

[Source: Introduction to Management Science, 5th edition, by Bernard W. Taylor III, Prentice Hall, Englewood, New Jersey]

9.5 PROJECT CRASHING AND TIME-COST TRADE-OFF

Project duration can be reduced by assigning more labor to project activities, often in the form of overtime, and by assigning more resources (material, equipment, etc). However, additional labor and resources cost money and hence increase the overall project cost. Thus, the decision to reduce the project duration must be based on an analysis of the trade-off between time and cost.

Project crashing is a method for shortening the project duration by reducing the time of one or more of the critical project activities to a time that is less than the normal activity time. *This reduction in the normal activities times is called 'crashing'*. Crashing is achieved by devoting more resources (in terms of money) to the activities to be crashed.

Many times it is felt that the project duration as estimated from arrow diagram is long and it is desired by management to accomplish the project in a shorter duration of time in order to secure progress payments or to avoid lateness penalties, etc. To do so various possibilities are explored. Work study techniques of systematic questioning (as in critical examination under method study) are employed to every (critical) activity to seek the possibilities of reducing their duration.

The critical path activities as classified as *Do* and *Ancillary* activities. Ancillary activities are those which support *Do* activities. For example, cutting of threads on a bar is Do activity whereas making the set up for cutting threads is an Ancillary activity. After identification, Do activities are subjected to systematic questioning technique embodying series of questions as regards purpose, place, sequence, person and means.

The second method is to *trade off* or transfer some resources from the activities having float to the critical activities, in order to reduce their duration. Trading-off redistributes the resources and accompanies changes in duration. The resources maybe workforce, amount of equipment and machinery, money, (better and more suitable) materials, etc.

Even by using work study techniques, trade off and other possible methods, if efficiency does not improve and the project duration is not shortened, then the only alternative left is network contraction or compression.

In other words, when all those techniques, which can reduce project duration at almost zero additional cost, fail then network, contraction, expedition or crashing of activities is resorted to. *This system of improvement involves extra cost because extra money is spent on overtime engagement of workforce, purchase of additional machinery, use of better materials, skilled workers, etc.* The cost increases, as more and more activities are crashed and in turn, of course the project duration decreases. One has to strike a balance between the extra money spent and the project time saved.

There are two types of activities- critical and non-critical. Crashing non-critical activities does not serve any purpose as they do not serve any purpose because they do not control the project duration. Completing the non-critical activities earlier does no benefit rather it increases work-in-progress. Therefore, crashing is centered on critical activities only which can reduce project duration if completed earlier.

Crashing of critical activities is started from that critical activity which has least cost-time slope, *i.e.*, which is cheapest to crash. Activities are crashed one after the other till the activity duration cannot be reduced further or the duration of original critical path gets shortened beyond a certain limit that another path becomes critical. In that case, one activity in each of the critical paths is chosen for crashing by the same amount of time. The crashing continues to the point whereafter further decrease in project duration is not possible, because either the network reaches the compression limit or the cost of crashing is more than the amount of saving in return.

The following terms should be conceptualized before actually crashing the network.

Normal Cost (Nc): It is the lowest cost of completing an activity in the minimum time, employing normal means, *i.e.*, not using overtime or other special resources.

Normal Time (NT): it is the minimum time required to achieve the normal cost.

Crash Cost (Cc): It is the least cost of completing an activity by employing all possible means like overtime, additional machinery, proper materials, etc.

*Crash Time (C_T): **It is the absolute minimum time associated with the crash cost.***

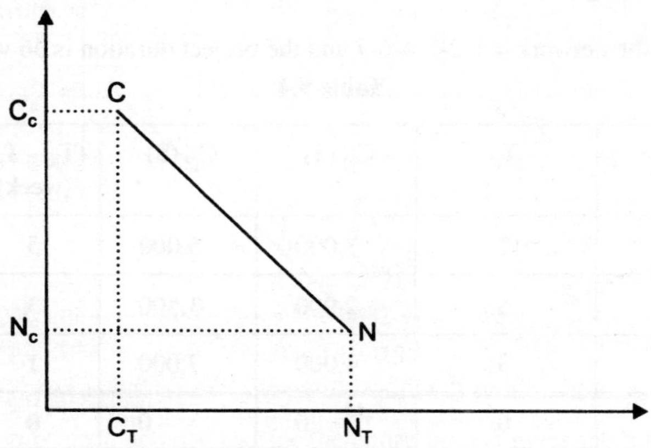

Cost-time slope of activity, $s = (C_c - N_c)/(N_T - C_T)$

As seen from the figure above, as the time to complete a project is reduced the cost involved gets increased. There are two types of cost in a project: *Direct* and *Indirect* or overheads. When the project time is reduced, the *indirect cost* decreases while the *direct cost* increases.

Example 9.3. For the given information in Table 9.3, the critical path of the project is 36 weeks. The builder wants to complete the project of house construction in just 30 weeks. How much extra cost would be incurred to complete the house by this time.

Table 9.3

Activity	*Description*	*Normal time (weeks)*	*Crash time (weeks)*	*Normal cost ($)*	*Crash cost ($)*	*Allowable crash time (weeks)*
1-2	Design house & get financing	12	7	3000	5000	5
2-3	Lay foundation	8	5	2000	3500	3
2-4	Order materials	4	3	4000	7000	1
3-4	Dummy	0	0	0	0	0
4-5	Select paint	4	1	500	1100	3
4-6	Build house	12	9	50000	71000	3
5-6	Select carpet	4	1	500	1100	3
6-7	Finish work	4	3	15000	22000	1
Sum				75000	110700	

Solution: Let

T_N = Normal time (weeks)
T_C = Crash time (weeks)
C_N = Normal cost ($)
C_C = Crash cost ($)
$T_N - T_C$ = allowable crash time (weeks) – $(C_N - C_C)/(T_N - T_C)$ = Crash cost/ week

If we assume that the relationship between crash cost and crash time is linear, then activity 1-2 can be crashed by any amount of time (not exceeding the maximum allowable crash time) at a rate of $400 per week as shown in Table 9.4.

The critical path of the network = 1-2-3-4-6-7 and the project duration is 36 weeks.

Table 9.4

Activity	T_N	T_C	C_N ($)	C_C ($)	$(T_N - T_C)$ (week)	$(C_N - C_C)/(T_N - T_C)$ $/week
1-2	12	7	3,000	5,000	5	400
2-3	8	5	2,000	3,500	3	500
2-4	4	3	4,000	7,000	1	3,000
3-4	0	0	0	0	0	0
4-5	4	1	500	1,100	3	200
4-6	12	9	50,000	71,000	3	7,000
5-6	4	1	500	1,100	3	200
6-7	4	3	15,000	22,000	1	7,000
Σ			75,000	110,700		

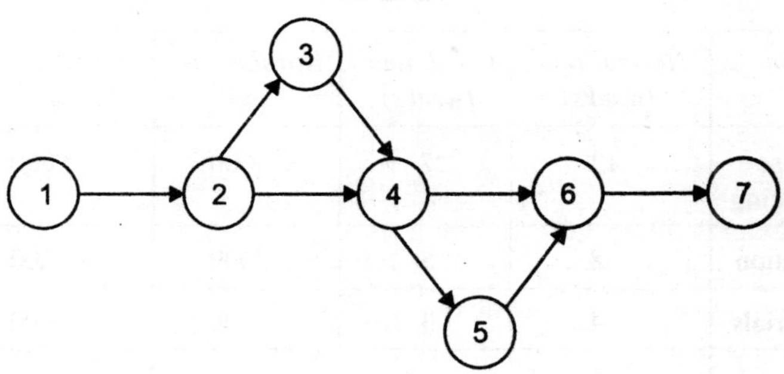

Figure 9.3

- The objective of project crashing is to reduce the project duration while minimizing the cost of crashing. Since, the project completion time can be shortened only by crashing activities on the critical path, it may turn out that not all activities have to be crashed. However, as the activities are crashed, the CP may change, requiring crashing of previously non-critical activities to further reduce the project completion time.

- We start the crashing process by looking at the CP and seeing which activity has the minimum crash cost per week. We see from the Table-9.4 that activity 1-2 has the minimum crash cost of $400 (excluding the dummy activity 3-4, which cannot be reduced). Thus activity 1-2 will be reduced as much as possible (5 weeks), but we can reduce activity 1-2 only to the point where another path becomes critical. When two paths simultaneously become critical, activities on both must be reduced by the same amount.
- If we reduce the activity time beyond the point where another path becomes critical, we may be incurring an unnecessary cost. This means we must keep a watch on the total network, when we reduce the individual activities. This makes the manual crashing very cumbersome.
- It turns out that activity 1-2 can be crashed by the total amount of 5 weeks without another paths becoming critical, since activity 1-2 is common in all four paths in the network. Crashing this activity gives the new project duration of 31 weeks at a crashing cost of $2,000.
- The process must now be repeated. The CP remains the same, and the minimum CC on the CP is $500 for activity 2-3, which can be crashed a total of 3 weeks, but since the contractor only desires to crash the network to 30 weeks, we only need to crash activity 2-3 by one week. Crashing activity 2-3 to 7 weeks (i.e., a one week reduction) costs $500 and reduces the project duration to 30 weeks.
- The total cost of crashing the project to 30 weeks is $2500.

Example 9.4. Given the following network and PERT activity time estimates, determine the expected project completion time and variance, and the probability that the project will be completed in 28 days or less.

Table 9.5a

	Time estimates (weeks)		
Activity	t_o	t_m	t_p
1-2	5	8	17
1-3	7	10	13
2-3	3	5	7
2-4	1	3	5
3-4	4	6	8
3-5	3	3	3
4-5	3	4	5

Solution:

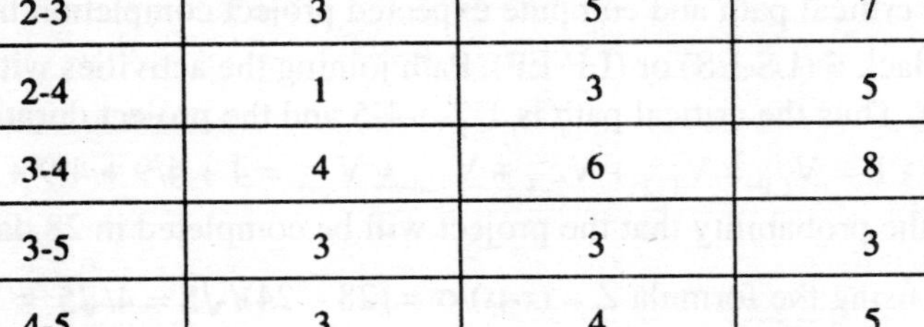

Figure 9.4

Compute the expected activity times and variances using the formulae discussed before. These are shown in the Table 9.5*b*.

Table 9.5b

Activity	$T_e = (t_o + 4t_m + t_p)/6$	$V_t = \{(t_p - t_o)/6\}2$
1-2	9	4
1-3	10	1
2-3	5	4/9
2-4	3	4/9
3-4	6	4/9
3-5	3	0
4-5	4	1/9

Determine the earliest and latest time at each node as shown below in the order of (ES, EF, LS, LF).

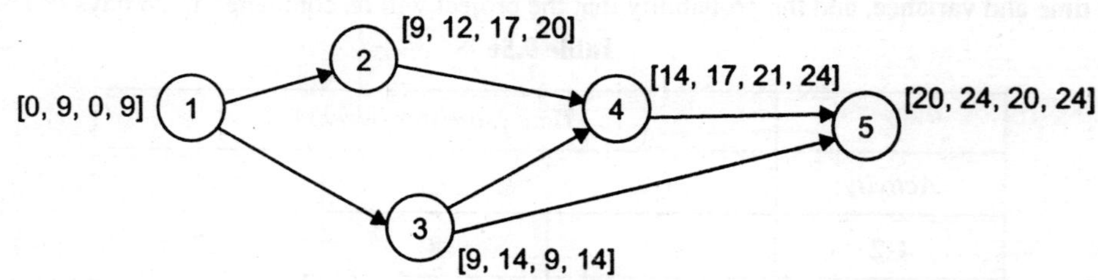

Figure 9.5

- Identify the critical path and compute expected project completion time.

Slack = (LS-ES) or (LF-EF). Path joining the activities with slack = 0 is called the critical path. Thus the critical path is 1-2-3-4-5 and the project duration is 24 days

Variance of CP = $V_{CP} = V_{1-2} + V_{2-3} + V_{3-4} + V_{4-5}$ = 4 + 4/9 + 4/9 + 1/9 = 5 days

- Determine the probability that the project will be completed in 28 days or less.

Compute Z using the formula $Z = (x-\mu)/\sigma = (28 - 24)/\sqrt{5} = 4/\sqrt{5} = 1.79$

The corresponding probability is 0.4633; thus $P(x \le 28) = 0.50 + 0.4633 = 0.9633$

Example 9.5. Three different time estimates for various activities of a project are given in Table 9.6. Construct a PERT network and find out (*a*) The earliest possible time (T_E) to complete the different activities, (*b*) The latest allowable time (T_L) for them, (*c*) The slack values, (*d*) The critical paths, and (*e*) The probability factor for completing the project in 30 weeks.

Table 9.6

Activity i – j	*Optimistic time*	*Most likely time*	*Pessimistic time*
1 – 2	1	2	3
2 – 3	1	2	3

2 – 4	1	3	5
3 – 5	3	4	5
4 – 5	2	3	4
4 – 6	3	5	7
5 – 7	4	5	6
6 – 7	6	7	8
7 – 8	2	4	6
7 – 9	4	6	8
8 – 10	1	2	3
9 – 10	3	5	7

Solution: The calculations are shown in Table 9.7

Table 9.7

$i-j$	t_o	t_m	t_p	t_e	σ_t	V_t	*C.P.*
1 – 2	1	2	3	2.00	0.33	0.11	0.11
2 – 3	1	2	3	2.00	0.33	0.11	
2 – 4	1	3	5	3.00	0.67	0.44	0.44
3 – 5	3	4	5	4.00	0.33	0.11	
4 – 5	2	3	4	3.00	0.33	0.11	
4 – 6	3	5	7	5.00	0.67	0.44	0.44
5 – 7	4	5	6	5.00	0.33	0.11	
6 – 7	6	7	8	7.00	0.33	0.11	0.11
7 – 8	2	4	6	4.00	0.67	0.44	
7 – 9	4	6	8	6.00	0.67	0.44	0.44
8 – 10	1	2	3	2.00	0.33	0.11	
9 – 10	3	5	7	5.00	0.67	0.44	0.44
						V_{CP}	2.00
						σ_{CP}	1.41

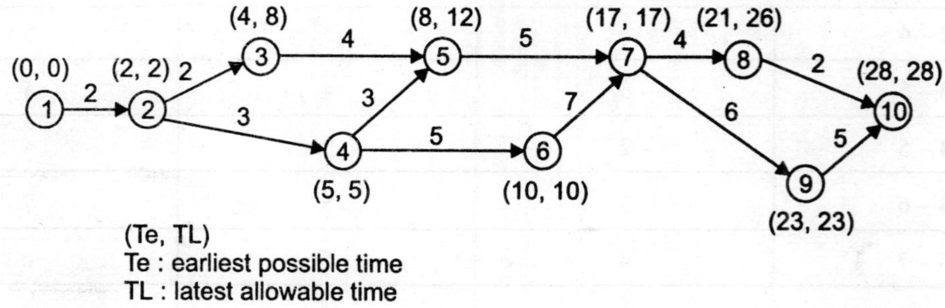

Figure 9.6

(*iv*) Critical Path

1–2–4–6–7–9–10 = 28 weeks.

$V_{CP} = 2$ and $\sigma_{CP} = 1.41$

(*v*) The probability factor for completing the project in 30 weeks.

$$Z = \frac{X - \mu}{\sigma} \quad \text{where } X = 30 \text{ weeks, } \mu = 28 \text{ weeks and } \sigma_{CP} = 1.41$$

Hence, $$Z = \frac{30 - 28}{1.41} = 1.41$$

Z is the number of standard deviations by which X exceeds μ

$\mu = T_e$ is the total project duration, and

X = due or scheduled date or time

From the table of *Standard Normal Distribution Function*, the corresponding percentage probabilities are given as follows:

For Z = 1.41 the probability is 92.07 % and for Z = 1.42 the probability is 92.22 %.

Interpolation

1.41 ....0.9207

1.414 .... *p*

1.42 ....0.9222

$$\frac{1.414 - 1.41}{1.42 - 1.41} = \frac{p - 0.9207}{0.9222 - 0.9207}$$

$$p = \frac{(1.414 - 1.41)(0.9222 - 0.9207)}{(1.42 - 1.41)} + 0.9207 = 0.9213$$

Therefore, there is **92.13%** probability that the project will be finished in 30 weeks.

Example 9.6. A reactor and storage tank are interconnected by a 3" insulated process line that needs periodic replacement. There are valves along the lines and at the terminals and these need replacing as well. No pipe and valves are in stock. Accurate, as built, drawings exist and are available. You are the maintenance and construction superintendent responsible for this project. The works engineer has requested your plan and schedule for a review with the operating supervision. The plant methods and standards section has furnished the following data. The precedents for each activity have been determined from a familiarity with similar projects.

Table 9.8

Symbol	Activity Description	Precedent	Time (Hrs.)
A	Develop required material list	—	8
B	Procure Pipe	A	200
C	Erect Scaffold	—	12
D	Remove Scaffold	I, M	4
E	Deactivate Line	—	8
F	Prefabricate Sections	B	40
G	Place New Pipes	F, L	32
I	Fit up Pipe and Valves	G, K	8
J	Procure Valves	A	225
K	Place Valves	J, L, F	8
L	Remove old pipe and valves	C, E	35
M	Insulate	G, K	24
N	Pressure Test	I	6
O	Clean-up and Start-up	D, N	4

(*i*) Sketch the arrow diagram of this project plan.

(*ii*) Make the forward pass and backward calculations on this network, and indicate the critical path and its length.

(*iii*) Calculate total float and free float (both early and late) for each of the non-critical activities.

The network (arrow diagram) is given in the figure below.

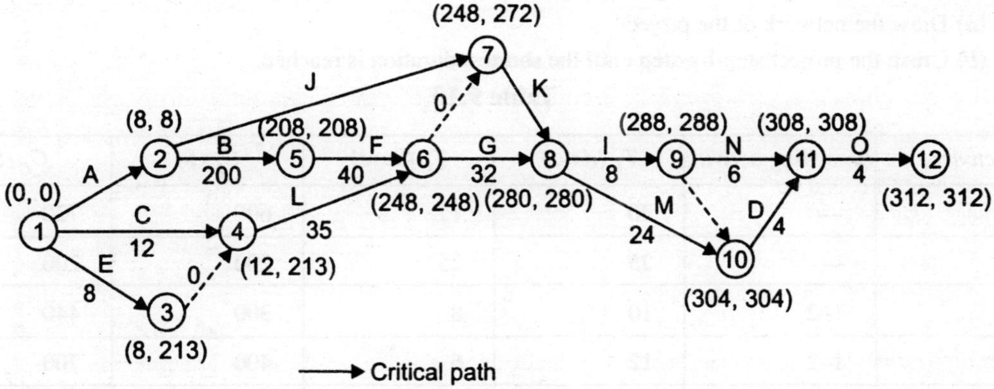

Figure 9.7

Critical Path: 1 - 2 - 5 - 6 - 8 - 10 - 11 - 12 = 312 Hrs.

Table 9.9

Activity	*Precedence*	*Earliest Start ES (hrs)*	*Latest Start LS (hrs)*	*Earliest Finish EF (hrs)*	*Latest Finish LF (hrs)*	*Total Slack (LF-EF) (hrs)*	*Free slack (FS)*
1–2	—	0	0	8	0	8	8–8 = 0
2–5	A	8	8	208	208	0	208–208 = 0
1–3	—	0	205	8	213	205	8–8 = 0
3–4	—	8	213	8	213	205	12–8 = 0
10–11	I M	304	304	308	308	0	308–308 = 0
1–4	—	0	201	12	213	201	12–12 = 0
5–6	B	208	208	248	248	0	248–248 = 0
6–8	F L	248	248	280	280	0	280–280 = 0
8–9	G K	280	294	288	302	14	288–288 = 0
2–7	A	8	34	233	272	26	248–233 = 15
6–7	—	248	272	248	272	24	248–248 = 0
7–8	J L F	248	272	256	280	24	280–256 = 24
4–6	C E	12	213	47	248	201	248–47 = 201
8–10	G K	280	280	304	304	0	304–304 = 0
9–10	—	288	304	288	304	16	304–288 = 16
9–11	I	288	302	294	308	14	308–294 =14
11–12	D N	308	308	312	312	0	0

Example 9.7. The following Table-9.10 gives the activities in a construction project with other relevant information.

(*a*) Draw the network of the project.

(*b*) Crush the project step-by-step until the shortest duration is reached.

Table 9.10

Activity	*Preceding activity*	T_N *(days)*	T_C *(days)*	C_N *($)*	C_C *($)*
1–2	—	20	17	600	720
1–3	—	25	25	200	200
2–3	1–2	10	8	300	440
2–4	1–2	12	6	400	700
3–4	1–3, 2–3	5	2	300	420
4–5	2–4, 3–4	10	5	300	600

Solution:

(*a*) **The Project Network is shown in the following figure using Normal Time (T_N).**

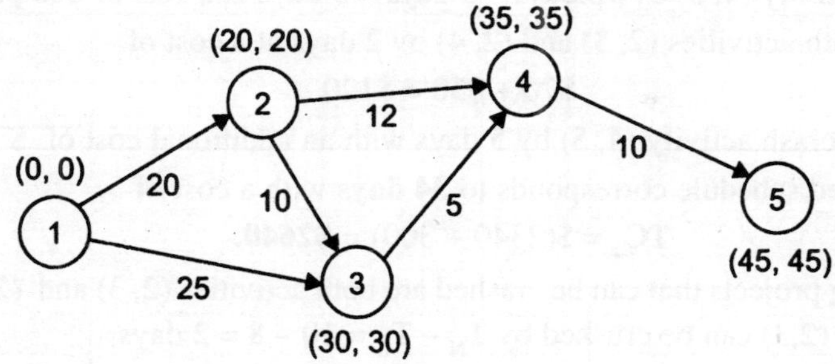

Figure 9.8

$$CP_1 = 1 - 2 - 3 - 4 - 5.$$
$$CP_2 = 1 - 2 - 4 - 5.$$

Normal duration of the project is **45 days.**

(*b*) **Compute the different min. cost schedule that can occur between normal and crash times, which are dependent on the cost time slopes for different activities. These are computed by the formula :**

$$\text{Cost slope} = \frac{\text{Crash cost} - \text{Normal cost}}{\text{Normal time} - \text{Crash time}}$$

The slopes of the activities of the above network are calculated as shown in Table-9.11:

Table 9.11

Activity	1-2	1-3	2-3	2-4	3-4	4-5
Slope (ΔC/ΔT)	40	0	70	50	40	60

Total Direct Cost (TC_1) = ΣC_N = \$2100.

Step 1. Since the project duration is controlled by the activities on the critical path, the duration of some activities lying on the critical path is reduced. First the duration of that activity is reduced which has the minimum cost slope. Since the activities (1, 2) and (3, 4) both give the minimum cost slope, the duration of activity (1, 2) is compressed from 20 to 17 days with an additional cost of \$ 3 × 40 = \$120.

Thus the revised schedule corresponds to **42 days** with a cost of

$$TC_2 = \$(2100 + 120) = \mathbf{\$2220.}$$

Thus the revised schedule corresponds to 42 days with a cost of

$$TC_2 = \$(2100 + 120) = \$2220.$$

Step 2. Further if the duration of activity (3, 4) of critical path is reduced from 5 days to 2 days = 3 days, the two critical paths of the project become the same. Therefore, we crash activity (3, 4) by 3 days with an additional cost of \$ 3 × 40 = \$120.

Thus the revised schedule corresponds to **39 days** with a cost of

$$TC_3 = \$(2220 + 120) = \mathbf{\$2340.}$$

It should be noted that I have chosen the activity (3, 4) because in doing so two parallel critical paths 1 → 2 → 4 → 5 and 1 → 2 → 3 → 4 → 5 are obtained.

Step 3. Now both CP1 and CP2 are equal and there are two possibilities of crashing the project duration.

- Crashing activity (4, 5) by 10 days – 5 days = 5 days at a cost of \$60 per day, and
- Crashing both activities (2, 3) and (2, 4) by 2 days at a cost of

$$\$70 + \$50 = \$120.$$

Therefore, we crash activity (4, 5) by 5 days with an additional cost of \$ 5 × 60 = \$300.

Thus the revised schedule corresponds to **34 days** with a cost of

$$TC_4 = \$(2340 + 300) = \mathbf{\$2640.}$$

Step 4. The remaining projects that can be crashed are both activities (2, 3) and (2, 4) at the same time.

Activity (2,3) can be crushed by $T_N - T_C = 10 - 8 = 2$ days

Activity (2,4) can be crushed by $T_N - T_C = 12 - 6 = 6$ days

Therefore, we can only crush both activities by 2 days at a cost of (\$70 + \$50) × 2 = \$240.

Thus the revised schedule corresponds to **32 days** with a cost of TC5 = \$(2640 + 240) = **\$2880.**

Conclusion: Just by paying $\Delta C = TC_5 - TC_1 =$ ***\$2880 – \$2100 = \$780,***

The project duration can be reduced from 45 days to 32 days or by **13 days.**

Example 9.8. In the project network shown in the Figure 9.9 below, the nodes are denoted by numbers and the activities by letters. The normal and crash durations of the various activities along with the associated costs are shown below in Table 9.12.

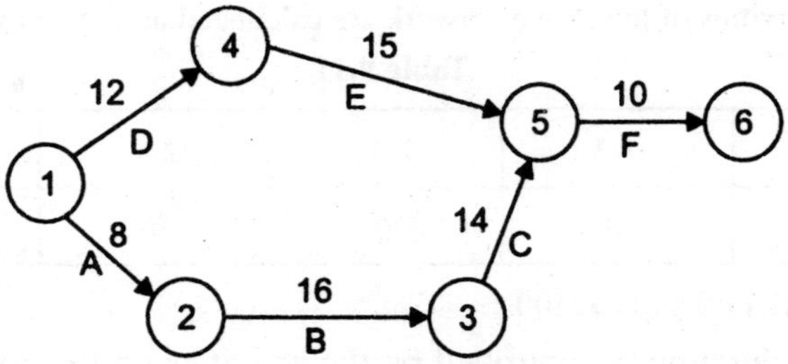

Figure 9.9

Table 9.12

Activity	*Normal Duration (days)*	*Normal cost (\$)*	*Crash duration (days)*	*Crash cost (\$)*
A	8	1800	6	2200
B	16	1500	11	2200
C	14	1800	9	2400
D	12	2400	9	3000
E	15	800	14	2000
F	10	2000	8	4000

Determine the least cost for 36 days schedule.

Solution : First assume that all activities occur at normal times. Then the following network shows the critical path computations under normal conditions.

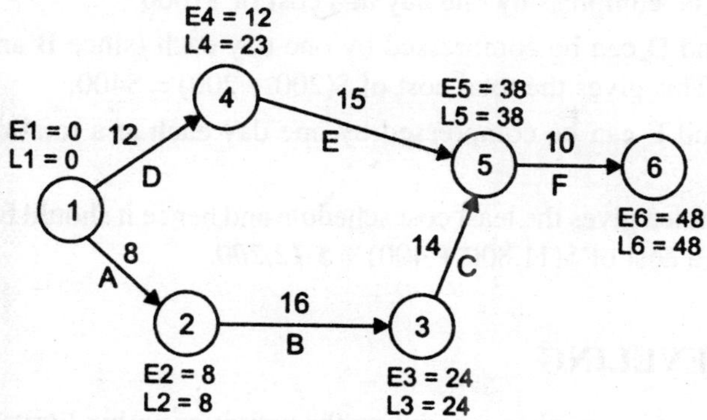

Figure 9.10

The critical path is A → B → C → F. The schedule of the project is 48 days and its associated normal cost becomes:

= $(1800 + 1500 + 1800 + 2400 + 800 + 2000) = **$ 10,300.**

The different minimum cost schedule that can occur between normal and crash times, which are mainly dependent on the cost time slopes for different activities. The cost time slopes can be computed by the formula:

$$\text{Cost} - \text{time slope} = \frac{\text{Crash cost} - \text{Normal cost}}{\text{Normal time} - \text{Crash time}}$$

The cost slopes for the activities of the above network are:

Table 9.13

Activity	A	B	C	D	E	F
Slope	200	140	120	200	1200	1000

Now we proceed step-by-step as follows:

Step-1. Since the present schedule consumes more time, the schedule can be reduced by crashing some of the activities. Since the project duration is controlled by the activities lying on the critical path, the duration of some activities on the critical path is reduced. First reduce the duration of that activity which involves minimum cost. Activity C with minimum slope gives the minimum cost. So the duration of activity C is compressed from 14 days to 11 days with an additional cost $ 5 × 120 = $600. There fore, the new schedule corresponds to ***43 days*** with a cost of $(10,300 + 600) = ***$10,900.***

Step-2. Now, it can be observed that the present schedule still consumes more time and also not all the activities on the critical path are at their crash durations. Hence the project duration can be reduced by crashing some other activity. Out of the remaining activities on the critical path, activity B has the least slope. So reduce the duration activity B from 16 days to 11 days at a cost of $ 5 × 140 = $700. Thus the new project duration becomes ***38 days*** with a cost of $(10,900 + 700) = ***$11,600.***

Step 3. This project duration is still more than the required duration of 36 days. So select some other activity lying on the critical path for crashing. Obviously, only activities A and F on the critical path can be considered for crashing. Since activity A has the smaller slope, the duration of A can be compressed. Compress A only by one day although it can be compressed by two days (from 8 to 6 days). Because, the path 1 → 4 → 5 → 6 becomes a parallel critical path as soon as A is compressed by one day. Thus the new schedule corresponds to ***37 days*** with a cost of $(11,600 + 200) = ***$11,800.***

Step 4. Since only 36 days schedule is required, compress some activity by one day. To do so compress one day in each of the two parallel critical paths. So there are three choices:

- Activity F can be compress by one day at a cost of $1000.
- Activities A and D can be compressed by one day each (since B and C are already at their crash points). This gives the total cost of $(200 + 200) = $400.
- Activities A and E can be compressed by one day each at a total cost of $(200 + 1200) = $1400.

But, the second choice gives the least cost schedule and hence it should be selected. This involves a ***36 days*** schedule with a cost of $(11,800 + 400) = ***$ 12,200.***

9.6 RESOURCE LEVELING

Resource leveling or smoothing implies scheduling the activities within limits of their total floats such that fluctuations in load or resource requirements are minimized. As a result of resource leveling, the peaks and valleys in the load chart are leveled in order to keep the workforce constant and stable throughout the project duration. Keeping unnecessary large workforce means extra cost, and dismissing the workers during lean period of the project brings dissatisfaction among the workforce and bad name to the organization. Moreover, getting the skilled workforce again during the peak period is not guaranteed.

Smoothing affixes actual dates to the activities, reallocates the resources between them and actually improves the utilization of resources. Of course there is a constraint in the case of resource smoothing and that is the total project duration, within which everything has to be managed.

The smoothing technique makes use of floats in different activities. The activities are adjusted within the period equal to their duration plus float (D + F). In other words an activity having float may be started at any time within this period and finished within the same period. The activity can be taken during the earlier, middle or later part of the (D + F) band of period. Various activities can be scattered so that no high peaks or low valleys are formed in the manpower loading chart.

Smoothing manually by juggling with available float of each activity may be alright for small projects, but large and complex projects definitely demand the use of a computer.

The *Heuristic* approach to smoothing is simply the testing of various arrangements to achieve the acceptable solution. Smoothing is very essential in the projects where overloading and under-loading is not easy to avoid.

9.6.1 HEURISTIC METHODS

A *heuristic* is a guide or method of reducing search in a problem solving situation. It is also called 'rule of thumb'. Some of the examples of heuristics could be:

- If the problem is how to drive to work in the least time, one might use the rule, "when the freeway is crowded, take the surface street to work." This avoids the complicated procedure of measuring traffic flows, obtaining highway bulletins, gathering statistical data, etc.
- The classic management rule, "Handle only the exception problems and let subordinates decide routine matters."
- A collection of such rules for solving a particular problem is called a *heuristic program.*
- While heuristics may not always lead to the best solution, they provide good solution to recurring problems with a minimum effort.

Heuristic programs for resource scheduling usually take one of the two forms:

(*a*) *Resource leveling programs*: These attempt to reduce peak resource requirements and smooth out period-to-period assignments, within a constraint on project duration.

(*b*) *Resource allocation programs*: These allocate available resources to project activities in an attempt to find the shortest project schedule consistent with fixed resource limits.

We shall discuss these two approaches in the next section:

9.7 RESOURCE LEVELING OF PROJECT SCHEDULES

It is usually wise to maintain relatively stable employment levels and to utilize resources at a more constant rate. In such situations resource leveling programs are most appropriate. We know that activity slack is a measure of flexibility in the assignment of activity start times. The scheduler may use activity slack as a means of smoothing peak resources requirements.

Resource Allocation Heuristics

- Allocate resources serially in time. It means, start on the first day and schedule all jobs that are possible, then do the same for the second day, and so on.
- When several jobs compete for the same resources, give preference to the jobs with the least slack.
- Schedule non-critical jobs, if possible, to free resources for scheduling critical or non-slack jobs.

The program is based on three rules (heuristics):

- Allocate resources serially in time. That is, start on the first day and schedule all jobs possible, then do the same for the second day, and so on.
- When several jobs compete for the same resources, give preference to the jobs with the least slack.
- Reschedule non-critical jobs, if possible, to free resources for scheduling critical or non-slack jobs.

Let us see these heuristics with some examples:

Example 9.10. (Resource Leveling) Figure 9.11 shows an arrow diagram, with activity duration and number of workers required to complete each activity being marked on all activities. In this case, the number represents both

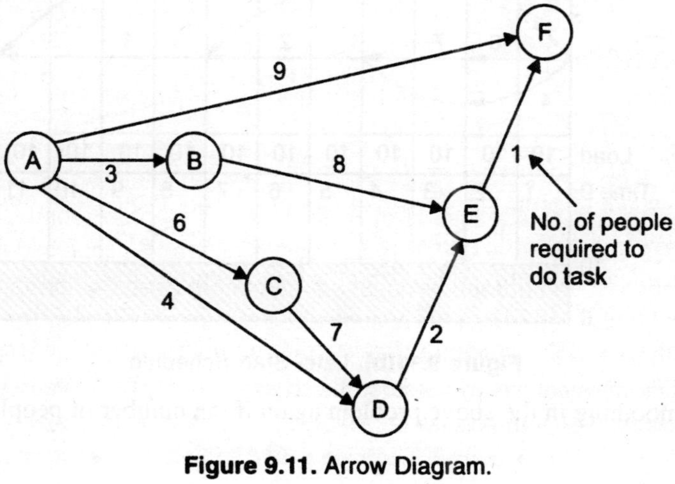

Figure 9.11. Arrow Diagram.

the number of men and the number of days to finish an activity. For example, activity E-F needs 1 man to finish it in 1 day, activity A-F needs 9 men to finish the job in 9 days, and so on.

Figure 9.11(*a*) shows the initial schedule graph in which various activities have been placed with the number of workers written on them. Do the resource leveling in the above problem if the number of men in a particular day is not to exceed (*a*) 10 and (*b*) 12.

Solution: **(*a*) Figure 9.11(*a*) is based on Earliest —Start Schedule. This chart shows that the minimum number of workers required on any day are 1 on day from 8 to 11, whereas the maximum number of men (24) is needed on day 3. This means there is a huge fluctuation of manpower demand from day to day in the project. We have to try to smooth this chart so that the manpower needed on any day remains within the given limit of 10.**

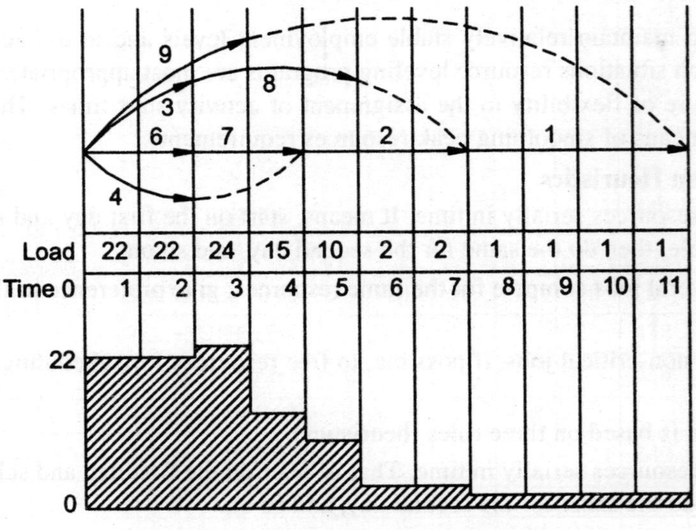

Figure 9.11(a). Earliest–Start Schedule.

Figure 9.11(*b*) shows a smoothing based on the floats available called **Late–Start Schedule.** This needs a lot of trial to reach this very smooth stage. As we can see, this gives the best load distribution. This kind of smoothness may not be possible always though.

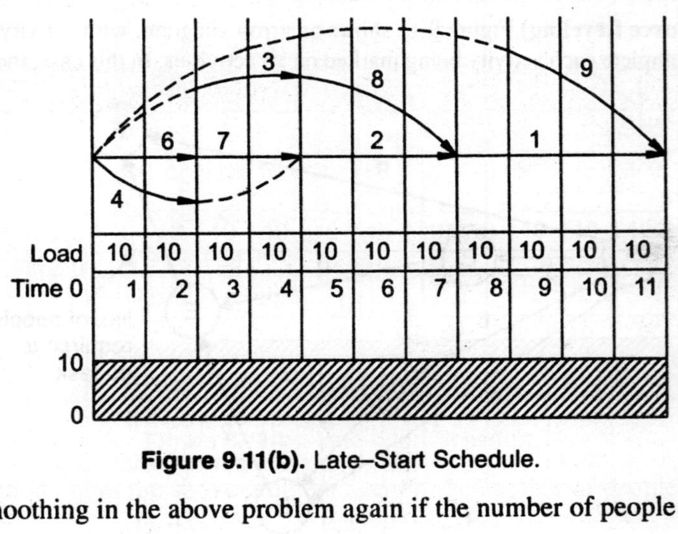

Figure 9.11(b). Late–Start Schedule.

(*b*) Do the smoothing in the above problem again if the number of people in a particular day is not to exceed 12.

The solution is shown in Figure 9.11(*c*).

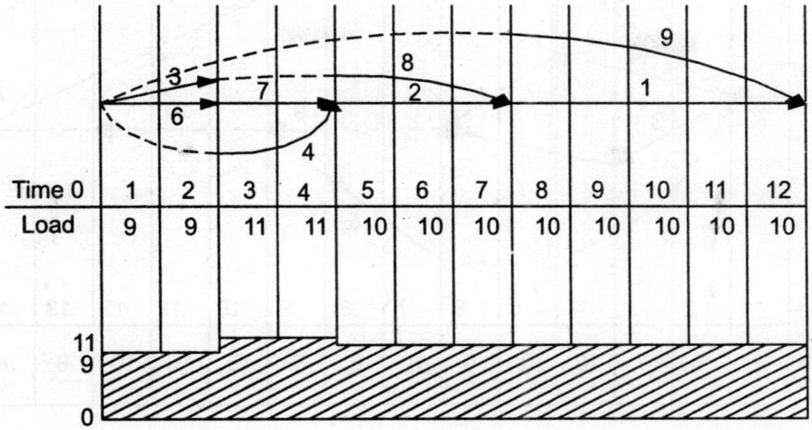

Figure 9.11(c). Late–Start Schedule.

Example 9.11. (Resource Allocation) The initial project schedule is shown in Figure - 9.12. How should the project be rescheduled so as not to exceed the **10 men** constraint but still to complete the project as soon as possible?

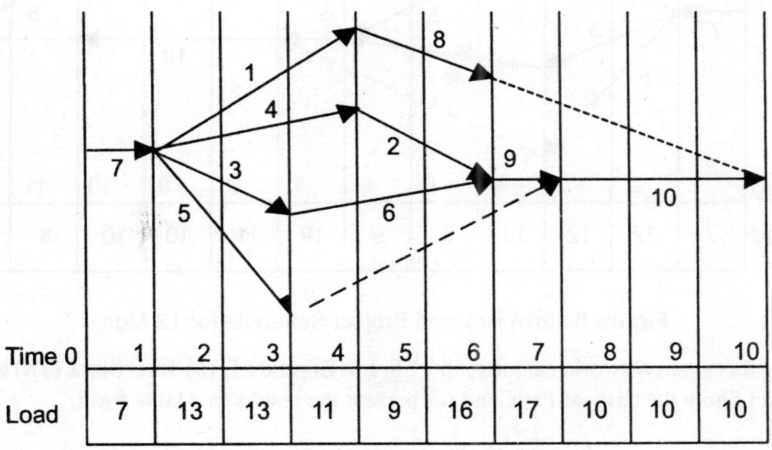

Figure 9.12. Initial Project Schedule.

Solution: After a lot of trials the final solution is shown in Figure 9.12a. The demand of manpower or the load is less than the limit of 12 men on any day. However, in meeting this constraint, the project duration is extended by 4 days. That means the project will be completed on 14th day rather on 10th day as previously planned.

Readers can try to do the resource allocation in the above problem if the maximum number of people available on any day is to be 12.

The solution is shown in Figure 9.12b. The project duration has now reduced from 14 to 12 days-quite logical: more men available means less duration the project should take to complete.

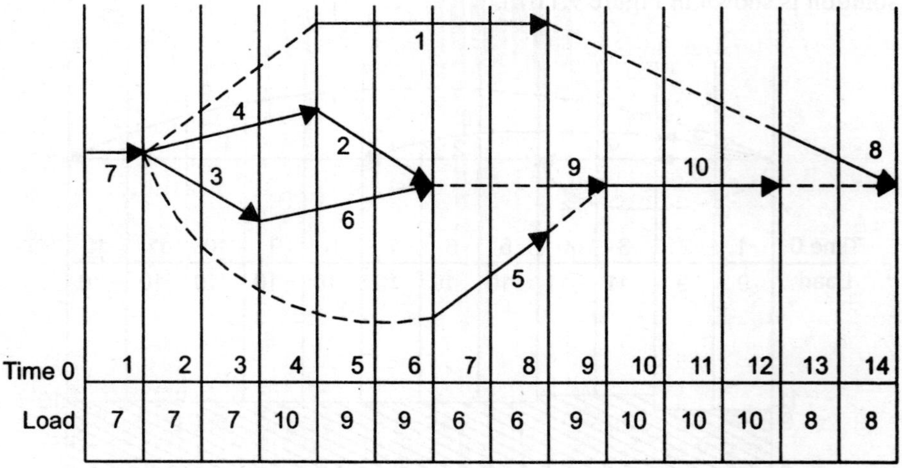

Figure 9.12(a) Revised Project Schedule for 10 Men.

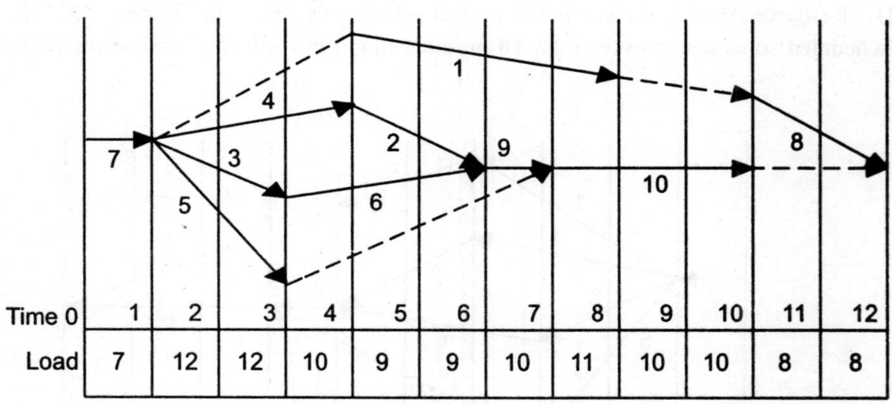

Figure 9.12(b) Revised Project Schedule for 12 Men.

Example 9.12. For this given network, calculate: (*a*) ES, LS, EF, and LF, (*b*) Total Slack (TS) and Free Slack (FS) for each activity, (*c*) Show the Critical Path, and (*d*) present the results in a table form.

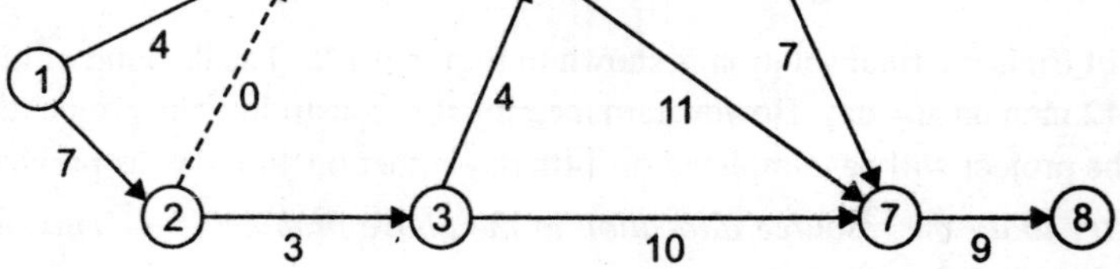

Solution:

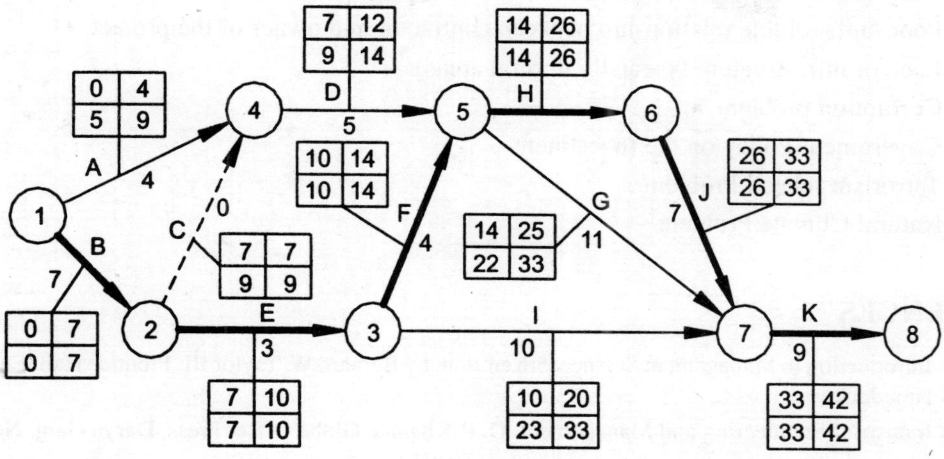

Figure 9.13

Table 9.14

Activity		*Duration*	*ES*	*LS*	*EF*	*LF*	*TS*	*FS*
A	1–4	4	0	5	4	9	5	3
B	1–2	7	0	0	7	7	0	0
C	2–4	0	7	9	7	9	2	0
D	4–5	5	7	9	12	14	2	2
E	2–3	3	7	7	10	10	0	0
F	3–5	4	10	10	14	14	0	0
G	5–7	11	14	22	25	33	8	8
H	5–6	12	14	14	26	26	0	0
I	3–7	10	10	23	20	33	13	13
J	6–7	7	26	26	33	33	0	0
K	7–8	9	33	33	42	42	0	0

CP = B → E → F → H → J → K.

9.8 PROJECT DELAY

Most of the projects suffer from time and cost overruns due to one reason or another. The possible reasons for the project delay in general are:

- Power interruption or under-supply of it,

- Limited Resources (money, men, machine and lack of will power),
- Poor /unfavorable relationship between contractor and workers,
- Poor /unfavorable relationship between contractor and owner of the project,
- Lack of infrastructure (specially in rural areas)
- Corruption problem
- Government Policy on the Investment
- Terrorism related Problem
- Natural Climate Problem

REFERENCES

(*a*) Introduction to Management Science, 5th edition, by Bernard W. Taylor III, Prentice Hall, Englewood, New Jersey.

(*b*) Industrial Engineering and Management, O. P. Khanna, Globe Offset Press, Darya Ganj, New Delhi.

10

Quality Control

10.0 INTRODUCTION

Quality is a very frequently used term by almost all of us. However, it is very difficult to define quality in a unique way. Some believe that quality products are invariably costly products. For some quality signifies the degree of perfection. In fact, quality, like beauty, lies in the beholder's eyes. But technically speaking, *Quality is the totality of features and characteristics of a product or service that bear on its ability to satisfy stated or implied needs.* A quality product is not necessarily a good product. In fact all products have quality, though the level of quality may be very low in some products and very high in others. It is not always true that a product with high quality will also be costly. Conversely, many times an expensive product is low in quality. A cup of tea or coffee taken in a highway cafe may taste better than what one gets in a five star hotel-though the cost in the two places will be remarkably different.

A high quality product is often expensive because more time and efforts go into manufacturing such product with its close tolerances and fewer defects. Product quality level also reflects the image of the company that produces it. For example, some companies in the electronic fields (*e.g.* Philips, Sony, JVC, etc.) leave an imprint on users' minds as *'first class companies'* while others are not seen in favorable lights and are considered as mediocre companies. The factors that affect the ultimate quality level of a product are: theoretical perfection, lower selling price, and the manufacturability.

10.1 INSPECTION

Inspection is the art of determining actual conformity of product to the specifications laid down for it. It is a tool to control the quality of a product. Thus, inspection means checking the acceptability of the manufactured product. It measures the quality of a product or service in terms of predefined standards. Product quality may be specified in terms of strength, hardness, shape, surface finish, etc.

10.1.1 TYPES OF INSPECTION

Inspection can be either *preventive* or *corrective*. **Preventive** inspection is concerned with discovering defects, the cause of defects, and helping in the removal of such causes. **Corrective** (remedial) inspection, on the other hand, deals with sorting out good parts from the bad ones. Its primary purpose is to discover the defective parts that have already been manufactured and prevent their use in the final product. Many firms use both types of inspection, but the emphasis is often on preventive inspection. The idea is to prevent the inferior parts from further processing down the production line. This, in turn, will reduce the labor cost.

10.1.2 PURPOSE OF INSPECTIONS

- It separates defective components from non-defective ones and thus ensures the adequate quality of products.
- It locates the defects in raw materials and flaws in process which otherwise cause problems at the final stage. For example, detecting parts with improper tolerances during processing itself, will minimize the troubles at the time of assembly.
- It prevents further work being done on semi finished products already detected as spoiled.
- It ensures that the product works without hurting anybody.
- It detects sources of weakness and trouble in the finished products and thus checks the work of designers.
- It builds up the reputation of the company with the customers by reducing the number of complaints from them.

10.2 SOME QUALITY RELATED TERMS

Quality assurance: All those planned or systematic actions necessary to provide adequate confidence that a product or service will satisfy given requirements for quality.

Quality audit: A systematic and independent examination to determine whether quality activities and results comply with planned arrangements, and whether these arrangements are implemented effectively and are suitable to achieve objectives.

Quality control: The operational techniques and activities that are used to fulfill requirements of quality.

Quality system: The organizational structure, responsibilities, procedures, processes, and resources for implementing quality management.

10.3 STATISTICAL QUALITY CONTROL (SQC)

Inspecting all the items is very time consuming and costly affair. An alternative to this is statistical control which is a type of inspection based on probability and mathematical techniques. In many instances it may be used in place of ordinary inspection procedures. Its objective, like that of inspection, is to control quality level of product without doing 100 percent inspection.

SQC uses statistical methods to gather and analyze data in the determination and control of quality. It is based on sampling, probability, and statistical inference, i.e., judging an entire lot by the characteristics of a sample.

The question often raised is 'whether a sample always reflects the true characteristics of the production lot'. The answer is no. However, the sampling may be the only way to estimate the quality of a lot. For example, the only way to determine the life of an electric bulb is to burn it until it burns out or the only way to test a rifle shell is to fire it. In each of these cases, inspection is destructive, and sampling is obviously required if the product is to be marketed.

10.4 ACCEPTANCE SAMPLING

In a nutshell, acceptance sampling is a system that determines whether an entire lot of goods should be accepted or rejected. In the simplest case of acceptance sampling, we draw a random sample of size n from the total lot N and decide whether or not to accept the entire lot based upon the sample. If the sample signals to reject the lot, it may then either be subjected to 100 % inspection, sorting out bad parts, or to be returned to the original supplier, which may be a vendor or another department within the organization.

Acceptance sampling techniques available for different situations are:

- *Sampling by attributes*: where we simply classify parts as good or bad.
- *Sampling by variables*: Where we make an actual measurement of some kind which indicates how good or bad a part is.

10.4.1 WHERE DO WE USE SAMPLING ?

Acceptance sampling attempts to control the quality that passes an inspection point after production. In general, acceptance sampling is appropriate when:

- Possible losses by passing defective items are not great and the cost of inspection is relatively high. In the limiting situation, this can mean no inspection at all.
- Inspection requires destruction of the product.
- Further handling of any kind is likely to induce defects, or when mental or physical fatigue is an important factor in inspection. In either instance, a sampling plan may actually pass fewer defective items than would 100 percent inspection. But, it costs less.

10.4.2 ADVANTAGES AND DISADVANTAGES OF ACCEPTANCE SAMPLING

Advantages of Acceptance sampling:

- It is very useful in mass production.
- It is economical, easy to understand, and easy to conduct.
- It causes much less fatigue to inspectors.
- Computation work is simple.

Disadvantages:

- It does not give definite assurance for confirmation of the specification.
- Decision of acceptance or rejection is based only on the sample drawn from the batch.

10.4.3 REPRESENTATIVE SAMPLE

The rule of sampling is that the sample be properly drawn from the batch. It means that the sample must be representative of the batch or the lot. For example, if we need a sample of 25 units from a production run of 250 units, then it implies that these 25 units represent the entire lot of 250 units. This would not be so if all 25 were taken from the units produced during the last fifteen minutes of the operation. Similarly, the sample would not be representative if all 25 came from the units produced during the initial fifteen minutes of operation. Sampling, in fact, should be on a random basis where all possible samples in the production lot have an equal chance of being included. Then the sample of 25 would probably be more nearly representative if the individual units were chosen at more or less periodic intervals throughout the entire production run.

Acceptance sampling tries to assure the quality rather than control the quality. It is an inspection technique. Procedure of sampling inspection consists of the following steps:

- Making inspection batches of the total quantity.
- Drawing random samples from each batch.
- Carrying out proper inspection to determine the quality of the random samples.
- Selecting a sampling plan and establishing an allowable percent defective.

10.5 SAMPLING PLANS

1. Single Sampling Plan
2. Double Sampling Plan
3. Sequential Sampling Plan

10.5.1 SINGLE SAMPLING PLAN (SSP)

A lot is accepted or rejected on the basis of a single sample of n items drawn from the lot of N items. The following steps are involved in this:

- Draw a single sample of size *n*. The sample size may either be calculated or found from tables.
- Inspect the sample and find the number of defective pieces.
- If defective pieces exceed the acceptance number *c*, the lot is rejected else the lot is accepted.
- In case the lot is rejected, inspect each and every piece of the lot and replace the defective pieces or salvage and correct the defective pieces.

A sampling plan is specified by the values of n and c. The sampling plan is supposed to separate good lots from bad lots. There are bound to be some errors in sampling. We will study the probabilities of such errors graphically, using an Operating Characteristics Curve (OCC) shown in Figure 10.1.

Figure 10.1 shows OCC for two single sampling plans (SSP) A and B with $n = 35$, $c = 1$; and $n = 150$, $c = 6$ respectively. Assume that a lot with F = 10% defectives is considered to be a *bad lot* and a lot with $f = 2\%$ defectives is considered to be a *good lot.* From Figure, it is clear that Plan A would stand a 14% chance of accepting a bad lot. The same unfortunate error can occur with Plan B, with larger sampling size also, but the probability of error is just 1%. Plan B is also better at not rejecting a good lots ($f = 2\%$). Plan A has 16% chance of rejecting a good lot whereas Plan B has only 3% chance of rejecting a good lot.

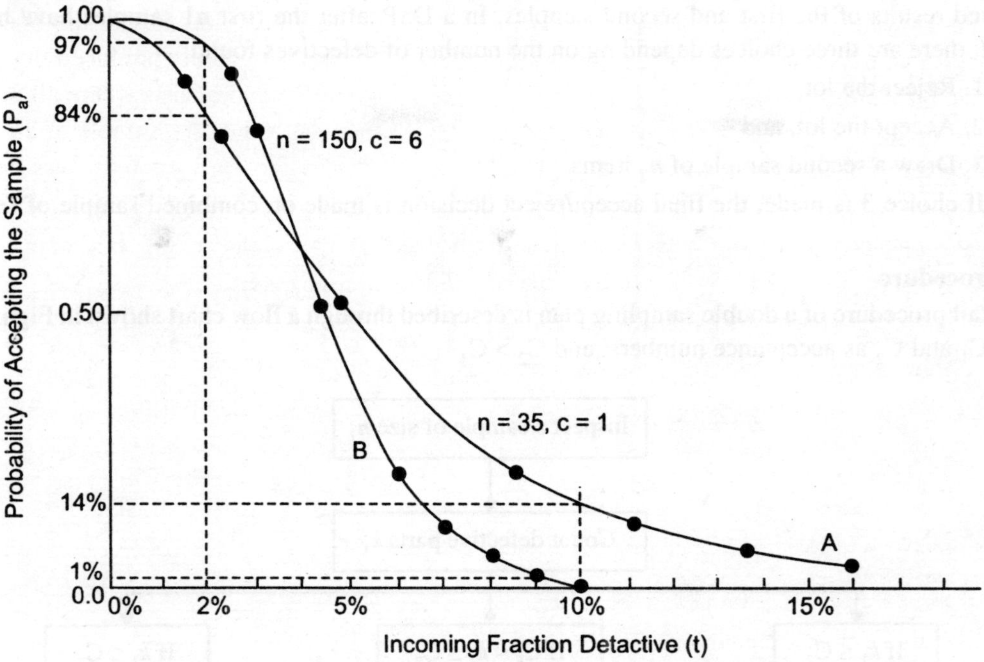

Figure 10.1. Operating Characteristics Curve (OCC).

So, it is obvious that a larger sample does a better job of discriminating between good and bad lots. It has more information. However, the price for increased accuracy is higher inspection costs. The design of a sampling plan has to optimally **trade-off** cost with discrimination. The values of the ordinates of the OCC are determined from the Poisson distribution. The actual details are available in the advanced texts listed in the reference.

Characteristics of a SSP

- It is easy to design, explain, and conduct.
- It is the only practical type of sampling plan under conveyorized production conditions when only one sample can be selected.
- It involves a lower cost of training and supervising employees, transporting and sorting samples, etc.
- It estimates the lot quality very accurately.
- It is more economical than double sampling plan when lots have their percent defectives close to acceptable quality level (AQL).
- It involves a bigger sample size than that of double sampling plan.
- It involves lesser record keeping than that of double and multiple sampling plans.
- It provides maximum information about the lot quality because each sample can be plotted on the control chart.

10.5.2 DOUBLE SAMPLING PLAN (DSP)

If it is not possible to decide the fate of the lot on the basis of the first sample. So, a second sample is drawn out of the same lot, and the decision whether to accept or reject the lot is taken on the basis of the combined results of the first and second samples. In a DSP, after the first n1 samples have been inspected, there are three choices depending on the number of defectives found:

1. Reject the lot,
2. Accept the lot, and
3. Draw a second sample of n_2 items.

If choice 3 is made, the final accept/reject decision is made on combined sample of $(n_1 + n_2)$ items.

DSP Procedure

The detail procedure of a double sampling plan is described through a flow chart shown in Figure 10.2. Given C_1 and C_2 as acceptance numbers, and $C_2 > C_1$

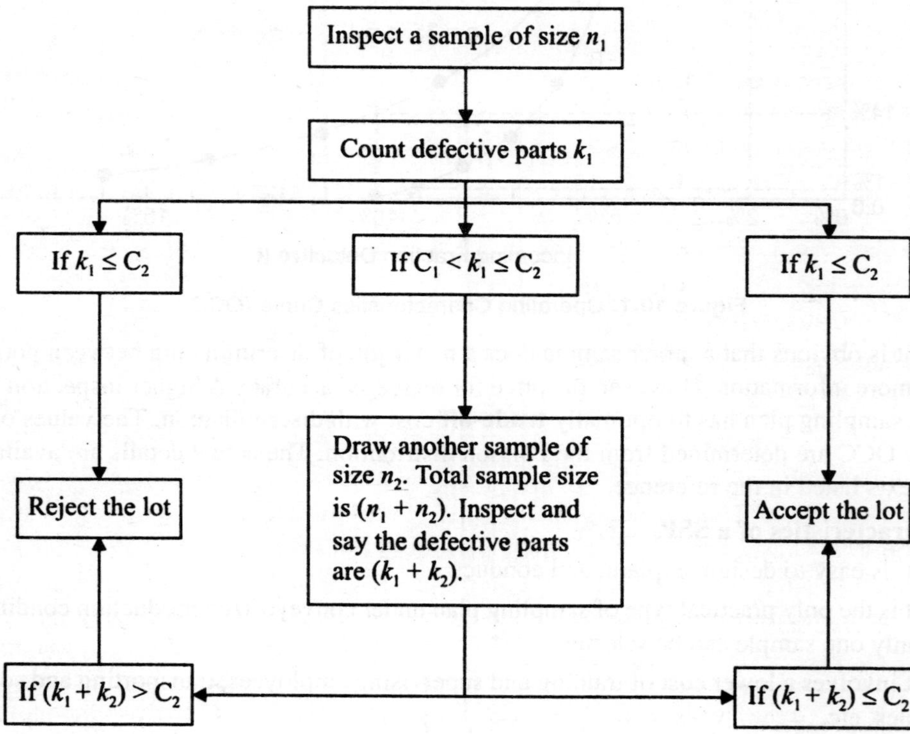

Figure 10.2. Flow Chart for DSP.

Characteristics of DSP

- It is more expensive to administer than a comparable single sampling plan.
- It involves less inspection than that required for a single sampling plan.
- It is more appealing to the personnel because it gives a second chance to a lot before rejecting.
- It permits a smaller first sample than is needed in the corresponding single sampling plan.
- It involves more overheads than a single sampling plan.
- It involves more record keeping than a single sampling plan.
- It does not give as accurate estimation of lot quality as is provided by a single sampling plan.

10.5.3 SEQUENTIAL OR MULTIPLE SAMPLING PLAN

In this plan of sampling, one, two, three or more samples may be required to reach a decision regarding acceptance or rejection of a batch. A multiple sampling plan operates in the same way as the DSP, but with more than two samples. Double and multiple sampling plans reduce inspection costs because many accept/reject decisions are made based on the first sample which is smaller than that of the single sampling plan. However, SSP is more popular and easy to use.

10.6 PROCESS VARIABILITY AND CONTROL

Everything we do in life is a process, and everything in life varies. For example, brushing teeth is a process, and we have never brushed our teeth twice in exactly the same way. Variations that occur in an industrial process fall in two broad categories: (*a*) Variations due to **chance,** and (*b*) Variations due to **assignable** causes. We want to learn about variation and how it affects our work processes.

The **chance variations** may be due to minor causes, none of which can account for any significant part of the total variation. The result is that these variations occur in a random manner, and there is very little that we can do about them. When a process is in a state of statistical control, variations that occur in the number of defects, the size of a dimension, chemical composition, weight, etc are due to chance variation only.

On the other hand, variations due to **assignable causes** are relatively large and can be traced. In general, assignable causes are:

- Differences among workers' skills,
- Differences among machines,
- Differences among materials, and
- Differences due to interaction between any two or all three of these factors.

Put differently, In a process control, we try to determine whether variation is due to 'common causes' or 'special causes'.

Common causes are those that are inherent in the process over time, affect everyone working in the process, and affect all outcomes of the process. For example, studying engineering drawing is a process. Common causes that affect all students are: the text book, the class room, the drawing table, the drawing instruments, the lighting in the room, the teacher, the number of credit hours, and so on. The common causes can be eliminated by making fundamental changes in the system or the process (*e.g.* change classroom, better lighting facility, keep better instruments, modify the number of credit hours, etc).

Special causes are those that are not part of the process all the time. They do not affect everyone, but arise due to specific situations. These causes can be removed with the help of specific measures. For example, if someone is very weak in drawing he can take up some additional tutorial classes or help from his friends.

As opposed to the aim of acceptance sampling (to accept or reject products already produced), control charts help to produce a better product. The charts have three main applications:

- To determine the process capability to meet specifications.
- To guide modifications for improving the quality of the products.
- To help bring a process in control.
- To keep a process in control, and

- To monitor the output. Monitoring function shows the current status of output quality and provides an early warning of deviations from quality goals.

All products and services have a certain amount of natural variability because of variations in the input and imperfections in the process. This **process variability** may be measured by the process standard deviation s, which indicates how much the products will vary even if the process is in control.

Products have to meet *specified tolerances* imposed by their intended use. Accordingly, the natural variability must be substantially smaller than the specified tolerance. This is explained in Figure 10.3, in which the central line is desired average of the process and the dashed lines are the **3s limits** representing the natural process variability.

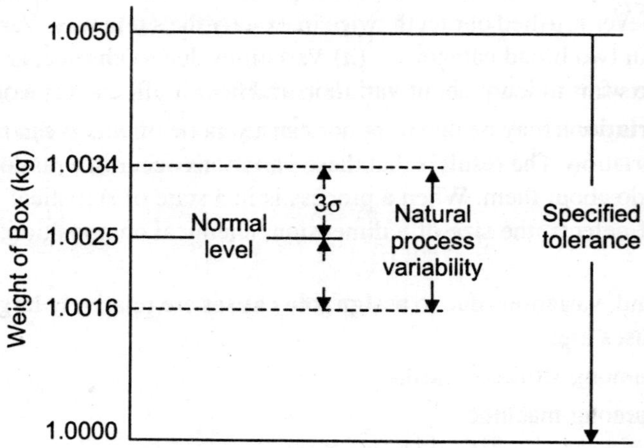

Figure 10.3. Process Variability.

It can be shown that variations of more than 3s from the process average are very unlikely. In fact, it is about 0.25% if the process follows the normal distribution and definitely less than 5% for most processes. The solid lines represent the tolerances specified by the intended use of the product.

Output from a process is sampled and a statistic is calculated which bears the name of the control chart on which it is to be plotted (*e.g.* the sample average $\overline{X}$ is plotted on the $\overline{X}$ chart). (*i*) When process variability is due only to *common causes*, the process is in a state of statistical control (SOSC) and the plotted pattern of data over time is reasonably well behaved, falling within predictable limits and according to predictable patterns. (*ii*) When process variability is due to common and special causes, such as people, equipment, and/or materials, the process is out of control (OOC) and nonrandom patterns appear on the control chart.

Within the specified tolerances, a certain amount of process variability is to be expected. However, it is the goal of the **statistical process control** (SPC) to determine when the process variability is getting out of hand, so that corrective action can be taken, preferably before the required tolerances are violated. This is generally achieved by a **Control Chart** which will be discussed next.

10.7 CONTROL CHARTS

Control charts are tools to study variability in the process. They tell us if a process is showing stability or consistent variation. A **stable process** is also called an *in-control*, a *predictable*, or a *'common cause'* process. It is said to be in a state of statistical control (SOSC). An **unstable process**, on the other hand, is called an *out-of-control* (OOC), *unpredictable*, or a *'common plus special cause'* process.

The control chart is based on the idea that the average of a sample of several items will tend to cancel out the normal process variability, so that undesirable changes in the process will be more visible.

Control charts have a center line plus upper and lower control limits. These control limits are usually spaced 3 standard deviations (of the sample statistic being plotted) above and below the center line. As such, it is highly unlikely that a plotted point will fall outside control limits as long as an SOSC exists. In addition to points outside control limits, the pattern of plotted points within control limits is equally important in identifying an OOC condition and its cause. Therefore, sample statistics are almost always plotted in time order.

Types of Control Charts

They are:

(*a*) Control Charts for measurable quality or **variables** ($\overline{X}$, and R Chart),

(*b*) Control Charts for fraction defectives or **attributes** (*p* chart, *np* chart)

(*c*) Control chart for **number of defects per unit** (*c* Chart).

When a record shows only the number of items that conform and number of items that do not conform to the specifications, then it is a record of *attribute* type. For example, a casting with a blow hole is to be rejected. The size and the shape of the blow holes are not to be accounted. Similarly, a pot with a crack will be rejected, the dimension of the crack is not important.

When a record is made of an actual measured quality characteristics, the quality is said to be expressed by *variables*. Actual measurements of length, diameter, temperature, weight, strength, etc are examples of measurement by variables.

$\overline{X}$ **and R charts** are used together on variable data (*e.g.* measurements of length, diameter, weight, etc) to analyze the central tendency and spread of a process on a single measurable characteristic.

p-chart is used to analyze attribute data (e.g. good or bad classification), such as the fraction nonconforming to a process. There are three ways of making p-chart: (*i*) fraction defective chart or *p-chart*, (*ii*) number of defective chart or *np-chart*, and (*iii*) percent defective chart or *100p-chart.*

c-chart is used when attributes data, such as a count of the number of defects per sample unit, is the focus.

Sometimes $\overline{X}$ chart does not give satisfactory results. This may occur due to old machine or worn-out parts or misalignment or where processing is inherently variable. Here, the range chart is used as an additional tool to control. The purpose of this chart is to have constant check over the variability of the process. The R chart does not replace the $\overline{X}$ chart but simply supplement with additional information about the production process.

10.7.1 THE p-CHART

A p-chart is used when individual units are judged acceptable or rejectable. This is the control chart for percent defectives or for fraction defectives. p-chart is based on binomial distribution.

The *p*-chart is an attribute data chart based on the fraction of product nonconforming to specifications. A subgroup of n items is selected from a process and each is inspected for nonconformities on multiple characteristics. Any item found to have one or more nonconformities is considered a nonconforming item. The number of nonconforming items *x* divided by the sample size n is the fraction nonconforming.

The *p*-chart, like $\overline{X}$ and R charts, is very popular in industry. It requires only attributes data, so the method like Go - No Go gauging, visual inspections, etc. provide with appropriate data. The p chart is particularly attractive where combining several characteristics into one chart is desired, unlike $\overline{X}$ and R charts. Unfortunately, common subgroup sizes are often in the range of 50 to 300 items.

p = fraction defective

= (number of defective units in each lot inspected/no. of units in the lot)

= x/n

Approximately $m = 20$ or 30 subgroups of size n are selected from the process, keeping in mind the desire for within-subgroup homogeneity, with production process differences, if any, showing up over time between subgroups. For each group *i*, the statistic $p_i = x_i/n_i$ is calculated.

We recall that the number of nonconforming items in a sample of size n from finite process is described by the binomial distribution with mean $\mu = np$ and variance $\sigma^2 = npq$, where $q = 1 - p$ and where p is the process fraction defective. Since we are interested in a p chart, the appropriate measure for each subgroup is x/n, or the subgroup fraction nonconforming which has mean $\mu = p$ and variance $\sigma^2 = pq/n$. Thus, 3σ control limits are established from m subgroups by using the following equations:

$$\text{Center line} = \overline{p} = \frac{\sum_{i=1}^{m} x_i}{\sum_{i=1}^{m} n_i}$$

$$\sigma_p = \sqrt{\frac{\overline{pq}}{n_i}}$$

$$\sigma_{np} = n\sqrt{\frac{\overline{pq}}{n_i}}$$

Control limits for p-chart

$$\text{Upper Control Limit, UCL} = \overline{p} + 3\sqrt{\frac{\overline{pq}}{n_i}}$$

$$\text{Lower Control Limit, LCL} = \overline{p} - 3\sqrt{\frac{\overline{pq}}{n_i}}$$

Control limits for np-chart

$$\text{Upper Control Limit, UCL} = n\overline{p} + 3n\sqrt{\frac{\overline{pq}}{n_i}}$$

$$\text{Lower Control Limit, LCL} = n\overline{p} - 3n\sqrt{\frac{\overline{pq}}{n_i}}$$

Example 10.1. The balls for ball bearings are inspected by attributes. A sample of 100 is inspected daily for continuously 10 days. The samples are taken randomly from the daily production of 1000 balls. Compute the control limits for p- chart based on the following data.

Date	1	2	3	4	5	6	7	8	9	10
Rejections	18	12	6	15	2	20	14	10	8	6

Solution:

Table 10.1

Date	1	2	3	4	5	6	7	8	9	10	Total
Rejections	18	12	6	15	2	20	14	10	8	6	111
$pi = x_i/n_i$	.18	.12	.06	.15	.02	.20	.14	.10	.08	.06	1.11

$\bar{p}$ = (Sum of total defectives or rejections in 10 days)/Total no.of bearings inspected in 10 days $= 111/(10 \times 100) = 0.111$

n = no. of samples inspected daily = 100

$$\sigma_p = \sqrt{\frac{\bar{p}\bar{q}}{n_i}} = \sqrt{\frac{0.111(1-0.111)}{n}} = \sqrt{\frac{0.111 \times .889}{100}} = 0.0314$$

Control limits for p-chart

Upper Control Limit, UCL = $\bar{p} + 3\sigma_p = 0.111 + 3 \times 0.0314 = 0.2052$

Lower Control Limit, LCL = $\bar{p} - 3\sigma_p = 0.111 - 3 \times 0.0314 = 0.0168$

Note:

- Since all the fraction defectives are within the control limits, the trial control limits are taken as the actual control limits.
- If any of the fraction defectives are out of control limits, then calculate new $\bar{p}$ and new control limits eliminating the reading which is out of control.
- If all the remaining fraction defectives are within the control limit, the new control limits are actual control limits.

10.7.2 THE c-CHART

This is a method of plotting attribute characteristics. In this case, the sample taken is a single unit of length, breadth, area or a fixed time, etc. In some cases it is required to find the number of defects per unit rather than the percent defectives. For example, a car or a radio in with a large number of small components form a large unit. The radio may have defects at various points. A *c*-chart is based on Poisson distribution.

Average number of defects, $\bar{C}$ is computed as follows:

$\bar{C}$ = Total number of defects/Total number of samples

Standard deviation, $\sigma_c = \sqrt{\bar{C}}$

Trial control limits

$$UCL = \bar{C} + 3\,\sigma_c$$

$$LCL = \bar{C} - 3\,\sigma_c$$

Example 10.2. The following table shows the number of point defects on the surface of a car body manufactured by a company on March 14, 2004. Compute the control limits for *c*-chart.

Table 10.2

Car no.	*No. of defects*	*Car no.*	*No. of defects*
1	2	11	3
2	2	12	0
3	4	13	5
4	7	14	1
5	5	15	3
6	6	16	10
7	7	17	4
8	14	18	3
9	2	19	12
10	9	20	11
Total	58	52	

Total number of defects = 58 + 52 = 110

Average number of defects = $\overline{C}$ = 110/20 = 5.5

Trial control limits

$$UCL = \overline{C} + 3\,\sigma_c = \overline{C} + 3\sqrt{\overline{C}} = 5.5 + 3\sqrt{5.5} = 12.54$$

$$LCL = \overline{C} - 3\,\sigma_c = \overline{C} - 3\sqrt{\overline{C}} = 5.5 - 3\sqrt{5.5} = -1.74 = 0$$ **as negative defects are not possible.**

If any of these points fall outside the control limits, calculate new $\overline{C}$ and new control limits eliminating the observation which falls outside. For example, observation number 8 with 14 defects falls outside the control limits. So, the value of $\overline{C}$ should be recalculated.

New $\overline{C}$ = (110 – 14)/19 = 96/19 = 5.05

10.7.3 STEPS IN CONSTRUCTING S-CHART

1. Select *k* successive subgroups where *k* is at least 20, in which there are n measurements in each subgroup. Typically *n* is between 1 and 9. 3, 4, or 5 measurements per subgroup is quite common.
2. Find the range of each subgroup *s*(*i*) where *s*(*i*) = biggest value – smallest value for each subgroup *i*.
3. Find the centerline for the *s* chart, denoted by

$$\overline{S} = \frac{1}{k}\,\Sigma s(i)$$

4. Find the UCL and LCL with the following formulas:

   UCL = B(4) $\overline{S}$ and

   LCL = B(3) $\overline{S}$

B(3) and B(4) can be found in the following Table 10.3:

Table 10.3 of B(3) and B(4)

n	*B(3)*	*B(4)*	*n*	*B(3)*	*B(4)*
2	0	3.267	6	.03	1.970
3	0	2.568	7	.118	1.882
4	0	2.266	8	.185	1.815
5	0	2.089	9	.239	1.761

5. Plot the subgroup data and determine if the process is in statistical control. If not, determine the reason for the assignable cause, eliminate it, and the subgroup(s) and repeat the previous 3 steps. Do NOT eliminate subgroups with points out of range for which assignable causes cannot be found.
6. Once the *s* chart is in a state of statistical control and the centerline $\overline{S}$ can be considered a reliable estimate of the range, the process standard deviation can be estimated using:

$$\sigma = \frac{\overline{s}}{c(4)}\sqrt{1-[c(4)]^2}$$

$c(4)$ can be found in the following Table 10.4.

Table 10.4

n	*c(4)*	*n*	*c(4)*
2	.7979	6	.9515
3	.8862	7	.9594
4	.9213	8	.9650
5	.9400	9	.9693

10.7.4 STEPS IN CONSTRUCTING THE $\overline{X}$ CHART

1. Find the mean of each subgroup $\overline{X}(1)$, $\overline{X}(2)$, $\overline{X}(3)$,... $\overline{X}(k)$ and the grand mean of all subgroups.

$$\overline{\overline{X}} = \frac{1}{k}\Sigma\overline{X}(i)$$

2. Find the UCL and LCL using the equations

$$\text{UCL} = \overline{\overline{X}} + A(3)\ \overline{S}$$

$$\text{LCL} = \overline{\overline{X}} - A(3)\ \overline{S}$$

3. A(3) can be found in the following Table 10.5:

Table 10.5

n	*A(3)*	*n*	*A(3)*
2	2.659	6	1.287
3	1.954	7	1.182
4	1.628	8	1.099
5	1.427	9	1.032

4. Plot the LCL, UCL, centerline, and subgroup means.
5. Interpret the data using the following guidelines to determine if the process is in control:
   - one point outside the 3σ control limitsb. eight successive points on the same side of the centerline
   - six successive points that increase or decrease
   - two out of three points that are on the same side of the centerline, both at a distance exceeding 2σ from the centerline
   - four out of five points that are on the same side of the centerline, four at a distance exceeding σ sigma from the centerline
   - using an average run length (ARL) for determining process anomalies.

Example 10.3. The following data consists of 20 sets of three measurements of the diameter of an engine shaft.

Table 10.6

n	*meas#1*	*meas#2*	*meas#3*	*Range*	$\overline{X}$
1	2.0000	1.9998	2.0002	0.0004	2.0000
2	1.9998	2.0003	2.0002	0.0005	2.0001
3	1.9998	2.0001	2.0005	0.0007	2.0001
4	1.9997	2.0000	2.0004	0.0007	2.0000
5	2.0003	2.0003	2.0002	0.0001	2.0003
6	2.0004	2.0003	2.0000	0.0004	2.0002
7	1.9998	1.9998	1.9998	0.0000	1.9998
8	2.0000	2.0001	2.0001	0.0001	2.0001
9	2.0005	2.0000	1.9999	0.0006	2.0001
10	1.9995	1.9998	2.0001	0.0006	1.9998
11	2.0002	1.9999	2.0001	0.0003	2.0001

12	2.0002	1.9998	2.0005	0.0007	2.0002
13	2.0000	2.0001	1.9998	0.0003	2.0000
14	2.0000	2.0002	2.0004	0.0004	2.0002
15	1.9994	2.0001	1.9996	0.0007	1.9997
16	1.9999	2.0003	1.9993	0.0010	1.9998
17	2.0002	1.9998	2.0004	0.0006	2.0001
18	2.0000	2.0001	2.0001	0.0001	2.0001
19	1.9997	1.9994	1.9998	0.0004	1.9996
20	2.0003	2.0007	1.9999	0.0008	2.0003

$\overline{S}$ Chart Limits:

$\overline{S} = 0.0002$

UCL = B(4) $\overline{S}$ = 2.568*.0002 = 0.0005136

LCL = B(3) $\overline{S}$ = 0 * .0002 = 0.00

$\overline{X}$ Chart Limits:

$\overline{\overline{X}} = 2.000$

UCL = $\overline{\overline{X}}$ + A(3) $\overline{S}$ = 2.000 + 1.954*.0002 = 2.0003908

LCL = $\overline{\overline{X}}$ − A(3) $\overline{S}$ = 2.000 − 1.954*.0002 = 1.9996092

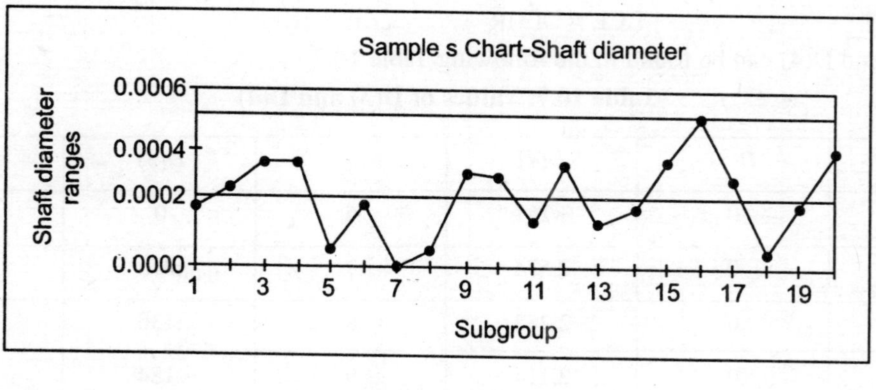

Figure 10.4. s-Chart.

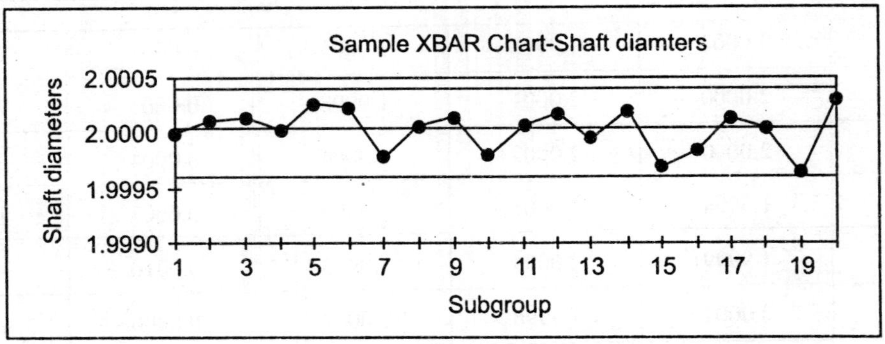

Figure 10.5. $\overline{X}$**-Chart.**

Although theoretically possible, since we do not know either the population process mean or standard deviation, these formulas cannot be used directly and both must be estimated from the process itself. First the R chart is constructed. If the R chart validates that the process variation is in statistical control, the $\overline{X}$ chart is constructed.

Steps in Constructing an R Chart

1. Select k successive subgroups where k is at least 20, in which there are n measurements in each subgroup. Typically n is between 1 and 9. Though 3, 4, or 5 measurements per subgroup is quite common.
2. Find the range of each subgroup R(i) where R(i) = (biggest value – smallest value for each subgroup i).
3. Find the centerline for the R chart, denoted by

$$\overline{R} = \frac{1}{k}\Sigma R(i)$$

4. Find the UCL and LCL with the following formulas:

$$UCL = D(4)\overline{R}$$

$$LCL = D(3)\overline{R}$$

D(3) and D(4) can be found in the following Table 10.7:

Table 10.7. Values of D(3) and D(4)

n	*D(3)*	*D(4)*	*n*	*D(3)*	*D(4)*
2	0	3.267	6	0	2.004
3	0	2.574	7	.076	1.924
4	0	2.282	8	.136	1.864
5	0	2.114	9	.184	1.816

5. Plot the subgroup data and determine if the process is in statistical control. If not, determine the reason for the assignable cause, eliminate it, and the subgroup(s) and repeat the previous 3 steps. Do NOT eliminate subgroups with points out of range for which assignable causes cannot be found.

6. Once the R chart is in a state of statistical control and the centerline RBAR can be considered a reliable estimate of the range, the process standard deviation can be estimated using:

$$\sigma = \frac{\overline{R}}{d(2)}$$

$d(2)$ can be found in the following Table 10.8:

Table 10.8

n	*d(2)*	*n*	*d(2)*
2	1.128	6	2.534
3	1.693	7	2.704
4	2.059	8	2.847
5	2.326	9	2.970

Steps in Constructing the $\overline{X}$ Chart

1. Find the mean of each subgroup $\overline{X}(1)$, $\overline{X}(2)$, $\overline{X}(3)$, ..., $\overline{X}(k)$ and the grand mean of all subgroups using

$$\overline{\overline{X}} = \frac{1}{k}\Sigma\overline{X}(i)$$

2. Find the UCL and LCL using the equations

$$\text{UCL} = \overline{\overline{X}} + A(2)\,\overline{R}$$

$$\text{LCL} = \overline{\overline{X}} - A(2)\,\overline{R}$$

A(2) can be found from the following table:

n	*A(2)*	*n*	*A(2)*
2	1.880	6	.483
3	1.023	7	.419
4	.729	8	.373
5	.577	9	.337

3. Plot the LCL, UCL, centerline, and subgroup means.
4. Interpret the data using the following guidelines to determine if the process is in control:
   - one point outside the 3σ control limits
   - eight successive points on the same side of the centerline
   - six successive points that increase or decrease
   - two out of three points that are on the same side of the centerline, both at a distance exceeding 2σ from the centerline
   - four out of five points that are on the same side of the centerline, four at a distance exceeding 1σ from the centerline
   - using an average run length (ARL) for determining process anomalies.

Example 10.4. The following data consists of 20 sets of three measurements of the diameter of an engine shaft.

Table 10.9

n	*meas#1*	*meas#2*	*meas#3*	*Range*	$\overline{X}$
1	2.0000	1.9998	2.0002	0.0004	2.0000
2	1.9998	2.0003	2.0002	0.0005	2.0001
3	1.9998	2.0001	2.0005	0.0007	2.0001
4	1.9997	2.0000	2.0004	0.0007	2.0000
5	2.0003	2.0003	2.0002	0.0001	2.0003
6	2.0004	2.0003	2.0000	0.0004	2.0002
7	1.9998	1.9998	1.9998	0.0000	1.9998
8	2.0000	2.0001	2.0001	0.0001	2.0001
9	2.0005	2.0000	1.9999	0.0006	2.0001
10	1.9995	1.9998	2.0001	0.0006	1.9998
11	2.0002	1.9999	2.0001	0.0003	2.0001
12	2.0002	1.9998	2.0005	0.0007	2.0002
13	2.0000	2.0001	1.9998	0.0003	2.0000
14	2.0000	2.0002	2.0004	0.0004	2.0002
15	1.9994	2.0001	1.9996	0.0007	1.9997
16	1.9999	2.0003	1.9993	0.0010	1.9998
17	2.0002	1.9998	2.0004	0.0006	2.0001
18	2.0000	2.0001	2.0001	0.0001	2.0001
19	1.9997	1.9994	1.9998	0.0004	1.9996
20	2.0003	2.0007	1.9999	0.0008	2.0003

R Chart Limits

$$\overline{R} = 0.0005$$

$$UCL = D(4)\ \overline{R} = 2.574 * .0005 = 0.001287$$

$$LCL = D(3)\ \overline{R} = 0.000 * .0005 = 0.000$$

$\overline{X}$ Chart Limits

$$\overline{\overline{X}} = 2.0000$$

$$UCL = \overline{\overline{X}} + A(2)\ \overline{R} = 2.000 + 1.023*.0005 = 2.0005115$$

$$LCL = \overline{\overline{X}} - A(2)\ \overline{R} = 2.000 - 1.023*.0005 = 1.9994885$$

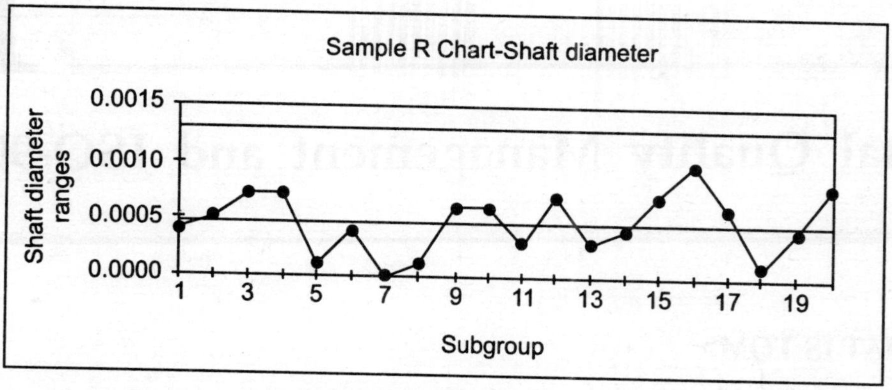

Figure 10.6. R-Chart.

10.7.5 THE $\overline{X}$ AND R CHARTS

Theoretical Control Limits for $\overline{X}$ Charts are:

$$UCL = \mu + \frac{3\sigma}{\sqrt{n}}$$

$$LCL = \mu - \frac{3\sigma}{\sqrt{n}}$$

Although theoretically possible, since we do not know either the population process mean or standard deviation, these formulas cannot be used directly and both must be estimated from the process itself. First the R chart is constructed. If the R chart validates that the process variation is in statistical control, the $\overline{X}$ chart is constructed.

10.8 USE OF COMPUTERS IN QUALITY CONTROL

These days software packages for quality control are available. In some cases, computers can be linked directly to take the sample measurements and control the process **on-line**. These packages are likely to take much of the chores associated with the lengthy calculations and make the application of quality control techniques far more easy and effective.

11

Total Quality Management and ISO-9000

11.0 WHAT IS TQM?

TQM stands for Total Quality Management. It is one of the most effective and least understood corporate strategies. It can affect every level, procedure and every person in a company. It is a comprehensive process that can bring a company to the forefront of the global market. TQM has been defined in many ways by various authors. Some of them are being presented here.

According to British Quality Association, 'TQM is a corporate business management philosophy which recognizes that customer needs and business goals are inseparable. It is applicable within both industry and commerce'.

TQM is a management philosophy for continuously improving overall business performance based on leadership, supplier quality management, vision and plan statement, evaluation, process control and improvement, product design, quality system improvement, employee participation, recognition and reward, education and training, and customer focus.

TQM is an operating philosophy, a goal, and a way of doing business. For many companies, it is a major cultural change; from 'solving a crisis' to 'not having a crisis'. The typical 'just do it' approach to business is replaced by clearly defined processes.

According to some common opinion, TQM is nothing new - it is just a common sense way of remaining in business. In fact, any well run company is already doing TQM without even realizing it. TQM is still the Japanese trick that the western firms are keen to copy.

11.1 TQM NEEDS COMMITMENT

TQM has methods, but the most important criteria for continuous improvement is *commitment.* The common reason behind the failure of TQM is the lack of commitment from the top management. If you are in middle management, then you must lobby your CEO or boss. You must prove why it is important and have him or her on your team talking up the plan. Your staff wants to see your commitment. You lead, they will follow.

The activities for each employee, including top management, should be directed towards the same purpose or the vision. If people in a company do not have the same purpose, the organization will be weak. Just as a cricket team loses fans when it loses games, a company that loses its purpose will miss its goal, will make too many mistakes, and will lose customers.

11.2 VARIOUS APPROACHES TO TQM

11.2.1 DEMING'S APPROACH TO TQM

Deming (1986) stressed the responsibilities of top management to take the lead in changing processes and systems. It is the top management's responsibility to create and communicate a vision to move the firm towards continuous improvement. Top management is responsible for most quality problems; it should give employees clear standards for what is considered acceptable work, and provide the methods to achieve it. These methods include an appropriate working environment and climate for work-free of faultfinding, blame or fear.

Deming (1986) also emphasized the importance of identification and measurement of customer requirements, creation of supplier partnership, use of functional teams to identify and solve quality problems, enhancement of employee skills, participation of employees, and pursuit of continuous improvement.

The means to improve quality lie in the ability to control and manage systems and processes properly, and in the role of management responsibilities in achieving this. Deming (1986) advocated methodological practices, including the use of specific tools and statistical methods in the design, management, and improvement of process, which aim to reduce the inevitable variation that occurs from "common causes" and "special causes" in production.

"Common causes" of variations are systemic and are shared by many operators, machines, or products. They include poor product design, non-conforming incoming materials, and poor working conditions. These are the responsibilities of management.

"Special causes" relate to the lack of knowledge or skill, or poor performance. These are the responsibilities of employees.

Deming proposed 14 points as the principles of TQM, which are listed below:

- Create constancy of purpose towards improvement of product and service, with the aim to become competitive and to stay in business, and to provide jobs.
- Adopt the new philosophy. We are in a new economic age. Western management must awaken to the challenge, must learn their responsibilities, and take on leadership for change.
- Cease dependence on mass inspection to quality. Eliminate the need for inspection on a mass basis by building quality into the product in the first place.
- End the practice of awarding business on the basis of price tag. Instead, minimize total cost. Move towards a single supplier for any one item, on a long-term relationship of loyalty and trust.
- Improve constantly and forever the system of production and service, to improve quality and productivity, and thus constantly decrease costs.
- Institute training on the job.
- Institute leadership. The aim of supervision should be to help people and machines and gadgets to do a better job. Supervision of management is in need of overhaul, as well as supervision of production workers.
- Drive out fear, so that people may work effectively for the company.
- Break down barriers between departments. People in research, design, sales, and production must work as a team, to foresee problems of production and in use that may be encountered with the product or service.

- Eliminate slogans, exhortations, and targets for the workforce asking for zero defects and new levels of productivity. Such exhortations only create adversarial relationships, as the bulk of the causes of low quality and low productivity belong to the system and thus lie beyond the power of the workforce.
- Eliminate work standards (quotas) on the factory floor. Substitute leadership. Eliminate management by objective. Eliminate management by numbers, numerical goals. Substitute leadership.
- Remove barriers that rob the hourly worker of his right to pride of workmanship. The responsibility of supervisors must be changed from sheer numbers to quality. Remove barriers that rob people in management and in engineering of their right to pride of workmanship. This means, inter alia, abolishment of the annual or merit rating and of management by objective.
- Institute a vigorous program of education and self-improvement.
- Put everybody in the company to work to accomplish the transformation. The transformation is everybody's job.

11.2.2 JURAN'S APPROACH TO TQM

TQM is the system of activities directed at achieving delighted customers, empowered employees, higher revenues, and lower costs (Juran and Gryna, 1993). Juran believed that main quality problems are due to management rather than workers. The attainment of quality requires activities in all functions of a firm. Firm-wide assessment of quality, supplier quality management, using statistical methods, quality information system, and competitive benchmarking are essential to quality improvement. Juran's approach is emphasis on team (QC circles and self-managing teams) and project work, which can promote quality improvement, improve communication between management and employees coordination, and improve coordination between employees. He also emphasized the importance of top management commitment and empowerment, participation, recognition and rewards. According to Juran, it is very important to understand customer needs. This requirement applies to all involved in marketing, design, manufacture, and services. Identifying customer needs requires more vigorous analysis and understanding to ensure the product meets customers' needs and is fit for its intended use, not just meeting product specifications.

Thus, market research is essential for identifying customers' needs. In order to ensure design quality, he proposed the use of techniques including quality function deployment, experimental design, reliability engineering and concurrent engineering.

Juran considered quality management as three basic processes (Juran Trilogy): Quality control, quality improvement, and quality planning. In his view, the approach to managing for quality consists of: The sporadic problem is detected and acted upon by the process of quality control; The chronic problem requires a different process, namely, quality improvement; Such chronic problems are traceable to an inadequate quality planning process. Juran defined a universal sequence of activities for the three quality processes, which is listed in Table 1.

Juran defined four broad categories of quality costs, which can be used to evaluate the firm's costs related to quality. Such information is valuable to quality improvement. The four quality costs are listed as follows:

- Internal failure costs (scrap, rework, failure analysis, etc.), associated with defects found prior to transfer of the product to the customer;
- External failure costs (warranty charges, complaint adjustment, returned material, allowances, etc.), associated with defects found after product is shipped to the customer;

- Appraisal costs (incoming, in-process, and final inspection and testing, product quality audits, maintaining accuracy of testing equipment, etc.), incurred in determining the degree of conformance to quality requirements;
- Prevention costs (quality planning, new product review, quality audits, supplier quality evaluation, training, etc.), incurred in keeping failure and appraisal costs to a minimum.

11.2.3 CROSBY'S APPROACH TO TQM

Crosby (1979) identified a number of important principles and practices for a successful quality improvement program, which include, for example, management participation, management responsibility for quality, employee recognition, education, reduction of the cost of quality (prevention costs, appraisal costs, and failure costs), emphasis on prevention rather than after-the-event inspection, doing things right the first time, and zero defects.

Crosby claimed that mistakes are caused by two reasons: Lack of knowledge and lack of attention. Education and training can eliminate the first cause and a personal commitment to excellence (zero defects) and attention to detail will cure the second. Crosby also stressed the importance of management style to successful quality improvement. The key to quality improvement is to change the thinking of top managers-to get them not to accept mistakes and defects, as this would in turn reduce work expectations and standards in their jobs.

Understanding, commitment, and communication are all essential. Crosby presented the quality management maturity grid, which can be used by firms to evaluate their quality management maturity. The five stages are: Uncertainty, awakening, enlightenment, wisdom and certainty. These stages can be used to assess progress in a number of measurement categories such as management understanding and attitude, quality organization status, problem handling, cost of quality as percentage of sales, and summation of firm quality posture. The quality management maturity grid and cost of quality measures are the main tools for managers to evaluate their quality status. Crosby offered a 14-step program that can guide firms in pursuing quality improvement. These steps are listed as follows:

- *Management commitment:* To make it clear where management stands on quality.
- *Quality improvement team:* To run the quality improvement program.
- *Quality measurement:* To provide a display of current and potential nonconformance problems in a manner that permits objective evaluation and corrective action.
- *Cost of quality:* To define the ingredients of the cost of quality, and explain its use as a management tool.
- *Quality awareness:* To provide a method of raising the personal concern felt by all personnel in the company towards the conformance of the product or service and the quality reputation of the company.
- *Corrective action:* To provide a systematic method of resolving forever the problems that are identical through previous action steps.
- *Zero defects planning:* To investigate the various activities that must be conducted in preparation for formally launching the Zero Defects program.
- *Supervisor training:* To define the type of training that supervisors need in order to actively carry out their part of the quality improvement program.
- *Zero defects day:* To create an event that will make all employees realize, through a personal experience, that there has been a change.

- *Goal setting:* To turn pledges and commitment into actions by encouraging individuals to establish improvement goals for themselves and their groups.
- *Error causal removal:* To give the individual employee a method of communicating to management the situation that makes it difficult for the employee to meet the pledge to improve.
- *Recognition:* To appreciate those who participate.
- *Quality councils:* To bring together the professional quality people for planned communication on a regular basis.
- *Do it over again:* To emphasize that the quality improvement program never ends.

11.2.4 FEIGENBAUM'S APPROACH TO TQM

Feigenbaum (1991) defined TQM as: An effective system for integrating the quality development, quality-maintenance, and quality-improvement efforts of the various groups in a firm so as to enable marketing, engineering, production, and service at the most economical levels which allow for full customer satisfaction. He claimed that effective quality management consists of four main stages, described as follows:

- Setting quality standards;
- Appraising conformance to these standards;
- Acting when standards are not met;
- Planning for improvement in these standards.

The quality chain, he argued, starts with the identification of all customers' requirements and ends only when the product or service is delivered to the customer, who remains satisfied. Thus, all functional activities, such as marketing, design, purchasing, manufacturing, inspection, shipping, installation and service, etc., are involved in and influence the attainment of quality. Identifying customers' requirements is a fundamental initial point for 5 Feigenbaum used the term TQC (total quality control) instead of TQM in his book. He claimed that it permits what might be called total quality management to cover the full scope of the product and service "life cycle" from product conception through production and customer service. According to ISO 8402 - Quality management and quality assurance -vocabulary, TQM is sometimes called "total quality", "company-wide quality control", "total quality control", etc. He claimed that effective TQM requires a high degree of effective functional integration among people, machines, and information, stressing a system approach to quality. A clearly defined total quality system is a powerful foundation for TQM.

Total quality system is defined as follows:

The agreed firm-wide operating work structure, documented in effective, integrated technical and managerial procedures, for guiding the coordinated actions of the people, the machines, and the information of the firm in the best and most practical ways to assure customer quality satisfaction and economical costs of quality.

Feigenbaum emphasized that efforts should be made towards the prevention of poor quality rather than detecting it after the event. He argued that quality is an integral part of the day-to-day work of the line, staff, and operatives of a firm. There are two factors affecting product quality: The technological-that is, machines, materials, and processes; and the human-that is, operators, foremen, and other firm personnel. Of these two factors, the human is of greater importance by far. Feigenbaum considered top management commitment, employee participation, supplier quality management, information system, evaluation, communication, use of quality costs, use of statistical technology to be an essential component of TQM. He argued that employees should be rewarded for their quality improvement suggestions, quality is everybody's job. He stated that effective employee training and education should focus on the following three main aspects: Quality attitudes, quality knowledge, and quality skills.

11.2.5 ISHIKAWA'S APPROACH TO TQM

Ishikawa6 (1985) argued that quality management extends beyond the product and encompasses after-sales service, the quality of management, the quality of individuals and the firm itself. He claimed that the success of a firm is highly dependent on treating quality improvement as a never-ending quest. A commitment to continuous improvement can ensure that people will never stop learning. He advocated employee participation as the key to the successful implementation of TQM. Quality circles, he believed, are an important vehicle to achieve this. Like all other gurus he emphasized the importance of education, stating that quality begins and ends with it. He has been associated with the development and advocacy of universal education in the seven QC tools (Ishikawa, 1985). These tools are listed below:

- Pareto chart;
- Cause and effect diagram (Ishikawa diagram);
- Stratification chart;
- Scatter diagram;
- Check sheet;
- Histogram;
- Control chart.

Ishikawa used the term TQC (total quality control) instead of TQM in his book. According to ISO 8402—Quality management and quality assurance—vocabulary, TQM is sometimes called "total quality", "company-wide quality control", "total quality control", etc. Ishikawa (1985) suggested that the assessment of customer requirements serves as a tool to foster cross-functional cooperation; selecting suppliers should be on the basis of quality rather than solely on price; cross-functional teams are effective ways for identifying and solving quality problems. Ishikawa's concept of TQM contains the following six fundamental principles:

- Quality first-not short-term profits first;
- Customer orientation-not producer orientation;
- The next step is your customer-breaking down the barrier of sectionalism;
- Using facts and data to make presentations-utilization of statistical methods;
- Respect for humanity as a management philosophy, full participatory management;
- Cross-functional management.

Table 11.1 Summary of TQM Gurus

Writer	*Definition of quality*	*Focus*	*Developed*
Juran	Fitness for use	Customer	Quality trilogy, five quality characteristics, internal customer, The 4 phases of problem solving, quality council, The quality spiral.
Deming	Fitness for purpose	Customer	14 points of quality, Deming PDCA cycle, 7 deadly diseases, system of profound knowledge.

Crosby	Conformance to requirements	Supplier	5 absolutes of quality, 14 points plan for quality.
Ishikawa	None specific	Supplier	Fishbone diagram, Classification of statistical quality tools, Company wide quality control, Quality circles.
Taguchi	None specific	Supplier	Quality of design methods.
Feigenbaum	Customer satisfaction at the lowest cost	Supplier	Industrial cycle, Utilization of the quality consultant.

11.3 SOME QUALITY AND TQM RELATED TERMS

What is Quality ?

Quality is a state of mind and can be delivered better by people who are having fun than by people who live dull, regulated lives surrounded by slogan and exhortations.

Quality means satisfying the customer. According to TQM, the quality is totally defined by the customer's perceptions. It doesn't matter what we think, it matters what our customers think, and the customers' perceptions are constantly changing. It is up to us to make sure our organization is fast and flexible enough to respond to their demand of better products/services.

Quality management, as specified in ISO-9000, is about managing our organization with the objective of satisfying our customers' needs.

According to Arnold Fiegenbaum (consultant), the cost of correcting mistakes can easily be 15 to 40 % of the plant's productivity.

What is ISO-9000?

ISO-9000 is the generic name used to describe the International Standard Organization (ISO) 9000 series of management system standards. The peak standard of ISO-9000 series is ISO-9001, which is titled 'Quality Systems—Model for quality assurance in design/development, production, installation and servicing'. This is the standard to which an organization can be certificated for the design, development, installation, and maintenance of products and services (*e.g.*, software development, operation, and support) [Jenner, Michael G.].

ISO-9001: is known by different names in different countries as shown below.

- ANSI/ASQC ISO-9001 in USA
- EN ISO-9001 in Europe
- BS/EN ISO-9001 in the UK
- AS/NZS ISO-9001 in New Zealand and Australia
- SS ISO-9001 in Singapore

ISO-9002

- For organizations that do not do their own design.
- Titled 'Quality Systems—Model for quality assurance in production, installation and servicing'.

ISO-9003

- Titled 'Quality Systems—Model for quality assurance in final inspection and test'.
- This is used by organizations that perform final inspection and testing of products purchased from external suppliers.

ISO-9000.3

- Titled 'Quality Management and Quality System elements—Guidelines for development, supply and maintenance of software'.
- Is a guideline on the use of ISO-9001 in computer software development.

ISO-9004.2

- Titled 'Quality management and quality system elements—Guidelines for services'.
- Is a guideline on the application of ISO-9001 and ISO-9002 to services. An organization cannot be certificated to ISO-9004.2 and it is not used during the certification process.
- This can be applied to the following:
  - **Hospitality services:** catering, hotels, tourist services, entertainments, radio, TV, etc.
  - **Communications:** airports, airlines, roads, rail, sea transport, telecommunications, post office, etc.
  - **Health:** medical practitioners, hospitals, ambulances, medical labs, dentists, opticians, etc.
  - **Maintenance:** electrical, mechanical, vehicles, heating systems, air-conditioning, building, computer.
  - **Utilities:** cleansing, waste management, water supply, grounds maintenance, electricity, gas and energy supply, fire, police, public services, etc.
  - **Trading:** wholesale, retail, stockist, distributor, marketing, packaging.
  - **Financial:** banking, insurance, pensions, property services, accounting.
  - **Professional:** architecture, surveying, legal, law enforcement, security, education, engineering, quality management, etc.
  - **Administration:** personnel, computing, office services, etc.
  - **Technical:** consultancy, photography, test labs, etc.
  - **Scientific:** research, development, studies, decision aids, etc.

ISO-9004.4

'Guidelines for quality improvement' provides a concise reference source for information and technique relating to quality improvement.

ISO-10011

'Guidelines for auditing quality systems' is a valuable guide for internal auditors.

ISO-10013

'Guidelines for developing quality manuals'

ISO-9126

'Information technology—software product evaluation—quality characteristics and guidelines for their use', defines the terminology to be used as the basis for software quality metrics.

Why ISO-9001 ?

Because it provides a clear way to structure your operation to empower your people, reduce paperwork and bureaucracy, constantly delight your customers, and survive in business over the long term.

Benefits of implementing an ISO-9000 based system can be two folds: (*i*) Financial, and (*ii*) Personal.

- Staff and customers are more satisfied because the services provided are close to customers' needs.
- We can achieve significant savings from satisfied customers. With our improved reputation and credibility, we can offer our services at premium prices.
- We will find ourselves being taken seriously when the prestigious contracts are being bid. In fact, being certified to international quality management standard is increasingly a prerequisite for bidders on Government and industry contracts worldwide.
- Indirect benefits include improved staff motivation and reduced management frustration.
- Winning more work-orders with less efforts due to enhanced credibility.
- Increase profitability due to better products at lower costs.

What does ISO stand for? Where is it situated?

ISO stands for International organization for Standardization. It has it's head office at Geneva, Switzerland and it comprises National Standard Bodies of 91 countries including India.

How does ISO-9000 emerge?

Over the past two decades it has been felt by big companies that there should be some efficient ways of assuring reliable product quality in advance of delivery rather than waiting to find the failures when it might be too late. As a result in early 70s many companies started specifying their own QA Standards to their suppliers. But this was not found economical by suppliers and the customers requirements were not consistently met.

Thus thinking developed to formulate a set of uniform Standards, on Quality systems and Quality management, which if implemented could satisfy all the customers. The UK and Canada took the lead and the success of these standards became known in other countries. The ISO then prepared a Standard in the form of ISO-9000 series of Standards.

What are ISO-9000 standards?

ISO-9000 Standards are the contractual, functional and technical requirements for all quality activities to ensure that a product, process, service or system is fit for it's intended purposes. It was developed in 1987.

What is it's Indian equivalent?

It's Indian equivalent is IS-14000.

How many standards are there in ISO-9000 series?

ISO-9000 Series has 5 standards, viz;

ISO-9000

ISO-9001

ISO-9002

ISO-9003

ISO-9004

What are the applications of each standard?

ISO-9000: provides guidelines for selection in use of a series of ISO-9001, ISO-9002, ISO-9003, and ISO-9004. This standard, therefore, is not to be used for contractual purposes.

ISO-9001: This is for use when the contract specially requires that the supplier assure quality throughout the whole cycle from the Design through Production, installation and Servicing.

ISO-9002: This is for use when the specified requirements for products are stated in terms of an already established design or specification.

ISO -9003: This is applicable in a situation where only the Suppliers' capabilities for inspection and tests (conducted on products as supplied) can be satisfactorily demonstrated. This standard is for contractual use.

ISO-9004: This is for internal use which describes a basic set of quality system elements which help to develop a sound and comprehensive quality management system.

What are the ingredients of a quality system?

The ingredients are:

- Clearly defined responsibilities and authority.
- Documented procedures, Instructions and controls.
- Knowledge and understanding of responsibilities, authority, procedures and instructions.
- Correct operation of procedures by the authorized and responsible personnel.
- Adequacy of personnel, equipment, facilities and general resources.
- Effectiveness of the system when correctly operated.

What type of systems are required?

ISO-9000 requires a documented quality system comprising the following:

- A policy document mentioning the Company's intention to ensure that the system exists and to guarantee consistent product quality.
- Operating procedures which are instructions on equipment operation, Inspection and tests, documentation, etc.
- Specific instructions relating to particular contracts which include drawings, specific test procedures, quality plans etc.

What are the quality system requirements specified by the Standard ?

The standard specifies 20 sections of quality systems requirements. They are:

Management Responsibility

Requires that quality Policy defined, documented and communicated throughout the organization; that responsibility regarding quality be clearly defined; that in-house resources are available for verification activities; that the management representatives be appointed to ensure quality system requirements are being met; and that the management representative lead a management review periodically to ensure the continuing suitability and effectiveness of the quality system.

Quality System

Requires a quality system that meets the criteria of the applicable ISO-9000 Series standard be established and maintained (documented as a quality system manual and implemented) as a means of ensuring that product conforms to requirements.

Contract Review

Requires review of contracts to ensure requirements are adequately defined and to ensure the capability exists to meet the requirements.

Design Control

Requires procedures for controlling and verifying product design to ensure that specified requirements are being met and to include procedures for design/development planning, design input/output, design verification, and design changes.

Document Control

Requires establishing and maintaining procedures for controlling documentation through approval, issue, change. and modification.

Purchasing

Requires that purchased products conform to specified requirements; ensure through subcontractor assessments, clear & accurate purchasing-data, and verification of purchased product.

Purchaser-Supplied Product

Requires procedures for verification, storage and maintenance of purchaser product.

Product Identification and Traceability

Requires procedures for identifying a product during all stages of production, delivery and installation, and individual product or batch-unique identification as needed.

Process Control

Requires procedures to ensure that production and installation processes are carried out under controlled conditions which include documentation, monitoring and control of suitable process and product characteristics, use of approved equipment, criteria for workmanship.

Inspection and Testing

Requires that procedures for inspection and test at receiving in process, and final stations be in place as documented in quality plan; must include maintenance of records and deposition of product.

Inspection, Measuring and Test Equipment

Requires procedures for selection, control, calibration and maintenance of measuring and test equipment.

Inspection and Test Status

Requires that marking, stamps or labels be affixed to product throughout production and installation to show conformance ,or nonconformance to tests and inspections.

Control of Nonconforming product

Requires control of nonconforming product to ensure it is not inadvertently used; includes identification, segregation and evaluation.

Corrective Action

Requires procedures for investigation of causes of nonconformance, taking action to rectify them, and creating controls to prevent future occurrence.

Handling, Storage, Packaging and Delivery

Requires procedures for handling, storage, packaging and delivery of product.

Quality Records

Requires procedures of identification, collection, indexing, filing and storage of quality records.

Internal Quality Audits

Requires a system of internal audits to verify whether quality activities comply with requirements and to determine the effectiveness of the quality system.

Training

Requires procedures for identifying training needs and providing for all personnel to meet those needs.

Servicing

Requires procedures for performing servicing as required by contract.

Statistical Techniques

Requires procedures for identifying the use of statistical techniques in process, product and service.

What are the elements of the total documentation for a Comprehensive quality system?

There are four elements namely:

- Quality policy, Organization structure for Quality, Responsibility and authority for quality across the Company.
- Quality Procedures.
- Work Instructions.
- Forms -Records -other documents.

What comprises a quality management system 'documentation' ?

It comprises a quality manual and procedures.

What is a quality manual?

It is a document which communicates the quality policy and objectives of the company to its staff and customers and outlines the Organisation Structure, the responsibilities and authorities for quality across the entire Company functions and documentation of activities undertaken to ensure a consistent approach to meet the specified quality goal. It is the foundation of the quality systems which should be acceptable by all. It contains quality procedures detailing the working practices in all the primary areas affecting quality and ensure that consistency in quality is achieved in these activities.

What is the purpose of a 'quality manual' ?

The purpose of this is to communicate the quality policy and objectives of the Management of a Company to its staff and customers and provide guidelines for consistent approach to meet the specified quality goals.

What does it explain?

It explains the manner in which the company intends to comply with the Standards say, in terms of direction, listing responsibilities and authorities and documenting the activities, to ensure a consistent approach.

What is an assessment of a 'manufacturer's quality system' ?

It is a formal appraisal to establish whether or not the system meets the criteria laid down in the quality system standard ISO-9000.

What is involved in the 'assessment process' ?

It involves a documentation review and physical checking to see if the quality management system (*a*) exists (*b*) is correctly operated and maintained and (*c*) is effective.

What does the assessment process look for ?

It looks to see whether the quality system is being correctly managed.

Is ISO-9000 only for an external assurance?

No, it is for both external quality assurance and the development of an internal quality system?

Who are the certifying agencies country wise ?

- Bureau Veritas Quality International, UK
- Intertek, USA
- Vincotte, USA
- AT & T's Quality Registrar, USA
- Lloyd's Register Q.A, USA
- ABS Quality Evaluations, UK

Which are the consulting agencies in India?

- CII
- Lloyd's Register Q.A.
- ABS Quality Evaluations.

Which are the Indian companies currently under the ISO certification?

- M/s. Sundram Fasteners, Madras
- M/s. Kirloskar Cummins Ltd, Pune
- M/s Ralliwolf Ltd, Mumbai
- M/s Kirloskar Brothers, Pune
- M/s Widia Industries, Bangalore

What must be ensured before calling a 'third party certification body' for an assessment of a manufacturer's quality system ?

The quality system must be allowed to run for a sufficient period of time. Procedures and work instruction must be available at the time of assessment. Management must ensure that the Company has been operating in the desired manner for a sufficiently high period of time to demonstrate that they can be effective.

Is this period same for all companies?

No, it varies from Company to Company.

What does this period ensure?

This period ensures that the system has become routine and its effectiveness has been reviewed.

Before a formal assessment, what should be done ?

The system should be internally audited prior to the formal assessment.

What is the certification maintenance procedure?

(*a*) Certification to be renewed every 3 years.

(*b*) System assessment by the certifying agency every 6 months.

In case of withdrawal of registration, the name of the company will be published in various publication media.

Why do we need ISO-9000 ?

- For export to European Countries.
- Other importing Countries may also like to align with the E.C. Requirements.
- ISO-9000 Standards may be asked for Self-Certification by Govt. of India.
- Domestic market may also require certification to this Standard.
- Strengthen System Discipline, which will help in the overall quality, leading towards World-class Quality.

What are some of ISO-9000 standard's advantages?

It ensures product interchangeability, reduces quality costs and other costs, and provides opportunity for evaluating supplier's goods and services consistently and uniformly regardless of the location of the supplier.

What are the benefits of the ISO-9000 standards?

- ISO-9000 Standards have universal acceptance.
- The supplier audits are fewer and have more focus.
- Easier, faster and more comprehensive learning, resulting in increased productivity and quality.
- Giving rise to better market sales.

What are some of the short-comings of the ISO-9000 standards ?

- It does not tell a Company how to document the Quality System.
- It does not specify what makes up an adequate quality policy.
- It does not mention or make provision for continuous improvement.
- It requires no evidence of a satisfactory track record of performance.
- It doesn't differentiate suppliers with respect to their Industry base, their Company size and what portion of the Company is being registered.

Is ISO-9000 ultimate in the road to quality?

No, it should be seen only as a first step in continuing improvement.

Is adherence to ISO-9000 standards sufficient to do business with Europe after 1992 ?

Not necessarily. The customer requirement may be more than the general application of the ISO-9000 Standards.

What is the requirement for world class quality?

We have to go much beyond ISO-9000 Standards, and look at continuous quality improvement and customer satisfaction.

Understanding ISO and ISO 9000

ISO is a nickname—not an acronym—for the International Organization for Standardization which facilitates the creation and voluntary adoption of world wide industrial and manufacturing standards. This international body developed the ISO 9000 Standards to ensure that products and services of member countries secure global acceptance.

ISO 9000 is a written set of standards which describe and define the basic elements of the quality system needed to ensure that an organization's products and/or services meet or exceed customer needs and expectations. The implementation of the standards will help ensure that products and services that are produced meet the required specifications on a continuous basis.

11.4 RELATIONSHIP BETWEEN ISO 9000 AND QUALITY

According to the ISO 9000 Standard, quality is defined as the totality of features and characteristics of a product or service that bear on its ability to satisfy stated or implied needs. The features and characteristics are identified based on the needs of the customer. It is the customer who evaluates whether the product meets the specifications that have been determined. Thus, quality really means meeting the needs of the customer. In the Civil Service, quality service that is capable of meeting the needs of the customer would among others include features such as timeliness, accuracy, politeness, reliability, informativeness and availability.

There are two principal approaches which can be adopted to ensure that products and services meet the needs of the customer. One is by means of quality control and the other is through quality assurance. Quality control refers to techniques which are used to identify products that do not meet the required specifications. The underlying philosophy behind these techniques is to carry out inspections after the product has been produced.

Consequently, the quality control approach to quality can result in very high costs as a lot of resources would have already been utilized to bring out the products that do not meet the required specifications.

The very high costs above can be avoided in the second approach to quality, namely quality assurance. In quality assurance the focus is on the process that results in the product and not on the product itself.

By focusing on the process to ensure that only products and services that meet customer needs will be produced, the approach seeks to eliminate the underlying weaknesses in the process that may give rise to defective products and services. In short, the fundamental principle in quality assurance is prevention and not remedial action after the defects have occurred. It is this quality assurance that is the principal goal of the ISO 9000 Standard.

For an organization to achieve quality assurance it must have an efficient process governed by a well-planned, well-documented, and well executed quality management system or 'quality system' in short. The ISO 9000 standard helps an organization to achieve quality assurance by creating such a quality system. The way in which the ISO 9000 standard achieves this is briefly summarized in the figure below:

ISO 9000 Concept

As shown in the figure, to achieve the goal of quality assurance, the needs of the customer must be understood and a quality system created based on the ISO 9000 standard. The comprehensive coverage and the detailed documentation requirements of the standard will help ensure that the input and the process for producing the output will be controlled and the output verified so as to ascertain that it meets customer needs. In this way the ISO 9000 standard will achieve a quality system that ensures that the products and services of an organization are of consistent quality.

11.5 RELATIONSHIP BETWEEN ISO 9000 AND TQM

ISO 9000 will help to build a strong foundation for the implementation of TQM. TQM is a quality management process that is based on the quality philosophy of customer orientation, continuous improvement, involvement of all aspects of the organization and an emphasis on teamwork. Among key organizational areas emphasized by TQM are management support, strategic quality planning and process management. ISO 9000 also covers these areas with a particular emphasis on process management.

The quality system developed by ISO 9000 will enhance the effectiveness and efficiency of process management, thereby considerably assisting in the implementation of TQM.

11.5.1 PRINCIPLES OF ISO 9000

ISO 9000 embodies a few key principles which are explained below:

- *Principle One:* ISO 9000 is a standard for a quality system. It is not a product or service standard which describes the specifications that the product or service must have. An example will best illustrate the difference. SMR is a standard for a type of rubber produced by Malaysia. This standard lays down the specifications that this type of rubber must have in terms of color, elasticity and the type of chemicals that it will contain. ISO 9000 on the other hand only lays down the standard for the quality system that produces this rubber.
- *Principle Two:* ISO 9000 is based on documentation and is premised on the following:
  - Document what you do;
  - Do what you document; and
  - Prove it.
- *Principle Three:* ISO 9000 emphasizes prevention. The objective is to prevent defects in quality and not attend to them after they have occurred.
- *Principle Four:* ISO 9000 is a universal standard. It is able to achieve this universality because it only spells out broad requirements and leaves the manner of fulfilling the requirements to the organization. In other words, the focus of ISO 9000 is on what needs to be done and not on how it is to be carried out. For example, the standard mandates corrective action to be carried out but does not delineate the nature or details of the corrective action itself. Being a universal standard ISO 9000 can be implemented in both product based and service based organizations, including the Civil Service.

11.5.2 BENEFITS OF ISO 9000

The implementation of ISO 9000 will bring about various benefits which among others include:

- reduces firefighting and frees managers from constant intervention in the operation of the business. This is achieved as the staff will be given the means to control their own operations;
- provides the means for enabling the right tasks to be identified and specified in a way that will yield the right results. The standard requires planning in advance of the work and putting in place procedures, standards and guidelines which help people choose the right things to do;
- provides a means of documenting the organization's experience in a structured manner that will provide a basis for education and training of staff and the systematic improvement of performance. This is taken care of by the documentation requirements under the standard which not only call for the quality system to be documented but also to be continually reviewed and maintained;
- provides a means for identifying and resolving problems and preventing their recurrence. The standard calls for the installing of measures for detecting deviations from practices and specifications, for discovering the cause of the deviations and for planning and implementing corrective actions;

- •provides the means for enabling people to perform tasks right the first time. This is achieved through the provision of work instructions, effective controls, appropriate and adequate resources, training, motivation and a conducive environment;
- provides objective evidence that can be used to demonstrate the quality of the organization's products and services and to demonstrate to any external evaluators that the various operations are under control. The standard enables this by identifying, producing and maintaining records of key operations; and
- provides data that can be used to determine the performance of operating processes, products and services and for improving organizational performance and customer satisfaction. This is made possible through the collection, analysis and review of the records generated by the quality system.

12

Linear Programming

12.0 INTRODUCTION

Linear Programming (LP) is a model consisting of linear relationships representing a firm's decision(s) given an objective and resource constraints. Steps of LP based solution are: (*i*) Observation, (*ii*) Problem definition, (*iii*) Model construction, (*iv*) Model solution, and (*v*) Implementation. The various terms related to LP model are given below.

The **objective function** is a linear relationship reflecting the objective of an operation. The objectives of a business are to maximize profit or minimize cost.

A **model** is a functional relationship including variables, parameters, and equations. A management science model consists of a set of mathematical relationship with numbers and symbols. For example, a firm sells a product at a price of Rs. 30. It takes Rs 10 to produce the product. A mathematical model that computes the total profit that will accrue from the items sold is

$$Z = 30x - 10x,$$

where Z = total profit, x = no. of units of the products sold out. Z and x are variables. The numbers Rs. 30 and Rs.10 are parameters.

A **constraint** is a linear relationship representing a restriction on decision making.

Variable is a symbol used to represent an item that can take on any value.

Decision variables: They are mathematical symbols representing levels of activity.

Parameters are known, constant values that are often coefficients of the variables in equations.

Data are pieces of information from problem environment.

12.1 THE LP FORMULATION AND UNDERLYING ASSUMPTIONS

A *Linear Programming* problem is a special case of a *Mathematical Programming* problem. From an analytical perspective, a mathematical program tries to identify an *extreme* (*i.e.*, minimum or maximum) point of a function $f(x_1, x_2, ..., x_n)$, which further satisfies a set of constraints, *e.g.*, $g(x_1, x_2, ..., x_n) \geq b$.Linear programming is the specialization of mathematical programming to the case where both, function f—to be called the *objective function*—and the problem constraints are *linear*.

For Linear Programming problems, the *Simplex* algorithm, discussed later in the text, provides a powerful computational tool. It provides fast solutions to very large-scale applications, sometimes including hundreds of thousands of variables (*i.e.*, decision factors). In fact, the Simplex algorithm was one of the first Mathematical Programming algorithms to be developed (George Dantzig, 1947), and its subsequent successful implementation in a series of applications significantly contributed to the acceptance of the broader field of *Operations Research* as a scientific approach to decision making.

As it happens, however, with every modeling effort, the effective application of Linear Programming requires good understanding of the underlying modeling assumptions, and a pertinent interpretation of the obtained analytical solutions. Therefore, in this section we discuss the details of the LP modeling and its underlying assumptions, by means of the following example.

Example 12.1. A company produces two types of products P_1 and P_2. Production of these products is supported by two workstations W_1 and W_2, with each station visited by both product types. If W_1 is dedicated completely to the production of P_1, it can process 40 units per day, while if it is dedicated to the production of P_2, it can process 60 units per day. Similarly, workstation W_2 can produce daily 50 units of P_1 and 50 units of P_2, assuming that it is dedicated completely to the production of the corresponding product. If the company's profit by selling one unit of P_1 is \$200 and that of selling one unit of P_2 is \$400, and assumning that the company can dispose its entire production, how many units of each product should the company produce on a daily basis to maximize its profit?

Solution: First notice that this is an *optimization* problem. Our *objective* is to *maximize* the company's profit, which under the problem assumptions, is equivalent to maximizing the company's *daily* profit. Furthermore, we are going to maximize the company profit by adjusting the levels of the daily production for the two items $P_1$and P_2. Therefore, these daily production levels are the control/decision factors, the values of which we are supposed to determine. Let

X_1 = number of units of product P1to be produced daily

X_2 = number of units of product P2 to be produced daily.

In the light of the above discussion, the objective function can be expressed as:

$$\max f(X_1, X_2) = 200\,X_1 + 400\,X_2 \qquad ...(1)$$

Eq. 1 will be called the *objective function* of the problem, and the coefficients 200 and 400 which multiply the decision variables in it, will be called the *objective function coefficients*.

Moreover, any decision regarding the daily production levels for items P_1 and P_2 in the company's operation context must observe the production capacity of the two worksations W_1 and W_2. Hence, our next step in the problem formulation seeks to introduce these *technological* constraints in it. Let's focus first on the constraint which expresses the finite production capacity of workstation W_1. Regarding this constraint, we know that one day's work dedicated to the production of item P_1 can result in 40 units of that item, while the same period dedicated to the production of item P_2 will provide 60 units of it. *Assuming that production of one unit of product type P_i, $i = 1,2$, requires a constant amount of processing time T_{1i} at workstation W_1*, it follows that: T_{11} = 1/40 and T_{12} = 1/60. *Under the further assumption that the combined production of both items has no side-effects, i.e., does not impose any additional requirements for production capacity of workstation W_1 (e.g., zero set-up times)*, the total capacity (in terms of time length) required for producing X_1 units of product P_1 and X_2 units of product P_2 is equal to $\frac{X_1}{40} + \frac{X_2}{60}$. Hence, the technological constraint imposing the condition that our total daily processing requirements for workstation W_1 should not exceed its production capacity, is analytically expressed by:

$$\frac{X_1}{40} + \frac{X_2}{60} \leq 1.0 \qquad ...(2)$$

Notice that in Eq. 2, the time is measured in days. Following the same line of reasoning (and under similar assumptions), the constraint expressing the finite processing capacity of workstation W_2 is given by:

$$\frac{X_1}{50} + \frac{X_2}{50} \leq 1.0 \qquad ...(3)$$

Constraints 2 and 3 are known as the *technological constraints* of the problem. In particular, the coefficients of the variables X_i, $i = 1, 2$ then, $1/T_{ji}$, $i = 1, 2$, are known as the *technological coefficients* of the problem formulation, while the values on the right-hand-side of the two inequalities define the *right-hand side (rhs)* vector of the constraints. Finally, to the above constraints we must add the requirement that any permissible value for variables X_i, $i = 1, 2$ must be nonnegative, *i.e.*,

$$X_i \geq 0 \quad i = 1, 2 \qquad ...(4)$$

since these values express production levels. These constraints are known as the variable *sign restrictions.*

Combining Eqns 1 to 4, the analytical formulation of our problem is as follows:

$$\max f(X_1, X_2) := 200X_1 + 400X_2$$

Subject To

$$\frac{X_1}{40} + \frac{X_2}{60} \leq 1.0$$

$$\frac{X_1}{50} + \frac{X_2}{50} \leq 1.0$$

$$X_i \geq 0 \quad i = 1, 2 \qquad ...(5)$$

12.2 THE GENERAL LP FORMULATION

The general form for a Linear Programming problem is as follows:

Objective Function:

$$\max/\min f(X_1, X_2, ..., X_n) := c_1X_1 + c_2X_2 + ... + c_nX_n \qquad ...(6)$$

Subject To

Technological Constraints:

$$a_{i1}X_1 + a_{i2}X_2 + ... + a_{in}X_n \begin{pmatrix} \leq \\ = \\ \geq \end{pmatrix} b_i, \quad i = 1, ..., m \qquad ...(7)$$

Sign Restrictions:

$$(X_j \geq 0) \text{ or } (X_j \leq 0) \text{ or } (X_j \text{ urs}), j = 1, ..., n \qquad ...(8)$$

where 'urs' implies *unrestricted in sign.*

The formulation of Eqns. 6 to 8 has the general structure of a mathematical programming problem, but it is further characterized that the functions involved in objective and the left-hand-side of the constraints are *linear.* It is the assumptions implied by linearity that to a large extent determine the applicability of the above model in real-world applications.

12.2.1 GRAPHICAL SOLUTION OF 2-VARIABLES LP

In this section, we develop a solution approach for LP problems, which is based on a geometrical representation of the feasible region and the objective function. In particular, the space to be considered is the n-dimensional space with each dimension defined by one of the LP variables x_j. The objective function will be described in this n-dim space by its *contour plots, i.e.*, the sets of points that correspond to the same objective value. To the extent that the proposed approach requires the visualization of the underlying geometry, it is applicable only for LP's with upto three variables. Actually, to facilitate the visualization of the concepts involved, in this section we shall restrict ourselves to the two-dimensional case, *i.e.*, to LP's with two decision variables.

12.2.2 A 2-VAR LP WITH A UNIQUE OPTIMAL SOLUTION

The 'sliding motion' suggests a way for identifying the optimal values for, say, a max LP problem. The underlying idea is to keep 'sliding' the isoprofit line $c_1X_1 + c_1X_1 = \alpha_0$ in the direction of increasing α's, until we cross the boundary of the LP feasible region. The implementation of this idea on the prototype LP of Eqn. 5 is depicted in Fig. 12.1.

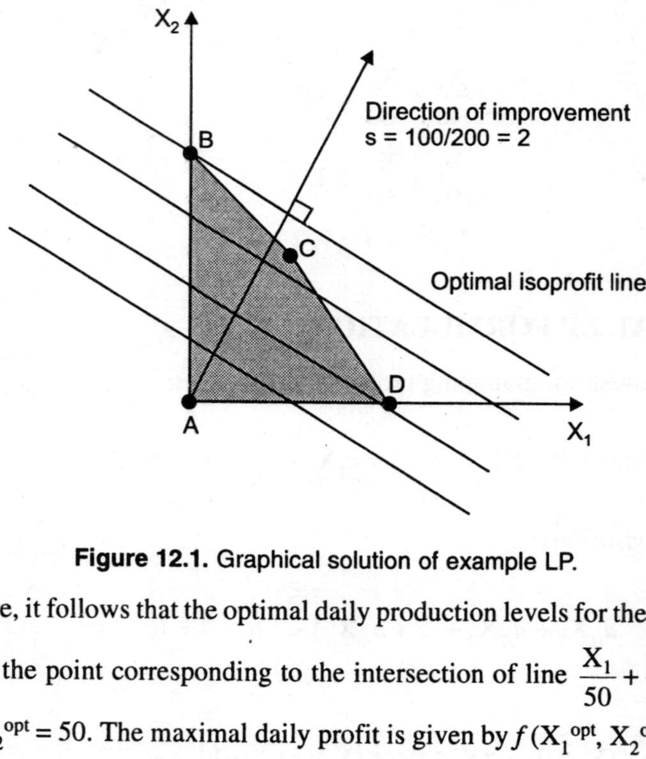

Figure 12.1. Graphical solution of example LP.

From this figure, it follows that the optimal daily production levels for the protoype LP are given by the coordinates of the point corresponding to the intersection of line $\frac{X_1}{50} + \frac{X_2}{50} = 1.0$ with the X_2 axis, *i.e.*, $X_1^{opt} = 0$; $X_2^{opt} = 50$. The maximal daily profit is given by $f(X_1^{opt}, X_2^{opt}) = 200x\,0 + 400x\,50 = 20{,}000$ \$.

Notice that the optimal point is one of the '*corner*' points of the feasible region depicted in Figure 12.1. Can you argue that for the geometry of the feasible region for 2-var LP's described above, if there is a bounded optimal solution, then there will be one which corresponds to one of the corner points? (This argument is developed for the broader context of n-var LP's in the next section.)

12.3 DIFFERENT FORMS OF LINEAR PROGRAMS

There are different ways of writing linear programs, and a variety of names to refer to them. We shall stick to two forms: the **standard and the canonical forms**. Each form has two versions: the maximization and the minimization versions. Fortunately, all versions and forms are equivalent.

The min version-**standard form** reads

$$\min c_1x_1 + c_2x_2 + \cdots + c_nx_n$$

subject to

$$\begin{aligned} a_{11}x_1 + a_{12}x_2 + \ldots + a_{1n}x_n &= b_1 \\ a_{21}x_1 + a_{22}x_2 + \ldots + a_{2n}x_n &= b_2 \\ \ldots \ldots \ldots \ldots &= \ldots \\ a_{m1}x_1 + a_{m2}x_2 + \ldots + a_{mn}x_n &= b_m \\ x_i \geq 0, \quad \text{For } i = 1, \ldots, n. \end{aligned}$$

The linear function $c_1x_1 + c_2x_2 + \ldots + c_nx_n$ is called the objective function. The constraints $x_i \geq 0$ are also referred to as the non-negativity constraints. If the objective is to maximize instead of minimize, we have the max version of the standard form.

In **canonical** form, the min version reads

$$\min c_1x_1 + c_2x_2 + \ldots + c_nx_n$$

subject to

$$\begin{aligned} a_{11}x_1 + a_{12}x_2 + \ldots + a_{1n}x_n &\geq b_1 \\ a_{21}x_1 + a_{22}x_2 + \ldots + a_{2n}x_n &\geq b_2 \\ \ldots \ldots \ldots \ldots &\geq \ldots \\ a_{m1}x_1 + a_{m2}x_2 + \ldots + a_{mn}x_n &\geq b_m \\ x_i \geq 0, \quad \text{For } i = 1, \ldots, n. \end{aligned}$$

and the **max version** is nothing but

$$\max c_1x_1 + c_2x_2 + \ldots + c_nx_n$$

subject to

$$\begin{aligned} a_{11}x_1 + a_{12}x_2 + \ldots + a_{1n}x_n &\leq b_1 \\ a_{21}x_1 + a_{22}x_2 + \ldots + a_{2n}x_n &\leq b_2 \\ \ldots \ldots \ldots \ldots &\leq \ldots \\ a_{m1}x_1 + a_{m2}x_2 + \ldots + a_{mn}x_n &\leq b_m \\ x_i \leq 0, \quad \text{For } i = 1, \ldots, n. \end{aligned}$$

The reason we change $\geq$ to $\leq$ in the max version is that it might be intuitively easier to remember:

if we are trying to minimize some function of x, there should be some 'lower bound' on how much x can get smaller, and vice versa. Obviously, exchanging the terms on both sides and the inequalities are reversed. Hence, beside being easier to remember there is no other value on which way the inequalities should go.

Example 12.2. A firm manufactures two types of products A and B and sells them at a profit of \$ 2 on A and \$ 3 on B. Each product is processed on two machines M_1 and M_2. Product A needs one minute of processing time on M_1 and two minutes on M_2. Product B requires one minute on M_1 and one minute on M_2. The machine M_1 is available for not more than 6 hours 40 minutes, while machine M_2 is available for 10 hours during any working day. Formulate the problem as a linear programming model.

Solution:

$$Z = 2x_1 + 3x_2$$
$$x_1 + x_2 \leq 400$$
$$2x_1 + x_2 \leq 600$$
$$x_1, x_2 \geq 0$$

Example 12.3. A firm manufactures three products A, B and C. The profits are $3, $2, and $4 respectively. The firm has two machines, and the required processing time in minutes for each machine on each product is given in the Table 12.1 below:

Table 12.1

Machine	*Products*		
	A	B	C
X	4	3	5
Y	2	2	4

Machines X and Y have 2,000 and 2,500 machine minutes respectively. The firm must manufacture 100 A's, 200 B's and 50 C's but not more than 150 A's. Set up an LP model to maximize profit.

Solution:

Maximize $Z = 3x_1 + 2x_2 + 4x_3$

Subject To

$$4x_1 + 3x_2 + 5x_3 \leq 2000$$
$$2x_1 + 2x_2 + 4x_3 \leq 2500$$
$$100 \leq x_1 \leq 150$$
$$200 \leq x_2$$
$$50 \leq x_3$$

Example 12.4. Find the maximum value of $Z = 7x_1 + 3x_2$

Subject to the constraints

$$x_1 + 2x_2 \geq 3$$
$$x_1 + x_2 \leq 4$$
$$0 \leq x_1 \leq 5/2$$
$$0 \leq x_2 \leq 3/2$$

Solution: The lines have been shown graphically on the X1 and X2 plane. The hatched area shows the solution space of the problem. The solution is shown in the following Table-12.2.

Table 12.2

Point	X_1	X_2	$Z = Z = 7x_1 + 3x_2$
A	2.5	0.25	ZA = 18.2
B	**2.5**	**1.5**	**ZB = 22.0**
C	0	1.5	ZC = 4.5

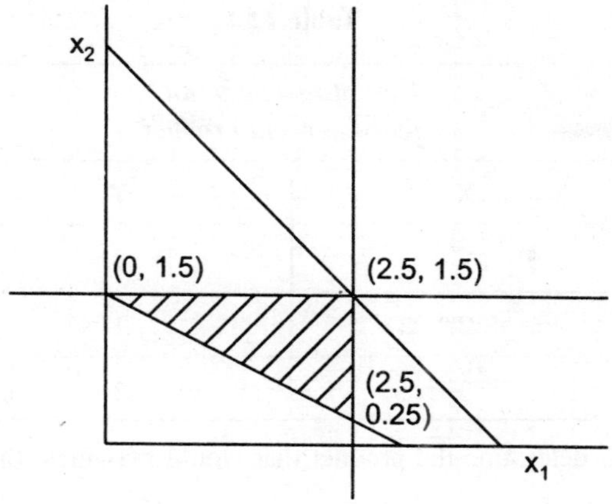

So, the objective function will have a maximum value of 22 at point B with

$$X_1 = 2.5, \text{ and } X_2 = 1.5$$

Example 12.5. A company produces Motor cycles and scooters. Production of these is organized in three departments whose maximum weekly capacities for producing either motor cycles or scooters are as follows:

Table 12.3

Department	*Capacities*	
	Motor cycles	*Scooters*
Forming and welding	90	120
Assembly	80	160
Painting	150	100

The profit contribution of each motor cycle is Rs. 600 and that of a scooter is Rs 400. Use graphical analysis to find the optimum number of motor cycles and scooters to be produced. If at least as many scooters as motorcycles are to be produced, what change in solution space results and what would be the new optimum solution.

Solution:

Let x_1 = number of motor cycles

x_2 = number of scooters

Then the objective function is

Maximize $Z = 600x_1 + 400x_2$

Subject To

$$x_1/90 + x_2/120 \le 1$$
$$x1/80 + x_2/160 \le 1$$
$$x_1/150 + x_2/100 \le 1$$

Ans: $x_1 = 73, x_2 = 94$

When no. of scooters = no. of motor cycles

Then $x_1 = x_2 = 76$.

Example 12.6. A company plans to manufacture and sell two types of products X and Y. These two products require the use of three different raw materials A, B and C which are available in limited quantities. The profit per unit of product X and Y is Rs 5 and 6 respectively. The other relevant data are given in the Table 12.4 below.

Table 12.4

Raw material	*Unit of raw material needed per unit product*		*Total units of raw materials available*
	X	Y	
A	2	3	18
B	2	1	12
C	3	3	27

The company wants to determine the product that would maximize the total profit. Fraction units are permissible.

Formulate as a linear programming problem.

Determine the optimal product mix.

Ans: $x = 9/2$, $y = 3$.

Example 12.7. A small manufacturer employs 5 skilled men and 10 semi-skilled men. He makes an article in two qualities, a deluxe model and an ordinary model. The making of a deluxe model requires 2 hours of work by semiskilled men and 2 hours of work by skilled men. The ordinary model requires 3 hours of work by semi skilled men, and one hour of work by skilled men. By union rules, no men can work more than 8 hours a day. The manufacturers profits on deluxe model and ordinary model are Rs 10, and Rs 8 respectively. How many of each type of model should be made in order to maximize the profit?

Solution:

Let x_1 = no. of deluxe model,

x_2 = no. of ordinary model

Then, the objective function is

Maximize $Z = 10x_1 + 8x_2$

Subject to the constraints

$$2x_1 + 3x_2 \leq 10x_8$$
$$2x_1 + x_2 \leq 5x_8$$
$$x_1, x_2 \geq 0$$

Ans: $x_1 = 10$, $x_2 = 20$.

Example 12.8. Use the simplex method to solve the following LP problem.

Maximize: $Z = 3X_1 + 5X_2 + 4X_3$

Subjected to: $2X_1 + 3X_2 < 8$

$$2X_1 + 5X_3 \leq 10$$
$$3X_1 + 2X_2 + 4X_3 \leq 18$$
$$X_1, X_2, X_3 \geq 0.$$

Solution:

Sept 1. Transform the equation into standard form.

$$Z = 3X_1 + 5X_2 + 4X_3 + 0.S_1 + 0.S_2 + 0.S_3$$
$$2X_1 + 3X_2 + S_1 < 8$$
$$2X_1 + 5X_3 + S_2 \leq 10$$
$$3X_1 + 2X_2 + 4X_3 + S_3 \leq 18$$
$$X_1, X_2, X_3 \geq 0$$

By normalizing the equation, we get

$$3X_1 + 5X_2 + 4X_3 + 0.S_1 + 0.S_2 + 0.S_3 = Z$$
$$2X_1 + 3X_2 + 0.X_3 + S_1 + 0.S_2 + 0.S_3 = 8$$
$$2X_1 + 0.X_2 + 5X_3 + 0.S_1 + S_2 + 0.S_3 = 10$$
$$3X_1 + 2X_2 + 4X_3 + 0.S_1 + 0.S_2 + S_3 = 15$$

Sept 2. Set up the tableau and identify the key row and key column.

Then for the simplex solution the matrix form of the above equations are as follows:

Iteration 0

			3	5	4	0	0	0	*b/cc*
			X_1	X_2	X_3	S_1	S_2	S_3	
0	S_1	8	2	**3**	0	1	0	0	8/3
0	S_2	10	2	0	5	0	1	0	8
0	S_3	15	3	2	4	0	0	1	15/2
			– 3	– 5	– 4	0	0	0	

Note. *X_2 is the entering variable and S1 is the leaving variables.*

Step 3. Compute the second iteration (tableau)

Here the selected row is the second and the selected column is the fifth, then the next matrix is as follows:

Note. *X_3 is the coming variable and S_2 is the leaving variables.*

Iteration 1

			3	5	4	0	0	0	*b/cc*
			X_1	X_2	X_3	S_1	S_2	S_3	
5	X_2	8/3	2/3	1	0	1/3	0	0	8
0	S_2	10	2	0	5	0	1	0	2
0	S_3	29/3	5/3	0	4	– 0.667	0	1	2.44
		40/3	1/3	0	– 4	5/3	0	0	

Since all the values on the bottom row are positive, therefore, it is an optimal solution with

$$X_1 = 0, X_2 = 8/3, X_3 = 2$$

Then
$$Z = 3X_1 + 5X_2 + 4X_3$$
$$= 3(0) + 5(8/3) + 4(2) = 64/3$$

Iteration 2

			3	5	4	0	0	0
			X_1	X_2	X_3	S_1	S_2	S_3
5	X_2	8/3	2/3	1	0	1/3	0	0
4	X_3	2	2/5	0	1	0	1/5	0
0	S_3	113/15	17/15	– 4/5	0	– 2/3	– 4/5	1
		64/3	29/15	0	0	5/3	4/5	0

Since all the values on the bottom row are positive, therefore, it is an optimal solution with

$$X_1 = 0, X_2 = 8/3, X_3 = 2$$

Then
$$Z = 3X_1 + 5X_2 + 4X_3$$
$$= 3(0) + 5(8/3) + 4(2) = 64/3$$

Example 12.9. Use the Big-M simplex method in order to solve the following LP problem.

Maximize
$$Z = 2.1X_1 + 4.8X_2 + 6X_3$$

Subject to:
$$10X_1 + 23X_2 + 26X_3 < 700$$
$$5X_1 + 13X_2 + 22X_3 < 550$$
$$7X_1 + 9X_2 + 11X_3 < 450$$
$$X_1 > 0$$
$$X_2, X_3 > 0$$

$$10X_1 + 23X_2 + 26X_3 + S_1 = 700$$
$$5X_1 + 13X_2 + 22X_3 + S_2 = 550$$
$$7X_1 + 9X_2 + 11X_3 + S_3 = 450$$
$$X_1 - S_4 + A_1 = 50$$
$$Z = 2.1X_1 + 4.8X_2 + 6X_3 + 0.S_1 + 0.S_2 + 0.S_3 + 0.S_4 - MA_1$$

BIG M-METHOD

$$Z = 2.1X_1 + 4.8X_2 + 6X_3 + 0.S_1 + 0.S_2 + 0.S_3 + 0.S_4 - MA_1$$
$$10X_1 + 23X_2 + 26X_3 + S_1 + 0.S_2 + 0.S_3 + 0.S_4 - 0.A_1 = 700$$
$$5X_1 + 13X_2 + 22X_3 + 0.S_1 + S_2 + 0.S_3 + 0.S_4 - 0A_1 = 550$$
$$7X_1 + 9X_2 + 11X_3 + 0.S_1 + 0.S_2 + S_3 + 0.S_4 - 0A_1 = 450$$
$$X_1 + 0X_2 + 0X_3 + 0.S_1 + 0.S_2 + 0.S_3 - S_4 + A_1 = 50$$

Iteration 0

			2.1	4.8	6	0	0	0	0	– M	
			X_1	X_2	X_3	S_1	S_2	S_3	S_4	A_1	
0	S_1	700	10	23	26	1	0	0	0	0	70
0	S_2	550	5	13	22	0	1	0	0	0	110
0	S_3	450	7	9	11	0	0	1	0	0	450/7
– M	A_1	50	1	0	0	0	0	0	– 1	1	50
		– 50M	– M – 21	– 4.8	– 6	0	0	0	M	0	

Iteration 1

			2.1	4.8	6	0	0	0	0	– M	
			X_1	X_2	X_3	S_1	S_2	S_3	S_4	A_1	
0	S_1	200	0	23	26	1	0	0	0	0	200/26
0	S_2	300	0	13	22	0	1	0	0	0	300/22
0	S_3	100	0	9	11	0	0	1	0	0	100/87
2.1	X_1	50	1	0	0	0	0	0	– 1	1	8
		105	0	– 4.8	– 6	0	0	0	– 2.1	2.1 + M	

Iteration 2

			2.1	4.8	6	0	0	0	0	– M
			X_1	X_2	X_3	S_1	S_2	S_3	S_4	A_1
6	X_3	200/26	0	23/26	1	1/26	0	0	0	0
0	S_2	3400/26	0	– 168/26	0	– 22/26	1	0	0	0
0	S_3	400/26	0	– 19/26	0	– 11/26	0	1	0	0
2.1	X_1	50	1	0	0	0	0	0	– 1	1
		1965/13	0	0.51	0	6/26	0	0	– 2.1	2.1 + M

From the table we can get that;

$$X_1 = 50$$
$$X_2 = 0$$
$$X_3 = 200/26$$

Then
$$Z = 2.1X_1 + 4.8X_2 + 6X_3$$
$$= 2.1(50) + 4.8(0) + 6(200/26)$$
$$= 151.1538$$

Example 12.10. Primal form

Maximize: $Z_P = 10X_1 + 6X_2.$

Subject to:
$$X_1 + 4X_2 = 40$$
$$3X_1 + 2X_2 = 60$$
$$-3X_1 - 2X_2 = -60$$
$$-2X_1 - X_2 = -25$$
$$X_1, X_2 = 0$$

One of the conditions for transferring a primal problem into dual is that the primal be in standard form. The above given problem is in standard form. However, it violates simplex restriction that all quantity values must be either zero or positive. The constraints are not converted so that it can be solved with the simplex method; rather, it is being converted into the dual form. In the dual, the quantity (right hand side) values of the optimal form the coefficient of the objective function and these can be negative.

The **dual form** of this model is formulated as follows:

Minimize $Z_d = 40Y_1 + 60Y_2 - 60Y_3 - 25Y_4.$

Subject to:
$$Y_1 + 3Y_2 - 3Y_3 - 2Y_4 \geq 10$$
$$4Y_1 + 2Y_2 - 2Y_3 - Y_4 \geq 6$$
$$Y_1, Y_2, Y_3, Y_4 = 0$$

Example 12.11. A manufacturing firm has discontinuous production of a certain unprofitable product line. This created considerable excess production capacity. Management is considering to devote this excess capacity to one or more of three products A, B, and C. The available capacity on the machines which might limit output, is summarized in the following Table 12.5.

Table 12.5

	Time (hours) required by Product			*Time available (hours)*
Machines	A	B	C	
Milling machine	8	2	3	250
Lathe	4	3	0	150
Grinder	2	—	1	50

The unit profit would be Rs. 20, Rs. 6, and Rs. 8 for products A, B, and C respectively. Find how much of each product the firm should produce to maximize the profit ?

Solution: *Mathematical formulation*

Let the management decides to produce x_1 units of A, x_2 units of B, and x_3 units of C respectively per week. Then the objective function will be to

Maximize $Z = 20x_1 + 6x_2 + 8x_3$

Subject to the constraints

$$8x_1 + 2x_2 + 3x_3 \leq 250$$
$$4x_1 + 3x_2 \leq 150$$
$$2x_1 + x_3 \leq 50$$

and $x_1, x_2, x_3 \geq 0$

By introducing $y_1 \geq 0$, $y_2 \geq 0$, and $y_3 \geq 0$, the inequalities of the constraints are converted into equations as follows:

Maximize $Z = 20x_1 + 6x_2 + 8x_3 + 0y_1 + 0y_2 + 0y_3$

Subject to the constraints

$$8x_1 + 2x_2 + 3x_3 + 1y_1 + 0y_2 + 0y_3 = 250$$
$$4x_1 + 3x_2 + 0x_3 + 0y_1 + 1y_2 + 0y_3 = 150$$
$$2x_1 + 0x_2 + x_3 + 0y_1 + 0y_2 + 1y_3 = 50$$

As this problem contains more than two variables, we will solve it by simplex technique. Now, let us make the following table for simplex solution.

Iteration 0

	x_1	x_2	x_3	y_1	y_2	y_3	*b*	*Ratio*
y_1	8	2	3	1	0	0	250	250/8 = 125/4
y_2	4	3	0	0	1	0	150	150/4 = 75/2
y_3	2	0	1	0	0	1	50	50/2 = 25 ← KR
Index	– 20	– 6	– 8	0	0	0	0	
	↑ KC							

KC = Key Column (Column with maximum negative)

KR = Key Row (Row with the minimum ratio)

Key number = the point of intersection between the KC and the KR

Iteration 1

	x_1	x_2	x_3	y_1	y_2	y_3	b	*Ratio*
y_1	0	2	– 1	1	0	– 4	50	50/2 = 25
y_2	0	3	– 2	0	1	– 2	50	50/3 ← KR
x_1	1	0	1/2	0	0	1/2	25	25/0 = ∞
Index	0	– 6	2	0	0	10	500	

↑ KC

Iteration 2

	x_1	x_2	x_3	y_1	y_2	y_3	b	*Ratio*
y_1	0	0	1/3	1	– 2/3	– 8/3	50/3	50 ← KR
x_2	0	1	– 2/3	0	1/3	– 2/3	50/3	– ve
x_1	1	0	1/2	0	0	1/2	25	50
Index	0	0	– 2	0	2	6	600	

↑ KC

Iteration 3

	x_1	x_2	x_3	y_1	y_2	y_3	b	*Ratio*
x_3	0	0	1	1/3	– 2	– 8	50	– ve
x_2	0	1	0			– 6	50	– ve
x_1	1	0	0			5/2	0	50
Index	0	0	0	6	– 2	– 10	700	

Check the table

Iteration 4

	x_1	x_2	x_3	y_1	y_2	y_3	b	*Ratio*
x_3	0	0	1	1/3	– 2	– 8	50	– ve
x_2	0	1	0			– 6	50	– ve
x_1	1	0	0			5/2	0	50
Index	0	0	0	6	– 2	– 10	700	

Check the table

Ans: $x_2 = 50$, $x_3 = 50$, $x_1 = 0$, and $Z^* = 700$

12.4 THE ASSIGNMENT PROBLEM

Example 12.12. There are n jobs for a factory and the factory has n machines to process the jobs. A job i ($i = 1, 2, ..., n$) when processed by machine j ($j = 1, 2, ..., n$) is assumed to incur a cost C_{ij}. The assignment is to be made in such a way that each job can be associated with only one machine. Determine an assignment plan of jobs to machines so as to minimize the total cost.

Jobs → / *Machines ↓*	*1*	2	*3*	*4*	...	*n*
1	C_{11}	C_{12}	C_{13}	C_{14}	...	C_{1n}
2	C_{21}	C_{22}	C_{23}	C_{24}	...	C_{2n}
3	...	...	...	...	...	...
4	...	...	...	...	...	...
...	...	...	...	...	...	...
n	C_{n1}	C_{n2}	C_{n3}	C_{n4}		C_{nn}

Solution: We will use Hungarian algorithm for the assignment. This consists of the following steps:

Step 1. Subtract the minimum cost of each row of the cost matrix from all the elements of the respective row. Then modify the resulting matrix by subtracting the minimum cost of each column from all the elements of the respective columns, obtaining the starting matrix.

Step 2. Draw the least possible number of horizontal and vertical lines to cover all the zeros of the starting table.

Let N = the number of lines required to cover all the zeros, and n = order of the matrix.

Case I: If $N = n$, then the optimum assignment has been achieved.

Case II: If $N < n$, then go to Step 3.

Step 3. Determine the smallest cost in the starting table not covered by N lines. Subtract this cost from all the surviving (uncovered) elements of the starting matrix, and add the same to all those elements of the starting matrix which are lying at the intersection of horizontal and vertical lines drawn, thus obtaining the 2nd modified cost matrix.

Step 4. Repeat steps 1, 2, and 3 till we get $N = n$.

Step 5. Examine the rows successfully until a row with exactly one unmarked zero is found. Encircle this zero, for an assignment to be made later. Mark a cross (x) in the cells of all other zeros lying the column of the encircled zero to show that they are not free for further assignment. Continue this way till all the rows have been taken care of.

Step 6. Repeat steps 4 and 5 successfully till one of the following arises:

(*i*) No unmarked zero is left, and

(ii) There lie more than one unmarked zeros in one column or row.

In case (*i*), the algorithm stops. In case (*ii*), encircle one of the unmarked zeros arbitrarily and mark a cross in the cells of remaining zeros in its row and column. Repeat the process till no unmarked zero is left in the cost matrix.

Step 7. We now have exactly one encircled zero in each row and each column of the cost matrix. The assignment schedule corresponding to these zeros is the optimum assignment.

Example 12.13. A department has five employees and five jobs are to be performed. The time each man will take to perform each job is given in the effectiveness matrix below. How should the job be allocated, one per employee, so as to minimize the total man-hours?

Table 12.6

Employee → / *Jobs ↓*	*1*	*2*	*3*	*4*	*5*
A	10	5	13	15	16
B	3	9	18	13	6
C	10	7	2	2	2
D	5	11	9	7	12
E	7	9	10	4	12

Solution: We use Hungarian algorithm for the assignment. This consists of the following steps:

Step 1. Subtract the minimum time of each row of the matrix from all the elements of the respective row. Then modify the resulting matrix by subtracting the minimum time of each column from all the elements of the respective columns, obtaining the starting matrix.

Table 12.7

10	**5**	13	15	16
3	9	18	13	6
10	7	2	**2**	2
5	11	9	7	12
7	9	10	**4**	12

The minimum in each row is shown in dark color. Following step 1, the matrix becomes as shown in Table 12.8.

Table 12.8 (After Row wise subtraction)

5	0	8	10	11
0	6	15	10	3
8	5	0	0	0
0	6	4	2	7
3	5	6	0	8

Step 2. Draw the least possible number of horizontal and vertical lines to cover all the zeros of the starting table.

Table 12.9 (After column wise subtraction)

5	0	8	10	11
0	6	15	10	3
8	5	0	0	0
0	6	4	**2**	7
3	5	6	0	8

N = the number of lines required to cover all the zeros = 4

n = order of the matrix = 5

So, here N < n, then go to Step 3.

Step 3. Determine the **smallest time** in the starting table not covered by N lines. We see that this number is 2. Subtract this time from all the surviving (uncovered) elements of the starting matrix, and add the same to all those elements of the starting matrix which are lying at the intersection of horizontal and vertical lines drawn, thus obtaining the 2nd modified time matrix.

Table 12.10 (after step 3)

5	0	6	8	9
0	6	13	8	**1**
10	7	0	0	0
0	6	2	0	5
5	7	6	0	8

Step 4. Repeat steps 1, 2, and 3 till we get N = n.

Table 12.11(after step 4)

6	0	6	9	9
0	5	12	8	0
11	7	0	1	0
0	5	1	0	4
5	6	5	0	7

Here, we see that N = n = 5, so the assignment can be done optimally as follows:

Table 12.12

	1	2	3	4	5
A		**0**			
B	**0**				**0**
C			**0**		**0**
D	**0**			**0**	
E				**0**	

0 = not free for assignment

0 = assigned with the job

A-2, B-5, C-3, D-1, and E-4

Minimum total man-hour = A2 + B5 + C3 + D1 + E4

= 5 + 6 + 2 + 5 + 4 = 22 hours

Example 12.14. A computer center has got three expert programmers. The center needs three application programs to be developed. The Chief of the computer center, after studying carefully the programs to be developed, estimates the computer time (in minutes) required by the experts to the application programs as follows:

Programs →	*A*	*B*	*C*
Programmers ↓			
1	120	100	80
2	80	90	110
3	110	140	120

Assign the programmers to the programs in such a manner that the total computer time the least.

Ans: 1 – C, 2 – B, 3 – A.

12.5 TRANSPORTATION PROBLEM

The transportation problem deals with the transportation of commodity from m *sources* to *n destinations*. Suppose the supply available at source i is a_i units, the demand required at destination j is n_j units, and the transport cost per unit from source i to destination j is C_{ij}. Then, if x_{ij} represents the amount transported (*i.e.*, level of activity from i to j), the problem can be expressed mathematically as

Minimize, $$Z = \sum_{i=1}^{m} \sum_{j=1}^{n} C_{ij} X_{ij}$$

Subject to the constraints:

$$\sum_{j=1}^{n} x_{ij} = a_i, \; i = 1, 2, ..., m$$

$$\sum_{i=1}^{m} x_{ij} = b_j, j = 1, 2, ..., n$$

and $x_{ij} \geq 0$ for all i and j.

The above formulation also requires the additional condition

$$\sum_{i=1}^{m} a_i = \sum_{j=1}^{n} b_j$$

which can always be satisfied by adding a fictitious source or destination to adjust the difference

$$\sum_{i=1}^{m} a_i - \sum_{j=1}^{n} b_j$$

Definition 1: *(Feasible solution):* A set of non-negative individual allocation ($x_{ij} \geq 0$) which simultaneously removes all the existing surpluses and satisfies all the existing deficiencies is called a feasible solution to a transportation problem (TP).

Definition 2: *(Basic feasible solution):* A feasible solution to a m-source, n-destination TP is said to be basic if the number of positive allocations equals $(m + n - 1)$.

Definition 3: *(Optimum solution):* A feasible solution (not necessarily basic) is said to be optimum if it minimizes the total transportation cost.

Table 12.13. Transportation Table

Source → *Destination ↓*	D_1	D_2	D_3	...	D_n	*Available*
S_1	C_{11}	C_{12}	C_{13}	...	C_{1n}	a_1
S_2	C_{21}	C_{22}	C_{23}	...	C_{2n}	a_2
S_3	C_{31}	C_{32}	C_{33}	...	C_{3n}	A_3
S_4	...	...	...	...	...	...
...	...	...	...	...	...	
S_m	C_{m1}	C_{m2}	C_{m3}	...	C_{mn}	a_m
Demand	b_1	b_2	b_3		b_n	

Methods for obtaining an initial basic feasible solution.

1. North-West (NW) Corner Rule

Step 1. The first assignment is made in the cell occupying the upper left hand (North-West) corner of the transportation table. The maximum feasible amount is allocated there. That means, $x_{11} = \min(a_1, b_1)$. This value of x_{11} is then entered in the cell (1,1) of the table.

Step 2. If $b_1 > a_1$, we move down vertically to the second row and make the 2nd allocation of magnitude $x_{21} = \min(a_2, b_1 - x_{11})$ in the cell (2, 1).

If $b_1 < a_1$, we move right horizontally to the second column and make the 2nd allocation of magnitude $x_{12} = \min(a_1 - x_{11}, b_2)$ in the cell (1, 2).

If $b_1 = a_1$, there is a tie for the second allocation. One can make second allocation of magnitude:

$$x_{12} = \min (a_1 - a_1, b_1) = 0 \text{ in the cell } (1, 2).$$

$$x_{21} = \min (a_2, b_1 - b_1) = 0 \text{ in the cell } (2, 1).$$

Step 3. Repeat steps 1 and 2 moving down towards the lower right corner of the transportation table till all the rim requirements are satisfied.

2. Matrix Minima Method or Lowest Cost Entry Method

Step 1. Determine the smallest cost in the cost matrix of the transportation table. Let it be C_{ij}. Allocate $x_{ij} = \min (a_i, b_j)$ in the cell (i, j).

Step 2:

- If $x_{ij} = a_i$, cross off the *i*th row of the transportation table and decrease b_j by a_i. Go to step 3.
- If $x_{ij} = b_j$, cross off the jth column of the transportation table and decrease ai by b_j. Go to step 3.
- If $x_{ij} = a_i = b_j$, cross off either the *i*th row or the *j*th column but not both.

Step 3. Repeat steps 1 and 2 for the resulting reduced transportation table till all the rim requirements are satisfied. Whenever, the minimum cost is not unique, make an arbitrary choice among the minima.

3. Vogel's Approximation Method (VAM)

This method takes into account not only the least cost C_{ij} but also the costs that just exceed C_{ij}. The steps of the method are discussed below:

Step 1. For each row of the transportation table, identify the smallest and the next-to-smallest costs. Determine the difference between them for each row. Display them alongside the transportation table in parenthesis against the respective rows. Similarly, compute the differences for each column.

Step-2: Identify the row or column with the largest difference among all the rows and columns. If a tie occurs, use any arbitrary tie breaking choice. Let the greatest difference correspond to *i*th row and let C_{ij} be the smallest cost in the *i*th row. Allocate the maximum feasible amount $x_{ij} = \min (a_i, b_j)$ in the cell (i, j) and cross off the ith row or *j*th column in the usual manner.

Step 3. Recompute the column and row differences for the reduced transportation table, and go to step 2. Repeat the procedure till all the rim requirements are satisfied.

Remarks: VAM determines an initial basic feasible solution which is very close to the optimum solution.

Example 12.15. Obtain an initial basic feasible solution to the following transportation problem.

From ↓ *To* →	D_1	D_2	D_3	D_4	a_i
S_1	11	13	17	14	250
S_2	16	18	14	10	300
S_3	21	24	13	10	400
b_j	200	225	275	250	

Method 1: NW Corner method

From ↓ *To* →	D_1	D_2	D_3	D_4	a_i
S_1	**200** / 11	**50** / 13	17	17	~~250~~ ~~50~~
S_2	16	**175** / 18	**125** / 14	10	~~300~~ ~~125~~
S_3	21	24	**150** / 13	**250** / 10	~~400~~ ~~250~~
b_j	~~200~~	~~225~~ ~~175~~	~~275~~ ~~150~~	~~250~~	

Transportation cost according to the NW corner rule is given by

$$Z = (200 \times 11) + (50 \times 13) + (175 \times 18) + (125 \times 14) + (150 \times 13) + (250 \times 10) = \text{Rs. } 12{,}200$$

Method 2: Matrix Minima (Least Cost Entry) Method

From ↓ *To* →	D_1	D_2	D_3	D_4	a_i
S_1	**200** / 11	**50** / 13	17	14	~~250~~ ~~50~~
S_2	16	**50** / 18	14	**250** / 10	~~300~~ ~~50~~
S_3	21	**125** / 24	**275** / 13	10	~~400~~ ~~125~~
b_j	~~200~~	~~225~~ ~~175~~ ~~125~~	~~275~~	~~250~~	

The transportation cost according to the above route is given by

$$Z = (200 \times 11) + (50 \times 13) + (50 \times 18) + (250 \times 10) + (125 \times 24) + (275 \times 13) = \text{Rs. } 12{,}825$$

Method 3: VAM (Vogel Approx Method)

From ↓ *To* →	D_1	D_2	D_3	D_4	a_i *(Penalty)*
S_1	**200** 11	**50** 13	17	14	~~250~~ ~~50~~ (2)(1)
S_2	16	**175** 18	14	**125** 10	~~300~~ ~~125~~ (4)
S_3	21	24	**275** 13	**125** 10	~~400~~ ~~275~~ (3)
b_j	~~200~~	~~225~~ ~~175~~	~~275~~	~~250~~ ~~125~~	
Penalty cost	(5)	(5)(6)	(1)	(0)	

From ↓ *To* →	D_1	D_2	D_3	D_4
S_1	**200** 11	**50** 13	17	14
S_2	16	**175** 18	14	**125** 10
S_3	21	24	**275** 13	**125** 10

The transportation cost according to the above route is given by

$$Z = (200 \times 11) + (50 \times 13) + (175 \times 18) + (275 \times 13) + (125 \times 10) + (125 \times 10) = \text{Rs. } 12{,}075$$

12.5.1 TRANSPORTATION ALGORITHM (MODI METHOD)

Step 1. Construct a transportation table entering the origin capacities a_i, the destination requirements b_j and the cost C_{ij}.

Step 2. Determine an initial basic feasible solution using any of the three methods, *viz.* NW corner rule, matrix minima or VAM. Enter the solution in the upper left corners of the basic cells.

Step 3. For all the basic variables x_{ij} solve the system equations $u_i + v_j = C_{ij}$. Starting initially with some $u_i = 0$ and entering succesively the values u_i and v_j on the transportation table.

Step 4. Compute the net evaluations $Z_{ij} = u_i + v_j - C_{ij}$ for all the non-basic cells and enter them in the upper right corners of the corresponding cells.

Step 5. Examine the sign of each $(Z_{ij} - C_{ij})$. If all $(Z_{ij} - C_{ij}) \leq 0$, then the current basic feasible solution is an optimum one. If at least one $(Z_{ij} - C_{ij}) > 0$, then select the variable xrs having the largest positive net evaluation to enter the basis.

Step 6. Let the variable xrs enter the basis. Allocate an unknown quantity, say θ, to the cell (*r*, *s*). Identify a loop that starts and ends at the cell (*r*, *s*) and connects some of the basic cells. Add and subtract alternatively θ, to and from the transition cells of the loop in such a way that the rim requirments remain satisfied.

Step 7. Assign a maximum value to θ in such a way that the value of one basic variable becomes zero and the other basic variables remain non-negative. The basic cell whose allocation has been reduced to zero, leaves the basis.

Step 8. Return to step 3 and repeat the process untill an optimum basic feasible solution has been obtained.

Example 12.16. Solve the following transportation problem.

From ↓ *To* →	*A*	*B*	*C*	*Availablity*
1	50	30	220	1
2	90	45	170	3
3	250	200	50	4
Requirements	4	2	2	

Example 12.17. A company has factories at A, B and C with supply warehouses M, N, P, and Q. Monthly factory capacities are 300, 400, and 500 respectively. Monthly warehouse requirements are 200, 240, 280, and 340 respectively. Unit transportation cost are given in the Table.

From ↓ *To* →	*M*	*N*	*P*	*Q*
A	7	9	9	6
B	6	10	12	8
C	9	8	10	14
Requirements				

Suggest the optimum transpotation solution.

13

Methods Engineering

13.0 INTRODUCTION

The term *methods engineering* connotes both *methods study* and *work measurement*. They try to answer respectively the questions like: 'How should a task be performed? And How much time should it take to perform the task including allowances?' *Methods Study* is the study of detailed design of workstations, and also to some extent the relationships between workstations.

Methods Study or Work study is the management technique to investigate all the factors affecting the efficiency and economy of an organization under review in order to improve it. It assumes that for every job there is always one best way of doing it. A scientific method is the best and surest way of finding this 'one best way'. The time taken for doing the job by the best way can be measured and set as a standard time. Work study can be applied in various sectors, viz: Industries (production, operations, research), Marketing, sales and distribution, Materials handling, Design, Building and other constructions, Transport, Hospital, Defense, Agriculture, etc.

In the planning stage, an estimate is made of the time taken by a typical employee to perform a given task at a workstation. Later, when the employee has learned the task and the conditions affecting the task have stabilized (*e.g.*, tooling, material, method, and conditions are available and are consistently applied), management requires a restudy of the job. Through observation and analysis, an industrial engineer or technician defines and documents the standard method and determines the time standard for performing the task, including nonproductive allowances. This time becomes a benchmark of how long it should take a typical trained employee at a normal rate of activity to perform the required operation, per unit of product, including prorated allowances. The sum of all operations for a product represents the expected direct labor time for a completed unit of product. This time serves the purpose of providing management with a basis for determining employee performance by comparing the actual number of units produced by an employee over a period of time and the number of units that the employee would have produced based on standard time. The process of determining the standard time for an operation is called *work measurement.*

13.1 OBJECTIVE OF WORK STUDY

The objective of work study is to avoid waste of any kind (time, human effort, materials, capital, etc.). Its slogan is 'work smart, not work hard' [Turner].

- To standardize the method of doing a task.
- To determine the standard time (ST) for doing a task to be used in wage payment.
- To minimize the unit cost of production by selecting proper machine tools, optimum parameters and proper process.
- To minimize the materials movements, operators movement, idle time of the workers and machines by proper plant layout.
- To eliminate the unnecessary human motions in performing a task.
- To utilize the facilities such as men, machines or materials most efficiently.

13.2 TOOLS AND TECHNIQUES OF WORK STUDY

Work study consists of **(a) Method study, and (b) Work measurement.** Which are discussed below.

13.2.1 METHOD STUDY

Method study is the process of subjecting work to systematic, critical scrutiny in order to make it more effective and/or more efficient. It was originally designed for the analysis and improvement of repetitive, manual work, but it can be used for all types of activity at all levels of an organization. Whenever one tries to find better ways to cut grass, cook food, wash cars, travel to work, and so on, he is doing a method study knowingly or unknowingly. However, a systematic approach is essential to do the method study. The **steps** of conducting method study are as given below:

1. **Select:** the job or work or method or operation for study.
2. **Record:** the various facts for the selected job.
3. **Examine:** the recorded facts for the selected job.
4. **Develop:** a better method by examining the recorded facts.
5. **Install:** the newly developed method, and
6. **Maintain:** this newly installed method to get the desired advantages.

Let's see these steps in more detail:

1. Select

Work is selected on the basis of it being an identified problem area or an identified opportunity (resulting from a systematic review of available data, high levels of dissatisfaction and complaint or as part of a change in policy, practice, technology or location), and usually because it meets certain conditions of urgency or priority. Selecting a job calls for the following considerations by the person concerned.

Economic consideration: Method study involves industrial engineers, supervisory staff, and equipment. So, it is a costly process for the organization which takes up the method study program. It is important to match the gain from this study with the cost that goes into it. If the job selected for study is not expected to run for long, or is very small, or a change in its design is likely in near future, then the gain due to this venture will be short lived and the expenses on this study may be greater than the gain. Therefore, the method study engineers should be careful in selecting the job for study.

Technical consideration: We must have enough technical expertise before taking up a job for method study. For example, in an assembly shop it's felt that the production rate is not as expected. The method study analyst feels that less production could be due to poor layout, the line balancing, and inefficient methods of working which needs to be investigated by expert industrial engineer. If the organization doesn't have this expertise to sort out this problem, then mere identification of the problem will be of no use.

Human reactions: They are very important and should be given due consideration. If the study of a particular job causes discontent or conflicts or likely to cause unrest among the workers, then it is wise to take into confidence all concerned or in a worst situation give up the study altogether, even if it would bring considerable gains to the organization.

2. Record

Recording is the second stage. After selecting a particular job for MS, the relevant facts regarding various processes, inspections, transportations, etc. are recorded properly. A wide range of techniques are available for recording; the choice depends on the nature of the investigation and the work being studied, and on the level of details required. Many of the techniques are simple charts and diagrams, but these may be supplemented by photographic and video recording, and by computer based techniques.

13.2.1.1 Methods Study Charting Techniques

Many of the traditional approaches in methods engineering can be classified as charting methods. In general, charting methods offer a graphic dimension to a problem and also channel data collection with respect to it. These charts and diagrams are discussed below:

(*a*) Operations Process Chart
(*b*) Flow Process Chart
(*c*) Flow Diagram
(*d*) Man-Machine Chart
(*e*) Multiple Activity Chart
(*f*) String Diagram.

(*a*) **Operation Process Chart (OPC):** This chart has been used for long time to display the operations, inspections, and their sequence for manufacture of a complete product in one figure. *Operation* includes all work performed by a worker or a crew at one location at one time.

(*b*) **Flow Process Chart (FPC):** In case of OPC, attention was paid only to operations, the flow process chart (FPC) includes additional components like transports or moves, delays and storages occurring during production. This also gives the information regarding the distance moved and time required for different items such as transportation, delays, and inspection, etc. It is usually prepared for one component of an assembly at a time. *Storage* indicates that the product has come out of production's control, and is under the control of another entity (*e.g.*, the stockroom or warehouse). *Delay* implies that the product remains under production's direct control. The different activities like: operation, transportation, inspection, storages, and delay are represented by the following symbols respectively.

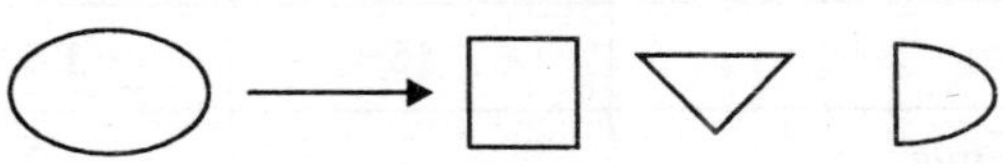

The flow process chart is particularly effective in tracing the incredible distance traveled by a part in plant specially if the plant is not designed scientifically. There are three types of flow process chart:

(*i*) *Flow Process Chart (machine type)*

(*ii*) *Flow Process Chart (man type):* This chart is based on man analysis. This is a graphic representation of different steps a person performs when doing a job and his movements from one place to another in performing that job.

(*iii*) *Flow Process Chart (product type):* This chart is based on product analysis. This is a graphic representation of different steps involved in performing the work required to pass a product from one stage to another.

The recorded data are subjected to critical examination and systems analysis. The aim is to identify, often through a structured, questioning process, those points of the overall system of work that require improvements or offer opportunity for beneficial change.

Example 13.1. A flow process chart is shown below for **vulcanizing for tires**. Vulcanizing means treating rubber under heat with sulfur or some compound to increase elasticity and durability. The symbols are short hand tools and serve as sign posts to wake critical areas for improvement. In this way by making flow process chart, a process or job can be analyzed step by step. Activity can be eliminated in some cases, combined in others or rearranged for effective processing.

Table 13.1

SN	*Description*	*Distance (m)*	*Time (minute)*	*Symbols*				
				O	→	D	□	▽
1.	Tires brought from store for dismantling of stepny	10	1		*x*			
2.	Stepney dismantled	—	14			*x*		
3.	Moved for removing old patches	3	0.5		*x*			
4.	Old patches removed	—	17	*x*				
5.	Taken for skiving operation	8	0.75		*x*			
6.	Skiving (to split or cut leather into layers)	—	5	*x*				
7.	Taken to flexible buffing	25	1.5		*x*			
8.	Buffing of inside surface	—	20	*x*				
9.	Taken for cutting operation	3	0.5		*x*			
10.	Cutting	—	5	*x*				
11.	Taken for mounting of new patch	16	1		*x*			
12.	New patch mounted	—	15	*x*				
13.	Patch inspected	—	5				*x*	
14.	Taken to vulcanizing m/c	15	1.5		*x*			
15.	Mounted on vulcanizing m/c	—	2	*x*				
16.	Vulcanized	—	24			*x*		
17.	Dismounted	—	2	*x*				
18.	Taken to tire spreader	10	1		*x*			
19.	Inspection on spreader	—	3				*x*	
20.	Sent for storage	10	1					*x*
21.	Total	94	121	7	8	2	2	1

Summary

Activity	*Present*	*Proposed*	*Savings*
Operation	7		
Transport	8		
Delay	2		
Inspection	2		
Storage	1		
Distance moved	87 m	33 m	44 m
Time taken	120.25 min	100 min	20.25 min

(*c*) **Flow Diagram**

- It is the plan view of a work to a certain scale and a line diagram which indicates the path followed by object under study. It shows the path followed by materials , man or machine. Where more than one floor is involved, an isometric drawing can be used.
- Flow process chart and flow diagrams are very simple and effective tools of methods study. They are very useful in establishing the overall sequence of operations and in determining the best layout.
- They present a clear picture of a process and are very effective tools to study and improve a complex job.

(*d*) **Multiple Activity Chart (MAC):** It is a graphic representation of the simultaneous activities of more than one man or machine on a common time scale to show their inter-relationship. These can be effective in analyzing situations in which at least two resources are employed within an operation. The objective is to group or arrange the sequence of events with respect to the resources employed so that a minimum unit production time is determined. MAC may be of the following types:

- One man—one machine chart (Man-Machine Chart)
- Two men—one machine chart
- One men—two machine chart
- Two or more men—one or more machine chart.

Man-Machine Chart. A *Man-Machine Chart* is illustrated in Figure 13.1. The general approach in such analysis is to try to use the resources in optimal manner. The focus of the analysis is to minimize the cycle time of man or the operator. Based on this study, one can propose a better method. Efforts are directed to reduce the idle times of man and machine.

Man				*Machine*	
S. N.	*Description*	*Symbol*	*Time*	*Symbol*	*Description*
1.	Loading work and setting tool		0.0 0.4		M/c idle
2.	Man idle (automatic feed)		0.4 1.0		Turning the w/piece

3.	Changing tool for thread cutting		1.0 1.6		M/c idle
4.	Auto feed (man idle)		1.6 2.0		Thread cutting
5.	Tool change for knurling		2.0 2.4		M/c idle
6.	Manual feed		2.4 2.8		Knurling

Summary

	Existing		*Proposed*	
	Man	*Machine*	*Man*	*Machine*
Idle time	1.0	1.4		
Working time	1.8	1.4		
Cycle time	2.8	2.8		
% Utilization	64%	50%		

Figure 13.1. Man-Machine Chart.

One Man—Two Machines Chart

There could be different variations of the man-machine chart. One of them is 'One man—Two machine chart' which is shown in Figure 13.2. This chart can be used:

- In finalizing the optimum number of machines an operator could attend for minimum overall machine idleness.
- In finalizing the optimum number of machines an operator can attend for his minimum overall idle period.
- In planning man power to attend the machines.
- In scheduling the jobs for overall maximum man-machine utilization.

Man				*Machine 1*			*Machine 2*		
S. No.	*Description*	*Symbol*	*Time*	*Description*	*Symbol*	*Time*	*Description*	*Symbol*	*Time*
1.	Loading the w/piece and setting tool on m /c1		0.0 0.4	M/c1 idle		0.0 0.4	M/c 2 idle		0.0 0.4
2.	Loading the w/piece and setting tool on m/c 2		0.4 0.8	Turning of the w/piece		0.4 0.8	M/c 2 idle		0.4 0.8
3.	Man idle		0.8 1.6			0.8 1.6	Turning the w/piece		0.8 1.6
4.	Groove cutting by manual feed		1.6 2.0	Groove cutting		1.6 2.0	Parting off		1.6 2.0

Summary

	Existing			Proposed		
	Man	*M/c1*	*M/c2*	*Man*	*M/c1*	*M/c2*
Idle time	0.8	0.4	0.8			
Working time	1.2	1.6	1.2			
Cycle time	2.0	2.0	2.0			
% Utilization	60%	80%	60%			

Figure 3.2. (One Man-Two Machines Chart).

(*e*) **Left Hand-Right Hand chart.** When the two hands of an operator are not moved simultaneously (in general), then it can be studied by a **'Left Hand-Right Hand chart'** as depicted by the following example.

Example 13.2. Finish hand filing (A Left hand - Right hand chart has been drawn for illustration):

- Searching, holding and lifting the work-piece to the vice table by LH = 0.2 min
- Opening the vice by right hand (RH) = 0.1 min
- Clamping the work-piece by both hands = 0.2 min
- Holding and lifting the file by RH = 0.1 min
- Hand filing by both hands = 1.5 min
- Bring the micro-meter by RH = 0.1 min
- Checking dimension by both hands = 0.4 min
- Opening the vice by RH = 0.1 min
- Removing the work-piece by left hand (LH) = 0.1 min

Description	*Symbol*	*Time (min)*	*Symbol*	*Description*
Lift the work piece		0.2		RH idle
LH idle		0.1		Opening the vice
Clamping the work piece by both hands		0.2		Clamping the w/p
LH idle		0.1		Holding and lifting the file
Hand filing by both hands		1.5		Hand filing
LH idle		0.1		Bringing micrometer
Checking dim. by both hands		0.4		Checking dimension
LH idle		0.1		Opening the vice by RH
Removing the work piece		0.1		RH idle

Summary

Left hand idle time = 0.3 min

Right hand idle time = 0.3 min

(*f*) **String Diagram.** For this diagram, a length of string is used to record the extent as well as the pattern of movement of a worker or piece of equipment within a limited area during a certain period of time. It is used to study where the journeys are irregular in distance and frequency. It is used in the following situations:

- When a group of operators is working.
- When a single operator is attending several machines.
- In process, where several sub-assemblies have to be moved to other assembly.
- Where processes require the operator to be moved from one work-place to another.
- For checking the relative value of various layout.

13.2.1.2 Micro-Motion Study

In certain types of operations and particularly those with very short cycles which are repeated thousands of time, micro-motion study is carried out. This study is made with much more details to find out the possibility of saving movements and efforts and thereby developing the best possible pattern movement. Gilbreth divided the human activities into 17 fundamental motions called 'therbligs' which are given in Table 13.2.

Table 13.2

S. No	*Operation*	*Abbreviation*	*Symbol*	*Example*
1.	Search	Sh		
2.	Hold	H		
3.	Select	St		
4.	Grasp	G		
5.	Release load	RL		
6.	Transport load	TL		
7.	Transport empty	TE		
8.	Position	P		
9.	Preposition	PP		
10.	Assemble	A		
11.	Disassemble	DA		
12.	Use	U		
13.	Inspect	I		
14.	Avoidable delay	AD		
15.	Unavoidable delay	UD		
16.	Plan	Pn		
17.	Rest for overcoming fatigue R			

This method originally used a constant speed (1000 frames per minute) 16-mm industrial camera; therefore the time between successive frames was 0.001 minutes. By examining and counting successive frames, usually with the help of a frame counter attached to the projector, one could break down the detailed human activity. A SIMO (Simultaneous Motion) chart is used to display a micromotion study analysis. By filming various alternative ways of performing an operation and analyzing their respective charts, it is possible to devise combinations of motion sequences that minimize unit cycle times. The employee is than trained to perform the operation using a better method.

Micromotion study can involve a considerable amount of film. Therefore, a technique known as memomotion study (similar to time-lapse photography) was developed, which employs a longer time interval between successive frames. It is often more feasible than micromotion study for medium- and long-cycle operations.

With the introduction video camera, it has become common practice to record the worker performance on videotape as part of the time-study process.

(*a*) SIMO Chart

SIMO stands for *simultaneous motion* cycle chart. It records simultaneously the various *therbligs* performed by different parts of the operator's body of one or more operators on a common time scale. The term 'therbligs' denote the fundamental motions of human activity. This was proposed by Frank Gilbreth and 'therbligs' (Gilbreth spelled backwards) include activities like search, find, transport empty, preposition, grasp, etc. SIMO chart could be used as a tool for reducing the work cycle, and reducing the fatigue due to excessive work done by only one hand or one part of the body.

(*b*) Cycle Graph

Gilbreth used this initially for analysis of work. It is a photographic technique usually made by a process of double exposure.

- The first exposure is a normal snapshot in which the workplace and the worker are photographed. Special lights are then attached to the hands of the operator and the lights are allowed to burn continuously and the operator has to perform his work.
- The second exposure is a time exposure that lasts for one complete cycle. Only the light from these bulbs is recorded as s continuous line on the photographic film - the other lights are switched off. Such a picture is called a 'cyclegraph'.
- This shows the workplace, the worker, his hands and a continuous line showing the motion patterns.

Limitations

In this cyclegraph, speed and direction of movement could not be determined from the continuous line of the light on the film.

(*c*) Chronocycle Graph

To overcome the limitations of the cyclegraph, Gilbreth used a relay circuit and made the lights attached to the operator to flicker (on and off). This caused on the film pear shaped dots from which the acceleration, deceleration and direction of movement by the increasing or decreasing length of the pear shaped dots and the direction of the tail formed by the moving light can be eliminated. The bulb is made slowly OFF and quickly ON and photograph is taken. The path of the bulb (path of man's movement) appears dotted, the dots taking pear shape. If the movement is fast, the dots are spaced far apart and they are closer if the speed is slow.

In both these methods, still films (either 8 mm or 16 mm, the later provides more clarity than the former) are used. Now a days, movie cameras are also being used in work study. They are widely used for the study of operations and for teaching purposes.

Install phase. The success of any method study is realized when actual change is made 'on the ground'. Hence, the **Install phase** is very important. Making theoretical change is easy; making real change demands careful planning, and handling of the people involved in the situation under review. They may need reassuring, retraining and supporting through the acquisition of new skills. Install, in some cases ,will require a *parallel running of old and new systems*, in others, it may need the *build-up of buffer stocks*, etc.

Maintain. Some time after the introduction of new working methods, it is necessary to check that the new method is working, that it is being adhered to, and that it has brought about the desired results. This is the *maintain phase*. Method drift is common—when people start to either revert to old ways of working, or introduce new changes. Some of these may be helpful (and should formally be incorporated); others may be inefficient or unsafe. A method audit can be used to formally compare practice with the defined method and identify such 'irregularities'.

13.2.1.3 Principles of Motion Economy

A number of common principles of good design have evolved over the years and are commonly referred to as 'Principles of motion economy'. Every work involves some or all of the 'therbligs'. Each 'therblig' absorbs time. This depends upon:

- Use of human body
- Arrangement of workplace, and
- Design of tools and equipment.

To reduce the time taken for performing any work some principles have been suggested by Barnes which are known as 'principles of motion economy'.

1. Rules concerning human body

- Both hands should be used for productive work (*e.g.* using steering wheel, lifting load, operating lathe wheels, etc).
- Both the hands should start and finish their motions at the same time.
- Except for the rest period, the two hands should not be idle at the same time.
- Motions of hands or arms should be symmetrical, simultaneous, and opposite (*e.g.* walking, running).
- Motions should be simple and involve minimum number of limbs (of course depending on the type of work) to have minimum time and less fatigue.
- It is desirable for a worker to use momentum to assist himself.
- Motions should be smooth and continuous—they should not involve frequent stops and sharp directional changes (*e.g.* traffic roundabouts).
- 'Ballistic' (free-swinging) movements should be preferred over controlled and restricted movements, *e.g.* driving a nail with a hammer.
- A worker may use mechanical aids to assist him to overcome muscular efforts (*e.g.* cranes, winches, levers, etc).
- Work movements should be rhythmical and automatic, if possible (*e.g.* exercising, jogging, cycling, etc).

2. Rules Related to work place layout and Material Handling

- For all tools and work-pieces, definite places should be fixed up (tool crib, racks, tool stand, pen stand, tray, etc).
- To reduce searching, tools and work should be pre-positioned (robot holding a job and transferring to other place).
- The workpiece should be delivered at the nearest to the workstation by gravity feed, or bins, or containers or transfer machines.
- Tools, materials and controlling levers should be located within easy reach of both the hands of operators.
- Tools and work-pieces should be arranged according to the sequence of operations.
- Arrangement should be made for automatic disposal of the finished workpieces.
- Adequate light, comfortable chairs, convenient height of the workplace should be provided.
- The workplace and the work-pieces should have color contrast.
- Working conditions—pleasant, illuminated, proper temperature, humidity, dust and fumes free, low noise level, color schemes, orderliness, etc.

3. Rules related to Tools and Equipment

- As far as possible, jig, fixture or foot operated device should be used instead of hands to 'hold' the work-piece.
- Tools should be combined, if possible, (hammer with provision of a screw driver and nail pulling, etc).
- If fingers are used, load to each finger should be given according to its capacity.
- Handles of levers, cranes or large screw drivers should be made sufficiently long so that there is maximum contact with the hands.
- The levers, cross bars, hand wheels, etc should be so arranged that the operators can use them with least change in their body position.

All the above principles are discussed in a separate subject called 'Ergonomics'. Some of the examples are as follows:

- Applications of most of the principles are made in 'automobiles'.
- Racing cycles have different types of handles and wheels (solid wheels).
- Racing cars with streamlined body, etc (movable roof, collapsible steering wheels, air bags, synchro-mesh gears, thermostatically controlled cooling fan in Maruti, etc).
- Levers of machine tools like lathe, drilling machine, etc. are colored in red while the body of machine in Grey to have the contrast.
- Cockpit of an airplane is ergonomically designed for the pilots.
- Hand operated cranes, remote controlled TV/VCR, digital radio, cordless telephones, walkman, mobile phone.
- Flexible back rest and neck rest of chairs.

13.2.2 WORK MEASUREMENT (TIME STUDY)

Methods study and W*ork measurement* are subsets of methods engineering. Time has always been one of the most important variables in engineering and science, including manufacturing. Galileo's experiments with falling bodies, for example, depended greatly on measurements of distance and time. It was

Taylor who offered the concept of measuring the time of human activity as a means of monitoring labor performance in industry.

Time study is a structured process of directly observing and measuring (using a timing device) human work in order to establish the time required for completion of the work by a qualified worker when working at a defined level of performance.

13.2.2.1 Stopwatch Time-Study

This was the first work measurement technique developed by Taylor. In this, the analyst breaks down an operation into elements. Then an operator performs the operation a number of times while the analyst observes elapsed time at the end of each element for a number of cycles of the study. The analyst also observes the rate of activity of the operator and records a 'performance rating factor', which is the observed pace of the operator compared to the analyst's concept of normal pace for the operation under study, considering applicable allowances for the operation.

The average time over several cycles is computed and adjusted for the speed and skill, or performance rating (PR), of the worker studied. Finally, an allowance factor (AF) is applied for personal needs, unavoidable delays, and fatigue. It typically represents a proportion of the normal time.

Steps in Conducting a Time Study

1. Select the job, inform the workers, and define the best method.
2. Time an appropriate number of cycles *n*. Use a sample size chart or graph to determine *n*.
3. Compute the sample size required.

   For desired level of accuracy, sufficient no of observations are required. For many kinds of measurements, a level of ± 5% accuracy is considered satisfactory. For this level of accuracy, the formula for determining the no of observations is

$$n = Z^2 \frac{p(1-p)}{h^2}$$

   where n = required sample size

   Z = standard normal deviate for the desired confidence level

   = 1 for 68 % confidence level

   = 2 for 95.45 % confidence level, and

   = 3 for 99.73 % confidence level

   p = estimated value of sample proportion (of time the worker is observed busy or idle)

   h = acceptable error level, in percent

4. Prepare a schedule to observe the worker at appropriate time. The concept of random numbers may be used to provide for random observations.
5. Observe, rate, and record the worker activities per schedule.
6. Record starting time, stopping time, and no. of acceptable units completed during the period.
7. Compute the normal time (NT)

$$\text{NT} = \frac{\text{total time} \times \%\ \text{working} \times \text{PR}}{\text{number of units completed}}$$

8. Compute the standard time (ST)

$$\text{ST} = \text{NT} + \text{Allowances}$$

Uses of Time Estimates and Work Standards

- Evaluation of present or past performance
- Worker payment/incentive payment, performance evaluation/productivity measurement
- Equipment and facility evaluation
- Evaluation of alternative work methods and operating procedures
- Prediction of future performance.

It follows the following steps:

- Analysis (*i.e.*, breaking of the work into small, easily-measurable elements);
- Measurement (of these components); and
- Synthesis (from those measured components to arrive at a time for the complete job).

The observer first undertakes preliminary observation of the work (a pilot study) to identify suitable elements which can be clearly recognized, and are convenient, in terms of their length, for measurement.

Subsequent studies are taken during which the observer times each occurrence of each element (using a stopwatch or other timing device) while at the same time making an assessment of the worker's rate of working on an agreed rating scale. (One of the prime reasons for measuring elements of work, rather than the work as a whole is to facilitate the process of rating. The rate at which a worker works will vary over time; if elements are carefully selected, the rate of working should be consistent for the relatively short duration of the element. More information on rating is given little later in work measurement.) This assessment of rating is used to convert the observed time for the element into a normal or basic time - a process referred to as 'extension'. It is essential that a time study observer has been properly trained in the technique and especially in rating.

Time study involves the use of specific control mechanisms to ensure that timing errors are within acceptable limits. Increasingly, timing is done by electronic devices rather than by mechanical stopwatch; some of these devices also assist in converting observed times into normal times.

Number of Observations

The **number of cycles that should be observed** depends on the variability in the work and the level of accuracy required. Since time study is essentially a sampling technique in which the value of the time required for the job is based on the observed times for a sample of observations, it is possible using statistical techniques to estimate the number of observations required under specific conditions. This total number of observations should be taken over a range of conditions (where these are variable) and, where possible, on a range of workers.

Once a normal time for each element has been determined, allowances are added (for example, to allow the worker to recover from the physical and mental effects of carrying out the work) to derive a standard time.

Time study is a very flexible technique, suitable for a wide range of work performed under a wide range of conditions, although it is difficult to time jobs with very short cycle times (of a few seconds). Because it is a direct observation technique, it takes account of specific and special conditions but it does rely on the use of the subjective process of rating. However, if properly carried out it produces consistent results and it is widely used. Additionally, the use of electronic data capture devices and personal computers for analysis makes it much more cost effective than previously.

Techniques of Time Study

There are **various ways** in which work may be measured and a variety of techniques have been established. The basic procedure, irrespective of the particular measurement technique being used, consists of three stages:

- an analysis phase in which the job is divided into convenient, discrete components, commonly known as elements;
- a measurement phase in which the specific measurement technique is used to establish the time required (by a qualified worker working at a defined level of performance) to complete each element of work;
- a synthesis phase in which the various elemental times are added, together with appropriate allowances (see below), to construct the standard time for the complete job.

The techniques used to measure work can be classified into those that rely on *direct observation of the work*, and those that do not. For example, some techniques, such as *predetermined motion-time systems(PMTS) and the use of synthetic or standard data* can provide times from simulation or even visualization of the work. However, the data on which such techniques are based were almost certainly based on earlier observation of actual work.

Performance Rating

Direct observation techniques (such as time study and analytical estimating) include a process for converting observed times to times for the 'qualified worker working at a defined level of performance.' The commonest of these processes is known as rating.

This involves the observer (after appropriate training) making an assessment of the worker's rate of working relative to the observer's concept of the rate corresponding to standard rating. This assessment is based on the factors involved in the work - such as *effort, dexterity, speed of movement, and consistency*. The assessment is made on a rating scale, of which there are three or four in common usage. Thus on the 0-100 scale, the observer makes a judgment of the worker's rate of working as a percentage of the standard rate of working (100).

The rating is then used to convert the observed time to the normal time using the simple formula:

$$\text{Normal Time} = \text{Observed time} \times \text{Rating factor}$$

Rating is a bit controversial area of measurement since it is a subjective assessment. Where different observers rate differently, the resulting normal times are not comparable. However, practiced rating practitioners are remarkably consistent. It is important that the raters are properly trained, and that this training is regularly updated (to maintain a common perception of standard rating).

Allowances

When carrying out work over a complete shift or working day, workers suffer from the fatigue due to the work undertaken and the conditions under which they are working. The normal practice is to provide some 'allowance' to allow the worker to recover from this fatigue and to attend to personal needs. The amount of allowance depends on the nature of the work and the working environment, and is often assessed using an agreed set of guidelines and scales.

Some suggest that relaxation allowances are unnecessary. With work like *carrying of heavy weights*, this school suggests that the observer automatically adjusts the concept of standard rating to allow for the weight. Thus, if the standard rate of performance for walking on level ground carrying no weight is equivalent to four miles per hour, then an observer rating a worker walking while carrying a weight will not expect the equivalent rate. Thus, it is argued that the weight has been allowed for in the adjustment of standard rating and any relaxation allowance is simply a duplication of this adjustment.

In many jobs there are small amounts of work that may occur irregularly and inconsistently. It is often not economic to measure such infrequent work and an additional allowance is added to cover such work and similar irregular delays. This allowance is known as a *contingency allowance* and is assessed either by observation, by analysis of historical records (for such items as tool sharpening or replacement), or by experience. This result in a standard time which includes the time the work 'should' take (when carried out by a qualified worker) plus additional allocations in the form of allowances, where appropriate, to cover relaxation time, contingency time and, perhaps, unoccupied time which increases the overall work cycle (such as waiting for a machine to finish a processing cycle).

13.2.2.2 Other Measurement Techniques

The choice of a suitable measurement technique depends on a number of factors including:

- the purpose of the measurement;
- the level of detail required;
- the time available for the measurement;
- the existence of available predetermined data; and
- the cost of measurement.

To some extent there is a trade off between some of these factors. For example, techniques which derive times quickly may provide less detail and be less suitable for some purposes, such as the establishment of individual performance levels on short-cycle work. These are popular techniques for the **Time Study**:

(*a*) Work sampling
(*b*) Predetermined Motion Time System (PMTS)
(*c*) Synthesis from standard data
(*d*) Estimating
- Analytical estimating
- Comparative estimating

(*a*) **Work Sampling.** This was first introduced in British Textile industry by L. Tippet in 1930s. It is used to estimate the percent of time that a worker spends on various tasks. It requires random observations to record the activity done by a worker. The results are used to find how employees allocate their time among various activities. This knowledge can lead to changes in staffing, reassignment of duties, estimates of activity cost, and the setting of delay allowances for 'labor standards'. When work sampling is done to establish delay allowances, it is also called a 'ratio delay' study. In a nutshell, work sampling can be used to know the following:

- % of the day a worker is working, and
- % of the day he is idle
- Working and idle time of a worker is used to fix up his performance rating.
- To establish the standard time for an operation.

Advantages Work Sampling

- It involves much less cost as compared to stop watch time study.
- It can be carried out with little training.
- It can time long operations which are almost impractical to be measured by stop watch time study.

- It's very good for timing group activities.
- It doesn't need any timing device like stop watch or micro-chronometer, etc.
- Even if the study gets interrupted in between, it doesn't introduce any error in the results.
- Observations can be made within the desired accuracy.
- Large no. of observations extended over days/weeks damp down the influence of day-to-day fluctuations on the results.
- It can improve efficiency by uncovering the sources of delay.

Limitations:

- It's uneconomical both as regards time and money to study activities of short duration by work sampling.
- It's also uneconomical in case one worker/one machine is to be studied.
- It doesn't break the job into elements and thus doesn't provide element details.
- It doesn't help in improving work method.
- It normally doesn't account for the speed at which an operator is working.
- Workers may not understand the principles of work sampling and hence may not trust it.

Applications:

- To determine working time and idle time of men and machines.
- To time long duration activities which are regular/irregular, frequent/infrequent.
- To estimate the % use of the inspectors and time standard for indirect labor.
- To estimate allowances for unavoidable delay.
- To estimate the time for which material handling equipment are actually operating in a day.
- In describing resource utilization patterns.
- For the purpose of cost control and accounting.
- In stores, hospitals, warehousing, offices, farm work, textile industry, m/c shop, etc.

Steps For Work Sampling

1. Select the job or group to be studied and inform the workers.
2. Take a preliminary sample to obtain an estimate of the parameter value (such as percent of time a worker is busy).
3. Compute the sample size required.

   For desired level of accuracy, sufficient no of observations are required. For many kinds of measurements, a level of ± 5% accuracy is considered satisfactory. For this level of accuracy, the formula for determining the no of observations is

$$n = Z^2 \frac{p(1-p)}{h^2}$$

where n = required sample size

Z = standard normal deviate for the desired confidence level

= 1 for 68 % confidence level

= 2 for 95.45 % confidence level, and

= 3 for 99.73 % confidence level

p = estimated value of sample proportion (of time the worker is observed busy or idle)

h = acceptable error level, in percent

4. Prepare a schedule to observe the worker at appropriate time. The concept of random numbers may be used to provide for random observations.
5. Observe, rate, and record the worker activities per schedule.
6. Record starting time, stopping time, and no. of acceptable units completed during the period.
7. Compute the normal time (NT)

$$NT = \frac{\text{total time} \times \% \text{ working} \times PR}{\text{number of units completed}}$$

8. Compute the standard time (ST)
9. ST = NT + Allowances.

Example 13.1. A company estimates that its employees are idle 25 % of the time. It would like to go for work sampling that is accurate within 3 % and wants to have 95.45 % confidence in the results.

Solution:

$$n = Z^2 \frac{p(1-p)}{h^2}$$

where n = required sample size

Z = 2 for 95.45 % confidence level, and

p = estimated value of idle proportion = 0.25

h = acceptable error level = 3 % = .03

$$n = Z^2 \frac{p(1-p)}{h^2} = 4 \times .25(1 - .25)/(.03)^2 = 833 \text{ observations.}$$

If the percent of idle time observed is not close to 25 % as the study progresses, then the no. of observations may have to be recalculated and increased or decreases accordingly.

Example 13.2. Calculate the no of observations necessary for an accuracy of ± 5%, and a confidence level 95% if $p = 0.25$.

Solution: For 95% confidence level, Z = 1.96

$$n = Z^2 \frac{p(1-p)}{h^2} = (1.96)^2 \times .25(1 - .25)/(.05)2 = 288.12 \text{ observations.}$$

(*b*) **PMTS (Predetermined Motion Time System).** It is a work measurement technique in which operations are divided into fundamental elements and time to complete each element is taken directly from the published Tables. Therefore before doing any operation, its standard time could be known. This is the difference with the time study where standard time (ST) is finalized after the operation is carried out. This is important to various organizations in setting time standards for various tasks.

Advantages of PMTS

- The standard can be determined from universally available data.
- The standard can be completed before a job is done.
- No performance rating is needed.
- There is no disruption of normal activities, and
- The methods are widely accepted as fair systems of determining standards.

Main uses of PMTS

1. Evaluation of method
   - To improve the existing methods
   - To evaluate the proposed methods in advance
   - To train the operator

- To evaluate change in design of tools, jigs, equipment, and the product to determine the standard time.

2. Establishing Time Standards
   - To get the standard time of any operation by the predetermined data
   - Comparison could be done with the values obtained by time study

Various Systems of PMTS

1. MTA (Motion Time Analysis)
2. WFS (Work Factor System)
3. BMT (Basic Motion Time-Study)
4. MTM (Methods Time Measurement)
5. 400 System (Western Electric)
6. DMT (Dimension Motion Time)

Time study elements can be quickly analyzed through **micro-motion process:**

Time Study Element	*Micro-motion*
Take a book from the rack	Reach, search, select, grasp
Place a part in a vice	Move, pre-position, assemble, release

1. MTA (Motion Time Analysis). A. B. Segur (Oak Park, Illinois) was the first to establish relationship between the time element and the motion itself. From his research, he discovered the law of fundamental times which says, "within reasonable limits, the time required by experts to perform a fundamental motion is a constant."

He emphasized that the time required to accomplish an act depends on how the work is performed (or the method used by the operator).

When an operation is studied, it is generally found that the operation consists of getting something, moving it to some location, processing or assembling it, and then releasing it.

Example 13.3. Operation of **writing with a pen** might be motion analyzed as follows:

Description (Right Hand)	*Motion*
Move hand to penholder	Transport empty
Grasp pen in penholder	Grasp
Move pen to paper	Transport loaded
Write on paper	Use
Move pen to penholder	Transport loaded
Pre-position pen to penholder	Pre-position
Assemble pen to penholder	Assemble
Release pen	Release
Move hand back to paper	Transport empty

In addition to analyzing the motions involved, certain other information must be collected, such as: the **distance moved**, the **type of grasp**, the **body members** required, and the **type of release**, etc.

- This information helps the analyst in answering questions like: *How was the transport empty, preposition, or grasp performed* ? This helps in defining the motions precisely and then choosing the proper time for performing the motions.

2. Work Factor System. In this system, the time for an operation is calculated on the basis of :

- **Body member used**: six body members are recognized and the time of an element depends on the particular body member used to perform the element. The body members are: *finger or head, arm, fore arm swivel, trunk, foot, and head turn.*
- **Distance moved:** the shortest distance between starting and stopping point of a motion or element is considered for time estimate.
- **Manual control**: can be of following types: *definite stop, directional control, carefulness, and change of direction.* Each type takes different type. One example could be passing a thread through the needle eye.
- **Weight or resistance involved:** weight has a positive effect on time. Again the time depends on the body member used to perform the element and also on ' whether an operation is made by male or a female'.

Example 13.4. If the time taken to move an empty hand through a distance of 10 inch is 0.0042 minute, the time to move a hand with 10 kg weight for the same distance would be 0.005 minute. If a lady does it, she may take 0.006 minute.

Time standards may be established by any one of the following three work-factor systems:

Detailed: when high accuracy is needed.

Simplified: some of the elemental work-factor motions are combined together to get quick measurement of standard time.

Abbreviated WF: where very high precision data is not required. It's generally applied for non-repetitive work with long time cycles, such as: *maintenance operation, material handling operation, m/c set up, and packing, etc.*

Work Factor	*Symbol*
Weight	W
Directional control	S
Precautions	P
Definite stop	D

3. Methods Time Measurement (MTM). This system is the most common form of PMTS. This divides any manual operation into basic motions, and then assigns predetermined time value to each. So it could be said that basically it is a technique of method analysis, however, it also does the work of time study by providing time values for each motion. The typical table of MTM system gives time in TMUs (Time Measurement Units). An analyst trained in MTM breaks down an operation into a sequence of elemental activities as classified by the MTM system. The sum the times for these detailed activities becomes the basis for establishing the standard time for the operation.

- One TMU = 0.00001 hour = 0.0006 minute = 0.0036 seconds.
- Time values were established by taking large number of motion pictures of various operations in different industrial organizations.
- The time standard depends on the use of particular fundamental motion required to perform an operation.
- Some TMU values for fundamental motions (for turn and apply pressure) are given as follows:

Weight (Pounds)	*Degree Turned*	*TMU*
0—2	30 45 60	2.8 3.5 13.1
2.1—10	30 45 60	13.4 5.5 6.5
10.1—35	30 45 60	8.4 and so on

19 fundamental motions are considered in this system:

8 Basic motions	*9 Pedal (leg) and truck motions*	*2 Eye motions*
Reach	Side step	Eye travel time
Move	Turn body	Eye focus time
Apply pressure	Walk	
Turn	Bend	
Grasp	Stoop	
Position	Kneel on one leg	
Disengage	Kneel on both legs	
Release	Foot motions	
	Sit	

Eye travel time = 15.2T/D TMU

Eye focus time = 7.3 TMU

where, T = distance between points from and to which the eye traveling, and D = perpendicular distance from the eye to the line of travel T)

4. BMTS (Basic Motion Time Study). "A basic motion is defined as a complete movement of body member", such as: *a hand moves from rest through space and again comes to rest.*

The following factors are considered for time estimation in this system:

The **distance moved** during any activity.

Visual attention needed to complete the motion or activity (*e.g.* taking temperature reading by thermometer, pressure guage, etc.)

The **degree of precision** needed in grasping or positioning (*e.g.* tuning in to BBC radio, microscope focusing, rifle shooting, holding a floppy, etc.)

The **amount of free space** required to handle weight or resistance.

Simultaneous motions (pulling out a bull worker spring, exercising with dumb bells, weight lifting, etc.)

Time for distance moved:

The following points are taken into consideration:

- Use of muscular control to stop the motion (*e.g.* stopping a cricket ball)
- No use of muscular control (touch control switches in calculators, etc.)
- Muscular control required to slow down the motion (driving car)

Unsolved Exercises

1. (*a*) Explain the different steps of method study with suitable examples.
   (*b*) Write the principles of motion economy.
2. A work-sampling study of customer service representatives in a telephone company office showed that a receptionist was working 80% of the time at 100 percent performance rating. This receptionist handled 200 customers during the 8-hour study period. Company policy is to give allowances of 10 percent of total on-the-job time. Find the normal time and standard time per customer.

13.3 STANDARDIZATION

Standardization is a strategic enterprise involving stakeholders having varying commercial and societal interests. Understanding the rules of the game, and the motivations of the other players, will help you to navigate the sometimes arduous terrain of standards development. As Yogi Berra, the great baseball player, once observed: "*If you don't know where you are going, you will wind up somewhere else.*"

13.3.1 WHAT IS A STANDARD?

It is a document, established by consensus, approved by a recognized body, that provides for common and repeated use, rules, guidelines or characteristics for activities or their results, aimed at achieving the optimum degree of order . . ."

However, it may be easier to understand by looking at some examples of products that conform to standards.

(*a*) *A roll of photographic film.* It works because of standard. The proof? It will fit into any 35 mm camera and provide you with color snapshots of your loved ones anywhere in the world. And if the flash didn't work because the battery was dead? Just put another battery in and you're all set.

(*b*) Why does *the battery* work? Because of Standards.

(*c*) An *ATM card* works due to Standard. Take it anywhere in the world. Stick in a bank machine. Out comes cash, so you can enjoy your vacation. Unless of course you've overextended your credit limit in which case what you really need is a personal financial planner. And lucky for you we now have international standards being developed for personal financial planners.

(*d*) The *lights in the room.* Something as vital to our everyday existence as electric lights, something we take for granted until we have to replace a bulb-or worse still, there's a blackout.

Now you say "wait a second, when I travel overseas, I have to bring an adaptor in order to plug my laptop into the electrical outlet." Well, let me ask you-What's that an example of? You guessed it-lack of international standards.

13.3.2 EXAMPLES OF STANDARDS

Now most of the examples given have been products because it is conducive to show-and-tell, but there are also standards for systems, processes and services. Pretty much anything can be standardized.

The *traffic lights* outside. Red means stop; green means go. Why? Standards.

In fact, since we've been focusing on travel, think about navigating your way through the airport when you first arrive in a country where you don't speak the language. Thanks to public information symbols, you are able to locate immigration, baggage claim, customs, and ground transportation.

Businesses follow standardized procedures for their quality and environmental management systems. For example, based on the ISO 9000 and ISO 14000 series of standards.

Increasingly, there is movement to develop standards for the service industries. And standards also exist for programs that certify professionals in various industries.

In short, standards are everywhere, impacting our daily lives in more ways than you probably ever imagined. Responsibility for the technical content of standards lies with the subject matter experts who participate in their development. Costs generally are borne by the participants and standards development organizations rely heavily on the sale of standards to support the standards infrastructure.

13.3.3 WHAT IS CONFORMITY ASSESSMENT?

Standards are only one side of the equation. Standards are just good ideas unless products, processes, systems and personnel conform to them. The process of evaluating whether or not they do is called conformity assessment. Let's look at another illustration.

A box of crayons

On the back, it says under "safety information":

"Art and Creative Materials Institute Certified. Conforms to ASTM D-4236. Meets performance standard ANSI Z356.1. Actually, that "ANSI Z356.1" is what's known as a standard's "designation." These declarations and seals on this box of crayons are known as "marks of conformity." In other words it's a manufacturer's claim-in this case, Crayola's-that these crayons are non-toxic to children, and that they meet the labeling and performance requirements set forth in the standards cited. In order for these claims to be made the product was tested against the standard by an independent third-party.

Now there are other valid methods for demonstrating conformity of products to standards, such as the manufacturer's or suppliers' declaration of conformity.

13.3.4 STANDARDS DEVELOPMENT, ACCEPTANCE/IMPLEMENTATION

Standards can be developed via a formal, fully consensus-based process, like ISO's, or by other means. Many multinational companies develop standards internally and use a combination of internally and externally-developed standards in their activities.

Companies in the IT and telecom sectors frequently partner with competitors to develop technical specifications aimed at solving a specific market need. Such consortia efforts are attractive to those industries because they enable them to keep pace with rapid advancements in technology and release new products more quickly into the marketplace.

For industry, the choice of what type of standards development process is used is largely a competitive, market-driven decision.

Standards can cut across industries. They can be national, regional or international in geographic scope. With the globalization of trade, the trend is increasingly toward international standards. While most standards are developed and used on a voluntary basis, they can become mandatory when they are incorporated into laws or technical regulations for health, safety, and protection of the environment.

Standards development involves . . .

- Research
- Gathering viewpoints
- Discussion
- Compromise
- Agreement on content
- Preparation of drafts
- Agreement on drafts
- Publication
- Ongoing maintenance.

13.3.5 BENEFITS OF STANDARDS TO INDUSTRY

As suggested in our earlier examples, standards help to ensure that product components work for their intended applications. Standards also help industry to:

- reduce costs and time -to-market
- ensure interoperability
- meet safety and regulatory compliance obligations
- access new markets, enhancing their competitive position, and
- reduce anti-trust and product liability exposure.

13.3.6 BENEFITS OF STANDARDS TO GOVERNMENT

- Partnering with the private sector to develop voluntary standards helps governments to meet public policy objectives relating to safety, health, the environment, and consumer protection.
- It provides government with access to private sector technology, and reduces regulatory and procurement costs.
- It promotes exports of goods and services, facilitates trade, and contributes to economic growth.
- And it helps to achieve WTO objectives to avoid the creation of non-tariff barriers to trade.

The extent of government involvement in standardization varies by country and region. In the European Union, for example, government plays a very proactive role in directing the European regional standards bodies to develop standards that will address societal objectives.

The United States standards system, on the other hand, is driven more by private sector, commercial interests, with public sector support. In the U.S., as a matter of law, federal government agencies are required to use private sector standards where feasible and to work with the private sector to develop needed standards.

13.3.7 BENEFITS OF STANDARDS TO CONSUMERS

I hope it's clear that standards make all of our lives simpler when they address basic human needs-needs such as interoperability, safety and accessibility.

Standards provide consumers with:

- a greater selection of goods and services, easier choices and lower costs
- better, more consistent quality, and
- enhanced safety and reliability.

Standards that take into account consumer requirements are more likely to result in products and services being accepted into the marketplace.

Let's look now at the fundamental principles of international standardization which will help to make clear why governments have come to embrace voluntary standards.

13.3.8 CARDINAL PRINCIPLES OF INTERNATIONAL STANDARDIZATION

The World Trade Organization has identified the following principles relevant to the work of organizations developing international standards:

Transparency:

- That all essential information regarding standardization work programmes, proposals for standards, and completed projects should be made easily accessible to all interested parties.
- That procedures should allow for early notification of standards activity, and adequate time and opportunity to comment on draft standards.

Openness:

- That any interested party may participate on a non-discriminatory basis at the policy level and at all stages of standards development.

Impartiality and Consensus:

- That the standard development process should not favour the interests of
- particular suppliers, countries or regions.
- That consensus procedures should seek to take into account the views of all parties concerned and to reconcile any conflicting arguments.

Effectiveness and Relevance:

- That international standards need to be relevant and effectively respond to regulatory and market needs, as well as scientific and technological developments.
- That they should not adversely affect fair competition, or stifle innovation and technological development.
- That whenever possible, they should be performance based rather than based on design or descriptive characteristics, and
- That international standards that have become obsolete or ineffective should be reviewed.

Coherence:

That international standards should not duplicate or conflict with standards developed by other international standards organizations. Cooperation and coordination is essential. Finally, international standards bodies should have a Development Dimension, meaning they should seek tangible ways of facilitating developing country participation such as through capacity building and technical assistance.

These principles are the hallmarks of international standardization.

The development of voluntary standards is both a challenging and a rewarding experience. Active standards participation is a serious commitment.

- It involves reviewing technical data, attending standards committee meetings, and commenting and voting on draft standards.
- It requires good listening skills and the ability to consider the viewpoints of subject matter experts from industry and other stakeholder groups, which may differ from your own.
- It involves negotiation and compromise.
- Consumers are not expected necessarily to have the same level of technical expertise as, say, a representative of a manufacturer. However, where consumers can add unique value to the standards process is by communicating the perspective of the ultimate end user of a product or service.
- The length of time it takes to develop a standard depends upon the amount of time it takes to achieve consensus and the urgency of the need. It can be anywhere from a matter of months to several years.
- The successful end result of these efforts is a document that makes a meaningful contribution to the public welfare, commerce, or understanding.

REFERENCES

1. Philip E. Hicks, 'Industrial Engineering and Management: A New Perspective', McGraw-Hill International Editions, Industrial Engineering Series.
2. Joseph G. Monks - Schaum's Outline of Theory and Problems of Operations Management).
3. 'Standardization Fundamentals—The Principles and The Players' by James McCabe, Director, Consumer Relations and Public Policy, American National Standards Institute (ANSI): Regional Seminar: "Making an impact: Consumer representation in standards-setting" 8 September 2003—Bangkok, Thailand.

14

Mechanization, Automation and Productivity

14.0 INTRODUCTION

Mechanization refers to the use of powered machinery to help a human operator in some task. It also *refers to the replacement of human (or animal) power with mechanical power of some form.* The driving force behind mechanization has been humankind's propensity to create tools and mechanical devices. The term is most often used in industry. The addition of powered machine tools, such as the steam powered lathe dramatically reduced the amount of time needed to carry out various tasks, and improved productivity. Today very little construction of any sort is carried out with hand tools. The term is also used in the military where it refers to the use of vehicles, notably *armored personnel carriers* (APCs), to move troops that would otherwise have marched into combat. Mechanization dramatically improved the mobility of infantry, and today what little infantry is not mechanized is airborne. The use of hand powered tools, however, is not an example of mechanization.

14.1 ASSEMBLY LINE

An assembly line is a manufacturing process in which interchangeable parts are added to a product in a sequential manner to create an end product. The assembly line was first introduced by Eli Whitney to create muskets for the U.S. Government. Henry Ford later introduced the moving assembly line for his automobile factory to cut manufacturing costs and deliver a cheaper product.

14.1.1 HISTORY OF THE ASSEMBLY LINE

Until the 1800s, craftsmen would create each part of a product individually, and assemble them, making changes in the parts so that they would fit together - the so-called English System of manufacture.

- Eli Whitney invented the American System of manufacturing in 1799, using the ideas of division of labor and of engineering tolerance, to create assemblies from parts in a repeatable manner.
- This linear assembly process, or assembly line, allowed relatively unskilled laborers to add simple parts to a product. As all the parts were already made, they just had to be assembled.
- While originally not of the quality found in hand-made units, designs using an assembly line process required less knowledge from the assemblers, and therefore could be created for a lower cost.

14.1.2 HISTORY OF MOVING ASSEMBLY LINE

Henry Ford installed the World's first moving assembly line on December 1, 1913, as one of several innovations intended to cut costs and permitting mass production. The idea was an adaptation of the system used in the meat processing factories of Chicago, and the conveyor belts used in grain mills. By bringing the parts to the workers, considerable time was saved.

14.1.3 PRE INDUSTRIAL REVOLUTION

Although Whitney was first to use the assembly line in the industrial age, the idea of *interchangeable* parts and the assembly line was not new, though it was little used. The idea was first developed in Venice several hundred years earlier, where ships were produced using pre-manufactured parts, assembly lines, and mass production; the Venice Arsenal apparently produced nearly one ship every day, in what was effectively the world's first factory.

14.1.4 INDUSTRIAL ROBOT

ISO standard 8373 defines an industrial robot as *an automatically controlled, reprogrammable, multipurpose manipulator programmable in three or more axes.* In a simple phrase, industrial robotics refers to the study, design and use of robots for manufacturing. Typical applications of industrial robots include welding, painting, ironing, assembly, palletizing, product inspection, and testing.

There are a small number of commonly used robot configurations for industrial automation, including articulated robots (the original, and most common), SCARA (Selective Compliance Assembly Robot Arm) robots and gantry robots (Cartesian robots, or x-y-z robots). In the context of general robotics, most types of industrial robots would fall into the category of robot arms (inherent in the use of the word manipulator in the above-mentioned ISO standard).

Industrial robot actions are determined by programmed routines that specify the direction, speed, and distance of a series of coordinated motions. For more precise guidance, robots are often assisted by machine vision systems acting as their "eyes". The setup of motions and sequences for an industrial robot is sometimes done by an operator using a teaching pendant, a handheld control and programming unit.

Manufacturers of industrial robots include: Epson Robots, Yaskawa, ABB, KUKA and FANUC. The first company to produce an industrial robot was Unimation.

14.2 POSTAL MECHANIZATION/EARLY AUTOMATION

At the turn of the 20th century, in spite of a burgeoning mail volume and limited work space, the Post Office Department relied entirely on antiquated mailhandling operations, such as the *pigeonhole* method of letter sorting. Although crude sorting machines were proposed by inventors of canceling machines in the early 1900s and tested in the 1920s, the Great Depression and World War II postponed widespread development of mechanization until the mid-1950s. The Post Office Department then took major steps toward mechanization by initiating projects and awarding contracts for the development of a number of machines and technologies, including letter sorters, facer-cancelers, automatic address readers, parcel sorters, advanced tray conveyors, flat sorters, and letter mail coding and stamp-tagging techniques.

As a result of this research, the first semi-automatic parcel sorting machine was introduced in Baltimore in 1956. A year later, a foreign-built multiposition letter sorting machine (MPLSM), the

Transorma, was installed and tested for the first time in an American post office. The first American-built letter sorter, based on a 1,000-pocket machine originally adapted from a foreign design, was developed during the late 1950s. The first production contract was awarded to the Burroughs Corporation for 10 of these machines. The machine was successfully tested in Detroit in 1959 and eventually became the backbone of letter-sorting operations during the 1960s and 70s.

In 1959, the Post Office Department also awarded its first volume order for mechanization to Pitney-Bowes, Inc., for the production of 75 Mark II facer-cancellers. In 1984, more than 1,000 Mark II and M-36 facer-cancellers were in operation. By 1992, these machines were outdated and began to be replaced by advanced facer-canceller systems (AFCS) purchased from ElectroCom L.P. The AFCSs process more than 30,000 pieces of mail per hour, twice as fast as the M-36 facer-cancelers. AFCSs are more sophisticated too: they electronically identify and separate prebarcoded mail, handwritten letters, and machine-imprinted pieces for faster processing through automation.

The Department's accelerated mechanization program began in the late 1960s and consisted of semi-automatic equipment such as the MPLSM, the single position letter sorting machine (SPLSM), and the facer-canceller. In November 1965, the Department put a high-speed optical character reader (OCR) into service in the Detroit Post Office. This first-generation machine was connected to an MPLSM frame and read the city/state/ZIP Code line of typed addresses to sort letters to one of the 277 pockets. Each subsequent handling of the letter required that the address be read again.

Mechanization increased productivity. By the mid-1970s, however, it was clear that cheaper, more efficient methods and equipment were needed if the Postal Service was to offset rising costs associated with growing mail volume. To reduce the number of mail piece handlings, the Postal Service began to develop an expanded ZIP Code in 1978.

The new code required new equipment. The Postal Service entered the age of automation in September 1982 when the first computer-driven single-line optical character reader was installed in Los Angeles. The equipment required a letter to be read only once at the originating office by an OCR, which printed a barcode on the envelope. At the destinating office, a less expensive barcode sorter (BCS) sorted the mail by reading its barcode.

Following the introduction of the ZIP+4 code in 1983, the first delivery phase of the new OCR channel sorters and BCSs was completed by mid-1984.

14.3 THE AGE OF AUTOMATION

Today, a new generation of equipment is changing the way mail flows and improving productivity. Multiline optical character readers (MLOCRs) read the entire address on an envelope, spray a barcode on the envelope, then sort it at the rate of more than *nine per second.* Wide area barcode readers can read a barcode virtually anywhere on a letter. Advanced facer—canceler systems face, cancel, and sort mail. The remote bar-coding system (RBCS) provides bar-coding for handwritten script mail or mail that cannot be read by OCRs.

The ZIP + 4 code reduced the number of times that a piece of mail had to be handled. It also shortened the time carriers spent casing their mail (placing it in order of delivery). First tested in 1991, the delivery point barcode, which represents an 11-digit ZIP Code, will virtually eliminate the need for carriers to case mail because mail will arrive in trays at the delivery post office sorted in "walk sequence." The MLOCR reads the barcode and address, then constructs a unique 11-digit delivery point barcode using the Postal Service's National Directory and the last two digits of the street address. Then barcode sorters put the mail in sequence for delivery.

Until now, most of the emphasis in automation has been processing machine-imprinted mail. Still, letter mail with addresses that were handwritten or not machine-readable had to be processed manually or by a letter sorting machine. The RBCS now allows most of this mail to receive delivery point barcodes without being removed from the automated mailstream. When MLOCRs cannot read an address, they spray an identifying code on the back of the envelope. Operators at a data entry site, which may be far from the mail processing facility, read the address on a video screen and key a code that allows a computer to determine the ZIP Code information. The results are transmitted back to a modified barcode sorter, which pulls the 11-digit ZIP Code information for that item, and sprays the correct barcode on the front of the envelope. The mail then can be sorted within the automated mailstream.

Letter mail represents approximately 70 percent of the Postal Service's total mail volume, so development of letter mail equipment has received the most attention. In addition to letter-mail processing, the Postal Service is taking steps to automate mail-forwarding systems and the processing of flats and parcels. The Postal Service also has accelerated installation of automated equipment in lobbies to serve customers better. The backbone of this effort is the integrated retail terminal (IRT), a computer that incorporates an electronic scale. It provides information to customers during a transaction and simplifies postal accounting by consolidating data. Postage validation imprinters have been attached to the IRTs to produce a self-sticking postage label that has a barcode for automated processing.

Competition and Change *(Delivery barcode sorter, Long Island, NY, 1992).* Despite improved technology, the Postal Service faced mounting financial and competitive pressures. Following a decade of prosperity in the 1980s that saw a dramatic increase in mail volume, the nation entered a period of slower economic growth in the 1990s. Bankruptcies, consolidations, and a general restructuring of the marketplace reduced the flow of business mail. In 1991, overall mail volume dropped for the first time in 15 years. The following year, volume rose only slightly, and the Postal Service narrowly avoided the first back-to-back declines in mail volume since the Great Depression.

Competition grew for every postal product. The rise of fax machines, electronic communications, and other technologies offered alternatives for conveying bills, statements, and personal messages. Entrepreneurs and publishing companies set up alternate delivery networks in an attempt to hold down the costs of delivering magazines and newspapers. Many third-class mailers, finding their mailing budgets reduced and their postage rates increased higher than expected, began shifting some of their expenditures to other forms of advertising, including cable television and telemarketing. Private companies continued to dominate the market for the urgent delivery of mail and packages.

To become more competitive, the Postal Service began to change and restructure. In 1990, the Postal Service awarded two contracts to private firms that now independently measure First-Class Mail service and customer satisfaction. The Postal Service also began working more closely with customers to identify ways to better meet their needs and expanded customer conveniences such as stamps on consignment. With the help of business mailers, the Postal Service continued support for rates reflecting customer work-sharing features, many tied to automation, to give customers more flexibility. At the same time, the Postal Service began implementing Customer Advisory Councils, groups of citizens who volunteered to work with local postal management on postal issues of interest to the community. By the summer of 1993, 500 Advisory Councils were in place.

In the summer of 1992, under the leadership of newly appointed Postmaster General Marvin Runyon, the Postal Service intensified its drive for competitiveness. After consulting with mailers, the Governors of the Postal Service, postal employees and their representatives, and Congress, Runyon set a 120-day agenda to reduce bureaucracy and overhead, to improve service and customer satisfaction, and to stabilize postage rates.

To help accomplish these goals, the Postal Service created a new organizational structure, starting at the top. The Postal Service reduced the officer corps by nearly one-half, eliminated layers of management to speed decision-making, and trimmed overhead positions by nearly one quarter, or 30,000 positions. By offering early-out retirements and other incentives, the Postal Service reduced overhead without layoffs or furloughs.

Throughout the country, the five regions and 73 field divisions were replaced by 10 areas, each with a manager for Customer Services and a manager for Processing and Distribution. At the local level, 85 Customer Services districts and 350 processing and distribution plants were established, and a marketing and sales office was set up in each area. The new structure allowed postal managers to focus their expertise, improved communications up and down the line, and empowered employees to meet the needs of their customers.

The Postal Service also took steps to improve service in 1993. It invested in service improvements in the processing and delivery of mail at every major postal facility, expanded retail hours, and developed a more user-friendly Domestic Mail Manual. In cooperation with business customers, the Postal Service began to develop new services to meet specific mailer needs and to overhaul and simplify its complex rate structure. In 1993, it awarded contracts for two additional external measurement systems, one to survey the satisfaction levels of business mailers, the other to track service performance of third-class mail.

Postal finances also improved. The restructuring eliminated some programs, cut costs, brought in new business, and reduced the Postal Service's projected deficit of more than $2 billion. This put the organization in a better position to try to hold rates steady, which means that rates will have remained stable for four years for the first time since the Postal Service began operations in July 1971. Furthermore, the independent measurement surveys already in place indicated that service was as good or better than ever since the restructuring.

Despite many challenges, the Postal Service plans to draw on its diverse strengths to become a model for government, a force to help American businesses be more competitive, and a more effective communications system that binds the nation together.

14.3.1 AUTOMATION

Automation or Industrial Automation is the use of computers to control industrial machinery and processes, replacing human operators. It is a step beyond mechanization, where human operators are provided with machinery to help them in their jobs. The most visible part of automation can be said to be industrial robotics. Some *advantages* are repeatability, tighter quality control, waste reduction, integration with business systems, increased productivity and reduction of labor. Some *disadvantages* are high initial costs and increased dependence on maintenance.

By the middle of the 20th century, automation had existed for many years on a small scale, using mechanical devices to automate the production of simply shaped items. However the concept only became truly practical with the addition of the computer, whose flexibility allowed it to drive almost any sort of task. Computers with the required combination of power, price, and size first started to appear in the 1960s, and since then have taken over the vast majority of assembly line tasks (some food production/inspection being a notable exception).

In most cases specialized hardened computers referred to as PLCs (Programmable Logic Controllers) are used to synchronize the flow of inputs from sensors and events with the flow of outputs to actuators and events. This leads to precisely controlled actions that permit a tight control of the process or machine.

HMIs (Human-Machine Interfaces) are usually employed to communicate to PLCs e.g., to enter and monitor temperatures or pressures to be maintained.

14.3.2 SOCIAL ISSUES OF AUTOMATION

Automation raises several important social issues. Among them is automation's impact on employment/unemployment.

Some argue automation leads to fuller employment. One author made that case here: When automation was first introduced, it caused widespread fear. It was thought that the displacement of human workers by computerized systems would lead to unemployment (this also happened with mechanization, centuries earlier). In fact the opposite was true, the freeing up of the labor force allowed more people to enter information jobs, which are typically higher paying. One odd side effect of this shift is that "unskilled labor" now pays very well in most industrialized nations, because fewer people are available to fill such jobs leading to supply and demand issues.

Some argue the reverse, at least in the long term. First, automation has only just begun and short-term conditions might partially obscure its long-term impact. For instance many manufacturing jobs left the United States during the early 1990s, but a massive up scaling of IT jobs at the same time offset this as a whole.

It appears that automation does devalue unskilled labor through its replacement with less-expensive machines, however the overall effect of this on the workforce as a whole remains unclear. Today automation of the workforce in the *western world* is quite advanced, yet during the same period the general well-being of its citizens has increased dramatically. What role automation played in these changes has not been well studied.

14.3.3 THE AUTOMATED WORKPLACE

Effect on skilled labour

Robotic machines can perform certain unpleasant and dangerous jobs, such as welding and painting, that can be injurious to a worker's health. They can handle loads of up to a ton or more and work efficiently in temperatures ranging from near freezing to uncomfortably hot. Automation has eliminated much of the worker's physical and mental drudgery and has allowed the worker to change from a machine operator to a machine supervisor.

At the same time, by increasing productivity as measured in output per man-hour, automation can reduce the number of workers. In the 1950s and '60s employment declined in the chemical, steel, meat-packing, and other industries in developed countries that achieved large increases in output. Except in certain older industrial areas in Britain and the United States, however, the widely feared onset of mass unemployment did not materialize. Although certain jobs and skills have been rendered obsolete, a vast array of new jobs calling for different skills has grown up.

Automation has brought about changes in the worker's relation to the job. Here the differences between labour practices in different countries proves instructive. *The old management principle that work should be broken down into the smallest operations, so that the worker would not have to use any intelligence in performing a job*, was based perhaps upon the notion that the worker is stupid. Hence, when full mechanization was introduced into American factories, the workers were not permitted to stop the moving assembly line if anything went amiss; that was presumed to be the task of supervisory engineering personnel. The result was both low productivity and a loss in quality control. In Japanese factories, on the other hand, assembly-line workers were allowed to stop the process when something went wrong. Indeed, the Japanese companies formed *quality circles*, wherein the workers were given a say in the performance of their tasks and in the process of problem solving—an application of Mayo's Hawthorne effect, which they had learned from American management consultants. These practices improved both productivity and quality.

A similar way of enhancing quality and work performance is what is known as *group assembly*, which started in Swedish automobile plants and was also adopted by the Japanese and then by the Americans. With this system a group of workers is responsible for the entire product, rather than individual workers doing only one small task. If something goes wrong on an assembly line, an individual worker can push a button and hold things in place until the problem is resolved. This approach to production is being increasingly employed throughout the world. It already has had major implications for the labour force and labour-management relations. For one thing, it allows smaller numbers of more highly skilled workers, operating sophisticated computer-controlled equipment, to replace thousands of unskilled workers in assembly-line plants.

As a consequence, the highly skilled worker, who began to disappear with the introduction of the old-fashioned mass production assembly line, again became indispensable. The increasing use of automated machinery and control systems placed new demands on both the technical skills and the intellectual aptitudes of production workers. While automation may have eliminated many unskilled jobs, it increased the demand for highly skilled mechanical labourers and knowledgeable technicians who could operate the newer automated devices. As a result, the early prophecies that automation would reduce the need for workers' skills have proved to be the contrary of what has been happening. Automation may be seen as improving efficiency and expanding production while relieving drudgery and increasing earnings—precisely the aims of *Frederick W. Taylor* at the turn of the 20th century.

The Office Workplace

The introduction of computers also affected the organization of work in the information sector of the production economy. File clerks, bookkeepers, and other skilled office personnel involved in information processing were replaced by semiskilled keypunch and tabulating-machine operators. Office automation represents a further mechanization of office work, a process that began with the typewriter and the adding machine in the 19th century.

The information flow in offices has been likened to the movement of materials in manufacturing. Information, like materials, must be stored; typing or keypunching changes the form of the information, just as a machine operation changes the form of the workpiece; the value of the finished product is changed by adding information to it; and there must be a measure of quality control to make certain that the information is accurate. Just as automated machinery has done away with the jobs of many machine operators, integrated information-processing systems have eliminated many clerical tasks. For the production operation, automation provides an exact control over the inventory of raw materials, parts, and finished goods. Applied to billing operations in the office, it often can drastically reduce accounting costs.

The combination of computers and telecommunications led some to believe that office workers would perform their required functions without leaving their homes, as the computer terminal would take the place of their usual paperwork. Such predictions generally have not materialized, however. Social psychologists explain this by pointing out the social aspect of the work process, in the office as well as on the assembly line. Office workers have revealed their nature as "social animals" who enjoy the companionship of their fellow employees at the workplace.

Nevertheless, office automation affects management-worker relationships in a number of ways. For middle-level employees it means that higher management can have the reports of production, costs, and inventory at their fingertips and on the computer screens at their desks instead of depending on their subordinates for information. Automation also gives managers the means to monitor the efficiency of office workers in a way hitherto impossible. Through computerized information they can, for example, count the number of times per hour that a typist strikes a letter on the keyboard or ascertain the number, times, and nature of a worker's telephone calls.

[source: http://www.willamette.edu/~fthompso/MgmtCon/Automation.html]

14.4 PRODUCTIVITY IMPROVEMENT STORIES

Examples from different sectors (agriculture, fire factory, painting factory and photographic industry) have been taken up to highlight the productivity stories.

14.4.1 STORY OF US AGRICULTURE

The story of US agriculture is a story of productivity growth; fewer workers producing more food and fiber from the same amount of land with more capital and other purchased inputs. Between 1960 and 1994, the quantity of farm output doubled, while farm employment shrank by 57 percent.

There were periods in US history in which farm output rose with more land and labor. However, for most of the 20th century, especially after World War II, the story of productivity growth in agriculture has been rising farm output- surpluses- associated with massive rural-urban migration. For example, throughout the US, crop output rose 2.3 percent a year, while farm employment shrank by 2.3 percent a year, and these national trends were mirrored in Iowa.

States with large labor-intensive fruit and vegetable sectors fared differently. For example, crop output rose 2.4 percent a year in California, and farm employment shrank by 0.6 percent a year. Florida had similar increases in crop output, shrinking in farm operator and family employment, and rising hired worker employment.

It is hard to make overall assessments of productivity trends in US agriculture because agriculture is diverse- some crops can be experiencing sharp productivity gains, while others do not, and these offsetting trends cancel each other out in productivity data. However, *there is no doubt that labor productivity rose faster in field crop agriculture* between 1960 and 1996 than fruit, vegetable and specialty agriculture.

In most cases, labor-saving mechanization responds to rising wages. There are a number of labor-intensive commodities whose harvests may soon be mechanized, including oranges, olives, raisins, peppers and cucumbers. *The mechanical harvesters used to harvest fruit are modifications of nut-harvesting machines, most of which grasp the trunk of the tree and shake off the nuts, which are then swept up from the ground.* The mechanical harvesters used to harvest vegetables were originally developed to harvest processing tomatoes in the 1960s. They are being modified to harvest peppers and cucumbers in a once-over pass through the fields. A pepper harvester can harvest two rows 30 inches apart at one time, and four to five acres a day. Peppers are harder to separate from the vine than tomatoes.

14.4.2 AUTOMATION IMPROVES PRODUCTIVITY IN A TIRE COMPANY

By automating the materials handling process between the curing and treading processes, a major tire company was able to decrease setup time and increase production line speed.

Background

This tire manufacturer produces tires for automobile manufacturers such as Nissan, Toyota, and Mitsubishi. It also manufactures replacement tires for repair shops, dealers, and vehicle owners. Further, it supplies curing machines to other manufacturers in countries such as China and Taiwan.

Production at the company's plants is just-in-time. The model and type of tires demanded by dealers and automobile manufacturers can change rapidly. Each plant must be able to adapt quickly to demand, instantly changing recipes and tread specifications to produce small batches of different tire models.

Challenge

To increase productivity and reduce product defects caused by human error, the tire company sought to automate the process between the curing and treading machines.

The curing machine forms the tire into a 'donut' shape. Tires come out of the curing process very hot, so they are put on cooling carts for approximately 30 minutes before they are treaded. Because the timing for cooling was estimated by the workers, it was subject to error, resulting in inconsistent tire quality and product defects.

After cooling, the tires are treaded by the treading machine. Workers manually matched the batch to the appropriate treading machine based on their own memory and knowledge, also introducing the prospect of human error and product waste.

Solution

Based on its outstanding reputation for engineering, products, and ability to provide local support, Rockwell Automation was selected to automate the materials handling process between the *curing* and *treading* machines.

The new automated materials handling system encodes each batch with the batch number, production time, recipe, and treading specifications. Bar code readers scan each tire as it comes off the curing machine.

An SLC500 PLC processes the information for each different batch. It then controls the speed of the conveyors to ensure proper cooling time, and ensures the batch is sent to the correct treading machine. The PLC also evenly distributes the tires among the treading machines, optimizing capacity.

The PLCs are linked together via a DH+ network. Operators and line managers can monitor and control the process using PC-based Panel View displays, which provide alarm messages and batch information.

Results

- By automating the materials handling process, the tire company improved plant flexibility through faster setup time.
- By optimizing capacity and increasing production line speed, it has increased productivity by 10%.
- By reducing human error, the company has ensured the consistent quality of its tires.
- Product waste due to defective tires has been reduced by 20%.
- Using Rockwell Automation's solution, the company has increased productivity while reducing human error and product defects. This has increased its customers' confidence in the company's safety standards, reliability, and quality.

14.4.3 AUTOMATION SENDS PRODUCTIVITY SOARING

An automated paint line has given Eagle® Window & Door the flexibility to finish more than 3000 aluminum parts in 10 to 20 colors during a single shift [Steven R. Kline, Jr., Editorial Director].

One reason for the high demand of Eagle's windows and doors is their resistance to a variety of environmental conditions. Once installed, the windows and doors are subjected to decades of extreme weathering, from direct sunlight to salty ocean air to cold mountain winds. Plus, the doors must withstand temperatures that range from – 20 to – 1000 F. "Through all of this, our finished product must continue to look great. After all," explained Brad Straka, facility engineer at Eagle, "an architect can build a $500,000 home and fill it with beautiful amenities, but most people will never see inside. However, the outside, including the windows and doors, can be seen by everyone who passes by. Naturally, expectations are very high."

However, this is not the only reason for the popularity of the company's windows and doors. "More and more, the marketplace wants special features that set their homes or buildings apart from the rest," said Mr. Straka. "They turn to us for customized shapes, sizes and colors that create a distinctive look. We have become the custom expert."

As market demand for special orders exploded during the last decade, Eagle was forced to keep up with the delivery schedules. Since Eagle's establishment in 1977, the company managed to meet delivery schedules by outsourcing the painting of its aluminum windows and doors to designated job shops. While the finish quality, consistency and durability from the paint shops were excellent, by 1997 outsourcing lead times became so extended that they were beginning to cost Eagle jobs.

In 1998, outsourcing lead times became too excessive, and Eagle eliminated outsourcing and established an in-house paint operation. Eagle contacted Midway Industrial Supply, St. Paul, MN, to help it establish and meet its basic engineering specifications. Two goals were established: reduce lead time and decrease the cost of painting the windows and doors. To do this Eagle installed a fully automated, in-house paint line to finish all its aluminum parts, including cladding, screen channels and accessories.

The new paint operation was designed to be completely self-sufficient. Eagle wanted it to be treated like an independent supplier to the company. Since Eagle would be the paint shop's only customer, the 30,000 sqft facility was equipped to meet very specific objectives.

Eagle selected rotary atomizers to accommodate a multitude of part profiles, handle frequent color changes, match colors consistently and continuously, provide a quality finish and minimize paint waste and touchup.

Eagle manufactures more than 100 aluminum window and door profiles that range in size from 0.1875 inches wide to 14 ft long. Most orders involve relatively small custom jobs, 20 to 30 windows in specific shapes and designer colors, and are run on a "per order" basis. "We needed to finish between 3,000 to 4,000 parts per day with the flexibility to apply two to 20 colors during a single shift," stated Mr. Straka. "In short, we needed a paint system that could accommodate a multitude of part profiles, handle frequent color changes, match colors consistently and continuously, provide a quality finish and minimize paint waste and touchup." Therefore, batching and inventorying solutions were out of the question.

The new paint facility is located less than a mile from Eagle's manufacturing operation. After the windows and doors are manufactured, they are "shipped" to the paint facility. At the paint shop, the windows and doors are presorted by individual orders, checked into a temporary holding area and manually loaded onto horizontal racks attached to an overhead conveyor moving at a constant speed of 8 fpm.

At the beginning of each day, Eagle knows that it will paint a certain number of orders this color and a certain number of orders that color, and it knows the order that the colors will be painted in. This information is then programmed into the paint line's control. Even though the control can be programmed to know that there are three white orders, two tan orders and five green orders, it cannot be programmed to know when one order ends and when the next one begins. So, to notify the control of an upcoming color change, Eagle places a color flag on the conveyor. Because the line moves at a constant speed, when the color flag breaks a line of light at a set distance from the booth, the control can calculate the exact time to make a color change.

With rotary atomizers, Eagle can now handle 10 to 12 color changes and produce 3,000 finished parts every day, eliminating the need to outsource and dramatically cutting lead time.

Eagle also uses an automated triggering system from Nordson to automate its paint line. The triggering system includes an operator interface, PLC controller, photo cells and conveyor encoder. The paint line operator enters trigger points and delay on/delay off times into the operator interface. As parts pass through the photo cells, a signal is sent to the PLC. Again, because the line moves at a constant speed, the signal triggers the spray guns on as the leading edge of the part approaches the spray devices and triggers the spray guns off as the trailing edge of the part passes through the spray booth. "Control is a key feature," said Mr. Straka, "since every order requires a fairly unique racking pattern. For example, it's not unusual to see a single half circle window frame hung on a rack. The controls will minimize any waste." The precise control of the spray gun triggering not only minimizes paint waste, it also reduces cleanup costs and helps control VOC emissions.

Another important part of Eagle's automated system is the spray guns. Based on the finish quality achieved by the job shops that Eagle previously used, the company's engineers knew that they wanted to use rotary atomizers in the new paint system. "We investigated Nordson RA20 rotary atomizers and were immediately sold on the finish quality, minimal paint over spray and consistency from piece to piece and rack to rack," stated Mr. Straka.

The rotary atomizers apply paint between 0.8 and 1.2 mil (dry) and are checked routinely to minimize the need for touchup. A manual spray booth is positioned immediately after the automated booths to reinforce coverage in unusual circumstances such as double hung parts with extreme configurations and recesses. "Rejects are virtually nonexistent," proclaimed Mr. Straka.

Durability of the finish is critical for Eagle. From excessive handling of parts throughout the manufacturing process to installation and beyond when windows and doors are subjected to decades of extreme weathering, Eagle's finished product must continue to look great.

Eagle currently uses an average of 110 gal of paint per day (shift) to coat 2,500 to 3,000 parts. "Rotary atomizer technology allows us to keep paint utilization very low," said Mr. Straka. "The ability to achieve close in painting gives us high transfer efficiency and good penetration. Likewise, spray pattern control of the rotary atomizers helps reduce over spray and paint waste." The rotary atomizers are positioned only 5 inches from the parts. This is possible because the spray guns do not have a minimum sparking distance.

"The automated paint line has given us tremendous flexibility," explained Mr. Straka. "We can now handle 10 to 12 different color changes and produce 3,000 finished parts every day. And, by eliminating the need to outsource, we've dramatically reduced our lead time on custom colors. Best of all, we've achieved all this and are only running at about a third of our capacity."

Looking into the future, sometime this year Eagle will make another big move to a new 400,000 sqft building that will house offices, manufacturing and an all new paint facility mirrored after the existing operation. "Based on the success and flexibility of our automated paint line, we will continue to expand our use of higher quality, higher durability paints, which means adding rotary atomizers into our primer coating booths," said Mr. Straka. "It's just another example of how we're 'Giving Vision to Great Ideas™'."

Productivity at Work: Processes, Productivity and Quality

Increased workplace productivity does not happen in a vacuum. The values that set high-performing companies apart from their competitors are consistent:

- Processes that represent the best way to accomplish a task
- Accountability from all partners in the work stream
- Quality assurance procedures.

14.4.4 STORY OF INCREASED PRODUCTIVITY IN PHOTOGRAPHIC INDUSTRY

Like many industries, the photographic equipment and supplies industry faces tough domestic and foreign competition. Although the industry enjoyed strong growth in the '60s and '70s, it has had to re-engineer itself during the last two decades to compete with imported products.

One factor readily linked to increased productivity is automation. The industry introduced sophisticated equipment and technology, such as CAD/CAM. Manufacturing photographic products, especially sensitized materials, requires high degrees of mechanization and automation.

Automation alone, however, was not enough to keep leaders in this industry competitive.

Processes

To improve their products, designers, engineers, shop floor managers and assembly workers met and talked about the tasks that went into manufacturing each of their products. As they talked to each other, they discovered new, Optimal Paths for product manufacturing.

As a result of these conversations, processes became less complex. At the assembly level, tasks were minimized. Effective communication among designers, engineers, and assemblers enabled simplification.

Corporate decision making was also streamlined. Ever increasing competition forced an increased responsiveness to customers.

Accountability

One successful process change was the introduction of workstations, which transformed the traditional assembly line process. This shifted accountability from a quality control position to individuals and small groups.

In the traditional setup a series of workers performed one or two tasks, then passed the product to a quality control specialist. In the new, workstation model, individuals or a small group of individuals performed either a partial or a complete assembly at a workstation. The same individuals or group monitored quality control.

Quality

To make the changeover from old process to new required training. Assemblers received training in the computer hardware and software required for precision assembly, equipment monitoring and quality control.

The new processes improved quality, increased production flexibility, and promoted accountability. The workstation assemblers now had responsibility for monitoring the quality of the products they made, and it changed the way they approached their jobs. Quality dramatically increased.

The photographic equipment and supplies industry is still reporting gains in productivity.

14.5 AUTOMATION SYSTEMS TODAY

Today, there are several levels of automation out there. Although it has received definition by many, its attributes and aspects continue to change. For the time being, however, for the sake of defining what we mean in automation systems, we shall attempt to plagiarize those before us who have pioneered us to this point.

There was a time when the competitive struggles for industrial survival took place within a country's borders. Worldwide barriers to transportation, communication, and trade provided a measure of insulation between a country's industries and their foreign competitors. Even more important was the financial and technological advantage possessed by a privileged few industrialized nations that seem impregnable to the leaders of industries of less developed nations. But the luxuries created for the rich nations by these competitive barriers have become their weaknesses - the chinks in the armor that formerly protected them from industrial competition. High wage rates, inefficient management, and obsolete factories are among these luxuries, which have allowed hungrier competition to break down the barriers and seize markets using low wages, determined management, and new factories that employ some of the latest technology developed by the very countries that are under economic seige.

The United States of America has seen its position as world manufacturing leader under serious question in the decades of the 1970s and 1980s. Some have seen robotics as a possible savior to reverse the trend. Others have despaired that even robotics will not impede what they consider to be the inevitable demise of the industrial colossus that has been the United States. However, toward the end of the decade of the 1980s, some rays of hope began to shine through.

Despite intense wage rate competition and the commitment to quality of such industrialized countries as Japan, the United States has a tremendous advantage over other countries in manufacturing. This advantage is the presence of a very large and ready domestic market for its products. Canada possesses nearly the same advantage as the United States because of its own market and proximity and excellent relationship with the large market of its neighbor to the south. Europe is seeking a similar advantage of its own by creating the European Common Market. The combined economies of the countries of Europe make up a large and powerful market base on which to build volume production with the associated economies of scale that U.S. industries have enjoyed.

For those industries that qualify, automation offers opportunities for quantum advances in productivity efficiency. - the kind of advances necessary to reverse trends, recapture markets, and break free from old constrictive ways. Automation is certainly not new, and in a broad sense it can be traced back to the Industrial Revolution when machines first began to multiply vastly the productive capability of workers. The history of automation, however, has not been characterized by a steady progression; instead, it has been a series of breakthroughs. One breakthrough was interchangeable manufacture; another was Henry Ford's assembly lines. One that is currently upon us a combination of robots, mechanized automation, integrated enterprise systems and business process engineering combined in various ways to yield above average results.

Regarding robots, they themselves are not the breakthrough, but are a product or result of the breakthrough. Robots have become the standard bearers of the current industrial automation movement and deserve the attention of any automation engineer who is involved in discrete-item manufacturing. The enterprise systems that have been developed in the automation of manufacturing facilities has now spilled out into many industries. An example of this is SAP.

SAP originated in manufacturing in order to assist in automating and expediting processes. The leap of R/2 (mainframe and functional oriented) to R/3 (client-server and business process oriented) allowed tremendous progress in expanding this manufacturing "automation tool" to have a broader application to overall industries. This has resulted in an explosion in SAP R/3 enterprise systems and some of its lesser competitors (Baan, etc.) to become the standard bearers for automation of businesses in ways not before contemplated, especially in a fully integrated way. On top of all of this, was the requirement to "reengineer" the workplace through business process engineering. This is a requirement in order to implement any enterprise system (using client-servers that needs business processes clearly defined and modeled in order to operate successfully and produce the expected results).

Labor's Role in Automation

Automation certainly is not the only way to break out of constricting environments. When the chips are down, the response of labor has been remarkable. Demands for higher wages formerly seemed almost insatiable. In the United States, the labor leaders of the 1960s would have been incredulous had they been afforded a glimpse of the wage and benefits concessions made by labor unions in the 1980s.

In recent years it has sometimes appeared that labor has more determination to meet world competition than does management. In the 1980s and early 1990s large U.S. companies have become bankrupt or suffered severe cutbacks in operations or corporate mission. These cutbacks have resulted in numerous plant closings, sometimes accompanied by severe hardship, especially in small towns in which the plant was the major employer. So determined are labor and local management in these crises, that, in some cases, employee groups have mounted drives to buy the facility from the parent company and continue operations.

Another weapon that is being used as a competitive weapon is *participative management*. The first arena for the display of this weapon was product quality, and the most popular term describing participative management is still *quality circles*.

REFERENCES

Shimon Y. N (editor) (1999), Handbook of Industrial Robotics, 2nd ed. John Wiley & Sons. ISBN 0471177830.

Ahearn, M. J. Yee, E. Ball, and R. Hehring. 1998, Agricultural Productivity in the United States. USDA,ERS, Ag. Information Bulletin No. 740, January

http://usda.mannlib.cornell.edu/data-sets/inputs/98003

15

Value Analysis and Value Engineering

15.0 INTRODUCTION

Value Engineering has its origin at the General Electric Company (GEC) USA. Due to the World War II, many materials were in short supply, and L. D. Miles was associated with a committee to identify substitute materials without sacrifice in quality and performance. It should be noted that material cost account for about 60 to 70 % of the total costs in many industries and it should be reduced by all concerned. Through a team approach, Miles brought about changes in products to lower their cost without affecting their utility and quality. Later on this method was known as Value Analysis. Value Engineering (VE) or Value Analysis (VA) is a technique to reduce materials cost by a scientific approach and analysis. It also tries to conserve the scarce material resources, foreign exchange reserves and promote the indigenous development of substitute materials. VE should not be seen as a mere cost reduction technique. It is more comprehensive and improves the value without sacrificing in quality, reliability, maintainability, availability, aesthetics, etc. VE was used in hardware projects such as product design, but now it is applicable for many areas like: software projects (the systems and procedures), urban slum development program, staff welfare, motivation enhancement and courtesy improvement plans.

According to **L. D. Miles**, '*Value analysis is an organized creative approach which has for its purpose the efficient identification of unnecessary cost i.e., cost which provides neither quality, nor use, nor life, nor appearance, nor customer features.*' [Techniques of Value Analysis and Engineering (1961)].

According to another definition: '*VA is an organized systematic study of the function of a material, component, product or service, with the objective of yielding value improvement through the ability to accomplish the desired function at the lowest cost without degradation in quality.*'

So, the main objective of VE/VA is to achieve same or better performance at a lower cost while maintaining all functional and quality requirements. It does this mainly by identifying and eliminating hidden, invisible and unnecessary costs.

15.1 SOME BASIC CONCEPTS

15.1.1 DEFINITION OF VALUE

The term 'Value' is often confused with price or cost of an item. However, value is not synonymous with cost. Value of an item is linked to its function, utility or purpose, viz. quality, elegance, prestige, etc.

Value of a product is the ratio of the worth or utility of the product to its price or cost.

$$\text{Value} = \frac{\text{worth}}{\text{price}} \text{ or } \frac{\text{function}}{\text{cost}} \quad ...(15.1)$$

It is obvious from above relation that the value of an item or service can be enhanced by

- Reducing the price for the same worth,
- Increasing the worth for the same price, and
- Reducing the price and increasing the worth simultaneously.

15.1.2 REASONS BEHIND POOR VALUE

One of the causes for poor value in products, systems and procedures could be the lack of organized effort in devising such systems. Many times the designs are created under highly compressed time frame and the designer may give more emphasis to the technical aspects, and may prescribe thicker, costlier materials and other unnecessary features which are not needed by the customer. Sometimes, ad hoc decisions take the permanent shape in the absence of the review of product designs.

Many a time poor value may result in product because the functions have not been precisely understood and redundant or unnecessary functions have been imposed.

15.1.3 TYPES OF VALUES

The term value can be divided into following types:

Use value: It is a monetary measure of the *qualities* of an item that contribute to its performance.

Esteem value: It is a monetary measure of the properties that contribute to its *stability or desirability* of ownership.

Cost value: The sum of labor, material and various overheads required to produce the item.

Exchange value: It is a monetary measure of the qualities and properties of an item that enable it to be *exchanged* for something else.

Thus, *Use value + Esteem value = Exchange value*

15.1.4 TYPES OF FUNCTIONS

According to VE approach, the functions can be of two types:

Primary functions: The basic purpose of the product.

Secondary functions: Other purposes not directly accomplishing the primary purpose but supporting it or resulting from a specific design approach.

15.2 VALUE TESTS

VE basically is based on questioning at the function and costs of the product. L. D. Miles designed a set of value tests to see if there is scope for value improvement. If these tests are applied sincerely, then there is bound to scope of improvement in most of the products, systems and procedures.

Some of these questions are:

1. Can the design be changed to eliminate the part?
2. Can you purchase it at lower cost?
3. Does it need all its features?

4. Can a usable part be made by a lower-cost method?
5. Can a standard part be used?
6. Could a less expensive material do the same function?
7. Is the function necessary?
8. Could it be eliminated?
9. Could other items serve the same function?
10. Can they be simplified?
11. Could the supplier reduce his price by a cooperative redesign or revised specifications?

15.3 STEPS IN VALUE ANALYSIS

This is also called the VE job plan. In the beginning, when **Miles** proposed VE job plan, it was simply the modified form of the steps involved in work study. There are three different techniques for VE program:

1. Job Plan due to Mudge.
2. DARSIRI Method (D-Data collection, A-Analysis, R-Record of ideas, S-Speculation, I-Investigation, R-Recommendation, I-Implementation).
3. FAST (Function Analysis System Technique).

In this section we will deal with the very well recognized **Job Plan due to Mudge** technique. The seven phases of Job Plan are:

1. General phase
2. Information phase
3. Function phase
4. Creation phase
5. Evaluation phase
6. Investigation phase
7. Recommendation phase

The Job Plan for VE should be applied on properly selected project. The chosen project should have potential for improvement. Brief description of each phase is given in the following section.

1. General phase

There are five techniques associated with this phase:

- *Use good human relations*: The use of good human relations means assistance in place of resistance.
- *Inspire team work*: It calls for subordinating personal prominence or ego in the interest of the group as a whole.
- *Work on specifics*: We should avoid generalities and work on specifics. Concrete data and information on specific problems must be secured.
- *Overcome roadblocks*: It is essential to recognize the roadblocks and then take steps to overcome them. Mudge has compiled a list of 'killer phases' which people use to kill an idea. It is very crucial to avoid such mental roadblocks.

- *Apply good business judgment*: Business decisions and judgments must be based on facts. Poor business decisions and poor judgment become prevalent when personal opinions and feelings take control. To apply good business judgment one must be resourceful, able to think, and able to pursue new knowledge.

2. Information phase

The objective of this phase is to gain an understanding of the project being studied and to obtain all essential facts related to the project to estimate the potential value improvement. This phase has three techniques:

Secure facts: The information gathered must be authentic which is a difficult task. Information needed will be:

- Technical specifications—dimensions, grades, tolerances, quality, appearance.
- Environmental specifications—Severity, test conditions.
- Engineering drawings
- Production sample—actual or its model
- Production data—operations, speeds, rates, output and stock level
- Cost data—material, labor, overhead-costs
- Work specifications—work place layout, standard times
- Features preferred by customers
- Development, testing, and service records
- Quantities involved
- Scrap rates.

Determine costs

- Complete and accurate cost must be secured to get the promising return on time and efforts.

Fix costs on specifications and requirements

- Accurate cost in relation to the specification should be collected.

3. Function or Analytic phase

The goals of this phase are:

- To define the functions that a product actually performs.
- To relate these functions to the cost and worth of providing them.

The two techniques of this phase are:

(a) **Define function.** The functions need to be described with only two words: a *verb* and a *noun*. This is done to get clear picture of the functions without frills. The rules of function description are:

- Determine user's need for a product or service.
- Use only one verb and one noun. The verb should answer the question: 'what does it do?
- Avoid passive or indirect verbs.

Example: Some functional definitions

Product	Function
Mirror	Reflect light
Brake	Arrest motion
Clutch	Transfer power
Cigarette lighter	Provide ignition
Light bulb	Emit light
Screw driver	Transfer torque
Coffee cup	Hold liquid

(*b*) **Evaluate function relationship.** This attempts to determine the relative importance of various functions. A *paired comparison technique* is used to determine the numerical value of various functions. In this, a pair of functions are compared and it is tried to determine which is more important and whether the degree of variation is major, medium or minor. Suppose we are comparing A and B. Then A-3 will mean that A is more important than B and there is a major difference in their importance. B-1 would have meant that B is more important than A but there is a minor difference only. This way a total number of $n(n - 1)/2$ pairs are compared and values entered in a cell if n-functions are to be compared. Then the score is obtained by adding all the numerals following a particular function. The function score divided by the total score gives relative importance of that function.

Function description should be derived for the product and all its components. The evaluation process also helps to find out whether it is a primary function or a secondary function. The primary function will have the highest score in the evaluation process. Generally, a product or component will have only one basic function and a number of secondary functions. If you have more than one basic function, it must be a mere restatement of the other.

4. Creative phase

The objective of this phase is to create ideas for value alternatives to accomplish the functions defined in the previous phase. The first steps is to try answering the question 'what else will do'? This phase requires creativity to be the focal point. *Brainstorming* is a very effective way to promote creativity. In the brainstorming, *free wheeling* is permitted. Two powerful techniques to promote creativity are:

a. Establish positive thinking

In this we allow people to create ideas and we do not attempt to judge an idea simultaneously when it is being created.

b. Develop creative ideas

This is done by developing a multitude of ideas and approaches for accomplishing the defined functions. The desired thing at this point is a large number of ideas, no matter whether they look ridiculous. Some of the questions asked at this phase are:

- What will the product do if new ideas and process are provided to it ?
- Develop various changes, optimize, and simplify.

5. Evaluation phase

The objective of this phase is to select the promising ideas of the creative phase for further analysis. They are subjected to the following criteria:

- Will it work?
- Is it less costly than the present design?
- Is it feasible to implement?

This phase requires us to be very objective in making the judgment. There are four techniques associated with this phase:

Refine and combine ideas

The ideas must be practicable and to make them so we may have to refine an idea or combine two or more ideas together.

Establish cost on all ideas:

While an idea or combination of ideas is being refined, an estimated cost should be calculated. Other questions to be asked are:

- What are the potential costs of implementing the idea?
- What are the resultant savings implied?

Develop function alternatives:

This makes further use of the information developed in the evaluation of functional relationships to mould the individual functional solutions into total solutions.

Evaluate by comparison:

The alternatives are compared to determine which one will provide the greatest value advantage.

6. Verification phase

Three techniques are used to further refine the selected ideas into workable and acceptable solutions providing lower cost methods for performing the desired function. The three techniques are:

Use company and industrial standards

Within a standard lies tried and proven solution to a problem. We should try to use standards to the extent possible.

Consult vendors and specialists

The vendor can be a source of help in VE program because he knows more about his product and its potential capabilities than most of his customers. We may decide to buy an item from the vendor rather than making it if it is a cheaper and better proposal. Suppliers should be asked for cost-reducing and quality improving ideas. Specialists can also suggest a better material substitute from their knowledge and experiences. In VE philosophy, consulting others is seen as strength and not a sign of weakness.

Use specialty products, processes and procedures

These in many cases could be a lower-cost way of accomplishing the function. But, they should be evaluated to ensure lower costs in relation to standard products, processes and procedures.

7. Recommendation

In this phase, the finally selected value alternative is recommended for acceptance and implementation. Many a time the acceptance of the suggested alternative depends on the way it is presented to the management. The two techniques to be used are:

Present facts

Facts usually speak for themselves. Summarize the proposed course of action and prepare a plan of implementation.

Motivate positive action

The presentation of accurate, specific and detailed facts and costs will motivate positive action. This technique needs follow-up to ensure that the action is taken to implement the ideas.

8. Implementation

This phase should address the following issues:

- Factors governing acceptance
- Requirements for acceptance
- Mechanism for implementation: who will monitor the implementation, who will do it, who provides the fund, who reports the progress, etc.?
- Determine the areas that are affected
- Determine time and sequence of effort and quantity at break-even point
- Follow up
- Measure results of gain in money and time. Compare net gains with the full cost of the value effort.

15.4 EXAMPLES OF VALUE ENGINEERING

VE has been extensively applied in product design, systems and procedures. In Indian industries VE applications have been reported from TISCO, TELCO, Escorts, Kelvinator, Railways, and other units. In many of these cases, large amount of savings have been achieved.

15.4.1 SOME SIMPLE CASE STUDIES OF VE

Example 1

Problem: Reduce the number of guards by combining entrances to classified areas.

Function: Monitor doors

General explanations and solutions: It was difficult to reduce the number of doors to the classified areas. However, it was found that each guard could monitor and control two entrance doors by using CCTV and electric door locks.

Example 2

Problem: Reduce the manufacturing cost of gasoline tanks for the landing aircrafts..

Function: Hold gasoline

General explanations and solutions: Initial design was inherently very costly. It was found that standard 55 gallon steel drums could be easily modified, coated and used.

Some concepts of VE have also been used in the following products:

- Cars used to have metallic bumpers, they have now been replaced by fiber or non-metallic ones.
- Computers used to have metallic case and parts. Now they have more of plastic parts. This has resulted in cost reduction of computers.
- Domestic equipment like mixer, grinder, hair drier, shaver, camera, gears in clocks, etc. are made of plastics or nylons to reduce the cost with same function. This enhances the value of these equipment.
- Leather belts in wrist watches in place of metallic chains.
- Car dashboards, cases of TV, VCR, radio are all made of plastics.
- 'Tooth brush with one handle and many spare brushes' in place of traditional single brush.
- 'Screw driver with one handle and many drivers' in place of the traditional single one.
- Thermostatically controlled radiator fans used in modern cars save lots of energy. The fan remains active only when the temperature goes up beyond a set limit. The old cars have the fans running all the time wasting so much of energy.
- Dot pens with replaceable refills.
- Carbide tipped tools with replaceable tool bits (one shank and many tool bits) in place of the single point cutting tool.
- Jackets with interchangeable sides or linings.

15.5 VALUE ENGINEERING AND SIMPLIFICATION ANALYSIS

This section contains: (1) Primary Questions, (2) Secondary Questions, and (3) Checklist.

15.5.1 THE PRIMARY QUESTIONS

The questioning sequence used follows a well-established pattern which examines:

- the *PURPOSE* for which the activities are undertaken
- the *PLACE* at which the activities are undertaken
- the *SEQUENCE* in which the activities are undertaken
- the *PERSON* by whom the activities are undertaken
- the *MEANS* by which the activities are undertaken

with a view to activity

- ELIMINATING
- COMBINING
- REARRANGING
- SIMPLIFYING

In the first stage of the questioning technique, the Purpose, Place, Sequence, Person, Means of every activity recorded is systematically queried, and a reason for each reply is sought.

PURPOSE:

- What is actually done?
- Why is the activity necessary at all?

in order to ELIMINATE unnecessary parts of the job.

PLACE:

- Where is it being done?
- Why is it done at that particular place?

SEQUENCE:

- When is it done?
- Why is it done at that particular time?

PERSON:

- Who is doing it?
- Why is it done by that particular person?

in order to COMBINE wherever possible or REARRANGE the sequence of operations for more effective results.

MEANS:

- How is it being done?
- Why is it being done in that particular way.

in order to SIMPLIFY operation.

15.5.2 THE SECONDARY QUESTIONS

The secondary questions cover the second stage of the questioning technique, during which the answers to the primary questions are subjected to further query to determine whether possible alternatives of place, sequence, persons and/or means are practicable and preferable as a means of improvement over the existing method.

Thus, during this second stage of questioning, having asked already, about every activity recorded, what is done and why is it done, the method study man goes on to inquire what else might be done? And, hence: What should be done? In the same way, the answers already obtained on place, sequence, person and means are subjected to further inquiry.

Combining the two primary questions with the two secondary questions under each of the head: purpose, place, etc., yields the following list, which sets out the questioning technique in full:

PURPOSE:

- What is done?
- Why is it done?
- What else might be done?
- What should be done?

PLACE:

- Where is it done?
- Why is it done there?
- Where else might it be done?
- Where should it be done?

SEQUENCE:

- When is it done?
- Why is it done then?

- When might it be done?
- When should it be done?

PERSON:

- Who does it?
- Why does that person do it?
- Who else might do it?
- Who should do it?

MEANS:

- How is it done?
- Why is it done that way?
- How else might it be done?
- How should it be done?

15.5.3 CHECKLIST

A check-list of questions which may be of use in applying the questioning sequence in method study. Most of the questions listed below apply generally to method study investigations. The questions are listed under the following headings:

- Operations
- Design
- Inspection Requirements
- Materials Handling
- Process Analysis
- Material
- Workplace Layout
- Tools and Equipment
- Working Conditions.

Operations

1. What is the purpose of the operation?
2. Is the result obtained by the operation necessary? If so, what makes it necessary?
3. Is the operation necessary because the previous operation was not?
4. Performed correctly?
5. Is the operation instituted to correct a condition that has now been corrected otherwise?
6. If the operation is being carried out to improve appearance, does the additional cost give extra saleability?
7. Can the purpose of the operation be obtained in another way?
8. Can the material supplier perform the operation more economically?
9. Is the operation being performed to satisfy the requirements of all users of the product, or is it made necessary by the requirement for one or two customers only?
10. Does a subsequent operation eliminate the necessity for this operation?
11. Is the operation being performed as a result of habit?

12. Was the operation established to reduce the cost of a previous operation, or a subsequent operation?
13. Was the operation added by the sales department as a special feature?
14. Can the part be purchased at a lower cost?
15. Would adding a further operation make other operations easier to perform?
16. Is there another way to perform the operation and still maintain the same results?
17. If the operation has been established to correct a subsequent difficulty, is it possible that the corrective operation is more costly than the difficulty itself?
18. Have conditions changed since the operation was added to the process?

Design

1. Can the design be changed to simplify or eliminate the operation?
2. Is the design of the part suitable for good manufacturing practice?
3. Can equivalent results be obtained by changing the design and thus reducing cost?
4. Can a standard part be substituted?
5. Would a change in design mean increased saleability, an increased market?
6. Can a standard part be converted to do the job?
7. Is it possible to improve the appearance of the article without interfering with its utility?
8. Would an additional cost caused by improved appearance and greater utility be offset by increased business?
9. Has the article the best possible appearance and utility on the market at the price?

Inspection Requirements

1. What are the inspection requirements for this operation?
2. Does everybody involved know exactly what the requirements are?
3. What are the inspection details of the previous and following operations?
4. Will changing the requirements of this operation make it easier to perform?
5. Will changing the requirements of the previous operation make this operation easier?
6. Are tolerance, allowance, finish and other standards really necessary?
7. Can standards be raised to improve quality without unnecessary cost?
8. Will lowering standards reduce cost considerably?
9. Can the finished quality of the product be improved in any way above the present standard?
10. How do standards for this operation/product compare with standards for similar items?
11. Can the quality be improved by using new processes?
12. Are the same standards necessary for all customers?
13. Will a change in standards and inspection requirements increase or decrease the defective work and expense in the operation, shop or field?
14. Are the tolerances used in actual practice the same as those used on the drawing?
15. Has an agreement been reached by all concerned as to what constitutes acceptable quality?
16. What are the main causes of rejections for this part?
17. Is the quality standard definitely fixed, or is it a matter of individual judgment?

Materials Handling

1. Is the time spent in bringing material to the work station and in removing it large in proportion to the time used to handle it at the work station?
2. If not, could material handling be done by the operators to provide a rest through change of occupation?
3. Should hand, electric or fork-lift trucks be used?
4. Should special racks, containers or pallets be designed to permit the handling of material with ease and without damage?
5. Where should incoming and outgoing materials be located in the work area?
6. Is a conveyor justified, and if so, what type would best be suited for the job?
7. Can the work stations for progressive steps of the operation be moved closer together and the material handling problem overcome by gravity chutes?
8. Can material be pushed from operator to operator along the bench?
9. Can material be dispatched from a central point by means of a conveyor?
10. Is the size of the container suitable for the amount of material transported?
11. Can material be brought to a central inspection point by means of a conveyor?
12. Can a container be designed to make material more accessible?
13. Could a container be placed at the work station without removing the material?
14. Can an electric or air hoist or any other lifting device be used with advantage?
15. If an overhead traveling crane is used, is the service prompt and accurate?
16. Can a tractor-trailer train be used? Could this or an industrial railway replace a conveyor?
17. Can gravity be utilized by starting the first operation at a higher level?
18. Can chutes by used to catch material and convey it to containers?
19. Would flow process charts assist in solving the flow and handling problem?
20. Is the store efficiently located?
21. Are truck loading and unloading stations located centrally?
22. Can conveyors be used for floor-to-floor transportation?
23. Can waist-high portable material containers be used at the work stations?
24. Can a finished part be easily disposed of?
25. Would a turntable eliminate walking?
26. Can incoming raw material be delivered at the first work station to save double handling?
27. Could operations be combined at one work station to save double handling?
28. Would a container of standard size eliminate weighing?
29. Would a hydraulic lift eliminate a crane service?
30. Could the operator deliver parts to the next workstation when he disposes of them?
31. Are containers uniform to permit stacking and eliminate excessive use of floor space?
32. Could material be bought in a more convenient size for handling?
33. Would signals, *i.e.* lights, bells etc., notifying men that more material is required, save delay?
34. Would better scheduling eliminate bottlenecks?

35. Would better planning eliminate crane bottlenecks?
36. Can the location of stores and stockpiles be altered to reduce handling and transportation?

Process Analysis

1. Can the operation being analyzed be combined with another operation? Can it be eliminated?
2. Can it be broken up and the various parts of the operation added to other operations?
3. Can a part of the operation being performed be completed more effectively as a separate operation?
4. Is the sequence of operations the best possible, or would changing the sequence improve the operation?
5. Could the operation be done in another department to save the cost of handling?
6. Should a concise study of the operation be made by means of a flow process chart?
7. If the operation is changed, what effect will it have on the other operations? On the finished product?
8. If a different method of producing the part can be used, will it justify all the work and activity involved?
9. Can the operation and inspection be combined?
10. Is the job inspected at its most critical point, or when it is completed?
11. Will a patrol form of inspection eliminate waste, scrap and expense?

Material

1. Is the material being used really suitable for the job?
2. Could a less expensive material be substituted and still do the job?
3. Could a lighter-gauge material be used?
4. Is the material purchased in a condition suitable for use?
5. Could the supplier perform additional work on the material that would improve usage and decrease waste?
6. Is the material sufficiently clean?
7. Is the material bought in amounts and sizes that give the greatest utilization and limit scrap, off cuts and short ends?
8. Is the material used to the best possible advantage during cutting, processing?
9. Are materials used in connection with the process-oils, water, acids, paint, gas, compressed air, electricity-suitable, and is their use controlled and economized?
10. How does the cost of material compare with the cost of labor?
11. Can the design be changed to eliminate excessive loss and scrap material?
12. Can the number of materials used be reduced by standardization?
13. Could the part be made from scrap material?
14. Can newly developed materials-plastics, hardboard, etc.-be used?
15. Is the supplier of the material performing operations on it which are not necessary for the process?
16. Can extruded materials be used?

17. If the material was of a more consistent grade, could better control of the process be established?
18. Can a fabricated part be substituted instead of a casting to save pattern costs?
19. Is the activity low enough to warrant this?
20. Is the material free from sharp edges and burrs?
21. What effect does storage have on material?
22. Could a more careful inspection of incoming materials decrease difficulties now being encountered in the shop?

Workplace Layout

1. How is the job assigned to the operator?
2. Are things so well controlled that the operator is never without a job to do?
3. How is the operator given instructions?
4. How is material obtained?
5. How are drawings and tools issued?
6. Is there a control on time? If so, how are the starting and finishing times of the job checked?
7. Are there many possibilities for delays at the drawing room, storeroom and at the clerk's office?
8. Does the layout of the work area prove effective, and can it be improved?
9. Is the material properly positioned?
10. If the operation is being performed continually, how much time is wasted at the start and end of the shift by preliminary operations and cleaning up?
11. Are tools prepositions to save mental delay?
12. How is material supply replenished?
13. Can a hand or foot air jet be supplied to the operator and applied with advantage?
14. Could jigs be used?
15. Could guides or bullet-nosed pins be used to position the part?
16. What must be done to complete the operation and put away all the equipment?
17. How thoroughly should the workplace be cleaned?

Tools and equipment

1. Can a jig be designed that can be used for more than one job?
2. Is the volume sufficient to justify highly developed specialized tolls and
3. fixtures?
4. Can a magazine feed be used?
5. Could the jig be made of lighter material, or so designed with economy of material to allow easier handling?
6. Are there other fixtures available that can be adapted to this job?
7. Is the design of the jig correct?
8. Would lower-cost tooling decrease quality?
9. Is the jig designed to allow maximum motion economy?
10. Can the part be quickly inserted and removed from the jig?

11. Would a quick-acting, cam-actuated mechanism be desirable for tightening the jig, clamp or vice?
12. Can ejectors be installed on the fixture for automatically removing the part when the fixture as opened?
13. Are all operators provided with the same tools?
14. If accurate work is necessary, are proper gauges and other measuring instruments provided?
15. Is the wooden equipment in use in good condition and are workbenches free from splinters?
16. Would a special bench or desk designed to eliminate stooping, bending and reaching reduce fatigue?

Working Conditions

1. Is the light even and sufficient at all times?
2. Has glare been eliminated from the workplace?
3. Is the proper temperature for comfort provided at all times; if not, can fans or heaters be used?
4. Would installation of air-conditioning equipment be justified?
5. Can fumes, smoke and dirt be removed by exhaust systems?
6. If concrete floors are used, is sacking or matting provided to make standing more comfortable?
7. Are drinking fountains with water provided and are they located nearby?
8. Has due consideration been given to safety factors?
9. Is the floor safe, smooth but not slippery?
10. Has the operator been taught to work safely?
11. Is the clothing suitable from a safety standpoint?
12. Does the plant present a near and orderly appearance at all times?
13. How is the amount of finished material counted?
14. Is there a definite check between pieces recorded and pieces paid for?
15. Can automatic counters be used?
16. What clerical work is required from operators for filling in time cards, material requisitions and the like?
17. How is defective work handled?
18. What is the economic lot size for the job being analyzed?
19. Are adequate records kept on the performance of operators?
20. Are new employees properly introduced to their surroundings and do they receive sufficient instruction?
21. When workers do not reach a standard of performance are the details in investigated?
22. Are suggestions from workers encouraged?
23. Do the workers really understand the incentive plan under which they work?
24. Is a real interest developed amongst the workers on the product?
25. Is the operation being performed by the proper class of labor?
26. Is the operator physically suited for the job.
27. Is the plant unduly cold in winter, or stuffy in summer, especially on the first morning of the week?

15.6 BENEFITS OF VALUE ENGINEERING

Value Engineering helps in improving efficiency and effectiveness of products, systems and procedures. In general, VE does the following:

- It helps us to pinpoint areas that need attention and improvement.
- It helps in generating ideas and alternatives for possible solution to a problem.
- It provides a method to evaluate alternatives.
- It provides a platform for dialogue.
- It records the logic behind the decisions.
- It improves the value of goods and services significantly.

REFERENCES

Miles, L. D., 1961; Techniques of Value Analysis and Engineering, McGraw-Hill, New York.

Mudge, Arthur E., 1971; Value Engineering: A Systematic Approach, McGraw-Hill, New York.

School of Management Studies, IGNOU; Value Engineering and Quality Assurance, December 1997.

Index

V

W